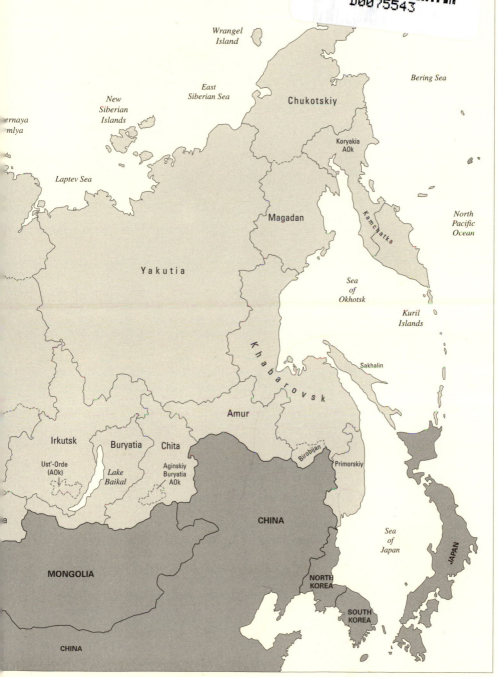

Wrangel
Island

East
Siberian Sea

Bering Sea

New
Siberian
Islands

Chukotskiy

ernaya
mlya

Koryakia
AOk

Laptev Sea

Magadan

Kamchatka

North
Pacific
Ocean

Yakutia

Sea
of
Okhotsk

Kuril
Islands

Khabarovsk

Sakhalin

Amur

Irkutsk

Buryatia

Chita

Birobijan

Ust'-Orde
(AOk)

Lake
Baikal

Aginskiy
Buryatia
AOk

Primorskiy

CHINA

Sea
of
Japan

JAPAN

MONGOLIA

NORTH
KOREA

CHINA

SOUTH
KOREA

Russia's Fate Through
Russian Eyes

RUSSIA'S FATE THROUGH RUSSIAN EYES

Voices of the New Generation

edited by

Heyward Isham

with

Natan M. Shklyar

with an introduction by

Jack F. Matlock Jr.

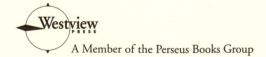
Westview
PRESS
A Member of the Perseus Books Group

Copyright © 2001 by Westview Press, A Member of the Perseus Books Group

Published in 2001 in the United States of America by Westview Press, 5500 Central Avenue, Boulder, Colorado 80301-2877, and in the United Kingdom by Westview Press, 12 Hid's Copse Road, Cumnor Hill, Oxford OX2 9JJ

Find us on the World Wide Web at www.westviewpress.com

Library of Congress Cataloging-in-Publication Data
   Russia's fate through Russian eyes / edited by Heyward Isham ; with Natan M. Shklyar ; with an introduction by Jack F. Matlock Jr.
      p.   cm.
   Includes index.
   ISBN 0-8133-3866-2
   1. Russia (Federation)—Politics and government—1991– . 2. Russia (Federation)—Economic conditions—1991– . 3. Russia (Federation)—Social conditions—1991– . 4. Russia (Federation)—Intellectual life—1991– . I. Isham, Heyward.II. Shklyar, Natan M.   III. Matlock, Jack F.

DK510.763 .R872   2000
947.086—dc21
                                                                                00-046224

The paper used in this publication meets the requirements of the American National Standard for Permanence of Paper for Printed Library Materials Z39.48-1984.

10   9   8   7   6   5   4   3   2   1

Dedicated to the memory of
Dmitry Sergeevich Likhachev (1906–1999),
intrepid investigator of the
Old Russian literary heritage from the tenth to
the seventeenth century and a source of
inspiration and wise counsel to the
new generation of Russian leaders of all ages.
"Our future lies in openness to
the entire world and in enlightenment."

Contents

Preface, by Heyward Isham   xi
Acknowledgments   xvii

Introduction, *by Jack F. Matlock Jr.*   1

PART 1
RESHAPING THE RUSSIAN STATE

1   A New Russia—Or the Same Old Russia? An Alternative
Worldview in the Making, *Yurii Plyusnin*   9

2   Protecting Fair Competition in the New Russia:
A Revolution in Thinking, Not Just Economics,
Natal'ia Fonareva   32

3   Reform in Russia's Regions: The View from Novgorod,
Mikhail Prusak   43

4   Federalism, Local Self-Government, and
National Renewal in Russia, *Aleksandr Voronin*   65

PART 2
COPING WITH NEW ECONOMIC RULES

5   The New Stage of Economic Reforms in Russia:
Thoughts on Policy and Practice, *Sergei Vasil'ev*   81

6   Building Houses for the Newly Affluent Near Moscow:
An Entrepreneur's Perspective, *Interview with
Kirill Gorelov*   99

7   A Pioneer in Russia's First Open Grain Market,
Interview with Arkadii Zlochevskii   107

8   Fighting for Labor Rights in a Transitional Economy,
    Interview with Aleksandr Sergeev   114

9   Transforming Russian Political Mores: The Key to
    Economic Evolution, *Aleksandr Auzan*   126

**PART 3
STRIVING TOWARD RULE OF LAW**

10 The Legal Profession and Civil Society in Russia:
    Problems and Prospects, *Vladislav Grib*   145

11 Freedom of Speech and the Rule of Law, *Andrei Richter*   162

12 Where Society Must Rein In Government:
    Restorative Justice and Preservation of the Community,
    Rustem Maksudov   171

**PART 4
CIVIL SOCIETY BUILDING BLOCKS**

13 Nongovernmental Organizations: Building Blocks for
    Russia's Civil Society, *Andrei Topolev and Elena Topoleva*   193

14 On the Path to a New Russia: The Youth Movement,
    Nadia Seriakova   202

15 Empowering Russia's Women: Will Their
    Potential Be Tapped? *Nadezhda Azhgikhina*   212

16 Reviving the Russian Orthodox Church: A Task Both
    Theological and Secular, *Interview with Hilarion Alfeev*   235

17 Caring for the Homeless in St. Petersburg,
    Interview with Valerii Sokolov   250

18 What Future Awaits the Russian Press? A Prognosis,
    Iosif Dzialoshinskii   258

19 My Life, My Fate: *Severiane* and Russia's North,
    Ol'ga Lobyzova   268

20 The Rise and Fall of Environmental Protection As a
    National Security Issue, *Aleksandr Knorre*   284

PART 5
PRESERVING THE CULTURE,
MODERNIZING EDUCATION

21 A Sad Tale About a Happy Fate, *Irina Prokhorova*   299

22 It's Not Easy Being a Scholar in Modern Russia,
    Vadim Radaev   308

23 Experimenting with Liberal Education in Russia:
    The Break with Soviet-Era Conventions,
    Nikolai Koposov and Dina Khapaeva   322

24 The Architecture of Humanism in Russian
    Higher Education, *Evgenii Kniazev*   342

25 A Theater for Oneself, *Vladimir Mirzoev*   357

26 Russia's Literary Revival: From Authoritarianism to
    Intellectual Freedom, *Aleksandr Ageev*   377

    Epilogue: Will Russia's Terrible Years Be Repeated?
    Vyacheslav Ivanov   396

Index   417

Preface

The young Russian men and women who record in these pages the hopes, fears, triumphs, and tragedies their country has undergone in recent years—altering their own lives profoundly in the process—all come from the first post-Soviet generation to achieve positions of leadership in Russia. They report on five challenges central to Russia's survival and stabilization: reshaping the state, coping with new economic rules, striving toward the rule of law, building a civil society, and preserving the national culture and educational capacity.

They love their country, while understanding all too well the crippling psychological legacy of seventy years of a dictatorship that was both cunning and cruel in dispensing a plausible utopian myth and exacting extraordinary sacrifices in the name of that myth. They understand the acute sense of disorientation that overcame all generations when the USSR abruptly dissolved in 1991 and the Communist Party simultaneously lost much, if not all, of its power. As several of our authors recall, it was like waking up one morning and finding yourself a citizen of an entirely different country, meanwhile discovering that your parents were not your real parents and that you had acquired a brand new surname.

But these young Russians waste no time in historical retrospectives. Unencumbered by fears of either a Communist restoration or a right-wing coup, they have no taste for recrimination or resentment: They go about their business briskly, boldly. From the voices caught in these pages we learn what the young generation of Russians are doing to help their country recover from its precipitous decline, and how they see the future. For example:

- a grain dealer deftly navigates the newly demonopolized commodities market and competes on the world market;
- a real estate developer, responding to pent-up demand, builds functional and affordable housing in the Moscow suburbs;

- an opponent of the compulsory registration system operates the first center for the homeless in St. Petersburg and publishes a newsletter advocating more humane treatment for them;
- a public-policy lawyer, using his advocacy and legislative drafting skills, protects consumers (unaccustomed to having a choice of goods and services) from buying defective equipment or succumbing to false advertisements;
- an anthropologist grounded in biology and philosophy explores the radically changed outlook among Siberia's urban and rural inhabitants who, with fortitude and ingenuity, struggle to adapt to the pervasive economic crisis, discounting any help from local authorities and meanwhile turning to the worship of nature as a traditional source of unity;
- an entrepreneurial couple organizes an agency to inform, educate, and support those engaged in the long process of building a civil society through a growing network of professional nongovernmental organizations;
- an independent publisher introduces readers to a wealth of undiscovered and unorthodox literary talents;
- a journalist directs a watchdog agency that publicizes reprisals against investigative journalists by government officials or businessmen exposed as corrupt;
- two scholar-administrators in St. Petersburg pioneer the country's first undergraduate program offering a cross-disciplinary liberal arts curriculum.

These are only a few of the articulate young leaders we meet in these pages.

The Russia they set their minds and energy to restore and modernize is a country that does not turn its back on the Bolshevik and Soviet past but acknowledges enduring bonds, common interests, and ethical values shared by every generation. It is a Russia that sets aside raw envy of others' entrepreneurial success, renounces the habit of subservience to the state, and distinguishes between universal principles of justice and cynical distortions of the law by bureaucrats. A Russia that can be roused from inertia to activism by reports of institutionalized torture, whether occurring under police interrogation, in Russia's overcrowded prisons, or in the army.

It is above all a Russia borne up in its many travails by a stubborn will to survive and by a capacity, especially in the new generation, to adapt ingeniously and swiftly to changes imposed by the need to compete at home and abroad under unforgiving market conditions.

It is, finally, a Russia that wants the West to demonstrate its interest in a more informed, balanced, and respectful relationship, shedding disparaging stereotypes and a priori assumptions. Although increasingly confident of its regenerative capacity, the new Russia, our authors believe, welcomes an intelligent, sensible helping hand as its citizens, with the new generation in the lead, rebuild their country "from under the rubble." The poet Boris Slutsky has written about the Russians: "worn out, like rails over which all the engines of the world have driven, they can still receive any signals sent out by good."

*   *   *

The genesis of this collection of original essays on Russia's future was probably my service as second secretary at the American embassy in Moscow during the mid-1950s, when I discovered firsthand that Western assumptions about the totalitarian controls imposed by the Soviet system failed to take into account the marvelously ingenious protective devices developed within society against secret police informers and other forms of political intrusion into private lives.

In those years, apart from chance (and often very instructive) encounters and conversations in parks, restaurants, markets, or train compartments, diplomats seeking the reality behind the stage props had, for example, to plow through politburo speeches or Party Congress transcripts, note a change of emphasis here or a telling omission there in the official press reports, and compare how news was handled in Moscow and in the provinces. The evidence of political disillusionment and intellectual resistance even then was greater than many Western observers assumed. I was struck, for example, by the buzz of debate among Moscow State University students caused by the publication of Vladimir Dudintsev's *Not by Bread Alone,* a novel that portrayed a Party apparatchik in subtly unflattering tones altogether inconsistent with approved iconic forms. Although Dudintsev's indictment pales when compared to the torrent of revelations about Stalin's repressions and the Party's degeneration that emanated from both official and samizdat sources during the 1960s and 1970s, the reaction to the book reflected the passing of an illusion and foreshadowed the role that opposition-minded intellectuals, some of them allied with Mikhail Gorbachev and his team, would play in the eventual destruction of the Party's monopoly on power and legitimacy in 1991.

The task of interpretation and analysis that faces foreign observers almost fifty years after Stalin's death and some fifteen years after the start of Gorbachev's glasnost and perestroika is of course altogether different. Deciphering post-Soviet puzzles requires a method that takes into account the proliferation and tendentiousness of print and electronic information, to the point that there seem to be not one but many Russias. Two of our authors, Sergei Vasil'ev and Vladimir Mirzoev, observe this phenomenon from the perspective of economic policymaker and theatrical producer. Fragmentation characterizes those who live in Moscow and St. Petersburg, the provincial cities, and rural villages and settlements; those over fifty and those under forty; citizens residing in republics or oblasts that border on West Europe, Central Asia, and the Far East; and those living in regions largely cut off from foreign ties, such as the Siberian North. Among the eighty-nine regions of Russia, a few are relatively stable and growth oriented but most are seriously impoverished and backward. And all such differences, of course, are compounded and manipulated by recurrent "information wars," the use of compromising material *(kompromat)* to crush political opponents, the hidden agendas of oligarchs who control much of the media, the intertwining of bureaucracy and organized crime, and mercurial changes in patterns of patronage. At the same time, the Internet links among universities and individual subscribers (some 3 million) are increasingly important in providing independent sources of information, although government monitoring is a latent threat. The rise and fall of confidants and courtiers, scoundrels and scholars, reformers and restorationists—such is the context in which these reflections, reminiscences, and observations must be viewed.

The approach I have taken in this book, therefore, follows that taken in my earlier volume, *Remaking Russia: Voices from Within,* published in 1995, which presented the views of some twenty outstanding intellectual figures of the older generation. For the present collection, I have concentrated on twenty-eight representatives of the new generation of Russian leaders, those roughly between the ages of twenty-five and forty, who were identified during field trips to Russia in March and May 1999 with the invaluable help of many in Moscow, St. Petersburg, and elsewhere (listed in the acknowledgments). Their perspectives find an arresting counterpoint and commentary in the epilogue contributed by one of Russia's most respected scholars, the historian and Slavicist Vyacheslav Ivanov.

My suggestion to the authors, once they were selected, was straightforward: Using your personal voice, as if you were writing a letter to American friends, share with us your professional evaluation of the profound changes in your country; note the implications for the future development of Russia; and describe what is necessary to move Russia toward a more civilized, responsible, and vibrant society. The classic questions—"Who are we? Where are we going? How do we get there?"—are within your power to answer.

The authors responded well to these proposals. Indeed, their written contributions (in some cases interviews) convey effectively the troubled, shocking, perplexing, contradictory evolution of their country from a coercive imperial system asserting a monopoly on faith and power to a national condition that seems far less clear, less predictable, less equitable, and certainly less effective than that which had preceded it, but one that increasingly offers new opportunities for independence of thought, collegiality of action, entrepreneurial boldness—and, above all, new hope for Russian society as a whole.

What these young leaders have to say also offers new ideas for the design and implementation of foreign assistance programs, for much has changed and continues to change since those programs were first initiated; and Russia under Vladimir Putin's presidency will present problems and opportunities of an altogether different order. The West more than ever will need to study the particular historical and psychological context, the nuances of words and actions, the smoke screens put up to mask weakness and confuse the potential antagonist—and it will also need to assess at its proper value the defiantly resilient and tenacious Russian character, imbued as it is with memories of a more coherent and authoritative past.

Heyward Isham

Acknowledgments

Many friends and colleagues in the United States, Europe, and Russia endorsed the concept of publishing a second *sbornik,* or anthology, of Russian "voices from within," suggested potential contributors, and in some cases helped arrange meetings. Their support and encouragement were invaluable. Special thanks go to John F. Tefft, deputy chief of mission at the American embassy in Moscow; Thomas E. Graham, former head of the embassy's Internal Political Section; Dr. John H. Brown and Sharon Hudson-Dean of the U.S. Information Service in Moscow; Mark Koenig and Lisa Petter of the U.S. Agency for International Development (USAID) mission in Moscow; Melissa Hudson, second secretary of the embassy; Elena Nemirovskaya, founder and director of the Moscow School of Political Studies, and her project director, Igor Gorely; Masha Gessen and Masha Lipman of *Itogi* magazine, Tatyana Zhdanova, director of the John D. and Catherine T. MacArthur Foundation's Moscow office; and Alan Rousso, director of the Carnegie Endowment's Moscow Center.

I am grateful as well to Celestine Bohlen of the *New York Times* Moscow Bureau; Irene Stevenson, director of the American Center for International Labor Solidarity in Moscow; Bernadine Joselyn, director of the Eurasia Foundation's Moscow office; Susan Wobst, director of the International Research and Exchanges Board (IREX) office in Moscow; Aleksei Barabashev, deputy director of the Institute of Public Administration and Social Studies at Moscow State University; Maksim Shevchenko, religious editor of *Nezavisimaya gazeta;* Evgenii Semenov, general director of the Russian Scientific Foundation for the Humanities; Susan H. Gillespie, director of the Institute for International Liberal Education at Bard College; Natal'ia B. Romanova, managing director of Jupiter Investments, Moscow; Ekaterina Genieva, director of the Soros Foundation, Russia; and Sergei Basov, director of the Soros Foundation's St. Petersburg branch.

To my program associate Natan Shklyar go my special thanks; he has been an indefatigable, resourceful, and highly knowledgeable editorial partner and has made major contributions to the book, including the recording and translation of four interviews and the care and feeding of our authors. As one who was born in the USSR in a military family, came to the American Midwest to get a college education, and then forged his way brilliantly to a respected position among Russia specialists, Natan epitomizes the entrepreneurial spirit and intelligent altruism characterizing the authors in this collection. His successor since May 2000, Marisa Robertson-Textor, has speeded the final stage of publication.

We were fortunate in having an experienced team of translators, Antonina W. Bouis, Marian Schwartz, and Anna Kucharev, who dealt expeditiously and lucidly with texts that seldom reflected Anglo-Saxon notions of brevity but always conveyed the thoughts of the authors forcefully.

Beyond the unflagging intellectual and operational support of my colleagues at the EastWest Institute, particularly John Mroz, the president, and Stephen Heintz, the executive vice president from 1990 to 1999, I owe an incalculable debt of thanks to the foundations and individuals who supported this project: the Annie Laurie Aitken Lead Trust, the John D. and Catherine T. MacArthur Foundation, the Rockefeller Brothers Fund, the Kennan Institute, and the Alida B. and Steven H. Scheuer Foundation. To all of them, the many other friends, colleagues, mentors, and family members who have lent me their encouragement and wisdom over the years, and especially to my beloved wife, Sheila, my profound thanks.

H. I.

INTRODUCTION

Jack F. Matlock Jr.

When Mikhail Gorbachev had introduced glasnost to Soviet society and perestroika was under way, I was sometimes asked by Soviet citizens how long I thought it would take before the Soviet Union could become a "normal" country. (By "normal," they meant to be like Western democracies.) My stock answer was, "two generations," which always brought signs of disappointment to the face of my questioner. I would hasten to explain: "You're going to have to create a system that in many respects is the opposite of what you have today. You will have to create democratic institutions. You will have to restore private property. You will have to develop the institutions and rules that make a market economy work. Most important of all, you will have to change the way people think, the way they deal with each other, and their attitude toward authority and personal responsibility. All these things take time, and nobody has a road map showing how to go from where you are to where you want to be. Inevitably, there will be much trial and error, steps forward and steps back. If your country is where you would like it to be in forty years, you'll be lucky."

This, however, was not the prevailing view among the reformers who suddenly metamorphosed out of once subservient academics, professionals, and even some Communist Party apparatchiks. The king—the Soviet system—had no clothes. Throw him out and, presto, we'll have the opposite, capitalism with all the freedom it has protected and affluence it has created elsewhere. Five hundred days of the right policies would do the trick, they thought. And, of course, even temporary sacrifice was out of the question. "We will

Jack F. Matlock Jr. is George F. Kennan Professor at the Institute for Advanced Study, Princeton, New Jersey. He was U.S. ambassador to the Soviet Union from 1987 to 1991 and is the author of *Autopsy on an Empire: The American Ambassador's Account of the Collapse of the Soviet Union*.

not carry out reform on the backs of the Russian people!" thundered Boris Yeltsin in the fall of 1990, as he attacked Gorbachev for not moving faster. It was going to be quick and painless, particularly if Russia could rid itself of those non-Russian Soviet republics that were considered drains on its economy and drags on its reconstruction. By the end of 1991, Yeltsin and his supporters had their way: no more Gorbachev, no more Soviet Union, no more communism. The road ahead seemed clear and unfettered. Free up prices, privatize state property, and then everything would fall into place, they reasoned.

The euphoria of 1991 of course could not last, and as problems developed it evaporated even faster than it had arisen. It was replaced by varying degrees of cynicism mixed with resentment and despair. "Democracy is not for us," many concluded. "Nothing but high prices, unemployment, a government of thieves, and constant change." And yet elections were held as scheduled, people kept coming out to vote, and few seemed to marvel that, for the first time in anyone's memory, they could say anything they wished without being thrown in jail, could form whatever associations they desired, and could travel anywhere they wanted, so long as they could afford the fare.

Since a few heady, optimistic months in 1992, Russia has been getting a bad press. Stories of organized crime, rampant official corruption, disastrous health conditions, a deteriorating education system, and pensioners on the brink of starvation were daily fare even before the 1998 financial collapse and renewed war in Chechnya exacerbated many problems. The privations and horrors are real, but they are not the whole story, for they fail to encompass changes that are under way in Russia, changes that may have a greater impact on the future than the sensational events that capture the headlines. The problem of comprehension is more than an unfortunate propensity to generalize from the sensational; it is also a matter of historical amnesia. Many observers remember only what has happened in the past few months, or even in the past few days. For some, it is as if Russian history began in 1992, all the problems since then being the product of bad government or—a few would even suggest—the innate depravity of the Russian people.

In fact, nobody can begin to understand what is happening to Russia today unless they grasp the enormous damage seventy years of communism inflicted on the country, the economy, the society, and the mores and mentality of the people. Totalitarianism exacted a toll in many dimensions, not just by its irrational and inefficient economic system, designed to feed a military behemoth rather than provide a better life for its people. It also atomized society, uprooting the fragile shoots of a civil society that had begun to sprout before the Bolshevik Revolution. It mocked legality with its "telephone law," exercised by Communist Party apparatchiks dictating to government officials, courts, and legislators as organized criminals would: behind the scenes, secretively, protected by vows of silence. It created a system that not only inhibited creativity and change, but encouraged the proliferation of economic enterprises that absorbed more resources than the value of the goods they produced. It became, ultimately, an economy of negative value. As the late Mancur Olson remarked in his insightful book *Power and Prosperity,* "As communism devolved, it was bound to collapse."[1]

Russia's political leaders in 1992 inherited not only the rubble of the collapsed economic system, the institutional fragments of totalitarian rule, and a society already mired in organized crime and corruption, but also a population conditioned to believe that prosperity and a better life depended on government, not on themselves. To become free and prosperous, Russia required simultaneous revolutions at the top of government and society, in the way the government ruled, in the structure of the economy, and, indeed, in the way the people thought. Not adjustments or modifications, but *revolutions.* Furthermore, if these revolutions were to succeed at all, they had to be peaceful. A country chock full of weapons of mass destruction could hardly have survived a violent revolution that brought on a civil war.

One can argue whether economic or political reform should have come first, and also whether either is possible in a society full of special interests determined to resist change. But this is a chicken-and-egg argument, since one revolution could not occur without the others. One can argue whether privatization of the economy was too fast or too slow, or whether it was conducted fairly.[2] But one cannot reasonably argue that Russia could have created a democracy and a market economy without privatization. At least there is no evidence that any country has been able to do that, and there are sound theoretical reasons that explain why this is so.

None of the required revolutions could be completed in months, or even a few years. The time they require is measured in generations. In a process that could only be gradual, steps along the way to reform the political system created barriers that delayed or blocked change in the economic structure. Increasingly, people came to blame the miseries caused by the Soviet economic collapse on the policies necessary to save them from that collapse. Their attitude created a hostile environment for the changes that were needed. Nevertheless, short-circuiting the democratic process has rarely brought lasting results. A civil society cannot be built top down, but must develop out of the successful efforts of individuals to form associations and groups to satisfy their interests and their needs. Although adopting appropriate laws is an essential element in any transition, the laws a market economy requires to function efficiently (for protection of property rights, enforcement of contracts, and disinterested resolution of disputes) do little good if their enforcement is subverted by corrupt bureaucrats or if they are flouted by the rich and the criminal. Russia's transition leaders faced a multitude of contradictions and vicious circles as they tried to create several revolutions simultaneously, none of which could be totally successful until they all were.

We are now almost halfway through the first transitional generation, and it is time we paid some attention to voices from that generation, rather than those of the gaggle of foreign journalists and self-styled "experts" whose vision rarely reaches past the newsworthy event, and whose historical perspective, in the words of American scholar Leon Aron, is that "of a fruit fly." The purpose of this collection of articles is to give voice to that generation.

What do we find? Not extended arguments about the past, or about who is responsible for the problems of today, subjects that seem to preoccupy many of the older generation of Russian intellectuals. Also absent is any penchant for facile theorizing, or of praising or blaming the "impenetrable Russian soul," topics that have of late absorbed so much attention of the chattering classes, East and West. This is not a place to look for grand schemes or transcendental speculation. What we have are descriptions of specific efforts in many different fields to create a Russia in the future that will differ greatly from that of the past, yet preserve the enduring values of the Russian tradition. Scholars, a provincial governor, federal officials, bankers, an entrepreneur, union leaders, lawyers, journalists, educators, leaders of fledgling nongovernmental organizations, a young Russian Orthodox priest—these authors represent a gamut of professions and offer a variety of points of view. They are doubtless exceptional, but not unrepresentative of their generation.

These authors neither gloss over difficulties nor yield to despair. They simply describe what is happening in their lives and their professions, and what they are contributing to their society and nation. Each story, each study, each interview is interesting and important in itself. Collectively they provide us with insights into today's Russia that are usually ignored in our periodical press. What impressed me most in this varied cornucopia of ideas and experience is the implicit confidence most of the authors have in the future. They seem to understand—in contrast to many of their elders—that the future is in their hands. They have set about the job of taking control of it, without bombast, without unreasonable expectations, and yet with confidence that what they do can make a difference. This does not mean that all their messages are comforting. Yurii Plyusnin's study of rural attitudes in Novosibirsk oblast is distressing in many respects, yet just such thoughtful and objective studies are necessary for an informed public policy. The sort of policies Governor Mikhail Prusak has introduced in Novgorod oblast seem designed to prevent the preoccupation with mere survival that Plyusnin's research revealed among peasants in Siberia, but whether Prusak's policies are working to that effect or not cannot be determined as yet.

One thing, however, is certain. Russia is so vast and so varied that examples can be found of almost anything. There have been atrocities in Chechnya by soldiers in uniform and also the encouraging growth of voluntary welfare agencies in many of Russia's cities. These opposites neither balance nor justify one another, but in the first instance (the war in Chechnya) conditions are—one would hope—unique, whereas in the other (poverty and homelessness), more general. The new Russia is a work in progress, and its success will depend on its ability to diminish the role of violence and expand the role of social service, whether private or public. This will not happen without a healthy, productive economy, a strong, though limited and honest, government, and a civil society with a significant proportion of public-spirited citizens.

The authors of this volume are busy creating just such a society. If they are typical of their generation, a "normal" Russia of the sort my questioners in Gorbachev's Soviet Union sought may not, in fact, take all of the forty to fifty years I predicted.

Notes

1. Mancur Olson, *Power and Prosperity: Outgrowing Communist and Capitalist Dictatorships* (New York: Basic Books, 2000), p. 153.

2. Those who debate the timing rarely address the question: How can privatization occur and also be "fair" if there is no legitimate private capital, and if many of the "assets" themselves are not assets but burdens? The attempt to transform the economy in the former German Democratic Republic, which was beset with less severe problems than the Soviet economy, has cost the German Federal Republic hundreds of billions of deutsche marks, and even after ten years many in Germany's eastern Laender are dissatisfied with the result. Most of the industrial enterprises were in fact not viable in a market economy and rather than representing value to an investor required a greater infusion of capital than an entirely new enterprise would have.

Part One

Reshaping the Russian State

1

A New Russia — Or the Same Old Russia?

An Alternative Worldview in the Making

Yurii Plyusnin

"Our life is like a tear trembling on the tip of an eyelash." For almost the entire 1990s, this maxim has proved to be true for most ordinary Russian citizens. During this time we have all lost a great deal and we have acquired a great deal.

A great many people have said many things about the losses and gains of the past decade, which (following Nikolai Berdiaev's well-known periodization) I would call the Sixth Great Turning Point in Russian history. If we were talking about changes "external" to the lives of ordinary people—the economic, social, and political transformations in Russian society—there would be little I could add. My aim, though, is to talk about the "internal" changes that have occurred, and are still occurring, in the psyche, consciousness, and behavior of the ordinary people of the Russian nation. And here there

Born in 1954 in a village near Kostroma, **Yurii Mikhailovich Plyusnin** studied zoology and sociology at Tomsk State University and has lived in Novosibirsk since graduation. He holds doctorates in both biology and philosophy, has had a long academic career, and is now a professor of sociology at Novosibirsk State University. The author of more than 150 publications, Plyusnin sits on the editorial boards of several academic journals. His research and writing focus on human behavior in differing physical and social environments. Translated by Anna Kucharev.

is much that is not known, either by the broad public or by specialists, including social scientists, politicians, and government officials. These issues—the personal life, feelings, and experiences of the common man—are usually ignored, considered immaterial against the backdrop of global social processes.

Which changes am I planning to discuss here? First: the magnitude and direction of emotional changes, the nature of the psychological experiences undergone by the general population, and those experiences engendered by the crisis of Russia's social and governmental system. Second: the transformation of social attitudes, the changes in value systems, and the ensuing slow evolution of the worldview and stereotypes held by ordinary Russians. Third: the particular, often situationally adaptive changes in the Russian people's behavior in response to changes in the external, the "big" life.

Of course, in this essay I will only be able to examine superficially a few of the numerous and diverse adaptations Russians have made to the new conditions in their lives. As a social psychologist, I was able to record these changes during the 1992–1999 period, when I organized and conducted nineteen sociological expeditions, studying problems in towns, regions, and the nation generally.

I began my observations of the changes occurring in the very depths of social life in 1992, the first and perhaps most difficult year of "shock therapy," whose consequences our society experienced suddenly and painfully. At first my observations were episodic and unsystematic, partly because I lacked funds and partly because local officials had no interest in my work. But by 1995, the research became more systematic, thanks almost entirely to the assistance of the Russian State Foundation for the Humanities in Moscow, and later the Novosibirsk municipal administration as well.

In order to make the picture of changes taking place in Russia objective and complete, I chose as subjects for permanent observation members of three social-professional strata sharply differentiated by lifestyle and type of work (and who therefore reacted differently to external changes and understood the prospects of the social reforms and their own place in society in different ways). These groups were: (a) *professional scholars,* who are more capable than others of reflecting on the changes taking place in society; (b) *the work force of a major industrial city,* as the "locomotive of contemporary history"—the main driving force of any social change (here my research was limited to Novosibirsk, with a population of 1.6 million);

and (c) *ordinary folk living in the villages and small towns* of provincial Russia. This last group accounts for most of Russia, not only in the quantitative sense (no less than 60 percent of the population[1]), but also as the most extensive social substratum. In this essay I will primarily discuss the results of my observations of the third category of the population. From my point of view, it is precisely the changes that remain hidden or go unnoticed by those at the "heights" of society, those changes taking place among society's ordinary members, that will create, sooner or later, what will be the "Sixth Russia."

To be sure, the risk of error in extrapolating a multitude of individual facts is always great, but (to paraphrase Goethe) a fact, even when confirmed many times over, is worth nothing without intellectual intuition. That is why, relying exclusively on my own research—on interviews with more than 5,000 people conducted over the course of the past eight years—I will permit myself to suggest several general observations about the "internal flow of life" in Russia and give my highly subjective prognoses about its future direction.

Which changes, from my point of view, in the psyche of the ordinary Russian are most important to consider? Three points seem essential: (1) how well adapted people feel to the new life; (2) how they plan their personal futures; and (3) their everyday emotional states.

Adaptation to the New Life

A significant number of my compatriots, in spite of a decade of changes, simply cannot yet adapt to the "new life." There are far too few people in society who consider themselves well adapted or completely adapted to present-day economic and even social conditions. Scholars lacking empirical data about public opinion and self-evaluation usually assume that in Russian society approximately one-fifth of the population is well adapted to the new life ("the favorites"); approximately one-fifth to one-fourth is poorly adapted ("the outsiders"); while the remaining one-half to three-fifths remain in an uncertain transitional state.

However, according to my observations based on annual surveys of the population of provincial Russia, as opposed to people living in major Russian cities and the capital, the picture turns out to be much more dismal. No more than one out of every ten persons (one-tenth, by no means one-fifth of the population) considers that he is one of "the favorites" of the new life and has already completely adapted to it. No fewer than five or six out of every ten persons simply cannot adjust at all (three-fourths are "outsiders," not one-quarter, as is commonly thought, although only about 10 percent consider that they are completely incapable of mastering the new rules of the game). The remaining three to four out of every ten persons (from one-third to two-fifths) are in an uncertain state: They themselves are not entirely sure whether or not they have adapted to this life during the past ten years.

Thus there are grounds to think that up to 90 percent of the ordinary people in the nation not only do not consider themselves "masters of their lives," but do not even expect the slightest success. The reasons for this are numerous. The primary and most obvious reason is economic.

Perhaps the paradox of present-day life among ordinary people in Russia will be more understandable if I say that up to 60 percent of them are "Thoreaus" who live in more dangerous and remote woods than Henry David Thoreau did. In his classic book *Walden, or Life in the Woods,* Thoreau mentions with some pride that he managed to spend only about $62 during the eight months he voluntarily spent in the woods in the cabin he built on the shores of Walden Pond.

If you accept the accuracy of an estimate made by the Federal Reserve Bank of Minneapolis calculating the level of inflation from the 1860s to our time, one dollar in 1860 is equivalent to $19.44 in 1999. Thoreau's expenses would thus be about $1,200 today, or nearly $150 a month (excluding food he grew on his own, such as potatoes, beans, peas, and corn). Measured by this standard, most of my compatriots in Russia's villages and small towns far outstrip the great American romantic in terms of thriftiness and endurance. Because when it comes to hard cash (not money that accrues as unpaid wages and remains only "paper money" for years—people often have many thousands of paper rubles, but this is akin to an interest-free loan to the government), these rural people have only 20 to 100 rubles in cash each month—not $150, but only $1–$4 per person in a family per month. And they have lived the Walden recluse's life (I have in mind only its material side) not for two years, but for nearly a decade. And like him, they grow and process their own food themselves. (So that the reader does not reproach me for citing excessively low figures, I will add that according to my estimates, for the past two years the monthly income of a resident of Novosibirsk has averaged between $45 and $80.)

Sadly, it is significant that the number of people who consider themselves adapted to the new life has not increased throughout almost the entire decade. In surveys taken from 1994 on, their numbers remain within the 5 to 10 percent range. And the number of people who consider themselves incapable of fitting into the new economic and social environment is not decreasing, either.

However, simple straight-line reasoning assumes that an increasing number of people will feel comfortable in the new socioeconomic conditions as they "enter the market." Perhaps this outcome would have been expected if the reforms had been sustained and positive, and if they had ultimately promoted the stabilization of society. Unfortunately, the chaos of reforms and complete uncertainty about the future causes people to choose behavior strategies that are adaptive only to the short term, and may even turn out to be maladaptive over one or two years. This is why people feel unable to adapt. They understand this well, they see that "external life" tosses them ever newer surprises, each more unpleasant than the last, in the form of contradictory laws and government directives. For this reason they are not at all certain that the weapon they choose to use in the battle for survival today will be as useful tomorrow.

Planning the Future and Emotional Stress

People always want peace and stability. And many are irritated and disoriented by the fact that in Russia most of us must constantly invent numerous, diverse, but essentially the most basic survival strategies and tactics in the battle for daily existence. The immediate response to this dilemma is that people sharply cut back any long-range planning in their personal and professional lives. Their emotional state, the basis for their everyday moods, suffers a steady decline.

My observations, especially since 1994, give, on the whole, a highly pessimistic picture of how drastically people's ability to plan ahead has been curtailed. According to the estimates of social psychologists, ordinary people in the Soviet period planned their futures one to three years ahead on average, and many planned five and more years ahead. The onset of the economic crisis, the emergence and growth of unemployment, and the government's nonpayment of wages, threatened everybody with the loss of all means of survival and caused most Russians (not only, say, factory workers or village dwellers, but even professional scholars) to cut back on their advance planning to periods of months and even weeks. It can be said with certainty that people's overall prospects diminished greatly within a very short period of time. By 1996–1998, a short but steady increase in long-term advance planning occurred; in some social groups the average estimates approached eight to ten months and one year. Starting in 1999, however, people found their prospects illusory once again and sharply curtailed advance planning to time periods similar to those of 1994.

I will cite some facts that sum up the mood from 1998 to 2000. Up to half of the population (more than 49 percent) completely refuse to plan their lives ahead in any fashion; another 15 percent plan no further than six months in advance. Almost three-quarters of the population do not see any long-term personal prospects under the still evolving social, political, and economic conditions. Only one-fourth of the population evaluate their life prospects in normal fashion (looking ahead one to five years) or extended fashion (looking ahead five to ten years or more).

The situation is somewhat better when it comes to advance planning for work. Here, one-third of the people (36 percent) refuse to plan their future employment in any way, and another 14 percent plan their work activity from one to six months in advance—exactly half the population. Of the remainder, a third of the population (34 percent) view their future work plans in segments of one to five years, and 12 percent look even further ahead.

A sharp reduction in the time segments used for life planning is, in my view, one of the most reliable markers of social instability. As soon as instability increases, most people cut back the duration of these time segments. The life perspectives I recorded among ordinary people attest to the depth of the psychological crisis in Russian society.

The second psychological reaction I noted is a deterioration in emotional state. People feel badly. But how badly? Here sociologists, psychologists, and physicians all agree in their opinions and in quantitative estimates. I will cite my own survey data for 1999. Only one person in every ten (more precisely, about 9 percent across the entire sample) responded that he is usually in a good or fine frame of mind (naturally, this group closely corresponds to those who consider themselves as having more or less successfully adapted to the new life). Less than 30 percent describe themselves as being in a normal psychological state. Thus, just under 40 percent now feel normal or good, that they are not experiencing emotional stress. But nearly two-thirds of the populace, about 62 percent, evaluate their frame of mind pessimistically, of whom 13 percent consider that they are experiencing severe emotional tension.

The same group of respondents, however, when asked to characterize the moods of kith and kin in their immediate surroundings, give less favorable evaluations. In their opinion, only one in every seven persons close to them (making up nearly 13 percent) lives with feelings of certainty about the future and with heart-felt optimism. Six out of every ten (63 percent) are seen as experiencing tension and uncertainty, while every fourth person (nearly 25 percent) is judged to be on the verge of a nervous breakdown (respondents refer to alarm and fear, irritation and aggression, apathy and ennui).

An increase in the level of emotional stress in the population was observable almost as soon as the economic reforms began in 1991–1992 (actually, at that time such research was episodic). Emotional tension appears to have reached its most severe level in 1995 and 1996. To use medical language, observations showed that from one-half to two-thirds of the population were in a state of acute emotional tension, while one-fifth to one-quarter or more had reached a stage of chronic tension capable of developing into the most diverse somatic illnesses and neuropsychiatric disturbances. Over time, as they adapted psychologically, those experiencing acute emotional tension began to decrease in number. To this day, however, no less than one quarter of the population experience a pathological emotional reaction to stress characterized by depressive phenomena. Moreover, the two methods used for assessing the level of chronic emotional tension in society, public opinion surveys and psychological testing, coincide, registering 25 and 24 percent, respectively. To put it in dramatic terms: One quarter of Russia's population are on the verge of breakdown. This is the sorrowful reality.

The Importance of Being Human:
Spontaneous Safety Nets

Given Russian society's extremely gloomy and dismal psychological state, is there at least something reassuring on the horizon?

Of course there is. Positive, favorable psychological aspects of our lives do exist, and they are just as obvious and visible as the signs of emotional stress. I will point out only two facts that I consider to be particularly significant.

First, people tend to get support from family, close friends, and colleagues at work. In our society (and specifically in the environment of ordinary people, different from that in Western society in many ways), an individual gets tremendous moral, emotional, and material support from kith and kin. After all, it is very important to know that you won't perish if something happens to you and that there are many people who will come to your aid, lend you a helping hand, and pull you out of the abyss.

What proportion of Russian society, then, is confident of help and support from their family and close friends? According to my observations, no less than three-quarters (75 percent). Only a handful of individuals (up to 5 percent) admit that they do not receive any material help or moral support at all from their close ones. Less than 10 percent of nonelderly adults in our society feel lonely. As far as I know, this is a much smaller percentage than, say, in western Europe, where up to 40 percent of people in that age group consider themselves lonely.

And a second positive fact: Respondents everywhere, no matter where they live, note that their relations with their neighbors remain normal and sincere, no matter what difficulties and cataclysms "external" life brings their way. Their community of neighbors, be it a small village or town, rural district, or major city, retains its cohesion and mutual altruism, people's willingness to help one another. For more than four-fifths of all the people I polled, the immediate social environment they inhabit is genuinely close, and relations between people are friendly and well meaning. Less than 15 percent report that they live in a tense relationship with their immediate surroundings. And only a few individuals, less than 3 percent, consider relations between people in their communities bad or tense.

From my point of view, these two circumstances—the considerable psychological support people give one another and the high degree of social cohesion in communities of neighbors—stand out as the most crucial factors that support and hold together our society at its deepest, most grassroots level, no matter what disasters the outside world may bring.

The issue of change in the worldview and the socially instilled values of contemporary Russian society, which social philosophers have interpreted as a structural crisis of values in a society that is itself in crisis and undergoing reform, is gradually losing both acuteness and novelty. Everybody already knows that something is occurring in the mentality of Russian society. But what is it specifically? In what direction are the shifts in worldview moving, especially where it concerns "ordinary people?" The opinions of researchers reflect uncertainty and conflict in direct proportion to the multitude of studies undertaken. Nearly all social psychologists direct their attention to studying the transformations in the consciousness of the general population living in midsize and large cities. But this is by no means the same as the mentality of those living in small towns and villages. I will introduce several areas of change in everyday consciousness (mentality) that have emerged, primarily changes in the hierarchy of basic values and meanings of life for ordinary people in provincial Russia. In fact, knowledge of these changes makes it possible to predict, at least to some degree, our society's tendency to move either in the direction of modernization and structural renewal or toward traditionalism and further disintegration.

Subtly Changing Kaleidoscope of Values

Studies of the structure of peoples' value preferences are usually based on the well-known concepts of Abraham Maslow.[2] According to Maslow, five categories of values are present in each individual's basic value system, ranging from the simplest values related to biological needs and physical safety, to the values of social ties, to the highest values of the individual's self-realization and self-actualization. Although clusters of values are ordered hierarchically on a social-normative scale, each person has his own hierarchy of preferred values. Society's ideal is for the normative and the individual hierarchies to coincide. But the higher groups of values are dependent on the extent to which the lower values have been satisfied. If the lower values are not satisfied, the individual will prefer them to the higher values.

This significant implication of Maslow's theory, although logically obvious, has not been verified in a mass sampling, since it is impossible to create experimentally the conditions in which significant groups of people would be simultaneously deprived of opportunities to satisfy their higher needs. Ronald Inglehart's widely known research,[3] which deals specifically with the stable societies of western Europe, demonstrates the distinct shift in the individual hierarchy of values of Europeans away from the material (generally speaking, lower values) and toward the postmaterial (higher values).

In my research into the dynamics of basic values, I have drawn data from the uniquely sad situation in my country, where virtually everyone is forced to think primarily about the means for obtaining nourishment and securing safety for self and family on a daily basis. My observations confirmed that the decrease in opportunities for satisfying their lower needs has forced people to alter their individual value systems. From year to year, during the entire period of my observations (begun in 1995), a rapid shift in this structure occurred for both men and women. Larger numbers of people began to find the values of physical safety and material well-being more important. The intensification of the economic crisis in August 1998, unexpected by many, influenced this shift especially strongly. For example, by the end of 1998 the number of people who considered the values of material well-being and safety most important had risen from 42 percent in 1995–1996 to 81 percent for women and to 74 percent for men.

The cluster of values associated with people's primary social status (social relations with family and close friends, family, love), which should occupy a significant place in the individual's value structure, now retreats further and further into the background. (The number of people for whom these values remain most important in their individual hierarchy does not change, however; they remain at 25 to 30 percent of the population.) Above all, the relative importance of such values as freedom, beauty, understanding, creativity, equality among people, and social justice declines. These values are all pushed lower and lower, to the very bottom of the list of the individual's values, and become insignificant.

What immediate consequences can such a shift in the value hierarchy have for most Russians? The process apparently is moving in a direction opposite to that which Inglehart records for Western societies. The hypothesis of "social swings of values," which I developed in 1995, may help answer the question. When social structure is stable, society strives, with the aid of socioregulatory mechanisms (above all education), to attain an uninterrupted and steady movement "up" the scale of values and to secure the most favorable conditions for individual growth. When stable social development is disrupted, however, "social swings" occur. Regulating and controlling mechanisms begin to weaken, traditional socializing arrangements begin to fail, and the individual has fewer incentives to make "positive social efforts." During the shift of priorities downward in the value hierarchy, the value of physical safety gradually moves to the fore.

But the downward movement cannot last indefinitely, nor can it be massive, since that would threaten society's very existence. As a self-organizing system, society is forced either to sue for more powerful methods of control and regulation or to form analogous new ones (such contingencies are extremely rare and always leave scars in the social consciousness; witness the Inquisition, and fascist and other dictatorships). These instruments are switched on as the final means to accomplish a mass "homecoming" of a society's members to an acceptable level of ritual and social behavior. If the mechanisms prove to be ineffective, the process evolves to its extreme point, which leads to the destruction of that society.

But just as the "lower" pole brings with it the destruction of societal structure, so the "higher" pole ends in social stagnation. In attaining the level of "socially valuable individuality," society evolves into a system organized along lines of expediency, as described in Plato's *Republic*. We do not know whether there are examples of societies that possessed mechanisms powerful enough to achieve an "ideal state" for their members. Since the meaning of life is defined only in ideological and religious terms, this "ideal" state eliminates the goals of life for each person. In a real society, however, the individual is in a state of "stable disequilibrium," forced by virtue of "social drive" to move up the scale of values but constantly aiming to roll downhill because of natural factors. The instability of the social development that periodically arises in any given society forces most of its members to balance on the "social swings" of values development. We are now witnessing such a pendulum swing in Russian society, where these "swings" have essentially reached their lowest point.

The Transformation of Life Meanings

Another important sign of the transformation of social consciousness in Russia is the change in the meaning of life. C. W. Morris's classic culture-independent typology of basic life meanings,[4] supple-

mented in the 1960s and 1970s by the work of Carl R. Rogers,[5] provided the methodological basis of my research into the meaning of
life for ordinary people in this country. I initially planned to study
only the structure of people's preferences with respect to the meaning of their private lives. However, the recorded structure proved to
have a certain temporal trend. The observations made during
1995–1996 indicate that, in four cases, a definite direction can be
traced, thanks to reasons of a social nature.

There has been a marked increase in the number of people in
Russian society who consider that a simple, uncomplicated life
based on the satisfaction of fundamental organic and material needs
is most desirable. The proportion of those thinking this way has
grown from 17 to 20 percent over the past several years. An obvious
interpretation suggests itself: The pushed-to-the-limit difficulties of
ensuring physical survival have increasingly forced people to reevaluate the meaning of life in favor of the most simple forms of existence.

At the same time, the number of people in Russian society for
whom the meaning of life is found in activity, in an individualistic
striving toward success, toward the achievement of a result, irrespective of difficulties, is also increasing. This type of goal, often considered uncharacteristic of Russians (in our mentality it is usually associated with the "American individualistic model of life"), turns out
to be a priority now for every fourth person! I do not possess reliable data for any period earlier than 1995, but, by indirect estimates, this life meaning was a priority then for only about 7 to 10
percent of ordinary people. One can believe that the reform years, in
spite of all the negative consequences for vital human activities, have
influenced this two- to threefold growth in the number of those who
rely primarily on themselves in their choice of life direction, rejecting
the usual paternalistic patterns of Russian socialism.

At the same time, public preference for a paternalistically determined life direction, such as living for the sake of other people and
aspiring to be of service to society, is decreasing. The number of people who identify this direction as the most important element in their
lives has decreased over the past five years by a factor of two: from
10 to 11 percent down to 5 to 6 percent.

Another socially oriented goal, to live honorably and in good conscience, participating responsibly in the affairs of society, has also
declined in importance. According to my 1995–1996 research, those

who indicated a preference for such goals made up 15 to 16 percent of the population. By the end of the 1998–1999 period, however, their number had decreased to less than 10 percent.

All these changes in preference in central life goals (impermanent and reversible, I think) can be easily interpreted. The internal social ties that support Russian society's stability through the deep programming of its members' worldview are weakening. People feel less and less obligated to make unconditional sacrifices for the sake of society and its prosperity. At the same time, external circumstances such as material hardships and the undeniable appeal of ideologies once unacceptable or forbidden also exert a powerful pressure on people's consciousness and force them to reevaluate life's meanings and priorities.

Meanwhile, I cannot ignore another important factor: Russians, especially those living in villages and small towns, show a marked preference for what might be called a "Rogerian" meaning of life. In his day, the great psychiatrist Carl R. Rogers suggested adding to Morris's list of five basic life meanings a sixth very important category: "to be who you actually are, to remain yourself under any and all circumstances." This meaning of life is precisely the one preferred by nearly 40 percent of ordinary Russians (although residents of major cities express a substantially lower preference).

I think that the explanation is easy to find here as well. During years of social instability and disorder, individuals are subjected to many trials and dangers that threaten their dignity. Under these circumstances, it is essential to maintain respect toward oneself as an individual, to sustain one's unique identity. Indeed, that is why preserving their own uniqueness and personality is now a primary aim for many Russians.

Media Addictions and an Archaic Religious Revival

Although it is extremely complicated and sometimes even impossible to record changes in the worldview of my compatriots, I will focus on three superficial and thus easily observable aspects: the *mentality of ordinary Russians;* their *susceptibility to the influence of the mass media;* and their *religious and ecological awareness.*

Russian perceptions of the world are now powerfully influenced by the mass media; this influence has increased since the Soviet period.

An average Russian whose perception of the world was formed in a "homogeneous" information environment, who has in his blood a reverence for the printed word (and a comparable respect for the word as spoken from the television screen), is now often incapable of responding critically to the pluralism of opinions. In the flood of highly distorted news broadcasts carried over the various mass media channels, he has lost his reference points. The ideological vacuum, now more than a decade old, coupled with the lack of objectivity and prevalence of disagreement in the news, offers ordinary Russians a less integrated perception of a world increasingly subject to market forces. This difficulty especially affects the young, the under-thirty. Moral traditions and ideological prisms for perceiving the world are being increasingly destroyed through the rise of deviant (addictive) forms of behavior, which are widely portrayed in the mass media (smoking, alcoholism, drug abuse, and sexual promiscuity).

Russians themselves concede that their immersion in the mass media is excessive, and may be harmful. More than half (53 percent) of the inhabitants of villages and small towns admit that they watch television and listen to the radio constantly every day (they hardly ever subscribe to newspapers now). Only about one quarter of the people "immerse themselves" in the mass media "from time to time"; no respondents said that they were not involved with the mass media at all. Without exception, everyone watches two types of television programs: the news and soap operas. News programs support the sense of participating in the world, of not being too isolated; soap operas help people to "forget themselves," to become distracted from distressing experiences and the need to engage in activities required for survival.

Russians admit that the influence of the mass media is harmful. The most striking example that ordinary people everywhere in the country cite in support of this conclusion is the presidential elections of the summer of 1996. Right after the elections and as long as twelve to eighteen months later, I was told again and again in interviews that most people were opposed to the president, but voted for him under the massive influence of the mass media. They then immediately regretted their choice. In nearly every local community the electorate was divided virtually in half, irrespective of age or sex. In almost all the interviews, the respondents who had voted for the president expressed regret about it, thereby providing an indirect indicator that no less than half of the population is subject to the influence of the mass media.

Most ordinary people equate religiosity with devotion to the Russian Orthodox Church, and in this form, religion ranks very low. But true believers are also few in number. Many respondents are certain—as far as they and their fellow villagers are concerned—that there is no true faith. If something of that order does indeed exist, then it belongs more to the realm of newfangled superstitions and remnants of pagan notions. Judging from the opinions of the people themselves, as well as from external evidence, it should be acknowledged that the level of religious feeling in Russia has not significantly increased over the past decade, notwithstanding the well-known church restoration projects undertaken by the authorities.

Extremely little authentic religious activity (attending churches and praying—matters about which it is possible to judge by the presence of icons in people's homes) takes place either in small towns or in villages. On the basis of certain episodic observations, it is possible to conclude that genuine, actively religious believers make up only 2 to 5 percent of the Russian population.

The active religious propaganda of the late 1990s notwithstanding, the number of true believers has apparently not grown at all. It has become fashionable, however, to be a believer not only in an urban setting, but even in a peasant one; as a rule, the younger a person is, the more likely he will draw attention to his religiosity.

The decline of religious feeling and the unexpected lack of receptivity to Orthodoxy can be explained to some extent by the fact that religious "surrogates" are developing in the public consciousness. First and foremost among these new forms is what might be called "ecological feeling."

This feeling (customarily termed "ecological awareness") is another indication of the nascent and radical change in the Russian worldview. In Soviet times, public indifference to ecological problems was as widespread as "ecological activism" became in the late 1980s and early 1990s. In my opinion, this turnaround was caused by the superficiality and "political correctness" of the ecological views that were shaped principally by the mass media. This relativity of ecological notions brought about a rapid change in these notions themselves. The public's ecological awareness derived primarily from utilitarian and to a lesser degree ethical attitudes to nature as a private domain (I would say, more precisely, to nature as a private pantry and warehouse of useful items). Russians see nature from the standpoint of its usefulness, profit, and harmfulness; less often, from the standpoint of its preservation and protection against destructive human activities. By the early 1990s, the ecological awareness of most village dwellers was based on the dichotomies of "pollution-purity" and "usefulness-harmfulness."

In recent years, however, the ecological awareness of ordinary Russians has changed perceptibly. The aesthetic and ethical components of relating to nature have grown in significance very rapidly and have become dominant, sharply diminishing the significance of the utilitarian component. Nowadays, for example, up to 50 percent of Russians consider aesthetic principles, and another 28 percent ethical principles, as the primary determinants of their attitude to nature and their interaction with it. Only about 10 percent maintain the primacy of utilitarian or negative principles. Relating to nature as one relates to beauty and peace, not just to something that is useful, is becoming increasingly important for broad circles of ordinary people. In this trend I see an indication that formerly suppressed religious feelings are undergoing a renaissance.

It would probably be accurate to say that the needs felt by many Russians for religion and religious feelings find expression not so much in seeking out the Church (this is why, in spite of all the official efforts, the level of people's declared religiousness is so low), as in expressing a renewed ecological sensibility, one that profoundly appeals to the Russian sense of archaic unity with nature. Given the vacuum of a worldview in Russia, especially a religious one, and given the absence of the Orthodox Church's essential authority (not only that of the Christian church, I think), it is entirely possible that these ecological notions can in the future serve as the foundation on which a new worldview will be constructed.

Even the examples I have described of the changes that have occurred in the three aspects of societal consciousness over the past decade seem to me sufficient grounds for appreciating how profoundly the Russian mentality has changed and for sensing how latent these processes still are.

The Decline in Government
Authority in the Provinces

Over the past decade, fundamental changes in Russian attitudes toward state power and in political preferences have occurred. Until 1994, one could say with assurance that among ordinary people, especially in village society, nearly everybody sympathized with Communist ideology. But by 1996–1997, a strong political polarization had developed, with nearly half of the members of any given community remaining loyal to the former ideology and the other half gambling cautiously on the new organizational and political formations and moving over to the camp, if not of the democrats, then of the "pluralists."

The political bacchanalia of 1997–1998 fostered among ordinary Russians an almost complete loss of interest in politics. The conflict between the Communist and democratic mindsets, in all its magnitude, disappeared into the depths of society: Neither philosophy was popular any longer. However sharply the popularity of communism has declined, sympathy toward its ideology and the Party still remains, whereas a deeply negative attitude has now developed toward democratic goals. This attitude is everywhere. One can mourn, but things have come to this: The word "democrat" has become a bugaboo in the provinces. This is why practically every local politician who hopes to succeed diligently avoids practically all democratic slogans. The overwhelming majority of Russians in rural areas and small towns is now completely apolitical. They intend to support whichever political movement can offer them, above all, strong authority.

During the 1990s, Russian attitudes toward state power developed along the same lines as their political passions. Throughout the entire decade, government, both local and federal, steadily lost authority, and in the eyes of ordinary people it continues to lose it. If fear of the government was strong until 1993–1994, when memories of Soviet times were fresh and when people expected a swift change in the economic and political situation, by 1996–1997 an attitude close to indifference predominated. At the local level the government possessed ridiculously little authority, or none at all.

The power of the state wound up quietly and imperceptibly in the hands of the "brigadiers": the foremen—both in the literal and metaphorical senses of the word—of agricultural cooperatives, which succeeded *kolkhozes* and *sovkhozes,* and the leaders of criminal organizations. "Nature abhors a vacuum." Although their actual relations toward the local authorities are complicated, ordinary Russians generally see the semicriminal, semiproductive organizations in every region and district as the reference points of real power.

In recent years, the attitude of ordinary Russians toward central government authority has even become contemptuous, which never used to be the case. The complete impotence of the government is seen not just in the fact that people do not take it into account (even if local officials do not rely on the authority and power of criminal structures); rather, it is as if the government did not exist at all. (An amusing paradox: The executive branch in most regions has completely lost its power, but the number of its representatives has grown two- or threefold almost everywhere. Now there are as many as eighty staff members in almost every regional administration.)

Very frequently (I think that this has now become the rule, although it is difficult for the outside observer to ascertain), regional leaders are tightly linked with local industrial and commercial firms, and through them to shadow organizations. At least, respondents everywhere often allude to such a chain of influence linking local officials with the shadow economy and in turn with the criminal world. In the eyes of the people, such relationships are justified, as they have had a chance to develop, consolidate, and take root. More than that, from the people's point of view, these relationships are even expedient. In one of his final interviews with me, one midlevel entrepreneur from Tver oblast expressed himself in frank terms:

> Why should I be afraid of racketeers? They are not the same as they were five or seven years ago; now they are people with understanding, they are always ready to see things from your point of view, make concessions, even help you. But when it comes to our government, that is the main racketeer, and the cruelest one. Any one of us is the enemy: Give it everything and it will strip you, deceive you, kill you.

This opinion is not unique; it is fairly typical among those who try to do business in the provinces. People have no positive expectations whatsoever from the present government.

But state authority and order are undeniably necessary, and many people emphasize this in their interviews. The dominant theme in people's political preferences remains the same as it was at the beginning of the decade: "Give us a Boss—then we'd make an effort." People don't care in the least about specific parties and programs. They need central state authority. Strong and consistent. Punitive, but also able to protect the ordinary person.

There is no state authority like that now. That is why people give in to two customary choices. In the first and simplest case, they appeal to representatives of the criminal world; finding protection and patronage there, they increasingly gravitate toward them. Although only a "pseudoauthority," criminal organizations are consistent and effective. Locally, the criminal world is more powerful than governmental authority. And more, with the passage of time the criminal authorities in the regions (where they are often major businessmen and merchants) are beginning to realize that they have become invested with a new function, one that has been imperceptibly transferred to them by government authorities. Frequently there are situations in which not just ordinary people but regional bureaucrats openly take pride in their connections with the criminal "authorities": This increases their influence and power. How can this situation not be compared with the Sicily of old or with present-day Colombia? But only since the late 1990s has this process accelerated and become evident.

In Self-Defense:
The Appeal of Local Self-Government

The population's second choice, in a situation where there is either little central government authority or none at all, is the aspiration toward local self-governance. This trend emerged very clearly between 1992 and 1994. One of the most important reasons for it was the disintegration of collective and state farms, when Russians, especially in small villages, found themselves suddenly confronted with the necessity of ensuring their own physical survival, without either the money or an adequate farming system to do so.

The objective of supporting livelihood with one's own efforts gave rise to an entirely natural aspiration: to regulate the life of the community independently of local governmental authority. In 1994, during my research in the Altai Mountain region, the resident of one village (Saidys) told me how, thanks to the self-rule organization that the village had formed, they were protecting their rights in the face of hostile government authorities. This was a time of illegal activity by corrupt officials, who aided "shadow businessmen" in solving their problems at the expense of the local population. One of these businessmen, who was breeding Siberian reindeer in order to sell their antlers abroad illegally, tried, with the support of regional officials, to fence in an enormous stretch of woods that belonged to two neighboring villages. This land was the people's source of livelihood. The conflict, in which ordinary rural dwellers opposed the combined forces of the criminal world, the local administration, and the militia, was resolved when the villagers dispatched two mounted detachments of young men armed with rifles to defend their territory. For a week, armed men from both sides stood at the boundaries of the forested area, until the businessman finally gave in. Does this situation recall the romanticism of the American Wild West? This particular case had a happy ending. And that was as unusual back then as it is now.

Most residents of small communities are turning to the idea of self-rule slowly, but with ever increasing attention. The degree of sympathy for the idea is, naturally, directly proportional to the weakness of the legally constituted local officials and the arbitrary rule of their criminal deputies. In the past few years no less than two-thirds of our respondents stated that self-governance is either desirable or essential for their village or small town. Less than one-fifth of the population opposed the idea of local self-rule. Very few actual steps have been taken in this direction, however. Judging by the survey responses, fewer than one in ten inhabited localities has put together the operational elements of self-governance; the institutions necessary for such a system to function normally are lacking everywhere.

This deficiency is understandable. Only a handful of Russians have an idea of what really constitutes self-governance, or what political, social, and economic conditions are needed if a small Russian town or village should want it. Not a single respondent expressed any notion whatsoever about specific mechanisms for implementing the idea of self-governance. At the present time, we see only that the need for it is acknowledged, but its implementation is not understood. The need is great, however. How long will it take to design an effective organizational model?

Survival Tactics in a Time of Trouble

Foreign scholars err when they talk about the low standard of living and the low quality of life in Russia. What they actually should be talking about is survival, simple biological survival, a problem that much of the nation's population has faced for many years now. Survival means creating the minimal conditions that ensure the basic physical preservation of the individual. These minimal conditions at present are a small plot of land on which a family (a household) can grow potatoes, vegetables, and fruit, as well as store hay for domestic cattle and fowl. In addition, a no less important task for many is stockpiling fuel (firewood or coal) for the long, cold winter. And, naturally, for all this one must have the strength to grow, store, process, and preserve one's natural products. Most of the life energy of a great many Russians is now being expended in this way.

During the first years of the economic reforms, many people found themselves utterly unprepared to support themselves and their families in such autonomous fashion. In that period quite a few people starved to death, even entire settlements of people. Many families lived only on their salaries and had no possibility of setting up farm plots right away. According to my data, in 1994–1996 up to one-third of the children in the provinces were starving—not only in the forest settlements (where personal farm plots were not traditionally cultivated and people lived on their earnings and from hunting and fishing), but even in the villages (where personal plots had always been maintained). The data on children was easier to obtain, but it implies that the adults in every third family were also starving. For example, in the Russian North, where economic activity was based on the large fishing collectives, the population traditionally had no personal plots; on average they had about 0.01 hectares of arable land per person and less than 0.3 head of any type of domestic livestock (in 1996 I counted only six pigs for 2,400 rural households).

The catastrophic state of household economies felt everywhere in the first half of the 1990s was offset quickly—it couldn't have been otherwise—by the active search for new forms of life support. Many diverse methods of autonomous survival were discovered and put into practice in every settlement and region. In one case, people began to prepare and sell hay because a neighboring oblast had experienced a bad harvest. In another case, they joined together into something resembling a cooperative for a time to raise calves and pigs so that they could sell the meat in town in the winter, bypassing middlemen. In a third case, people acted as impoverished landlords, renting out their fishing boats for a minimal price or hiring crews from among the even poorer workers from Ukraine and Estonia.

Natural Farming: A New Life Support Model?

There are a great many new forms of economic activity in Russia today. They are all extremely simple. And the simplest, as well as the most widespread (and the most astonishing), is the model of life support based on a return to natural farming, which provides a full life cycle for a family. Within one or two years, many Russians went from large-scale industrial agricultural production to the form of natural farming described by historians as typical during the sixteenth to eighteenth centuries and even recorded in chronicles of twelfth- and thirteenth-century Russia! An enduring image of our contemporary socioeconomic life took shape long ago. During the Soviet period, society resembled a massive, durable, homogeneous platform built on a foundation of almost completely uniform economic activity, like congealed fat in a cast-iron pot. In our difficult time of crisis, the fat has melted and come to a boil and is now roiling, a multitude of bubbles constantly forming and rising to the surface—new, hitherto unseen forms (more accurately, models) of life support. Nearly all these bubbles burst instantly and disappear; but the pot will stop boiling at some point—crises pass—and some of the newly formed bubbles—new models of life support—will not burst, but will have a chance to set, harden, and become a point of crystallization for a new economic, and perhaps also societal, order in Russia.

What is the nature of these possible points of economic growth? Will they be justified politically, socially, and morally? The question is not a frivolous one. With each year I observe the appearance or development of new "models of survival" that make me increasingly apprehensive. One sees, for example, entire communities, including women and children, beginning to support themselves by participating in the transport and sale of drugs. And if this "model of survival" spreads widely, the government will be powerless to eliminate it. Isn't it better, while it's not too late, to promote the dissemination of other models for living?

Beyond Present Tribulations: A Heroic Legacy

I am not inclined to make prognoses or study the long-term prospects for the development of Russian society. In writing this essay, I saw my objective as merely to record empirically the changes taking place in our society. Changes had to occur in any case because they constitute the fertile ground of any social development. It is another matter that these changes have turned out not to be the ones that we (I have in mind not the politicians, but the scientific and creative intelligentsia) enthusiastically forecast as long ago as 1989 and even 1991. Truly, it's like the old saying, "We wanted to do better, but it turned out to be just the same."

And at the same time, all these changes are a completely explainable reaction of society to its own disease (and perhaps a predictable reaction, if only we could have known ahead of time). And because these changes can be explained, we can draw one seemingly trivial conclusion. We see that Russia is changing, changing hastily, without getting its bearings. But what is the nature of these hurried changes? New political and economic institutions. Perhaps the elements of a new morality. But we discover that everything born within the depths of society, apparently out of nothing, had always existed there in its potential form. In any new political constellation, the same archetype of the national spirit that defines both the uniqueness of a people and the transformations they are undergoing reveals itself—independently of whether society experiences good times or tribulations during these transformations.

It is often the case that sorrowful times for the people living through them turn out to be heroic times for their descendants. A changing Russia still remains the same Russia.

Notes

1. In Russia, major cities have populations of 500,000 and more, and smaller towns have, as a rule, populations of 12,000 to 100,000. Residents of worker and resort settlements are included in city populations.

2. Abraham Maslow, *Motivation and Personality* (New York: Harper and Brothers, 1954).

3. Ronald Inglehart, *Culture Shift in Advanced Industrial Society* (Princeton: Princeton University Press, 1990).

4. C. W. Morris, *Varieties of Human Value* (Chicago: University of Chicago Press, 1956).

5. Carl R. Rogers, *On Becoming a Person: A Therapist's View of Psychotherapy* (Boston: Houghton Mifflin, 1961).

2

PROTECTING FAIR COMPETITION IN THE NEW RUSSIA

A Revolution in Thinking, Not Just Economics

Natal'ia Fonareva

Probably no single piece of economic reform legislation has had more trouble taking root in Russian soil than the Law on Competition. Throughout the twentieth century and right up to the 1990s, the national economy of the USSR and therefore of Russia followed the principle of "one country, one factory." And the Soviet economy, in turn, was built on the highly monopolized industrial base of pre-revolutionary Russia. The organization of a manufacturing system based on a strictly centralized system of administrative command and on the totalitarian control of state property required well-trained personnel. Drawing upon the old imperial mindset, therefore, a management corps was formed in a relatively brief time, and

Born in 1957, **Natal'ia Evgen'evna Fonareva** studied economics at the Plekhanov Economics Institute and earned her doctorate on the topic of consumer demand. Following a decade-long academic career in a research institute affiliated with the USSR Ministry of Trade, she worked in various government bodies tasked with economic reform, until in 1997 she was appointed chair of the State Antimonopoly Committee, which later became a ministry. After earning another advanced law degree from the Presidential State Service Academy, Fonareva was appointed in November 1998 first deputy minister for antimonopoly policy. Translated by Antonina W. Bouis.

these people were well adapted to the tasks of vertical planning and centralized management.

World War II, which created the need for swift mobilization and extreme centralization of human and material resources, strengthened the centrist and monopolist thinking of the management corps. This centrist tendency was reinforced during the postwar years, when the devastated wartime economy was being repaired, virgin lands conquered, the space program initiated, a transcontinental railroad constructed, and the arms race launched. Nor should we forget that the habit of state patronage, ingrained over many decades in the populace, had resulted in a lack of experience in making independent decisions and developing private initiatives.

Thus, when economic reforms began, it was hard to find people who knew the basics of entrepreneurship or managers in any field who could function in a decentralized market economy under conditions of competition.

I should add that a centrally planned economy is characterized by a total and stable shortage of everything—except money. As a result, no director of an enterprise had ever faced a real problem moving products to market. Almost everything was sold as it came off the assembly line. Coupled with the monopoly on foreign trade, this system led to a lack of interest in the development of a distribution system, marketing services, strategic planning, modernized production, or lower production costs. The price that Russian manufacturing has to pay today for almost a century of "hothouse conditions"— that is, the absence of competition—is enormous. Therefore it is no accident that the enterprises that had exported a significant part of their production (raw materials, arms, military technology) were in much better shape once the Russian market opened up.

Laying the Legal Groundwork

These preconditions determined the great difficulties faced in drafting and enacting legislation governing competition and in executing that legislation. Nevertheless, despite the relatively short period of its existence, several stages in the history of Russian competition legislation are already notable.

The Preliminary Stage. The passage in 1991 of the Russian Federation Law "On Competition and Limitation of Monopolistic Activity

in Trade Markets" marked the beginning. This law determined the
basic positions of government policy on competition, including antimonopoly policy aimed at preventing and stopping abuses of a dominant position in existing markets, forms of unfair competition, and
limits on allowable economic concentration of production and sales.

In July 1991 the government began establishing antimonopoly
agencies. The Supreme Soviet of the Russian Soviet Federal Socialist
Republic (RSFSR) promulgated a resolution on the creation of a
"State Committee of the Russian Federation on Antimonopoly Policy and Support of New Economic Structures." Its essential powers
were defined by the Law on Competition.

In its first version, this law existed until May 30, 1995. It drew
upon the broad legislative and practical experience in regulating anti-
monopolistic actions acquired in countries with developed market
economies: the United States, Canada, Great Britain, and Germany,
among others. However, despite the common principles of antimonopoly regulation, every country has its own historical traits in the
formation of its economy. For the Russian Federation, one of the most
important is the extreme monopolization of the economy. The Law on
Competition proved unable to deal with the economic processes in
Russia that were to be subjected to antimonopoly regulation. By
1993, therefore, it was clear that the law needed to be revised. A new
draft of the law, enacted in 1995, retained the initial policy concept,
even though almost every article had been changed to some extent.

The Second Stage.   The next stage involved the formation of a constitutional foundation for competition law. The new Constitution of
the Russian Federation, ratified on December 12, 1993, guaranteed
a single economic space; free movement of goods, services, and financial methods; *support for competition;* and freedom of economic
activity. This constitutional norm was also supported by another:
No economic activity directed toward monopolization and unfair
competition was allowed.

The Third Stage.   This stage in the development of competition legislation began in October 1994 and was related to the development
and passage of new civil legislation. Article 10 of the Civil Code of
the Russian Federation stated that the claim of civil rights could not
be used to limit competition, nor could a dominant position in the
market be abused.

Today, on the average, Russian antimonopoly agencies examine each year roughly a thousand cases dealing with abuse of dominant market positions, approximately thirty to forty cases of cartel arrangements and coordinated actions, and two to three hundred cases of unfair competition. These agencies are working intensively to control economic concentration and counteract the monopolization of the economy (8,000–9,000 appeals a year on average).

Along with the introduction and implementation of special legislation on competition, the government throughout the years of economic reform has tried to affect the fluctuations of prices and tariffs of the most important goods and services, particularly in economic sectors that influence organizational changes. This can be considered a special, *permanent stage* in the formation of a competitive environment.

The beginning of economic reform was characterized by an extraordinary upsurge in prices. The basic problem was that the increase in prices in individual branches and at individual enterprises was unequal. This provoked a crisis in sales for some enterprises and simultaneously a crisis of payments for others. Inflation inevitably led to a precipitous decline in production and the withering away of entire branches of industry. As early as 1992, therefore, the government considered whether to introduce price regulation for enterprises holding dominant positions in the market. In 1992, a special decree of the Russian government was passed, "On State Regulation of Prices and Tariffs on Production and Services of Monopolistic Enterprises in 1992–1993."

In practice, however, this kind of price regulation only stimulated higher operating costs among enterprises and reduced to zero their interest in developing a competitive edge, while also undermining the tax base. In 1994, the decree was not renewed. However, the government did not reject completely the implementation of its own price policy. At the present time, policy is being implemented primarily as it affects the energy and raw materials monopolies, under the authority of the Federal Law "On Natural Monopolies" as well as a number of special laws (for example, the Federal Law "On State Regulation of Tariffs on Electric and Fuel Energy").

Passage of the Law on Natural Monopolies proved extremely difficult. The legislation's authors encountered enormous counterlobbying from the enterprises affected. As a result, enterprises in the housing system were stricken from the category of natural monopolies during the time that the State Duma was seeking to overcome the president's second veto. Thus, housing reform in Russia began in 1997 without adequate legal support at the federal level. Nowadays it is the local authorities who regulate housing construction and services, often resulting, as audits have shown, in unjustified rent increases, unequal progress in housing reform from one region to another, limited use of competitive bidding for municipal contracts, alienation of the public, and insufficient public control over the actions of local government officials.

To implement the Law on Natural Monopolies, presidential decrees in 1996 established federal services to regulate the electricity, communications, and transport monopolies. However, by 1998, during the Evgenii Primakov government, two of the three regulatory agencies (transport and communications) were abolished by presidential decree and their functions handed over to the newly created Ministry on Antimonopoly Policy and Support of Entrepreneurship (MAP). This ministry assumed the responsibilities of the abolished State Committee of the Russian Federation on Antimonopoly Policy (GAK) and the State Committee of the Russian Federation on Support of Entrepreneurship (GKRP). Of the three agencies originally regulating natural monopolies, only the Federal Energy Commission of the Russian Federation (FEK) has remained independent, even though there have been numerous attempts to abolish it and turn its functions over to the MAP.

Foreign specialists in competition law, including experts from the World Bank, severely criticized this reorganization on the grounds that a single executive branch agency cannot be both controller (antimonopoly agency) and controlled (agencies on regulating the activity of subjects of natural monopolies), without compromising the checks and balances system in establishing prices and tariffs. Moreover, the critics argued, the political independence of a collegial organ—the board, which makes all important decisions on prices and tariffs for the production and services of the natural monopolies—could not be guaranteed within the framework of a federal ministry: A change in government could occur before the expiration of the four-year term set for board members.

In 1999, the government of the Russian Federation promised to reinstitute independent agencies to regulate the natural monopolies in transport and communications. Government regulation of the natural monopolies has led to a significant reduction in the rate of growth of prices and tariffs for these products and services as compared to the general index of industrial prices. However, this sphere of regulation is so large that many of its parts remain virgin soil, so to speak. This applies in particular to the activities of ports, transport terminals, and so on. There are many problems in devising modern accounting methods for these prices and tariffs.

Protecting Consumers from False Advertising

Once competition developed, advertising began to play a greater market role. The content of advertising, aimed at servicing commercial turnover with the goal of stimulating sales, in the early 1990s generalized excessively and revealed an obvious disregard of the norms on unfair competition, specified in Article 10 of the Law on Competition. Therefore, with the aim of protecting consumers against unfair competition in advertising, preventing and stopping inappropriate advertising that could deceive or harm consumers, the Federal Law on Advertising was passed in July 1995. The passage of this law can be considered the *fourth stage* in the development of competition law in Russia.

The need for such a law had become obvious by 1993. Particular alarm was caused by the sharp activation of so-called financial pyramids, which promoted business through a kind of "agitational" advertising that was unrestricted because of a legal vacuum in that area. The State Antimonopoly Committee did not manage to get adequate funding from the federal government then, so the draft law was developed in its early stages by members of the committee under my leadership.

By late 1993 a more or less balanced draft of the Law on Advertising was shared with representatives of the advertising business. Their reaction was unexpectedly strong and childishly egoistic. "We don't need a law like that!" We had to explain patiently that the law's main goal was to find a balance between the interests of advertisers, consumers of advertising, and the government. The law's framers, headed by me, spent a long time persuading the advertising and mass media representatives that the role of advertising in Russian society had grown so much that it was impossible to continue without a legislative balancing of interests. Having accepted this unhappy circumstance, advertising executives decided to take the textbook approach: develop an alternative draft law and present it through deputies in the State Duma. This alternative version, naturally, had a rather declarative character.

At the same time, the activities of the financial pyramids were assuming threatening proportions. As an emergency measure to fill the legal void, a version of the law in the form of a presidential decree was proposed: "On Protecting Consumers from Unfair Advertising." Promulgated in June 1996, the decree played a significant part in putting a brake on the financial pyramids, but it could not change the situation radically, since limitations on the legality of institutions, as required by the legal measures that could be applied in these cases, could only be effected by federal law, as specified by the Russian Constitution.

In August 1996, the government of the Russian Federation approved a draft federal law on advertising and sent it to the State Duma as a legislative initiative. Mikhail Poltoranin, then head of the Duma Committee on Information Policy and Communications, presented an alternative draft law at the same time. The government draft was presented in the Duma by Leonid Bochin, chairman of the Committee on Anti-Monopoly Policy. The battle was fierce. A major role was played at the Duma session by Sergei Kalashnikov, chairman of the Duma Committee on Labor and Social Policy (he is now minister of labor and social development). In a brilliant speech, Kalashnikov put the issue plainly: If you are for state control over advertising, vote for the government draft; if you are for business control over advertising, vote for the alternative. The government version won. Poltoranin was invited to join the expert group for further work on the government draft, but he replied with a sharp refusal, calling the government draft a "police law."

At the same time, the mass media started a propaganda campaign against the government draft law and its drafters, including me personally. We were inundated by direct and veiled accusations of corruption. We had to take one newspaper and one journalist to court in order to defend our name and integrity (we won the suit, of course). However, even after this, the war in the press did not abate. Among the "opponents" were several authors of the alternative draft law, who were quite vociferous. Despite everything, in July 1995 the Federal Law on Advertising was signed by the president of the Russian Federation. Thereafter, according to reports in the Russian mass media, the Law on Advertising received high marks from experts in the European Commission and the Trade and Industry Chamber of the Russian Federation.

Like all laws designed to manage competition, the Law on Advertising has had difficulties. In order to inculcate its basic tenets into business practice and to teach entrepreneurs the new rules of the game, the Antimonopoly Committee had to deal with quite a few precedent-setting investigations and win a series of difficult arbitrations. In 1995–1997, the most painful arbitration, in terms of obtaining compliance with the law, was advertising of services relating to the use of financial resources by juridical and physical persons (including advertisements for the so-called financial pyramids), as well as television advertising for alcoholic drinks and tobacco products. Nevertheless, this stage in the formation of advertising legislation was passed successfully.

However, we could not rest on our laurels. Advertising belongs to a sphere where too many people consider themselves experts (most people agree that in the past this kind of expertise was confined to economics, teaching, and medicine). Therefore, soon after the Law on Advertising was passed, various laws prescribed advertising standards (pertaining to medical preparations, regulation of the production and sale of ethyl spirits and alcoholic products, and others) that contradicted the Law on Advertising. This trend complicated not only the work of the advertising business but that of the antimonopoly agencies as well, because they monitored adherence to advertising legislation. Moreover, several regional legislatures tried to pass their own laws on regulating advertising initiatives, a practice not envisaged by federal legislation. In order to obtain unified rules of market economics in the production and distribution of advertising, we had to go through the Constitutional Court of the Russian Federation (the Moscow City Duma and the Legislative Assembly of Omsk oblast had asserted the right to regulate advertising on their own). We won the case, but some regional governments did not abandon their attempts to interfere illegally in the legislative process. Many illegitimate normative acts had to be rescinded through the procurator's office and the judicial system.

I had a reason for describing at length the drafting, passage, and implementation of the Law on Advertising. Its history is typical of all laws that are part of the system of Russian competition law. Unremitting attempts by the business community to revise competition legislation present a real problem; businessmen are trying to repeal standards that do not suit them, despite the fact that these standards are just, meet the goal of balancing social interests, and conform to international practice.

Fighting Obstacles to Entrepreneurship

Although they do not directly regulate competitive relations, Article 55 of the Constitution and Articles 1 and 49 of the Civil Code are important provisions designed to stop any illegal and unjustified limitations of the rights of organizations and individuals as well as to guarantee the normal development of entrepreneurial activity. Without such legal instruments, especially in a state with a federative structure, the effective safeguarding of many constitutional guarantees—including support for a single economic space; the free movement of goods, services, and financial assets across the national territory; and the free use of one's assets and property for entrepreneurial and other economic activity not banned by law—would be impossible.

In attaining the goal of supporting a single economic space, the antimonopoly agencies face formidable obstacles. When we turn to foreign experts in competition law, we often find that they do not understand the specifically Russian problems in applying legislation on competition. For instance, foreign agencies have the greatest difficulty (and spend a significant portion of their time) applying "classic" antimonopoly (antitrust) legislation to detect, prove, and prevent anticompetitive (cartel) agreements. Russian antimonopoly agencies, on the other hand, find that the lion's share of their time and effort goes into the struggle to surmount administrative barriers to entrepreneurial activity. These barriers derive from the various actions and agreements of the federal executive branch, the executive branches of regional administrations, and the local government agencies that all limit competition. On average, the Russian antimonopoly agencies review around 1,500 applications a year relating to such violations. The source of these difficulties is the federative structure of the state and the weakened influence of the federal center over the regions under conditions of economic crisis and budgetary deficits.

Just as executive branch agencies are establishing standards in a more orderly fashion, legislative branch agencies are enacting more laws that actually limit competition. Because this activity falls outside the jurisdiction of antimonopoly agencies, we must turn to the procuracy and the judicial system for help. However, these court trials are prolonged and often result in significant losses for Russian or foreign businesses.

This state of affairs suggested the title of this article. It is not enough for the government to proclaim a transition to a market economy, even though it would be more accurate to speak not of a "transition" but of the legalization of market relations that had been smothered by the administrative command system. Market relations are objective, and they cannot be repealed or changed as readily as day changes into night. However, when market laws are suppressed or ignored, the economy begins to produce negative results and lose ground. Nor is it enough to develop and pass good laws and to form an appropriate governmental apparatus. In order for these laws to work steadily throughout the country there must be a revolution in people's minds. People must rid themselves of the psychology of dependence that was imbued by a system of total state ownership and state patronage.

There are two aspects to overcoming such an all-encompassing social defect. One the one hand, it is important for people to learn to count primarily on themselves. On the other hand, people with power should stop using that power, whether by design or in error, for evil purposes; that is, by creating illegal benefits and advantages for "their" enterprises (enterprises in their region, or where relatives work, or where they have other connections) and squeezing out the outsiders. Government agencies must be reliably separate from business and must make fair decisions, without violating anyone's legal rights or interests.

It is no accident that both the Law of the Russian Federation "On Competition and Limiting Monopolistic Activity" and the Federal Law "On the Bases of State Service in the Russian Federation" prohibit entrepreneurial activity on the part of government officials. But is this ban always observed in practice? The experience of the anti-monopoly agencies shows that it is not. What seems understandable and obvious in countries with a developed market economy often is not seen the same way in Russia. The use of inside connections between the authorities and individual enterprises, groups of enterprises, and even entire branches of industry and the habit of resolving personal issues without considering the legal interests of market competitors leads to lost economic ties, unfair competition, unjustifiable losses, and limitations on the progress of reform. One can easily find politicians who say (especially during elections) that they support the concept of a single nation, strengthened statehood, the development of market principles, and assistance for Russian manufacturers—but who in fact behave in a completely different way. As a result, the problem of regional separatism today is just as acute as it was during the Tatar-Mongol invasion of the thirteenth century.

It is important for the country to have a broadly developed system of civilized rules and mores in business. Russian traditions in this area are extremely rich and interesting. However, the economic crisis, an unbearable tax burden, mass nonpayment of salaries, corruption, and racketeering, force many entrepreneurs who truly wish to live and work honestly to function in the shadow or semishadow economy. Until these problems are solved, the best-written codes of business ethics, loudly and publicly supported by everyone, will be nothing more than good intentions.

In speaking today of Russia's future, I would like to believe that the country will be preserved as a single state, with an economy reborn on market principles, with a population that will feel worthy and respected not only at home but abroad. Without solving the problems of political unity and corruption, and without endowing a new generation with a fundamentally different mentality, this goal will be impossible to achieve. Therefore, government officials in Russia's antimonopoly agencies see their main tasks as developing healthy competition in the economy, overcoming regional separatism, helping Russia join the world economy, and creating a stable and flourishing state.[1]

Notes

1. I should like to take this opportunity to thank Mrs. S. Reynolds and Mr. B. J. Phillips, of the Organization of Economic Cooperation and Development (OECD), for kindly providing the interesting materials on legislation governing advertising in various countries. Foreign experts from the United States, Germany, France, and Great Britain, as well as members of leading international organizations, especially the OECD, the United Nations Conference on Trade and Development (UNCTAD), and the European Commission, have given us invaluable and multifaceted support in developing and implementing specific legislation throughout the years of economic reform.

3

REFORM IN RUSSIA'S REGIONS

The View from Novgorod

Mikhail Prusak

Seven years of Russian market reforms have led to a number of fundamental changes in the landscape of Russia's sociopolitical and socioeconomic systems.

The transition from a centralized distribution system to market methods of managing the economy is almost complete, even though the market medium that has been created as a result of that transformation, its methods of functioning, and the legislative and legal base regulating, it all still require adjustment.

Russia's economy has taken on such market characteristics as free price formation, a two-level banking system that includes commercial banks, and competition among manufacturers; a majority of Russian enterprises have achieved true economic independence. A sweeping privatization of state property has taken place in all re-

Born in 1960 in Ukraine, **Mikhail Mikhailovich Prusak** worked briefly as a schoolteacher before launching his career in the Komsomol in Novgorod. After a few years as director of a collective farm near the city, he was elected to the first freely elected Soviet parliament in 1989, where he quickly joined forces with the reformers. In October 1991 he was appointed governor of Novgorod oblast and in 1993 was elected to the Federation Council. After completing his advanced degree from the Academy of People's Economy in 1994, Prusak was elected governor of Novgorod oblast in December 1995 and reelected in September 1999. Translated by Antonina W. Bouis.

gions of Russia, and as a result corporate and private forms of property predominate in the means of production. Property has been classified into federal, regional, and municipal forms. Conditions have been created for the primarily territorial management of the economy and the social sphere. Regional organs have developed significant capabilities for self-government. Private enterprise in small, medium, and large forms has been given legal shape and has significantly developed.

All these transformations were not goals in themselves; reform was meant to produce social results, manifested first of all in guaranteeing an economic upswing and the growth of personal wealth. In the first stage, these results have been more negative than positive. This, however, has been typical for the early stages of radical socioeconomic transformation in most postsocialist countries.

The positive results of the first stage of Russian reforms include:

- nearly total eradication of the chronic shortages of goods and services that were prevalent under the Soviet system, which many experts called "the shortage economy";
- reduction of inflation (which had reached critical levels in 1992–1994) to approximately 10 percent annually, price stabilization, and the equalization of price levels in Russia's regions;
- transfer of most housing to private ownership;
- emergence of real opportunity for citizens and families to own land, expansion of private farms, and introduction of the private farm system;
- significant expansion of opportunities to take initiatives in business;
- easing of restrictions against moving about, changing one's residence within the country, and traveling abroad;
- retention of free school education and medical services, state and municipal subsidies for housing and communal services, and transport subsidies; and
- preservation of a low retirement age comparable to international norms (fifty-five for women, sixty for men), and state support of pensioners' security.

Among the positive economic results of the first stage are: stabilizing the exchange rate of the ruble; reversing the decline of industrial production; partially restructuring industrial branches; preserving most operational assets in vital support sectors (energy, transport, and so on); increasing levels of exports in proportion to imports, and concurrently generating the creation of hard currency reserves.

At the same time, economic reforms require a more mature approach. Russian socioeconomic reforms of the past decade typically were introduced from the top down. The reforms were conceived and implemented through legislative decisions made in Moscow, and then sent out to the regions. The federative principle clearly predominated in the first stage of reform, which initially addressed management on the federal level. The regions, by which I mean the eighty-nine administrative territories of the federation (oblasts, krais, and republics), were forced to implement locally the legislative and other normative and legal acts and resolutions that determined and regulated the course of reform, based on decisions made at the federal level. In a number of cases, the federal acts and resolutions had no regional continuity at all and simply became the general rule for all regions—a procrustean bed.

While recognizing that centralizing principles are necessary to reform the economy and that only a common federal policy can implement reforms regionally, it is important to understand the dangers of misinterpreting true federalism, underestimating regional differences, and overlooking regional interests. The Soviet system of managing the economy, which was organized along both territorial and industrial lines, was in practice more sector oriented, under a management chain leading from state to sector to branch enterprise. Overlooking the regional factor was in my view one of the main reasons for the unsatisfactory development of reforms in Russia and for their loss of momentum.

Relying on foreign experience was inherent in the initial reform strategy. No one should believe that this strategy was imposed by "evil forces" from abroad in order to send Russia down a false and destructive path, as opponents of the reforms contend. The opinions of foreign advisers played an important part in developing a reform program. Unfortunately, these highly qualified specialists did not adequately understand or take fully into account the nature of Russia's history, the low starting point of its command economy, the political situation in the country, the complex regional fabric, or the tendency (ingrained over years of Soviet rule) to rely on a command process administered by the Party and state leadership in order to control all socioeconomic activity. Being most familiar with modern market systems in western Europe and the United States, the foreign advisers convinced Russian reformers to impose such a model upon the Russian economy as quickly as possible.

Whenever public dissatisfaction and outrage over those national policies that affect state property or local industry are directed at the regional agencies, we are the ones who must try to ease social tensions, find ways of localizing conflicts, and avoid socially unacceptable consequences.

Any movement forward requires a clear picture of the departure point. What were the starting conditions in Novgorod? I admit that we frequently acted on intuition. But we held to a few key principles in taking our first steps, and we have tried not to betray them since. The first is to encourage *broad dialogue.* We agreed from the start that not a single strategic decision would be made without discussion with the heads of *raion* (district) administrations. If even one objected, then we would not take that course. It may seem that we thus complicated the operational decisionmaking process, but practice has shown that team members, given the right to veto, use their veto with a great sense of responsibility.

The second principle we have relied on is that of *de-ideologizing.* We refused from the start to divide people into "former" and "present," "Communist" and "Yeltsinist." Instead, we looked for professionalism. Thanks to that principle, we brought in the best people from the former Communist Party Oblast Committee, the Executive Committee, and the legislative Soviet. At the same time, we worked closely with marketers, bankers, and representatives of small and midsize businesses. The government officials had practical experience and knowledge of local conditions, whereas the businesspeople had developed new methods of operating and could find their way in the rapidly changing economic milieu.

And our third important principle: Realizing that the basis of stability in every modern society is the *middle class,* which was only nascent at that point, we tried to concentrate on its formation. We defined our point of view as healthy centrism—the commonsense middle way—rejecting all radicalism, be it left or right. I must admit that sober common sense is my strongest human quality.

Of course, we know that there can be no swift or significant economic results from privatization alone. The change of property forms by itself solves nothing. Therefore we developed an array of measures to support entrepreneurship. We also took steps, now well known throughout the country, to attract foreign and domestic investment, and we created an informed and innovative infrastructure.

What were the first steps in creating a beneficial investment climate? First, we focused on how we could attract investment to our oblast, which had few natural resources, a weak infrastructure, a militarized industry, and a crisis in agriculture. Under accepted criteria for judging economic potential, Novgorod ranked sixty-third out of eighty-nine federation territories. We had only two trump cards: a favorable location on the Moscow–St. Petersburg route, and qualified people. But other regions had similar trump cards. To beat out the others, we had to create exceptionally attractive conditions for investors.

And then we came up with the bold idea of tax holidays, freeing investors from local and oblast taxes until their project had paid itself off, but no longer than a stipulated term. The idea was controversial; let us not forget that this was taking place in very difficult times, when the oblast treasury was empty. In those conditions, voluntarily giving up the collection of taxes from wealthy companies seemed almost blasphemous. There were accusations that we were selling the homeland down the river. People started adding up the alleged lost revenues. But if we had not decided to grant those benefits, there would never have been any revenues.

The Oblast Duma approved the draft bill on tax breaks for investors much more easily than would have been expected. Most of the Duma representatives were practical people, and they had come to understand a good deal about market economics. It was much harder to create a methodology for calculating a project's break-even point. What seemed to be an uncontroversial working document triggered protracted disputes with future investors. We then turned to a respected auditing company, Arthur Andersen, and commissioned them to design the accounting methodology—thereby eliminating half the problems in our negotiations with investors and shortening the long process of reaching an agreement.

By now, Novgorod's investment legislation is known in business circles in Russia and abroad. The World Bank ranks our oblast among the top six regions of Russia in terms of providing a beneficial investment climate. The oblast law of December 1994, "On Tax Benefits for Enterprises and Organizations Located on the Territory of Novgorod Oblast," exempts enterprises benefiting from foreign investment that are producing and are registered on oblast territory from paying regional taxes until they break even. Regardless of the size of foreign investment, new enterprises are partially exempted from paying territorial road taxes. They also receive a rebate of that portion of the value-added tax that goes into the oblast budget.

The legislation also provides for:

- reducing the profit tax for marketing costs;
- exempting banks from paying profit taxes on assets allocated to direct investments; and
- preserving the same legislative conditions provided when the enterprises made investment decisions.

In January 1997, four regions of the oblast were declared economically preferential zones enjoying special tax regimes. A system of guarantees for investors was created, with an investment insurance fund in the oblast budget.

Investors can now choose from among a wide selection of unused manufacturing space, equipped with infrastructure matching the investor's technical specifications (gas, water, electricity, pollution controls, and so on). They can use a databank called Free Industrial Spaces covering all the cities and districts in the oblast. Administrators of the oblast, cities, and districts follow up on prospective projects, help solve problems, and coordinate with federal agencies. Liaison officers from the oblast and local administrations help projects get under way without interfering in the company's internal affairs; they work with investors from project inception through the registration of the enterprise until the start of production and beyond.

There are different ways of seeking foreign investment. You can advertise in the mass media, you can knock on the doors of various companies, you can simply sit and wait. In my opinion, the most effective way is to invite an intermediary or a matchmaking company that knows potential investors well. That approach suits us, because the staffs of these intermediary firms are usually Russian.

A classic example of a successful investment project is the construction in Chudovo of a Cadbury's chocolate factory. This British company is one of the largest in the world, with twenty-six factories in sixteen countries. The founding fathers came from an old Quaker family with strong religious traditions and high moral standards. When Cadbury's decided to build one of Europe's largest chocolate factories in Russia, they were flooded with proposals from various regions. And yet Cadbury's chose Novgorod. The deciding factor was the system of benefits for investors we had already introduced. The site for the factory is Chudovo, a small town happily situated at the crossroads of major transportation lines.

The basic reasons for the passivity of Western investors in the Russian market include: the desire of various agencies to improve their lot at the expense of a rich Western "uncle," bureaucratic red tape, the absence of a business culture, the unreliability of potential partners, and occasional ordinary bribery. If a region wishes to attract foreign investors, it must act forcefully and ruthlessly to remove bureaucratic barriers, whoever created them.

The Chudovo factory was built in one year with an investment of $151 million, and today it is one of Russia's most modern factories. Dirol, which manufactures Stimorol gum, is completing construction of a factory in Novgorod costing over $100 million. Taking Cadbury's and Dirol as examples, we are convinced that we chose the right strategy for attracting foreign investment. And now, several years later, we can talk about the results.

As of March 1, 1999, the oblast had registered 170 enterprises with foreign capital amounting to $264 million and employing 18,600 people. The average salary at these enterprises is twice the oblast average. They produce almost 62.4 percent of the oblast's total volume of industrial production. These enterprises manufacture goods that are acceptable by world standards, meet consumer demand, and help the oblast sustain a positive foreign trade balance. Foreign investments during the 1994–1998 period grew from $153 million to $552.5 million.

Also as of March 1999, industrial enterprises were implementing forty-seven investment projects supported by the oblast administration, with time frames for recouping the investments ranging from one to six years. In effect, the oblast is acting as an investor. Over the period of the realization of these projects (1997–2003), the enterprises will be able to use around 585 million rubles saved from taxes they otherwise would have paid. We expect 36.1 million rubles to be paid in taxes from completed projects whose recoupment period comes in 1998–1999, while the tax benefits for these investment projects are valued at 24.6 million rubles.

The events of August 17, 1998, did not affect the attitude of foreign investors toward Novgorod oblast. Even in that extremely difficult crisis of confidence in Russia, none of our partners started packing their bags. And now, around thirty new projects with a total cost of $500 million are being developed. The fact that the World Bank ranked us in the top six most attractive regions of Russia for investment, sharing first place with Moscow on investment dollars per capita, helps us. In 1997 the American Chamber of Commerce in Moscow recognized us as the Region of the Year.

Although I have been discussing foreign investment, I must stress that our approach toward domestic investors is almost exactly the same. The nationality of capital should not matter, as long as it works for the oblast. Thanks to this approach, domestic investors have fundamentally changed their attitude toward us. In 1996, the volume of financial resources derived from domestic manufacturers exceeded the level of budget financing for the first time. The investments of such famous companies as the Cherkizovskii Meat Processing Plant and Dovgan Corporation added up to 73 million denominated rubles in just eighteen months. Cherkizovskii's Novgorod Meat House received tax breaks in the first half of 1997 in the amount of 10.4 million rubles, and it invested 62 million in the reconstruction of their plant. This allowed them to start production of sausages at such a level that 10 percent of their products suffices to meet the demand of the oblast, while the rest will be sold outside. Domestic enterprises in 1997 alone spent 532 million rubles of their own money on modernization.

Thus, if we place tax breaks for investors on one end of the scale and economic benefits for the region on the other, it is clear that both sides win. I would like to emphasize this point to everyone involved in establishing a beneficial investment climate for the country as a whole.

Investment may be the most important link in the chain of economic reform, but it is not the only one. There are a few other key components without which we cannot move further. First of all comes full-scale privatization. Much has been said about so-called voucher privatization; unfortunately, the "young reformers" chose far from the best way to revive private property, leaving out most of the country's population. (I do not rule out the possibility that a certain part of state property that was hastily handed over to private hands will be returned sooner or later to the state.) But the big mistake the privatizers made was not establishing a link between the privatization process and the production of goods and services. We at the local level smoothed out the process, but we could not have decisive influence, even though we did try to involve a greater part of the population in the benefits of privatization than was the case in the country as a whole. Be that as it may, in just five or six years the regional program of privatization begun in 1992 had reversed the proportions of the state and nonstate sectors in the economy.

Simultaneously, we were dealing with another strategic goal—the formation of the middle class, a stratum of the population that understood and accepted market conditions, adopted them, and at the necessary moment will support those who guarantee those conditions—thereby ensuring its own viability. Throughout the world the middle class is a pillar of society, a guarantor of its stability. In our country it is just finding its legs; without government support it may take decades to develop. Here I must add that we decided to support not just a future bourgeoisie, who don't care how they make money as long as they get rich. We focused instead on the manufacturers—small, midsize, and large—who are involved in productive business and not in clipping coupons.

If we had not systematically decided to support small business from the start, I doubt we would have had a stable social situation today. New jobs don't appear on their own.

Investment in small business is more effective, requires fewer expenses, is recouped quickly, and responds to demand more flexibly. The best example is a network of small bakeries that helped us solve perhaps the most painful problem in Novgorod. When we appealed to entrepreneurs to submit proposals to deal with the bread shortage, we were inundated with projects for creating bakeries. With financial support, small businesses were able to furnish bread to every town and village in the oblast within two years. Today almost a hundred bakeries operate in the oblast; instead of the five or six types of baked goods we used to have, they provide Novgorod residents with a wide assortment of fresh baked goods.

In order to ensure effective contact between local authorities and business, the Chamber of Commerce and Industry helps entrepreneurs get started, consolidate, and exert a measure of real social power. Our chamber today plays a notable role in developing economic strategy and regularly participates in almost all negotiations with foreign and domestic business partners.

Developing infrastructure to support small businesses is another priority. A network of twelve infrastructure systems comparable to those in Moscow and St. Petersburg supports both new and established businesses, and has earned the oblast a ranking among Russia's top five regions in this category. The Novgorod State Fund for Support of Small Business and the Novgorod Leasing Company in 1997–1998 gave 16.9 million rubles in financial support to 190 projects. This, in turn, had a marked effect on the revenue base of oblast and municipal budgets. Every fifth ruble of income in the oblast was earned in 1997 by small businesses.

Of course, these results are hard to obtain and just as hard to maintain. In this connection, we have to seek means of support for business from within the region. We have stopped giving interest-free subsidies to small businesses, but we tripled our budget resources for insuring small businesses through the oblast investment insurance fund—a measure that will help solve the problem of securing collateral for a needed loan.

Small businesses provided more than 50 percent of the oblast's new jobs during 1997–1998—affecting about 70,000 people. For our region, this is a significant number. But there is something else. Investors, particularly foreigners, are sensitive to the attitude of regional authorities to the development of small business. After all, 40 to 60 percent (and perhaps more) of the global economy is constituted by small business. Investors seek out these oases of stability.

So small business, I want to stress, is a strategic instrument for Novgorod's policy of attracting investments. The more people are involved in entrepreneurship, the higher the business activity of the territory. And if we do not have development resources in the form of rich mineral deposits, we do have people with initiative who can use their hands and their heads.

The administration is also working on bringing in foreign resources for the development of small business. For instance, together with three regions in Germany, Scotland, and Ireland we are creating the International Center for Regional Development designed, in particular, to promote the development of small and midsize businesses. Financing is planned to come entirely from foreign sources. We have developed a land cadastre that will give a complete picture of land resources and therefore prospects of activity. A logical follow-up step was the creation of an ecological cadastre.

How do we make money? In the oblast, we earn money principally from exports: mineral fertilizers and weapons, legally produced vodka, timber and wood products, construction materials, and manufactured products for the domestic market.

I would like to draw attention to a few new aspects of our economic policy. Our priorities in allocating organizational and financial support for specific sectors of the economy favor enterprises that pay taxes on time, reliably contribute to the oblast budget, and have sound development programs. In particular, this priority ranking favors timber-processing enterprises, which are planning to establish in the year 2000 several plants for processing lumber and producing new products for the oblast: plywood, large-format veneer, and medium-thickness planks, and new styles of upholstered furniture.

This focus on the lumber industry will lead in the near future to an increase in the profitability of timber, one of the oblast's most important natural resources. Even now this is happening because we have introduced timber auctions and leasing of forests, and we promote the development of entrepreneurship in wood processing. In 1998, the annual decline in the area of cleared timber reversed and became an increase. The timber auction accounted for more than 20 percent of the total clearing, which was ten times higher than in 1997. In the year 2000 we plan to introduce mandatory certification of secondary forest resources and of timber at the root, measures that will help increase lumber exports.

A very important factor in increasing product competitiveness is quality. In order to stimulate an increase in the quality of production and services, and to help introduce effective quality management, we have instituted an annual Quality Prize, the winners of which can for compete in the national quality contest. Industrial enterprises are hampered not only by unfavorable economic conditions but also by outdated management. For example, the restructuring of the Splav company into the financial and industrial group Kontur has allowed the firm to perfect its wares, expand its client list, and conquer new markets.

But any financial support of enterprises has to have the support of the banking system. Since cooperation with financial credit institutions depends on agreement on both sides, a coordinating council for banks has been established. In order to reduce risk to financial credit institutions who want to give long-term credit to Novgorod enterprises, the oblast budget includes an investment insurance fund, now in its third year. We plan to form a tax fund for oblast and municipal property in order to secure the collateral of oblast, city, and regional administrations.

At the turn of the century, Russia is moving from one kind of state to another, a transition that affects everyone in every city and village. How it will take place and how painless it will be depends in great part on the people working today in the regions. The role of the "human factor" is becoming rapidly more important, as is the role of administrators and the teams they head. And the price of mistakes is rising, too, especially strategic mistakes.

We have encouraged the development of new means of communication. Today, Novgorod is one of the few smaller cities in Russia that has practically every modern form of communications, such as Moscow and St. Petersburg have. Cellular phones, speedy fiber-optic lines, electronic mail, the Internet, and other digital systems for processing and transferring information are helping our business partners adapt to Russian conditions.

After infrastructure comes the analytical base necessary for modern business. We have established an information and analytical center to quickly process all incoming economic information and a geoinformational system that provides a database on land, forests, water resources, raw materials, and the ecology. With this system in place, an electronic map of the oblast can instantly retrieve a full description of any geographical point. We can now move from an intuitive approach to reforming the economy toward a fully reasoned, instrumental approach.

It is a slow, painfully slow, process, but the traditional Novgorod industries are coming back to life. The young designers at the Kvant corporation have developed a competitive seventh-generation television. Armatures for atomic energy, produced by Splav, are back on the world market. Producers of chemicals, alcohol, and wood products have stood up under intense competition. Each enterprise has devised its own recipe for survival, but there is one factor they all have in common—they are headed by talented, enterprising people.

And the reverse is true for other companies. Some enterprises did not enter the market economy; management could not or did not want to take initiatives and wasted time waiting for someone else to come along and solve their problems. The Volna company, once known throughout the country for its professional television equipment, wasted resources, let qualified personnel depart, and lost unique technologies. That is the price of inertia.

In the early 1990s, following the collapse in prices, another collapse occurred—one of public confidence. In an instant, people lost the all-encompassing patronage of the state. This paternalism had irritated and confined people, but without it, a great many people felt uncomfortable. Previously the state, in taking away almost everything from its citizens, gave them back a pathetically small but at least guaranteed minimum of support, from cradle to grave. Now people were forced to take their lives into their own hands; the state retained merely a subsidiary role in guaranteeing—and only sometimes—targeted support for social strata unable to take care of themselves. For our population, which had grown up in a fundamentally different society from that of western Europe, this was a powerful psychological shock. Russians saw that the government, without any explanation, was shedding one social obligation after another: housing, free medicine, compulsory free education. Realizing that they could expect nothing from Moscow, people turned to the local authorities. We became hostages to a situation that was exacerbated by an obsolete and imperfect legal base.

It was clear that if we wanted to keep the oblast governable, we had to take care of local government first. But in order for local government to become a real entity rather than something that existed in name only, it had to have four components: law, organization, property, and financial security. Under federal law any settlement, be it city, town, or village, regardless of the number of residents, can have property, elected organs, and a budget. In principle, all 278 localities of Novgorod oblast could have declared themselves independent. But we could not allow responsibility to be blurred through endless disputes among various agencies about which had primacy and which cared more about the populace. While giving regional administrative heads greater powers and making them key figures in local self-government, we retained a necessary counterbalance in the form of an elected Duma.

The question of property arose in the very first months after my appointment. At one of my first meetings with the district administrative chiefs, it was asked: Who would be in charge of the former state property located on the territory of the districts? I responded almost intuitively, by inviting the districts to take as municipal property whatever they felt was necessary for normal activity. On receiving this unexpected gift, the administrators, who had been prepared to battle for the property, paused to think. They saw that no one was

planning to pull the wool over their eyes, that the oblast wasn't trying to take the lion's share but was inviting them to make the decision from below. The ball was in their court. The matter ended with
the districts getting almost everything they had asked for as municipal property: industrial and agricultural enterprises, schools, hospitals, stores, sports complexes, houses of culture, means of transport,
and so on. A short time later, without any particular enthusiasm I
might add, the districts took over as their property all housing and
communal services as well as children's institutions, which had previously been divided among various agencies and therefore had become seriously dilapidated.

Once they had assumed responsibility for almost the entire social
sphere, however, the districts immediately raised the question of revenue. Once you say A, you have to say B. In reforming the local self-
government system, we had to make radical changes in the regional
budget. First, it became the real budget of the region, developed and
confirmed there, and not sent down from above. Further, it became a
single budget, not a consolidated one, and it was no longer broken
down into small "baby budgets" of village and town councils. The
result: In 1995 we had nearly 300 budgets for local councils of various levels; in 1997, only 22, one for each district. The strengthened
oblast budget gives much more opportunity for reallocating resources, a particularly important option when there is a deficit. It
has a more stable revenue base and allows decisions to be made on a
single administrative level.

The next decision—giving the districts a significant part of their
own revenues from the oblast budget—was particularly difficult.
The oblast is federally subsidized and has no spare cash. But we realized that the districts could not support social services on their own,
and we decided to share honestly. We increased the quota of revenues diverted into the budgets of cities and districts, including revenues from taxes on personal incomes and the property of enterprises, and we increased support for the budgets of educational
institutions. For institutions that were not helped by transferred revenues, we planned direct subsidies from the oblast budget.

Once they began receiving real income, local authorities felt they
could take on the responsibility of paying salaries and supporting
schools, hospitals, and cultural institutions. Now the residents of
districts do not have to seek what they want in Novgorod. Here is
your money, we said, now you handle it. Today, local authorities

work much more clearly and professionally than they did two or three years ago.

Another important shift has occurred in relations between the oblast and district administrations. A high level of mutual trust has developed, allowing us to solve problems without resorting to bureaucratic procedures. For instance, all the heads of administrations who supported our investment policy have announced the same tax holidays for investors in their local budgets, an action that has greatly heightened the attractiveness of the oblast as a whole.

Some districts, however, for all their desire to do so, could not guarantee even minimal budget expenditures with their own revenues. In order to ensure the disbursement of salaries (for those working in the public sector), pensions, child allowances, and other protected categories, we created a stabilization fund of subsidies. This fund, formed from oblast revenues and donations from two of Russia's more affluent regions, has helped reduce social tensions in the oblast's less developed areas and has helped to buffer these areas from the uncertainties of the extremely irregular payments from the federal budget. Federal officials in Moscow, unfortunately, are ready to share power with the regions but are unwilling to share money. Their second mistake is to have artificially separated local self-government from the vertical hierarchy of state power. They have put fancy clothes on a bare skeleton.

The Russian countryside has endured a painful evolutionary period accompanied by many shocks. The new village must be born naturally, without a cesarean section, and the authorities must help, like an experienced midwife. Until a new generation of farmers arises that is capable of working in market conditions, we need a transitional period during which the state- and collective-farm structure will gradually yield to a private-farm system.

Here is what this means in practice. The agricultural infrastructure developed over past decades (tractors and other equipment, granaries, workshops, gas stations; that is, the basic production resources except for animal breeding farms) will remain indivisibly in the hands of an agricultural group. It doesn't matter what the group will be called: association, fraternity, cooperative. That infrastructure cannot be privatized and divided up.

Livestock belonging to unprofitable farms should be parceled out among private holdings. At first this will lead to a reduction in the general number of animals, but soon afterward this number will be restored and grow. Farmers will decide for themselves how much livestock they want to keep—cows, pigs, sheep, chickens, and so on. In my opinion, the optimal number for a personal farm in our zone is three to five cows. That is the number that a farming family can service, given the conditions of a Novgorod village with its pastures, feed base, and means of small mechanization. And that is the number that guarantees the profitability of a small farm.

In essence, the process of transferring public livestock to private farms in the oblast has become irreversible. Today more than half of the meat and milk produced in the oblast comes from the private sector. As for efficiency, a cow pastured in a private farm yields two and a half times more milk than one in a collective farm.

The real challenge lies in combining the efforts of these small family-run farms, inducing them to coordinate their efforts, since it is obvious that they cannot function alone. That is the role assigned to the former collective farms, which retain extensive infrastructure but have been transformed into classic agricultural cooperatives—in terms of production, marketing, and processing—based on models of farming cooperatives throughout the world. Management, freed of inappropriate functions, can be reduced to five or six specialists who work on contract. Housing, communal services, and social services are now the responsibility of the local government. The president of the cooperative and the specialists deal exclusively with production.

And what work could such a cooperative do? Why, almost anything. It can prepare hay for privately owned cattle. It can produce seed for its own use and for sale, it can grow flax, it can hire itself out to work other people's land with the equipment it has retained. There would be no salaries paid as such, but a distribution of produce or the money obtained from its sale.

The next level of cooperation is regional. It is important to preserve the existing stockbreeding, seed-developing, and soil-improvement stations, upgrading them to comply with modern market conditions. We must allow the former state and collective farms to determine their areas of specialization themselves. We tell them: If you decide to concentrate on planting flax, fine—organize yourselves around a flax-processing factory. If you want to concentrate on meat products, good—consolidate around a dairy or meat-processing plant. But no coercion and no help! Whatever help is necessary must come from the village in the form of tax breaks, reduced tariffs on electricity, and low-interest loans, as well as through the state's participation in providing infrastructure, schools, and medical and veterinary institutions.

As to whether buying and selling land should be made legal, I agree with the necessity of such legislation, but I have three essential caveats. First, the price of land must include the added value in fertility created by its former owner. For this we need a comprehensive land cadastre. In our oblast this work is almost complete, enabling us to consider the issue on a practical level. Second, agricultural land, once sold, should not be removed from agriculture. This point must be an inalienable part of any land contract, since we are dealing here with the country's strategic interests. I nonetheless support in every way the idea of selling land to foreign partners for industrial construction, which for the present is not allowed in Russia.

Therefore, the key points in our approach to agrarian reform are:

- the evolutionary character of reform;
- a comprehensive approach, including a full selection of governmental, legal, organizational, financial, and technological measures intended to be applied over the entire period of reform;
- the retention of indivisible ownership of equipment by state and collective farms for their joint use;
- support for the private farm as the basic social and production nucleus in the village;
- the transfer of the entire rural social complex to local government authorities;
- the creation of a system of government support for all viable forms of agricultural production as well as of enterprises engaged in manufacturing equipment for villages, stimulating investment in this sphere and creating a network of processing enterprises for villages;
- land reform legislation that retains agricultural land for those who work it;
- the training of farmers both in local schools and abroad (through internships, exchanges, and so on);
- the provision of low-cost housing in the villages for local residents and migrants; and
- the creation of mortgage mechanisms for loans in the villages, bringing in Russian and foreign banks.

The question arises: Why didn't we force the implementation of agrarian reforms earlier? Briefly, the conditions were wrong, and above all, people in the villages were not psychologically prepared to take their lives into their own hands. Now we sense their readiness.

If we wish to create a modern society, and we do, then the regional and federal authorities must be willing to encourage a lively, resilient, and dynamic sociopolitical life. Political parties, unions, nongovernmental organizations and movements, religious communities, and the press must all function legally and freely. Their relationship with the government must be built not on arbitrary bureaucratic rule but on a civilized, constitutional basis. Close cooperation and mutual understanding among all government agencies, political parties and movements, trade unions, and manufacturers, regardless of the forms of property, have allowed our Novgorod team to develop a single economic policy, set priorities, and guarantee consistency and continuity in the transformation process.

In fact, how can one not be interested in politics if it is everywhere? Politics flows from television screens and newspaper pages, lurks at election polls, and becomes the eventual topic of every casual chat among friends. And people who work in government cannot escape from politics, since politics is nothing more than relationships among people with respect to power. Nearly any administrative decision of any consequence has political ramifications, since it touches on the interests of some strata of the population and therefore can determine their future social behavior.

Of course, that is a rather vague sentiment with which few would take issue. But in practice, when different interests clash and the authorities are threatened with losing their power, the temptation arises to create under some pretense a regime that is extremely beneficial for some and much less so for others. From my own experience I can state that such temptations must be overcome, because an illness that is hidden will reappear later in a much more virulent form. Sometimes political opponents deliberately provoke authorities to take hostile action, knowing that once the government takes part in a blind exchange of blows, it loses the trust of the people by lowering itself to the level of society's irresponsible elements. To keep that from happening we must apply not only well-considered tactics but a style of human behavior that allows us to maintain a normal dialogue with everyone, regardless of their views.

And how does the present sociopolitical situation look in our oblast? More than four hundred public organizations are registered, including fifteen regional branches of national Russian political parties and ten branches of public movements. Almost the entire spectrum of the country's political life is represented on the local level.

We see no fundamental differences in strategy and tactics between these local branches and their central headquarters, but judging by their behavior and their relations with the local government, I think there is a better articulated desire for dialogue than on the federal level. We have had almost no extremist forms of political competition, though we can't claim universal consensus either. During our personal contacts with representatives of various political parties, they tell us directly that they would like to get rid of us so they can then carry out their own policies. Of course, we tell them just as frankly that we don't want to permit that, naturally within the framework of a civilized political process. During elections, various coalitions form; for instance, all the parties and movements with a democratic orientation formed an alliance called the United Democratic Center. And the left-wing parties and movements formed their own bloc.

In recent years, nonpolitical public organizations have been quite active: a veterans' committee, a women's council, a consumer association, a committee of veterans of foreign wars, and a regional human rights center. Entrepreneurial associations are quite influential, for instance the Chamber of Commerce and Industry, a manufacturer's foundation, an association of peasant farms, a public council of entrepreneurs, and a league of businesswomen.

The nationalities question has become more acute, and the migration of forced refugees from areas of the former Soviet Union has given additional impetus to the formation of ethnic cultural societies, such as the German Union, the Russian Congress, the Jewish Culture Society, the Armenian Community, and the Chechen-Ingush center, Vainakh. But even here the situation is quite stable, with no extremist manifestations.

We place great stress on relations with trade unions. Despite all the shocks of recent years, unions remain the largest and consequently the most influential social organizations. I cannot say that there is total unity between the oblast administration and the unions as there was in Soviet times, when the unions were called the "schools of communism." Society has changed, and so has the role of unions. Today they are in opposition to the authorities. And at first, our relations with the unions developed along lines of conflict. The unions peppered the administration with demands, without thinking about realities. The administration, on the other hand, tried to weaken the role of the unions, seeing them only as a source of unconstructive opposition.

This confrontation continued until we understood that the axis of resistance had to be converted into a triangle of cooperation. This triangle engages the government, the unions, and the employers. Taking this new approach, our relations changed sharply. We have a tripartite agreement; there is a permanent commission on regulating socioeconomic relations. When a hotspot of social tension develops in a particular enterprise, we all go there together to deal with the specific situation and find a solution.

Of course, it's not all sunshine. Even with apparent calm, the potential for socioeconomic tension exists. And even though we almost never have labor walkouts, even though people don't lie down on railroad tracks or go on hunger strikes, we feel acutely that if the economic instability continues, this calm might be misleading. Only when the economy is strengthened, only when we guarantee stable incomes for everyone, can we be assured that the social conflicts that have already cost our country so much will cease.

And yet, no matter how important the economic transformation may be, the primary changes must take place in the minds of the people. Only there can change genuinely be made irreversible. Reform will be successful only when people come to believe in it.

In conclusion I would like to note the following: The guarantee of economic development lies in international integration. As for Russia's foreign policy concepts, I think that there is no point for the time being in inventing some new global strategy. It is much more important to start cleaning up the old piles of debris, come to terms with foreign partners on the simplest issues, establish normal, mutually beneficial relations, remove unnecessary barriers with countries, guarantee our citizens the right to trade and travel, create conditions for attracting capital, and cooperate more on the "people's diplomacy" level. Once we achieve such purely practical goals, we will advance along the path to strategic partnerships. Why should someone aim his missiles at Novgorod oblast, where hundreds of millions of dollars of foreign capital is invested? In other words, international cooperation must be built brick by brick from the bottom up. The trouble with our diplomacy is that it is so focused on broad policies that it pushes specific issues into the background. Yet it is the small problems that could hinder the development of relations between enormous countries.

Traveling as I frequently do to various countries, I see that more and more foreigners are freeing themselves of the "Russian threat" syndrome. Farsighted politicians understand this and will help improve conditions for Russia's return to international standing. And yet much can be done for integration by developing direct international contacts in the regions. For instance, Russia's long-awaited entry into the Council of Europe was a success not only for the government's diplomacy but for people's diplomacy as well, thanks to the commercial, economic, and cultural ties among regions, which could not be ignored. We are particularly proud that the Banner of the Council of Europe in 1997 was awarded to our oblast for special contributions to the development of European cooperation. It was a great honor for me to be elected deputy chairman of the Parliamentary Assembly of the Council of Europe (PACE).

Blair Ruble, director of the Kennan Institute in Washington, D.C., invited me to give a lecture on Russian reform, and in analyzing our situation, he wrote:

> With a renewed interest in the Russian market, the Russian regions will be in strong competition for investment and trade dollars. The winners of the competition will be those regions that create the best legal and stable environment for investment. Some regional leaders are creating their strategic groups, have concentrated on that, and it is the leaders of these regions who are the rising stars in today's Russian politics. Other oblast leaders are paying more attention to domestic problems, and these regions continue to be backward. In the Soviet system power was centralized and more importantly reduced to homogeneity. Like the housing built for people, local Soviet authorities were also standardized and weak. The post-Soviet Russian experience of governance on the regional level is amazingly varied. The regions are getting a greater ability to set their own course. In trying to measure the successes and failures of market reforms in Russia as a whole, it is important to look at individual regions because of the differences in the economic policies of the regions.

This citation reflects a fundamentally different approach to dealing with Russia. In the past, foreign investors focused almost exclusively on the federal level, a completely understandable approach given the extremely centralized Soviet system. Now these investors are selective, preferring to work directly with the regions—but only with those that have created beneficial market conditions. And that strategic shift on their part has served as yet another stimulus for our efforts to advance reforms in Novgorod.

4

FEDERALISM, LOCAL SELF-GOVERNMENT, AND NATIONAL RENEWAL IN RUSSIA

Aleksandr Voronin

The Making of the Russian State

Russian statehood owes its genesis above all to factors of climate and geographic space. Situated on a vast but lightly populated land mass that embraces many different climatic conditions and economic arrangements, and is home to over 180 ethnic groups, each with its own traditions, language, and culture, Russia throughout its history has been more the exception to the rule than the rule itself.

The making of the Russian state reflected a profound contradiction.

On the one hand, its enormous area meant relatively great autonomy for the territories from the very beginning. On the other

Born in 1962 in Kostroma, **Aleksandr Gennad'evich Voronin** studied to be a history teacher at the Kostroma State Pedagogical Institute, where both of his parents had taught. After many years of teaching history in Kostroma secondary schools, Voronin ran for city council in 1990, and in 1991 became its chairman. After he helped found the Union of Russian Cities in 1992, Voronin represented this organization during the Constitutional Convention, helping draft the Constitution of 1993. In March 1994 he was recruited to the Ministry of Federal and Nationality Affairs to start up and head a special department on local self-government. In July 1996 Voronin was promoted to deputy minister in charge of local government issues. Translated by Marian Schwartz.

hand, its geopolitical orientation toward both Europe and Asia and its lack of natural boundaries such as mountains or seas constantly generated external threats that in turn required a relatively harsh central authority. According to military historians of the ninth through eighteenth centuries, Russia was at peace only twenty-five years out of each century. The rest of the time it was forced to defend its borders against invaders. For example, in most of the southern princely states of ancient Rus', which were constantly at war with nomads, monarchical or princely regimes emerged, whereas in the north the Novgorod Republic invited a prince only in order to assume military leadership against a foreign enemy.

Under Ivan the Terrible, the central administrative system combined harsh despotism and relatively broad local autonomy. The "feeder" system functioning at the time obliged the official *(voevoda)* sent out to govern each territory to pay a fixed sum into the czar's treasury and to maintain a number of czarist institutions. In all other respects, though, the territorial administration was organized at the discretion of the ruler himself in accordance with local conditions.

This system of state administration lasted until the *guberniya* reforms of Peter the Great, which introduced some uniformity in the administration of Russia's regions, although the *guberniya* (province) system acquired its final form only in the first half of the nineteenth century. At the time, Mikhail Speransky, Alexander I's favorite statesman, succinctly formulated the basic principle of the relationship between the center and the regions: "Leave them enough to survive and just a little more."

The *guberniya* reforms completed in the nineteenth century did not establish uniformity of rule. The Grand Duchy of Finland, the Kingdom of Poland, and the Cossack troops occupying an immense territory in southern Russia, Siberia, and the Far East enjoyed incomparably greater rights than any *guberniya*. Central Asia, whose traditional despotic regimes were retained as the region joined the empire in the late nineteenth century, was more a protectorate of Russia than a part of it.

The democratic reforms carried out by Alexander II significantly adapted the system of administration to the demands of the huge state. The main reason for changing the entire state structure was the agrarian reform of 1861, which abolished serfdom, produced a large number of small-property owners, and accelerated the emergence of a free market in goods. Social relations became more complicated, calling for a fundamental change in the system of administration, a change that gave the new estates access to central authority and led to the devolution of many government powers.

The urban and land reforms carried out in the 1860s and 1870s created institutions of popular representation at the regional and local levels. The reform most consistently granted affected municipal self-administration. Towns received their own sets of authorities and responsibilities and also acquired extremely broad economic rights and property. Thus, in 1913, on average only 50 percent of municipal budgets in Russia came from the collection of taxes; the balance came from the towns' own economic activities.

The main form of local self-government in rural areas was the village commune. In accordance with the state's 1861 Manifesto on agrarian reform, the rural commune was composed of "one or more settlements bound together by common economic interests." The commune bore immense responsibility for regulating all of life in the local community; it also performed a number of legal and administrative functions.

The model for local self-government that took shape under Alexander II proved unexpectedly resilient. Attempts to destroy the rural commune failed during the Pyotr Stolypin reforms of 1907–1910 and under the Provisional Government of 1917. Even the Bolsheviks could not wipe out urban and rural self-government until the early 1930s.

The Bolsheviks' rise to power fundamentally changed the approaches to governance. The 1917 Revolution interrupted the natural process of forming a Russian state based on regional and local autonomy.

By 1919, the work of the special commission established in 1903 to determine the best model for Russia's *guberniya* system was for all intents and purposes complete. The commission envisioned changing the administrative arrangement of the state to conform with the principles of the highest economic efficiency. It proposed a sharp expansion of economic rights for the regions and a smooth transition to broad regional autonomy.

The Bolsheviks held other views of the state when they came to power, however. At the core of their notions of power were two fundamental postulates:

- the state is a means of violence perpetrated by one social group, the dictatorship of the proletariat, against another; and
- all economic life is based on the dominance of publicly held property.

Several basic conclusions followed from this approach.

First, given the dogma of just one property owner as personified by the state, all of Russia was transformed into a single unified enterprise, administered on the principles of centralized coordination and industrial branch management.

Second, this approach made it possible to ignore economic factors in determining administrative-territorial arrangements. Hence the ease with which entire territories were transferred during the Soviet period from one administrative subordination to another—the reason why there are today many conflicts in the Caucasus, the Crimea, and other former Soviet territories. For example, the criteria for designating a rural district included the principle that a specific number of Communist Party members must reside in the given territory.

Third, under this approach, any local political organ was a branch of central power. This resulted in hypercentralization, since only the highest echelon of power could make the final decision on any matter.

Public interest in self-organization persisted nonetheless and found an outlet in various forms of community self-administration, which achieved their greatest popularity in the 1930s, when the Stalinist model of the state was being shaped.

I would also like to say something about one extremely important consequence of the Soviet reforms. Because economic factors had lost their significance in determining administrative-territorial arrangements, Stalin in 1922 proposed putting the ethnic factor at the center of the national government system. It was during this period that many of our existing Russian Federation subjects—the republics and the autonomous okrugs—were established.

In this manner, the Soviet model envisioned a strictly hierarchical system of authority. Federal relations were reduced mainly to determining the needs of nation building.

Reforms in the State Structure, 1985–1993

The political and economic reforms that began in the mid-1980s also bore the stamp of the Soviet worldview. The first allusion to changes in the political course came in 1985. The logic of the first-wave reformers' ideas wholly corresponded to the logic of the system that produced them: an unlimited faith in the power of the state. In simplest terms, the entire reform movement relied on the thesis that a change in state power and strengthened public controls would lead to the increased effectiveness of state activity and, in turn, would fundamentally alter the very essence of the political system and, more importantly, the economic system.

Determining the effectiveness of the economic model was thus linked directly with developing civic institutions. However, this model almost wholly rejected the fundamental concept that government exists to serve specific interests of society and especially to regulate particular processes rooted in economic motivations. What is most interesting is that this model ignored a fundamental tenet of Marxist ideology, the correlation of the "base" and the "superstructure."

In the process of the subsequent search for a state model, the country was drawn into an endless series of reforms affecting the vertical lines of power in the state as well as the economy. Characteristic of such experiments were attempts to democratize industrial production activity itself. This boiled down not to liberalizing economic relations but to introducing democratic procedures in factory management.

Every successive change divorced the state system more and more from the system of economic relations, with results that were increasingly untenable. As a result, a paradoxical situation arose: The state, as the largest property owner, voluntarily removed itself from administering its property by giving the enterprises to themselves—or rather, by giving them to an absolutely uncontrolled caste of directors for plundering.

As it gradually lost its grip on the levers of the economy, state power seemed to hang suspended in midair. The Yegor Gaidar and Anatolii Chubais privatizations that followed were an extremely awkward attempt to bring these two discordant systems into alignment. Both of their attempts were accompanied by a centralization of political power and a decentralization of economic relations. In other words, the power pyramid was turned upside down, then flipped back on its base, and once again back on its apex. The power vertical based on cosubordination, which was strictly centralized in 1993, proved incapable of administering a decentralized economic system.

These contradictory processes manifested themselves especially vividly when the new Constitution of the Russian Federation was being drafted. The main discussions once again revolved around the state model. Unconsciously, many regional leaders began to understand the need to decentralize the power vertically, but each level of government felt, for completely subjective reasons, that decentralization had to stop at their own level. As one participating governor remarked, "The people can elect me, but I'll appoint the rest."

Ultimately, because its provisions were so nonspecific and relatively abstract, the Constitution approved in 1993 made it possible gradually to begin constructing an integrated system for structuring society through the process of legislation.

The Fates of Russian Federalism: Contemporary Views

The historical retrospective given in condensed form above is not arbitrary. Russian notions about the best method of administering their country have been significantly influenced by the unitary tendencies of the Soviet period as well as by democratic principles. This whimsical combination, enriched by the political interests of various social groups, has engendered disparate patterns of interpreting a given social phenomenon or aspect of public life.

Even today in Russia there are still many supporters of the "firm hand," who perceive the changes under way as just more "playing at democracy," and who see federalism and local self-government as artificially introduced from abroad. Such moods have been actively exploited by opposition parties and movements in their struggle with the existing political regime.

However, a return to the previous model is hardly possible. Even the Communists would not dare propose a blind return to the old system; instead they have limited themselves to appeals for a more balanced parliamentary republic and the partial nationalization of former state property.

All the current errors and myths about Russia's state structure are rooted in its history. As a rule, these views exaggerate the role of one of the factors in the formation of a state model.

Let us examine this observation, using modern conceptions of the federative structure as an example. There are three basic groups of conceptions:

- the ethno-state approach to the construction of federative relations;
- economic federalism and local autonomy; and
- the symmetrical federation.

The first conception stems from the idea that the federation should be founded on ethnic boundaries for the settlement of the ethnic groups residing in the Russian Federation. This assumes a distinction in the state structure between the ethnic republics and the Russian oblasts. This conception is the legacy of the Stalinist idea of the ethno-state structure.

Supporters of the second concept assume that only economically self-sufficient territories have the right to regional autonomy. This approach, as is well known, was propounded throughout the nineteenth century.

The third approach is based on the postulate that all subjects of the federation are equal among themselves and in their relations with the center. This approach has been inherited from Soviet times, when the legislation of the union republics was copied from the legislation of the Soviet Union.

As can be seen from the example cited, all these points of view are extreme, and none could be implemented in pure form.

It is impossible to make federation subjects equal in the full sense of the word when the richest and poorest regions differ in wealth by as much as a factor of 17.

It is impossible to base the federation's construction on the ethnic principle when ethnic Russians account for 87 percent of the population and in many ethnic republics make up an absolute majority.

On the other hand, it is impossible to ignore the fact that many ethnic groups that inhabit Russia had their own statehood before becoming part of it; it would be extremely dangerous to build the federation on the principle of pure territorial self-sufficiency.

Consequently, the only path to constructing a stable state model is to consider all three of the above-cited conceptions. It is this path that the authors of the 1993 Constitution followed when they put at its core the primacy of human rights and property rights. In addition, the Constitution assumed the existence within the federation of both administrative-ethnic subjects and administrative-territorial subjects. In formal legal terms, they are equal among themselves and in their relations with the federal center. However, the national republics have their own attributes of statehood and under their constitutions are explicitly recognized as states within the Russian Federation.

Constitutional reinforcement of the diversity of property forms predetermined the economic model, which is based on the decentralization of territorial administration. Anything else, in a state as big as Russia, would be impossible.

The federal structure that was proposed as a model for Russia's governance was not merely the only feasible solution to the turmoil after the breakup of the Soviet Union; it was an objective necessity: This is how Russia preserved its unity.

Disputes over the forms and degree of autonomy appropriate for the subjects of the Russian Federation were most contentious when the Constitution was being written, and they continue even now. The 1993 Constitution still has its share of critics. For example, Vladimir Zhirinovskii, leader of the Russian Liberal Democratic Party, proposes reviving the *guberniya* as the basic administrative unit for Russia. Leaders of the Russian Regions faction in the Duma, on the other hand, talk about expanding the rights of the regions and prescribing the rights of federation subjects in the Constitution.

Unfortunately, both of these ideas are extremely dangerous.

Reexamining the territorial boundaries between federation subjects would be a very risky business. Not that long ago, in the early 1990s, the Supreme Soviet passed a law "On Territorial Rehabilitation for Repressed Ethnic Groups." This law had extremely harmful consequences. One can say with complete confidence that the subsequent conflicts in the northern Caucasus were a consequence of this law. Under current conditions, when local and regional elites have already staked out their claims, any redivision of territory or property is fraught with grave potential upheavals and conflicts.

A revision of the Constitution's articles to reallocate authority along different political levels is no less dangerous. Compromise between the center and the regions was the fruit of a prolonged and very sharp discussion at the Constitutional Convention and afterward, during the treaty negotiating process. This Gordian knot cannot be cut at one stroke. Prescribing a single standard of competence for all federation subjects would hardly succeed if only because of the huge economic, spatial, and other disparities among the federation subjects themselves.

Most important, we have not yet exhausted all the methods of improving the Constitution, notably by devising legislation that can reflect a consensus on defining the authorities of federation subjects. No less important are the treaty negotiations between the center and the federation subjects that have been going on for six years. These treaties and related accords can ensure that the individual characteristics of each territory are taken into account.

The distribution of legal and regulatory authority by treaty arrangements is closely connected with the legislative process. When the treaties and accords are drawn up, some points get repeated from accord to accord, from treaty to treaty. This is the first signal that the legislator has introduced the given norms into the corresponding law.

On the other hand, the development of federal legislation constantly acts as a constraint on treaty-based governance. In the long term, it may become necessary to add to the text of the Constitution a number of powers exercised by subjects of the Russian Federation.

For the time being, however, proposals to revise the Constitution seem strange. Not even six years have passed since the document was ratified. Fundamental legislation vital to its development has not yet been passed; the system of power envisaged in the Constitution has not been established; yet some are again proposing that we drag the country through another redivision of power.

It also seems to me that today, at least on issues affecting the state's federal structure, the statement that "Russia is burdened with a new Constitution," as a number of politicians declare, is not appropriate.

Local Self-Government in Russia: An Eclectic Mix

At the beginning of 1997, after spending a long time shaping our own Russian model of local self-government, the Russian Federation adhered to the European Local Self-Government Charter. In contrast to the way regional autonomy developed in Russia, this process proceeded logically and gradually.

Unlike the more sluggish evolution at the central and regional levels of power, the organs of local self-government that were elected in 1990 under the new law have come a long way from the Soviet system and are moving toward an understanding of the role and place of local self-government.

During this period, I was working as chairman of a city council. I remember very well how in the first council sessions each agenda would center on "the political crisis in the country" or "the current moment." City councils were utterly politicized. But a year later such issues had given way to problems of running the municipal economy, administering municipal property, and providing social assistance for the population.

City council leaders quickly realized the enormous potential of local self-government. It was during this period that municipal politicians quickly came forward and later defined quite clearly what local self-government should be like in Russia.

Any attempt to characterize briefly the constitutional model of local self-government must take note of its eclecticism. The right of the population to determine independently the structure of local organs of self-government is borrowed from the American model; the independent determination of the territory of local self-government, from the Japanese experiment of the mid-1950s; and broad economic independence, from prerevolutionary Russian experience.

Russian local self-government is regulated at two levels of legislation—federal and regional. This dual legislative purview, combined with fairly simple procedures for dividing up and combining territories at the local level, assumes that territorial characteristics are taken into account.

As a result, different models of local self-government have taken shape. Most Russian Federation subjects (about 70 percent) have preserved the town and the rural district as the basic municipal entity. Many large federation subjects, such as Tyumen oblast, Tatarstan, and Bashkortostan, where one *raion* (district) can dwarf some European states, have introduced local self-government through a smaller rural unit—the *volost* (made up, as a rule, of one or a few small settlements).

However, one can hardly say that the process of instituting local self-government is complete. On the one hand, given the stagnation of Russia's economy, the economic interests of the population of each specific municipality have yet to be determined. On the other hand, in many federation subjects that have retained the old administrative divisions inherited from Soviet times, the processes of decentralizing *raion* structures are still under way.

Once these processes are stabilized, the federal center will have to decide how to refine the procedures for combining and dividing municipalities under a more permanent arrangement.

The municipalities had never encountered a number of these problems before. Previously, they had merely implemented decisions sent down from the top; now they are being forced to look differently at their territory, especially from the standpoint of identifying resources.

Giving organs of local self-government the right to make independent decisions affecting a fairly wide range of issues has defined most of the problems they are encountering today.

And when we try to solve these complex questions, we encounter a large number of errors and myths held over from the past.

Regional and Local Finances: Intelligence Versus Myth

The struggle over the allocation of resources is the most painful and complex issue in the interrelations among levels of power. Because federal legislation makes no precise distinctions among the powers and responsibilities to be exercised at the central, regional, and local levels, it is a complex matter to ascertain and justify decisionmaking processes on resource allocation.

The thesis advanced everywhere is that budgetary payments are not supported by equivalent receipts. In other words: "There isn't any money." And this despite the fact that Russia is unusually rich in virtually every type of resource.

Russia is indeed a very rich country. And difficult as it is to admit it, we have been corrupted by this wealth. According to calculations made in 153 municipalities of various types, there is a 30 percent cushion in the expenses section of local budgets. That is, with some intelligent management, expenses could be cut by one-third very easily and in absolutely any kind of municipality.

The income section of local budgets conceals no less of a reserve. For example, in implementing work on the Federal Program of State Support for Local Self-Government in Bologoe, Tver oblast (one of the most backward municipalities in that region), the following results were achieved in a year and a half simply by organizing intelligent administration: a 27 percent reduction in budget expenditures and a revenue increase of 37 percent. By investing 600,000 rubles in training, the direct economic impact totaled 15 million rubles.

Without question, such unutilized resources exist at every administrative level. But what is also interesting is that the residents of Bologoe never did feel the beneficial effects of this work because every penny saved went into the regional budget, not their own.

This absence of economic and psychological stimuli is the reason that economic management in the territories is ineffective.

Unfortunately, we inherited our tax system for the most part from the Soviet unitary state. Graphically, it looks like this:

TAXES
central organs of state power
regional organs of state power
organs of local self-government

POPULATION

This chart clearly shows that each level of power has one way to acquire additional income—by taking it away from another level. Tax reform legislation, which is proceeding very slowly in the Duma, envisions boosting income at each administrative level so that other levels can stimulate development of their income base.

No less complex is the problem of leveling out budgetary income. This problem has been exacerbated by the tremendous differences I've already mentioned in the economic development of the territories. In this situation, the aggregate of funds not being redistributed by the federal center is significant. For this reason, it is of fundamental importance that we ensure transparency and clarity in the procedures for redistributing those funds. Otherwise, "budgetary wars" among different administrative levels are inevitable.

The myth about the shortage of budgetary funds stems from the absence of stimuli for efficient economic management in the system of resource allocation. If to this problem we add the lack of a solution to the land question and the multiplicity of social benefits granted to various groups of the population (70 percent of the urban population, for example, enjoys benefits in the form of low-cost public transit), then the reasons for the shortage of budgetary funds become obvious.

The Myth of the "National Legacy at Risk"

One of the errors of inherited Soviet economics is the notion that the basis of economic potential consists of fixed capital—in other words, buildings and installations. However, in the postindustrial society in which we live, property that cannot produce income or satisfy society's demands has no value.

This notion is understandable because over the entire Soviet period, the industrial potential we still have today was created through an immense concentration of effort by entire generations of Russians. They have an emotional stake in that brick and mortar.

On the other hand, however, such notions constitute the most powerful of brakes on attracting investments to the productive sector of the economy, because:

- local politicians look on foreign investors as "buying up the national legacy," and consequently from day one they try to extract as much income as possible from a business that has not yet started;
- local officials see their main task as the creation of fixed capital, not jobs;
- local officials have a hard time understanding ideas and projects, such as energy conservation, that are not aimed at obtaining direct economic effects;
- local officials concentrate on obtaining state investments in viable projects rather than investing in projects that will create favorable conditions for business; and
- local officials fail to evaluate properly firms engaged in consulting and banking services and telecommunications, for example, and in organizing business infrastructure.

Unfortunately, such misconceptions create unfavorable public attitudes toward foreign entrepreneurs, since most people think they are not providing jobs but "appropriating the national legacy."

Casting Illusions Aside and
Restoring Faith in the Future

An oriental proverb says: "God forbid you come to live in a time of change." It is in such a condition that present-day Russia now finds itself. But I'm not so sure this proverb is correct. One must pay for everything in life. It seems to me that another Russian proverb suits modern Russia better: "The only free cheese is in the mousetrap."

It is a time of change, a time when we must part with the illusions inculcated in us during the Soviet period. It is a time when we should make sense of our journey, when new elites can emerge, when thousands of talented people will have the chance to rise to the top of the political and business elite.

But this is also an extremely difficult time. It's not easy to let go of your habits, especially your convictions and hopes. For seventy years we believed blindly in the might of the state. Now we have to believe in ourselves.

What is hardest, after all those years during which the Communist authorities tried to convince us that the state would take care of us and our families, is realizing that there is no one to do that now but ourselves.

Nonetheless, life is experiencing a revival. As we come to understand eternal truths about the value of labor and our responsibility for our own life, and with the rebirth and development of Orthodox values, Russia will take its proper place among the nations of the world and will provide, at last, decent living conditions for its citizens.

The main thing is not to be cajoled into changing the government structure yet again, into rocking the boat, which, however slowly, is sailing forward.

In this respect, it is hard to exaggerate the importance of expert and intelligent public administration for the country. It is also hard to exaggerate the role of federalism and local self-government, which is exactly what Russia needs.

Part Two

Coping with New Economic Rules

5

THE NEW STAGE OF ECONOMIC REFORMS IN RUSSIA

Thoughts on Policy and Practice

Sergei Vasil'ev

The crisis of August 17, 1998, signified a kind of intermediate termination of the economic reforms in Russia that had begun in November 1991 and lasted almost eight years.

Public opinion in Russia and beyond has tended to perceive the eight years of reform as largely a time of frustrated hopes. In fact, after an early period of high inflation and political instability from 1992 to 1995, the country stabilized to some degree over the next two years in its political and economic life, enjoying rising living standards and surging hopes for a full recovery.

Born in 1957, **Sergei Aleksandrovich Vasil'ev** holds a doctorate in economics from the St. Petersburg University of Economics and Finance. One of Anatolii Chubais's fellow reformers in the St. Petersburg city administration, Vasil'ev followed Chubais to government service in 1991 as the head of the newly established Working Center for Economic Reform, which drafted the legal foundation for the new market economy. Until August 1998 he held various high-level posts in the national government, including deputy minister of the economy. He is now chairman of the International Investment Bank and holds a chair in economic theory at the Higher School of Economics, as well as board seats in various foundations and research centers. Translated by Antonina W. Bouis.

Causes of the August 17 Crisis

The crisis of August 17, 1998, shattered these hopes. The trust that the reformers had been enjoying for quite some time, despite the many problems that arose in the course of reform—a trust that was reaffirmed in the presidential elections of 1996—was now completely exhausted.

And it does little good to refer to the objective difficulties of the reform process. The main difficulties occurred during President Yeltsin's first term, when reforms encountered the fierce opposition of the Supreme Soviet, the Central Bank executed its own policies at cross-purposes with the government, and the war in Chechnya began. It was nonetheless during this time that the initial accomplishments in the new economic policy were achieved.

In President Yeltsin's second term, objective conditions were much more favorable, yet the reforms bogged down. I cannot cite a single major achievement in reform policies during 1996–1999. Moreover, it was during that very period that conditions were created for the financial crisis of 1998. Contrary to the many recommendations made by the International Monetary Fund (IMF) as well as leading Russian and foreign experts, national budgets burdened by huge deficits were approved and implemented for several years in succession.

In order to cover the deficits, the government assumed enormous domestic and foreign debts at very high interest rates. The national debt rose at a rate that made the August crisis inevitable, whatever the developments in world financial markets.

The "vacuum cleaner" of government borrowing, switched to full power, sucked out money from current cash flows. After a decrease in 1994–1995, nonpayments rose again, as did barter operations. The Ministry of Finance compensated for the undercollection of taxes by issuing various surrogates for cash, and the use of such offsets became widespread. The money that the state could not raise in the form of taxes it borrowed at high interest rates.

The country's debt problems were magnified by the irresponsible policies of the major Russian banks, which set out to attract money from abroad on a large scale, and by the equally irresponsible policies of the Central Bank, which in effect exercised no control over the credit policies and risk exposure of the leading Russian banks.

The Results of the First Stage of Reform

Now, more than a year later, when the short-term consequences of the financial collapse have run their course, we can take stock of what was accomplished during the eight years of reform.

The first and fundamental result was the construction of a market economy. The most important evidence of that is the functioning of the Russian economy in the post-August period. Although the exchange rate of the ruble declined sharply and the domestic financial market disintegrated, the Russian economy adapted quickly to the new conditions, and a compensatory upswing began much sooner than expected. In fact, the economy resumed functioning normally within six months.

On the other hand, we see that throughout the entire reform period, basic economic indicators remained negative. Even though estimates of general domestic decline and the fall of gross domestic product (GDP) (-53 percent and -42 percent) are much greater than, say, that of retail trade (-13 percent), the national decline continues. Data on capital flight are particularly striking—around 20 billion dollars a year, a figure that appears to be almost totally independent of fluctuations in the exchange rate and changes in macroeconomic and structural policies. Those 20 billion dollars each year constitute a real reserve of investment in the national economy, a reserve of economic growth. The government's inability to halt that capital outflow characterizes the first stage of reform.

Analysts of the Russian economy also note that against the backdrop of a small decrease in the average standard of living (with the increase in the quality of consumption, there was no simultaneous decrease in consumption), the disparity in living standards of the populace increased sharply. The coefficient measuring the income gap between the richest 10 percent of households and the poorest 10 percent grew from 5 to 14—and this figure reflected only reported income, without including consumption in the shadow economy. Thirty-six percent of the population lives below the poverty line. And because basic natural resources are being used up, the inequality in income becomes an inequality in wealth.

This problem to a great extent derives from the structure of the Russian economy. Most of the added value in Russia occurs in a limited number of industries related to natural resources. In the course of creating a market mechanism, enterprises that exploited natural resources retained most of the income.

Moreover, the system of allocations to social support functions operates in a way that benefits those social strata who are better off rather than the poor. Such an inequitable system of transfers cannot be changed easily because the local interests who profit from the existing system block all attempts at change in the parliament.

To some degree, the increased stratification of Russian society according to wealth is a fiction. In the Soviet era, the privileged strata of society received basic (but scarce) goods at reduced prices. Now that system has almost vanished, and the former elite has converted its privileges into property and income. So even if their standard of living has not changed, statistically their wealth is growing.

In general, I feel that the problem of income and property stratification is secondary. As soon as the Russian economy begins to grow, poverty will decrease and new opportunities to help the needy will arise. Naturally, the system of social allocations will have to be restructured at that time.

One of the long-term problems of Russia's social development is the degradation of its human resources base. Historically, in comparison with the technological level of the economy, the quality of human resources in the USSR was higher than in other countries at comparable levels of development. Moreover, the quality of human capital was (and still is) the most important factor compensating for the low technological and organizational levels of the economy. Naturally, most of this human capital was focused on the needs of the military-industrial complex (MIC). At the same time, the MIC stimulated the development of many fundamental sciences and ensured a very advanced level of higher education.

The extended and persistent cutbacks of the MIC has had an extremely adverse effect on the financing of fundamental science and higher education and has led to the closure of scientific schools, reducing the country's scientific-technological potential, which will be needed once economic growth resumes.

Along with the underutilization of investment potential caused by capital flight, the severe national problem of individual savings hidden "under the mattress" is related to the workings of the Russian banking system. While most midsize and small banks grew to meet the needs of current payments (which is natural and normal), the principal large banks increased their potential by operating with monies from the state budget.

For it was these large commercial banks who were "empowered" by the Ministry of Finance to handle government accounts. As a result, these banks did not look for resources in the commercial sector but spent their time lobbying for money from the state. Incidentally, a significant part of the chronic delays in budget payments were due to the "use" of government funds by commercial banks. In a later period, the government represented not only most of the major banks' liabilities but also most of their assets in the form of domestic loans.

It is not surprising, then, that the largest Russian banks had a weak relationship with the productive sector of the economy, whether in attracting resources or in directing them there. The resulting crisis of internal loans was to be expected. Most of the large Russian banks went bankrupt, the banking system was set back several years, and the public's trust in Russian banks was severely undermined.

A basic reason for the 1998 crisis was the prolonged retention of significant budget deficits that were financed by domestic and foreign loans. Russia's partial default on foreign and domestic debt in 1998–1999 made it possible to balance current revenues and payments not tied to servicing and paying debt. However, a situation in which Russia does not fulfill its foreign debt obligations cannot continue for more than eighteen months to two years.

At the end of that period, the payments on foreign debt will rise again sharply, and efforts will have to be made to balance the budget, by reducing expenditures as well as by balancing payments and hard-currency deposits.

The Balanced Budget As
a Political Problem

The problem of a balanced budget is not a technical one. Nor is it a purely political one—as it now appears to certain advocates of liberal reforms, who maintain that the "good reformist government" tried everything to balance the budget, while the Communist-dominated State Duma tried everything to keep the government from doing it. In fact, the government played up to the leftist majority in the

Duma by regularly introducing soft draft budgets, and the Duma almost always approved the government proposals.

The deeper problem lies elsewhere—in the relations between society and the state that have been inherited from socialism. Under socialism, the state is totally separate from society, neither subordinate to it nor wholly responsible for the well-being of its citizens. As a result, social demands under socialism never became extensive.

As long as the repressive Communist apparatus remained in place, these demands never surfaced. The political collapse of communism, however, permitted growing social expectations to be openly expressed through a democratic political process, namely the election of a populist parliament.

In Russia, the situation is complicated by the fact that under the Constitution, the executive branch is independent of the legislature, while the parliament bears no responsibility for its own economic policies enacted in response to social demands. The formerly hidden conflict between society and state is now expressed in an open conflict between parliament and government.

Understandably, this conflict is a sign of the immaturity of civil society in Russia, a sign that citizens are not yet prepared to be responsible for the welfare of the country as a whole. But it is also clear that this conflict can be resolved only within the framework of the democratic process, through educating society and its elected representatives and giving parliament the responsibility for the formulation and implementation of economic policy.

In that sense, the experience of the left-of-center government of Evgenii Primakov is instructive. Primakov passed no populist measures and took an extremely hard monetary and budget line. It was the majority support of the parliament that helped his administration pass harsh measures that more right-wing governments could not have passed. (This phenomenon is not a purely Russian one; similar outcomes can be observed in central Europe and Latin America.)

The Reformers' Political Mistakes

In that sense, we can speak of the political mistakes and failures of the reformers. Excessive dependence on the president's power was a mistake. Yes, presidential power did guarantee for several years reform's continuity and its swift execution through a series of edicts.

But at the same time, the permanent conflict between the reformers and the parliament led to an extremely narrow and unstable legislative base for reform. A number of key issues in building a foundation for a market economy—private ownership of land, for example, and the creation of a rational tax system—remain as far from solution as they were five years ago. As for failures, the worst was the inability to create a major right-wing political party to press for the creation of an effective market economy.

The rightist liberal party Democratic Choice of Russia, strong enough in 1993–1994, lost the parliamentary elections in 1995 and now has minimal support. The right-centrist party Our Home Is Russia, which managed to create a large faction in the parliamentary elections of 1995, no longer has enough support among the general population. Yabloko, the largest democratic party, has the support of approximately 15 percent of the voters. However, that party alone is unlikely to be able to push pro-market ideas through parliament; besides which, in Western terms, Yabloko is a social democratic party.

The weak political support for rightist parties originates from the reformers' virtual defeat in the battle for public opinion over the results of the first stage of Russian reforms. Almost all the myths disseminated by the communists—the confiscation of people's savings during price liberalization, the thievery of privatization, and the stifling of domestic industry—have by now become ingrained in the public consciousness.

The reason for this defeat was that the reformers paid too little heed to explaining their strategy. The successful postcommunist transformations and reforms in other countries show that society's acceptance of reform is almost more important than the actual content of the reforms. People must receive information about what is happening directly from the main players. In Russia, unfortunately, the reformers always found policymaking more important than justifying their actions to the public. Their dislike of all ideology and propaganda, as vestiges of communism, also played a role.

The period of stalled reforms in 1996–1998 has made it clear that reforms based primarily on the exercise of presidential power are no longer an option. The essential condition for continued progress is the formation of a government based on a majority in the State Duma. Even if that government is not overly reformist, the exigencies of managing the national agenda will force it to take steps in the right direction, and the results achieved, grounded in legislation, will be more solid.

Priorities of Midterm Economic Policy for Russia

The Problem of State Debt

In light of the foregoing, the priorities of Russian economic policy over the midterm period become clear. Bearing in mind the relatively successful functioning of Russia's economy at the end of 1998 and the beginning of 1999 under conditions of freezing the foreign debt, the important issue becomes debt restructuring. In my opinion, the key to renewing economic growth in Russia is not so much writing off part of the debt as limiting the annual payments of the debt so that they correspond to the economy's true capacity.

The technical problem lies in the fact that the usual amortization schedules are made with equal payments every year, whereas Russia's ability to pay its debts depends primarily on how world prices for energy and raw materials correlate. Under those conditions, an unorthodox measure, such as tying Russia's debt payment schedule to the dynamics of world prices for oil, gas, and other exported products, might be appropriate.

In turn, domestic producers of export goods could be assessed a special tax whose rates would depend on the levels of export prices. A similar scheme is already in use in Russia for determining the level of customs duties for oil exports.

A flexible method of servicing Russia's foreign debt would solve many domestic economic and social problems. Currency policy and the exchange rate constitute one area that can benefit. The financial crisis of 1997–1998 showed, among other things, that no policy of fixed or tied exchange rates could be established in Russia. A sharp change in foreign trade conditions immediately made the "currency corridor" introduced in 1995 indefensible.

In the near future, therefore, while its primary exports remain energy and raw materials, Russia will have to maintain a floating exchange rate for the ruble. At the same time, to guarantee beneficial conditions for investments, especially foreign investments, the government must keep exchange rate fluctuations at a minimum. A special currency tax would be sufficient to accomplish this, since it would withdraw part of the exporters' added profit related to increased prices.

Another function of the currency tax would be to smooth out differences in per capita income in various branches of industry. If the special tax removes a significant part of the natural rents, it will lead to the equalization of income, for instance between industries exploiting natural resources and those processing them.

The Role of the West in Solving Russia's Debt Problems

No matter which scheme for Russian debt restructuring is considered, developing the necessary political conditions will not be easy. First of all, this process cannot begin until after the presidential elections in Russia in March 2000. Second, after a series of unsuccessful IMF programs in 1998, the West will want specific guarantees that an agreement on the restructuring of Russian debt truly will be the last in a series of debt agreements between the West and Russia and that the world community will no longer have to pull Russia out of a financial hole.

What would be an appropriate instrument for achieving such an agreement? Neither the IMF nor the World Bank are appropriate: They are primarily technical organizations and as such are best suited for solving technical problems. In my opinion, the numerous IMF programs in Russia failed precisely because the Group of Seven (G-7) countries expected the IMF to solve political tasks for which the IMF was generally not designed.

If the West seriously desires to solve Russia's debt problem in a radical way, it will have to create a separate instrument for doing so. Whether through the designation of a special representative or the establishment of a working group, the G-7 will have to enter into a direct economic and political dialogue with Russia.

For now, we can only imagine the rough outline of a future agreement. Most likely, it will involve legislative or constitutional amendments tied to nondeficit budgets at all levels; a total ban on foreign loans for all state or parastate institutions; the introduction of strict budgetary procedures; and an increase in banking controls.

One way or another, the agreement on restructuring foreign debt should guarantee certain minimal external conditions for the development of the Russian economy. No less important will be efforts to solve domestic problems.

A Balanced Budget and Tax Reform

The key issue is balancing the state budget. At present, revenues of the expanded government (in IMF terminology, an "expanded government" includes federal and regional budgets as well as nonbudget funds, primarily the state pension fund) are at a level slightly below 30 percent of GDP, whereas expenditures are slightly higher.

Even though some Russian liberal economists insist that the budget of the expanded government in relation to GDP should be significantly reduced, in my opinion there is no possibility of that. Most expenditures of the expanded government are for social purposes: state pensions, education, and public health. Even though all these areas need reform, such reforms will not lead to a reduction of expenditures over the next few years. It is the reduction in inefficient government allocations that will permit an increase in targeted assistance for the most needy.

It is also unlikely that in the next few years there will be a decrease in defense spending, another large part of the budget. A third budget sector—subsidies for housing and municipal transport—does, however, offer room for cutbacks. The scale of subsidies here is close to 4 percent of GDP, of which 3 percent could be saved. This sector offers probably the only single large reserve for reducing budget expenses.

Revenues are derived from an extremely inequitable system of taxation, although the level of taxation—less than 30 percent of GDP—is low by European standards. Honest taxpayers pay a very high (up to 70 percent) portion of their income, but a significant number of unscrupulous citizens pay no taxes at all. Therefore, the aim of reforming the tax system must be not so much a change in the tax rates as the creation of a simple, just, and effective system.

What should the framework of that system be? Since the most important goal of taxes, besides the mobilization of revenues, is the stimulation of economic growth, the tax system must focus on those mechanisms of economic growth that will be functioning in Russia in the next few decades.

However, current prospects for economic growth do not inspire optimism. The most important element of economic growth is the transformation of savings into assets through the national financial market, most significantly the banking system. Yet people's trust in commercial banks has been undermined, and most savings are kept in foreign currency or held as deposits in the largest state savings bank (Sberbank). Moreover, both hard currency savings and Sberbank ruble accounts are effectively kept out of investments. Sberbank, which has preserved its Soviet-era structures, is incapable of handling its assets in a flexible manner, much less giving credits directly to the economy. Even if Sberbank did nothing but attract people's savings, all decisions on its use of the money would be taken under powerful pressure from state organs.

In any case, given the absence of an interbank loan market and given the extreme instability of the securities market, it seems highly unlikely that Sberbank's assets will be used for investment needs. The only area in which there could be progress is mortgage lending.

The resources of commercial banks, which were established to guarantee payment flows for enterprises, could be used as investments, although by their nature and scale they are useful only for investing in working capital. Investment into basic capital assets in the near future will be accomplished by only a limited number of methods.

The first such method is financing from personal profit. Under the conditions of a developing market, the profits of successful companies will be quite high for a lengthy period of time. This will allow them, first of all, to expand and modernize their existing plants, and second, to diversify their profiles. Such high profits were in fact enjoyed by Russian industries after the August 17 crisis led to a sharp revival of investment activity.

The second method is secondary issuances of shares for strategic investors. In essence, this process involves the direct sale of enterprises under rational investment criteria. The investor receives a large (controlling or blocking) package of shares as a condition of his investment, because it is only then that he can influence the enterprise's management. In today's undeveloped stock market, buying small packets of shares is attractive only for a limited number of blue chip equities, but by the same token the ability of the blue chips to attract investments is much greater.

There is a third method, the establishment of an enterprise from scratch, known as greenfielding, which is much more common among foreign investors.

In this manner, the main source of assets will be the enterprises and not the population at large. In this case, the tax system must be oriented to give maximum tax relief to enterprises and to increase the actual collection of taxes from the populace. And this does not necessitate an increase in personal income tax.

Research done by the Bureau of Economic Analysis in 1998 shows a striking disparity between the actual income and expenditures of individuals and the total personal income tax collected. The income and expense data is based on surveys of families; this income is readily declared, and consequently does not include the significant shadow-economy income.

So, if the shadow-economy income were to be taxed even at a minimal rate, income tax collection in Russia would increase by two-and-a-half times.

The reasons for the low collection of income tax are simple. First, supplementary income is taxed through a mechanism of filling out tax declarations. Despite its best efforts, the Federal Tax Service cannot keep track of all the numerous sources of income. Second, Russia currently uses a system of progressive personal income tax with a limit of 45 percent, which is quite tolerable by European standards. However, because the amount of a paid salary determines allocations to social funds (pension, social security, and so on), the top limit is actually 75 percent. With tax rates like this, the stimuli to evade taxation become very strong, especially since successful businesses have the greatest incentives for not paying taxes in the first place.

There are dozens of schemes for tax evasion. Using purely administrative methods to combat them is pointless, because in Russia the people are more inventive than the state. Therefore I propose dropping the progressive scale of taxation and the entire system of tax declarations. There should be only two tax rates: 0 percent and, say, 20 percent (Russians will not pay more than 20 percent anyway). The 20 percent must be deducted at every source of income. The poor will have a minimum that goes untaxed. The Federal Tax Service should work not on discovering people's income but on recovering excess monies that were written off through tax loopholes created by legislation.

This scheme would at least double personal income tax collection.

It must be noted that a similar approach was considered for the Tax Code of 1997, but it was rejected by the State Duma as too liberal and not conducive to the deputies' aim of taxing the rich to the maximum. In that sense, restructuring the tax system will be one of the greatest challenges for the new president, parliament, and government. The degree to which these bodies can resist populism in reforming taxation will be an important indicator of the readiness of Russian centrists to execute a responsible economic policy.

Enforcing the collection of income tax from the population will also lighten the tax burden on manufacturers. This is now a heavy burden, not because of the high tax rate on profits (30 percent) but because of all the other taxes that must be paid on the entire manufacturing process—taxes on maintaining the local social infrastructure, for example, or payments to the road fund. Even though each of these taxes might be only a small percentage of revenues, in the end they can total 50 percent or more of profits. The liberal version of the Tax Code of 1997 proposed doing away with these taxes. That proposal, too, was rejected by the Duma.

In principle, the problem of taxation is not only a problem of rates but also of procedures. The strict tax collection procedures employed in developed countries will not work in Russia. Unfortunately, the concepts of human rights and freedom of enterprise are not generally accepted here. Laws giving broad powers to tax inspectors and tax police have created a situation in which regional authorities use these agencies to put political pressure on entrepreneurs, while semicriminal businesses use them to destroy competition. Thus, the legal and judicial protection of enterprises must be an important element in Russian tax legislation.

The Development of Russian Democracy: Scenarios

The coming decade will be a trial for Russian democracy. Here we see several possible scenarios. An optimistic scenario projects that the new Duma and the new government achieve consensus on fundamental issues; an agreement is reached on the restructuring of foreign debt; the reforms continue, albeit not very swiftly; and the democratic government is strengthened and stabilized. In such a political scenario, a rapid return of economic growth is feasible.

In a second scenario, there is no consensus among branches of power, economic policy leans toward populism, and long-term restructuring of the debt is not achieved. Such outcomes will lead to economic stagnation and political destabilization.

The chronic inability of the existing government to bring order to the economy and the growing instability in society could lead to a transition from the second to a third scenario—the introduction of "the strong hand." This presupposes the emergence, most likely through legitimate means, of a strong leader, one who at least for a time will change the rules of the game and secure the political authority to solve numerous problems that cannot be solved through democratic procedures. The consequences for economic policy could be either beneficial or catastrophic. Bearing in mind Russia's long authoritarian tradition, this scenario is highly likely, but extremely dangerous.

Thus, the politicians of the new wave have an enormous responsibility. The continuing decline and contentiousness of political life in Russia could plunge the country into a lengthy period of economic and political stagnation. Attempts to enact changes would be blocked by interest groups tied to various sources of income. Geopolitically, Russia would become a Third World country.

Who Determines Russia's Future, and How

This collection of essays seeks to show the future of Russia through the eyes of young Russians. I am reminded of the rebukes addressed to the reformers in 1992–1993, who were accused of not knowing (or of knowing, but refusing to tell) what kind of society they wanted to build. To tell the truth, the very thought that we reformers were supposed to show the path for all society irritated me. For the previous seventy years Russia had built a society according to a general blueprint—and nothing good came out of that.

The idea that leaders must choose a path for society's development is profoundly alien to me. Society chooses its own path of development—sometimes unconsciously, sometimes through public ideology and the political process. The Russian reformers of the 1990s naturally had, and still have, their own ideas about what they wish for Russia. But they did not want to impose their ideas on society. Their goal was different: As the socialist economic system disintegrated, they wanted to create the basic conditions for a market economy and, more broadly, for political democracy.

The key phrase for us was "freedom of choice." In economics, that meant freedom of pricing, freedom of choice of a business partner, freedom of selection of a contract type, freedom in foreign trade, and freedom in creating enterprises—economic freedom as the sole form of survival for the Russian economy, which had been almost choked to death by the former centrally planned system.

In politics, "freedom of choice" meant freedom of information, the priority of human rights, and democratic government—political freedom as the ability of society as a whole to choose the path of its own development.

These values do not have alternatives. If there is no economic freedom, there will be economic collapse. If there is no political freedom, then society has no voice. Therefore, economic and political freedom are not elements in a picture of Russia's future, but the conditions of its creation, and in that sense they are beyond ideology.

However, life played a cruel trick on the reformers. The reformers saw themselves as technocrats, the creators of the foundations of civil society, not of civil society itself. It was understood (without being said) that other people—politicians—would work on the development of an ideology. Moreover, it was thought that the first ideological push for Russian reform would come from the intellectuals of the older generation, whom the reformers viewed as teachers and older comrades and whose priorities in questions of ideology and politics they accepted without hesitation.

But it turned out that many of the liberals of the first wave were unprepared morally for the reforms they had demanded. The dramatic political dynamics of the transition period had severely disoriented them. Many of the "engineers of perestroika" took conservative positions. Some returned to academia, others moved abroad.

Therefore, at the decisive moments of political battles, the reformers were literally shoved out onto the political proscenium and forced to head a political party for reform. They had a clear economic program but had no developed views on any other issues: organization of government, federalism and municipal self-government, international relations, and social policies. And this, of course, is one of the reasons for the weak performance of the party of reform in the elections of 1993 and 1995.

The Crisis of Communication in a Postcommunist Society

The inability of the reformers to formulate their ideology is merely part of the larger informational crisis in Russian society. I attribute that crisis to the broad changes in the structure of society that have occurred in the process of reform.

The Role of a "Parallel" Information Field in the Collapse of Communism

As we know, one of the goals of the Communist regime was to achieve the social homogeneity of society. And to a significant degree this was achieved.

During the 1970s, a large middle class, educated and with a rising standard of living, took root in the major cities. The intellectual demands of that class outgrew the informational field of socialist society: the lies of official propaganda, the hypocrisy of social life, the low standards of official literature and art.

These people experienced a genuine informational hunger, greedily devouring everything that was the least bit different from the positions of official information channels. Because the Communist regime was gradually degenerating, the ideological pressure on the public did not remain absolute: Occasional critical articles appeared, ideologically incorrect authors published their books (albeit in small editions), unorthodox films were shown (on small screens). And because of this informational hunger, every new article, book, and film became an event and then a fashion.

Even under Leonid Brezhnev's style of socialism, a parallel non-Soviet subculture had formed. And since it was fashionable, this subculture involved ever-growing parts of the population, even those who were not so inclined by virtue of their social position (in the Soviet bureaucracy, or among the most educated of the workers). The growth of that stratum is reflected in the following statistic: The print run of Russia's only non-Soviet literary and political journal, *Novyi mir,* at the peak of the early Brezhnev thaw (1967), was 150,000 copies; at the start of perestroika, its circulation, as well as that of similar journals, ran into the millions.

In this non-Soviet subculture, an elite evolved: people who read samizdat and forbidden Western publications; whose creative work, even though it was subject to censorship, took place in an uncensored context that was obvious to its intended audience. These people were not simply non-Soviet, they were anti-Soviet.

By the mid-1980s, Russia had a well-educated and comfortable stratum of people living in a single information field (of both official and nonofficial culture), reading the same books, sharing the same non-Soviet values, and orienting ideologically toward the anti-Soviet intellectual elite.

In fact, the appearance of this class paved the way for perestroika and the downfall of socialism. In the eyes of the educated class, the Brezhnev regime had died as early as 1980. When censorship was lifted, the intellectual elite began speaking directly to the middle class, without resorting to Aesopian language. All the new ideas were disseminated through the information channels that already existed, and they were immediately absorbed by society.

The Disintegration of the Parallel Information Field

However, the moment of complete triumph for the alternative culture became, as often happens, the moment of the beginning of its disintegration. First of all, the basis for that culture—the social unity of its bearers—had vanished. Under socialism, the entire middle class had been equal in its lack of rights and its helplessness before the socialist Leviathan. But when a minority of the middle class, the most active members, went into business, the standard of living of those members rose.

The other, larger part of the middle class—affiliated with the defense industries, the fundamental sciences, and other sectors paid for by the state budget—found itself in dire straits. Both the absolute and the relative standard of living for that part of the middle class fell, as did its social status.

In any case, both groups became too busy (the one with business, the other with survival) for additional intellectual activities; they basically withdrew from the former subculture.

And finally, a significant number of the middle class chose to emigrate—their "non-Sovietness" had made them internal émigrés much earlier.

At the same time, the channels of informational interaction began dispersing. Representatives of the non-Soviet cultural elite had dominated the mass media during perestroika. In that period, the mass media truly were independent and guaranteed reliable communications between the elite and the middle class.

Beginning in 1992, however, the mass media, under pressure of circumstances, began commercializing rapidly. Although this was not in itself a threat, the danger lay in the fact that journalists as well as publications were becoming commodities. The mass media were transformed into influence-wielding loudspeakers for interest groups. The public trust was lost. Independent journalism was marginalized.

And the disintegration of the intellectual elite followed.

In fact, these circumstances represented the total collapse of the cultural environment that had given birth to perestroika and had guaranteed the fall of socialism. In the unverbalized plans of the reformers, this cultural environment was to have become the base for the development of a national reformist ideology and the foundation for further political action.

As a result, postcommunist society in Russia obtained in the form of the market a standard mechanism of economic communication, but it lost the ability to reflect, it lost the common voice by which public concepts of Russia's future had been formulated, and it lost its sociocultural unity.

Over the past few years I have had the opportunity to discuss Russia's economic problems with the most diverse people—governors, businesspeople, federal bureaucrats, and academic researchers. The problems were always the same—but the interpretations were so varied that I had the impression that my interlocutors were speaking different languages and talking about different countries. Theoretically, their solutions with regard to some particular problem might coincide, but their motivations were different. Therefore, it is harder for them to concur on ideology than to solve a practical problem together.

In that sense, for the near future, all actions of the government authorities as well as the political groups in Russia will be either reactive or modified by group ideologies. In these conditions, the feasibility of formulating and implementing long-term policies is dubious. A typical comment about Russia's future will sound like this: Here is what we would like to achieve—but things will develop in their own way.

6

BUILDING HOUSES FOR THE NEWLY AFFLUENT NEAR MOSCOW

An Entrepreneur's Perspective

Kirill Gorelov

> *Our Corporation is working to create a new kind of product—quality of life. We see our goal as not to build more houses, but to create a living habitat. In doing so, we are trying to combine a modern quality of life, the Russian worldview, and urban habits.*
> —from the Podmoskov'e Corporation's mission statement

I am twenty-nine years old and was born in Moscow, where I went to a special English-language high school. After graduation I started working in a bank, and a year later entered the Moscow State Institute of International Relations, where I studied interna-

Kirill Igorevich Gorelov, president of Podmoskov'e Corporation at the time of our interview, died in an accident while parachuting from a rocky cliff in Norway in August 1999.

Hundreds attended his funeral. As this interview makes abundantly clear, Kirill was a man of exceptional talents, the very model of an entrepreneurial leader who held strong values and lived by them. Russia is the poorer for his loss. His mother, Angelina, is now the president of Podmoskov'e. Interview recorded and translated by Natan M. Shklyar.

Interview: Monday, May 24, 1999, Moscow Oblast

tional economics at night while continuing to work at the bank. In 1987 I left the bank and entered graduate school at the Foreign Economic Relations Research Institute, where I had the good fortune to work in the department that helped develop the concept and practice of joint venture enterprises in Russia. This was a cutting-edge theme in a very interesting time, during the very beginning of economic reforms. Thus, I had a chance to work with the people who were at the inception of the new Russian economy, and the contacts and knowledge I acquired there helped me throughout the rest of my career.

I spent one and a half or two years there, learned a great deal, and in 1990, together with a friend, started my very first company. Our firm worked with information technologies, mostly selling electronic publications. At that time it was a difficult business, since there was no culture of selling this kind of information. Growth was slow. I left and began another career, in real estate, another new area that was emerging at that time. We started with simple land deals, buying and selling plots of land. Of course, at that time you could not legally buy and sell land. Instead, the negotiating parties would draft contracts for provision of services, and one of the clauses would specify unlimited access to the land. In fact, using just such legal loopholes, many people were buying and selling land. We made some good money on these deals, but eventually it got tedious and was no longer challenging. Aside from financial gain, there was no intellectual satisfaction from this business.

That is when I decided to move from land deals to comprehensive land development. This was a new topic at that time and even now remains relatively unexplored. Until very recently, land development fell within the sole purview of the state; private companies never ventured into this field. When in the Soviet days people would get their long-awaited apartment, they could expect to have it delivered with infrastructure, the stores, roads, gas stations, kindergartens, and everything else that people need for normal life. After the privatization of 1992, however, the state withdrew from these activities, and private firms began working in construction, road building, retail trade, the sale of gasoline, and the like. There was no comprehensive approach to residential living. We realized that this was a niche for us to fill.

We started in one of the Moscow subdivisions, working with the local administration, which was receptive to our plan. With the help of scholars, sometimes from as far away as Novosibirsk, we put together a development program, which was subsequently approved. After that we approached the Moscow oblast administration with a similar plan, but with the emphasis on construction of suburban houses and development of entire suburbs. Our firm was a pioneer in the movement to suburbanize Russian cities, an undertaking that is still in the early stages.

Because of its large and relatively affluent population, Moscow oblast is a leading region in the construction of private houses. Although people would prefer to build their own houses, there was no engineering or social infrastructure to support them. Our goal, therefore, was to give our clients everything they would need beyond their homes, ranging from plumbing, sewage, and electricity to schools, hospitals, gyms, churches, and shopping centers. Ideally, our customer should be able to live a full life in his neighborhood, instead of having to commute to Moscow for every kind of errand. In 1994 we submitted a comprehensive proposal to the Moscow oblast administration, and after it was approved, we became the main subcontractor in this project. Thus was created the Podmoskov'e Corporation,* an open joint stock company.

Our first major challenge was the lack of familiarity among our people with the technologies of suburban house construction. In Soviet times, most urban dwellers lived in high-rise concrete buildings, though some had custom-built dachas outside the city. People simply did not know what kind of private houses could be built using modern technologies. The challenge was to create an educated market of consumers; marketing became our number one goal. We started by creating an outdoor exhibition of model houses, where people would come and we would collect information about consumer preferences and the range of prices we could reasonably charge.

The next challenge was to set up facilities for the mass production of houses. Of course, domestic industry could not supply us with the necessary parts, so we had to import prefabricated housing kits for assembly from Sweden, Germany, the Czech Republic, and Finland. Eventually we realized that this was too expensive, and we built a plant to make our own kits, using Western technologies. We had visited many countries, including the United States, Canada, and Euro-

---

Podmoskov'e translates as the region immediately surrounding Moscow.

pean countries, and we eventually decided to adopt the technology used in Sweden.

Simultaneously, we had to find money to back up this project. Fortunately, the Ministry of Finance received a World Bank credit, part of which we borrowed from the government, and we used the money to build the plant in May 1998. Today we are the largest borrower from the World Bank's residential housing credit program. We have taken out three loans of $5 million each and have already paid off part of them. The plant is now producing about 200 houses a year, and simultaneously has begun to build whole suburban townships. Today our corporation has two such plants with their own procurement service, an architectural design bureau, a uniformed security service division, and our own advertising agency, as well as a subsidiary that provides our townships with support services. We employ about 400 people. Land development is a booming industry; we are not the only company involved in it. There are ten to fifteen others. However, we are the only company that has a comprehensive set of services and all the processes integrated in-house.

We have a very close relationship with the government. The firm helped create and is implementing two government programs: "Comprehensive Land Development" and "People's Housing." Among our largest clients are the Ministry of Defense, the Ministry of Emergency Situations, the State Committee on the North, and several regional administrations. The Moscow oblast administration is one of our founding shareholders, together with the local administrations of several districts in the city and several construction companies. No single party owns a controlling stake, nor does the staff own any part of the company.

The Ministry of Defense uses our services to build houses for retired officers. In 1999 we built about 50,000 square meters of housing; about half that was built directly by us, and the rest by secondary contractors. Usually we build whole townships ourselves, but sometimes clients invite us to work in existing subdivisions, where we build private homes for them. About half of our orders come from government agencies. We mostly work in Moscow oblast. If in 1995 our sales volume reached $700,000, in 1998 it totaled $20 million. During the same period, the price of a square meter of living space has halved, from $1,600 to $750 today.

In addition to servicing the domestic market, we are also exporting our product to Kazakhstan and negotiating an export contract for Germany. German clients find our products to be on the level of European standards, but much cheaper than what they can find on their own market.

If Russia is to develop a truly mass market for individual housing, we must introduce the institution of mortgage financing. Although Podmoskov'e Corporation is not a financial institution, we have drafted several mortgage system plans, but without much success. The main obstacles to mortgage financing are high interest rates, the lack of long-term credit practices, and the absence of a legislative framework. This is why there has been little or no development in the area of mortgage financing. Everybody likes to say that we need mortgage financing, but nobody wants to move beyond political statements.

Another even more fundamental problem is the legacy of the Soviet mentality. We have no laws today that would make it possible to evict a person from his house if he should fail to make his mortgage payments. To be sure, St. Petersburg has adopted a progressive law and even has built special housing for those who cannot keep up payments on their houses. In fact, the Russian mindset renders such a law useless. In the West, people think of their house both as real property and as a source of investment, perhaps to be sold at a later date. In Russia, on the other hand, people perceive housing as virtually a constitutional right and as a social prerogative. Thus, any Russian banker, even were he to be armed with an appropriate law, would think twice before kicking a family out on the street. Morally and psychologically, eviction would be very difficult. And in today's economic conditions, when people have lost much of their savings, as happened in August 1998, you can imagine how suddenly hundreds and thousands of people could find themselves unable to make their mortgage payments. How can a banker take on himself the burden of evicting all those people? After August 1998, when people lost their money and could not make payments on the houses we were already building for them, we did lose some of our customers. However, without mortgage financing, we cannot make private housing available to the public, and here the state must take a leading role and adopt appropriate legislation that can create conditions for this market to develop. Our clients today have to put down 30 percent of the price in advance and then can make payments over the course of construction.

At one point the United States Congress considered granting Russia $5 billion to help establish a system of mortgage financing. However, this initiative bogged down in the State Duma. Congress naturally wanted to have the Russian government guarantee this project with a special line in the federal budget, which must be approved in the State Duma. However, given the current budget deficit, when the government does not have the money to pay public-sector employees and pensioners, it is not realistic to expect the State Duma to approve such a "luxury" item as mortgage financing.

On the whole, private housing construction has made huge inroads in the past several years. Despite deficient legislation, harsh economic conditions, and a rigid public mentality, you can notice that people's ideas about housing are changing. Five years ago, wealthy people would build huge mansions to show off their wealth. Today the same people prefer to build medium-sized homes. Before, people would only consider the price of the house at the time of purchase, but today they tend to be more concerned with the cost of its upkeep. Thus, our consumer is changing very rapidly. Perhaps the greatest obstacle today is the low purchasing power of the mass market.

We are targeting the so-called middle class, a long-term vision for us. Both of our plants together could produce over 100,000 square meters of living space annually, enough for about 1,000 houses and apartments. We cannot limit ourselves to the very rich. However, the middle class today is economically strapped, not to mention the rest of the population. A square meter in one of our townships costs $750, so a typical apartment in one of our duplex houses costs $75,000. Today our typical clients are relatively young (thirty-five to forty years old), usually leaders of firms or organizations, second-tier managers of larger companies, well-known journalists, athletes, pop stars, and some state officials.

We own 350 hectares of land in Moscow oblast. When we look for new home sites, we already know all the landowners around, as well as everything about the land, for instance its value in a given location, the approximate cost of laying engineering infrastructure, and people's preferences as to distance from Moscow and landscaping. We buy land from various landowners, mostly local administrations, although there are more and more private owners, including collective farms. With some collective owners, like the collective farms, we have to strike special deals, because land ownership comes in different shapes and sizes these days. Some collective farms privatized all of their land and made each member a private landowner, free to sell his land or continue farming. In other instances, if a city dweller wants to farm, he can petition a local rural administration to sell him land at a low price. When we build houses for our clients, they also become owners of the land on which the house stands.

Very much like housing, considered to be a social right, people regard land as part of the public domain and a source of their livelihood. Russians are strapped for money today, and if the state were to allow the simple sale and purchase of land, very rich people or foreign companies could come in and buy up most of it. Russians, especially our impoverished peasants, are victims of a system that has prevented them from making money and has instead rewarded financial speculators. Russian society as a whole puts a premium on social justice.

In fact, there already is a functioning market for land in Russia. When in 1998 Governor Dmitrii Ayatskov of Saratov oblast signed a regional law allowing the sale and purchase of land, he was lionized as a pioneer in this area, especially since the State Duma had failed to adopt any federal legislation on the subject. In fact, it was just a populist gesture that is largely meaningless today.

In our management approach, we try to borrow the best practices of the West. For example, we have a mission statement that our entire staff helped draft. Because we operate on very thin profit margins, it is important for people to have nonmonetary incentives to work; one such incentive is allowing our employees to take ownership of the company's mission. All new staff members have to undergo a psychological assessment process, which we developed with the help of our partner, RHR International. Before we launched our plant, we sent staff members to Germany to study house construction. Our managers attend seminars on leadership development.

Many obstacles face our company, for example the lack of a coherent tax policy relating to housing construction. I think the government should stop taxing profits and added value, and instead start taxing property and land. It is also important to give people incentives to invest in housing by granting appropriate tax benefits. We have avoided conflicts with organized crime because we have kept our business completely clean and free of illegal operations.

We welcome Western investments in the Russian economy and in our industry in particular. Unfortunately, we have not seen much direct investment because of high risk and low levels of return. We operate with minimal profit margins. Foreign investment is not likely to pour in until the country has attained a degree of stability, and this will not take place until after the presidential elections. As to our own activities, we plan to continue to work hard and thus contribute to the process of transformation.

7

A Pioneer in Russia's First Open Grain Market

Arkadii Zlochevskii

I consider myself a very lucky man. Most of the important things that have happened to me in life have resulted from fortunate coincidences. In my early life I was a professional musician and composer, but when the reforms began I quickly realized that I could not feed my family that way. When in 1991 a friend told me about a job opening at OGO Corporation, I applied just to make some money. At that time, OGO bought and sold a wide variety of goods. I was hired as a salesman of strollers and cribs, but to this day I have not sold a single stroller. For whatever reason, selling merchandise did not click with me. Right away I was afraid that if I did not produce any revenue during my probation period, I would lose my job.

Fortunately, I came across a unique opportunity. OGO was one of the founding companies of the Russian Commodities and Raw Materials Exchange (RTSB), and as such we regularly received market price information for the goods that were trading at the exchange. At that time, in early 1991, enterprises across Russia were allowed for the first time to sell their products at market prices—but nobody really knew what a fair market price for their product was. They were used to state planning agencies determining prices by decree.

Arkadii Leonidovich Zlochevskii is the president of OGO Corporation and the chairman of the Grain Union of Russia. Interview recorded and translated by Natan M. Shklyar.
Interview: Monday, May 31, 1999: Moscow

When I realized that, I started selling printouts of RTSB price quotes to various producers, and I discovered a huge demand for this service. I started bringing buyers and sellers together and helped them strike market deals. At one point, our operations accounted for half of all the activity on the RTSB exchange. Ironically, another stroke of luck for me was the August 1991 coup. A few days earlier we had taken out advertising space in the *Pravda* issue of August 19. When the coup took place, all newspapers in the country were shut down except for *Pravda*. When it came out, we were the only firm in the entire country advertising our services. That day we could not handle the volume of incoming phone calls and deal offers. Between May and September 1991 I made more money for the firm than the rest of the firm's staff put together. In fact, eventually only my department survived. The rest of the firm's operations died out. Needless to say, I did not lose my job.

The shift in our business from selling market price information to grain production also happened in September 1991. That month, two major grain deals fell through, for no apparent reason—the sellers simply failed to deliver on their contracts. When we analyzed this situation we discovered that the country's grain market had collapsed, along with the state planning bodies that until then had been charged with bringing producers and consumers together. Chaos resulted. On the one hand, collective farms and independent farmers were not familiar with market conditions. On the other hand, traders had no knowledge of agriculture. OGO saw a market niche. We began running training seminars for traders, educating them in the basics of grain production. We also bought information on collective farms and compiled their profiles, which we then sold to traders.

Officially, OGO began grain operations in January 1992, giving up all activities on the RTSB, since we did not see much future there. Production and processing of grain, and to a lesser degree oil, became our main focus. Together with other managers I went to study in Zurich and Chicago, where we learned how Western commodity exchanges operate. Upon our return to Moscow, we even tried to speculate on the Chicago exchange ourselves; we lost money, but we learned valuable lessons. With the start of privatization in Russia in 1993, we bought shares of many agricultural enterprises. Although we did not participate in the first round of privatization, we bought the shares from financial companies, which had purchased the enterprises using voucher schemes. At the same time, once we had diversified our holdings with various enterprises, we began investing capital in production facilities. In many cases we outsourced production to other firms: For example, we pay them to process our grain into flour, and we retain the final product.

In assuming ownership of these enterprises, we immediately confronted the issue of human resources. Whenever we had to replace plant managers, we found that we really had to replace the entire staff in order to effect real change and boost productivity. Also, we soon realized the importance of creating a brand for ourselves, and we tried to invest in advertising. However, our experience showed that advertising by itself did not bring us more business, since our real market was out in the countryside, where sometimes people were not exposed to our ads. Advertising would generate a good response, but not from the people we wanted to reach.

We made a name for ourselves in 1993, when Americans were distributing grain as humanitarian aid in Russia. Grain auctions were held in Saratov, and we were invited to participate. When we arrived on the scene we found that the auction organizers had imposed conditions on the process that put buyers like ourselves at a disadvantage. At a meeting of buyers the night before, I stood up and sharply criticized these conditions. Virtually everybody else rallied behind me. The organizers backed down and agreed to our conditions, which included payment on delivery with assurance of high-quality grain. I was the one who stuck out of the crowd, and Americans and other observers present at the auction noticed me and OGO for the first time.

Ironically, on the day of the auction I realized that my earlier activities, although good for the buyers as a group, had been hurting my company's interests. As a result of the conditions we had forced the organizers to agree to, there was sharp competition among buyers, driving the prices of grain above OGO's top limit. It seemed that I had made a huge mistake and wasted much time and money. I have one guiding principle, however: Every defeat is an opportunity. When I learned that the next auction of American grain would take place in Moscow two months later, I decided to make up for my earlier mistake. In these two months we researched all potential buyers for this auction and struck deals with them, selling them grain at premium prices, thus making sure they would not come to compete at the Moscow auction. When the auction finally took place, representatives of only seven or eight companies, ourselves included, were present; we had a brief meeting and decided who would get how much, and we also agreed not to drive the prices up. As a result of this collusion, we all bought grain at a nominal price, well below the market level. For comparison, in Saratov the largest amount any company got was 30,000 tons of grain, whereas in Moscow our company got 180,000 tons out of the 500,000 tons sold.

Consequently, OGO made a name for itself in the Russian market and on the world scene. American observers were present all along to see how their foreign agricultural programs would help Russia develop a fair market economy. However, my actions showed how one can twist and turn the market to one's advantage. On the one hand, the Americans were upset that the ideas behind their assistance were being subverted, but on the other hand they were amazed at how quickly I was making money right before their eyes. I think this earned me a certain amount of respect among them. They were also surprised to learn that an organization other than government agencies could operate with such a large volume of grain. Finally, the Americans assumed that my actions in Saratov were part of an elaborate premeditated plan to make my competitors pay top dollar for their grain, thus exhausting their cash reserves and enabling me to later suck up the remaining grain in Moscow. Actually, all these events were coincidental, but we nevertheless made a name for ourselves as astute business operators.

Now that we were known in the Western business community, we were able to make contacts and begin working with several large Western companies. Having a respected brand name means that Western partners do not even ask for bank guarantees on deals: Our name and my signature on a contract is enough for our partners to give us money and assets. Our foreign partners include Continental Grain, Carolina Turkey, Cargill, Dupont, U.S. Wheat Associates, Exxon, Shell, and British Petroleum. We also became quite famous locally, since we handled such impressive amounts of grain at the Moscow auction. Today, OGO is one of the largest grain companies in Russia, employing more than 3,200 people across the country. We store, process, and sell grain and grain products. We are also one of the largest producers of mixed fodder in Russia. In the petroleum sector, we supply our partners with various oil products and inputs used in refining oil.

OGO is one of the founding members of the Grain Union of Russia, although at first I was among the skeptics: I thought that Russia first needed to develop a civilized grain market, and only then could we talk about an association of grain market professionals. However, for whatever reason members of the association elected me the chairman. One of our main priorities now is to develop lobbying skills, since we have clear interests, and it is important to influence the policymaking process. At first we tried to stay away from political authorities, and we have never accepted any financial involvement by the state. We eventually realized, however, that it is impossible to exist completely autonomously from the state. Although we still take no public money, we have to find common ground with regional authorities. For instance, the Astrakhan Bread Factory is a local monopolist: Although we own it, regional authorities have a keen interest in its work. At the same time, our refusal to accept any credits or subsidies from regional authorities, which many companies choose to accept, means that we can behave much more independently. Conflicts with regional authorities usually emerge when they owe us money or refuse to deliver on a contract.

It is true that political decisions are often made without regard for the interests of affected parties. And we can no longer simply rely on personal connections or our specialized knowledge of the grain industry. For instance, a government decision to raise pensions across the board seems at first glance far removed from any issues involving the grain industry, but in fact it affects the demand for grain products. Thus, in this instance we must have professional knowledge of pension issues to be able to influence policymaking. At the same time, we in the Grain Union try to stay away from party politics. We do not ally, for example, with the Agrarian Party, which represents the interests of collective farms. We are ready to address economic problems using political methods, but not the other way around. We would never finance any electoral campaigns or make political alliances. But we do work to educate legislators by helping them draft laws and programs that facilitate developing a sophisticated grain market. Several Western organizations, like the U.S. Grains Council, help us. We also promote professional education in the area of grain production, and we keep our members informed about the latest developments in grain markets in Russia and the world.

I have mentioned one of my guiding principles: Try to treat failures as opportunities. It is part of my general philosophy of life, and it has become OGO's philosophy of business. This philosophy rests on several tenets including efficiency and the drive to perfect it in our work, and the assumption of responsibility—"always blame yourself." If we cannot perform in a particular situation, we do not blame "circumstances beyond our control" but instead always look for ways to adapt to the situation and make it work. Thus, it makes no difference how unfavorable conditions may be, whether these involve taxes, regulations, or exchange rates—we simply need to find a way to cope and make it work. We never ask the question "What?" We prefer to ask "How?"

A good example of how this principle works in practice is our involvement in the barter system of exchange. Among economists and politicians, barter has earned a bad name for itself, but for us it is just another method of doing business. We do not sit around and blame the barter system as an obstacle to doing business—instead, we use it to make a profit. We have developed long and intricate chains of barter exchanges; our experience shows that the longer the chain and the more links it has, the better return we get on our investment, because with every transaction we accumulate profit. I cannot think like a politician, only like a businessman, so everything is a potential tool for making money. If I should encounter an instrument that I cannot use to make money, our guiding philosophy would tell me that I simply don't yet know how to make it profitable, although surely there is a way, and I need to discover it.

The third principle of our philosophy is a constant drive to educate ourselves. We encourage initiative and we penalize the lack thereof. We also believe in constant turnover of personnel; as a result, we rotate staff frequently, since some cannot handle the demanding nature of our business. Our system is designed to encourage talent and competitiveness. For example, in contrast to many companies, our employees compete not for salaries or positions but for each other's clients. We encourage internal competition among sales staff, so that everyone is always alert to opportunities and dangers. We even have subsidiary companies that operate independently and even compete with us on the market. Our company was not built from any blueprint design but has evolved in response to the constant problems and challenges that have confronted us. Some of our principles worked for a while but had to be dropped later in response to new challenges.

The August 1998 financial crisis hurt us considerably, mostly because we depend heavily on Western credits, which are cheaper than those obtainable in Russia. However, all our investments were tied up in domestic projects, and when the crisis hit, many of our partners simply refused to pay us and many banks made off with our money. Also, the rise of the dollar's value relative to the ruble increased our debt to foreign creditors. To be able to pay our creditors we were forced to use some of our cash reserves, although several credit deals were successfully restructured. At least we were able to stay afloat and retain most of our business, but our ability to invest in more production capacity has declined. Although many Western grain companies fled the scene after the crisis, it hardly helped our business, since we never saw much competition from them anyway. By now, though, we are firmly entrenched in our particular niche, and it would be very difficult for foreign competitors to pry us out of it.

8

FIGHTING FOR LABOR RIGHTS IN A TRANSITIONAL ECONOMY

Aleksandr Sergeev

The Making of an Activist

I am 39 years old and serve as the president of the All-Russian Confederation of Labor, one of Russia's independent unions. We are not allied with any partisan or ideological group. I also head the Independent Miners' Union, with 100,000 members employed at some 180 enterprises. Originally I am from Siberia, from Kemerovo oblast, also known as the Kuznetsk Coal Basin (Kuzbass). I have been a labor movement activist since 1989, when the Soviet Union first experienced miners' strikes and I was working in the first strike committees.

I have had the good fortune to witness and participate in all the developments that marked the end of the Soviet Union and the formation of the new Russian Federation. I was one of the organizers of the March 1991 strike demanding the resignation of President Mikhail Gorbachev. Ironically enough, our union held another strike in 1988, picketing the White House in Moscow and this time demanding the resignation of another president, Boris Yeltsin, whom we held accountable for the government's chronic delays in

Aleksandr Andreevich Sergeev is former president of the Independent Miners' Union. Since the end of his term in the fall of 1999, he has been a member of the union's governing council. Interview recorded and translated by Natan M. Shklyar.
  Interview: Friday, May 21, 1999, Moscow

salary and pension payments. For four years I served on the Presidential Council as one of Yeltsin's advisers. Needless to say, it was a difficult choice for me to make when in May 1998 I had to lead striking miners against the president.

At that time, radical leftist forces tried to use this action to advance their political interests. We insisted, however, that we supported the president's policy of economic reforms but demanded social justice in their execution. Then as now we understand that we too must take responsibility for the nation's future, although our political elites don't see it that way and often try to use us for their own purposes. In 1996 our union had supported Yeltsin's bid for the presidency, although we realized then that his course of reform was not ideal.

An Independent Labor Movement Arises

During the perestroika era, as more and more dissidents spoke out against the regime, government bureaucracy, and human rights violations, independent labor unions emerged in the Soviet Union. Dissidents, however, were only individuals. Many of their principles nonetheless influenced the formation of the independent labor movement in 1989, with miners across the country taking the lead. In some regions, for about a year, all government and Party authorities had to secure the approval of the local labor unions if they wanted to make any important economic decisions. Naturally, the KGB and the Party tried to infiltrate and control us.

Our discussions then turned to the future of our organization. First we tried to create a political organization, which we called the Laborers' Union, but it gained only limited support; most workers care more about their own parochial issues than larger political objectives. Region by region, miners came to realize that they needed to create their own union as an alternative to the official trade unions. Earlier, we had tried to reform the old Soviet-era unions from within, but they proved to be too bureaucratized and too connected to Party and enterprise managers.

In July and October 1990 we held two large congresses, bringing together representatives of every mine across the country. Immediately we came under Party and KGB pressure. However, we were strong enough to resist. At these congresses we decided to form an independent miners' union. In the old mineworkers' union, working miners made up only about 30 percent of the members; the balance were from administrative and support staff. Naturally, a structure of this kind did not represent or defend our interests.

In another breakthrough, we demanded the introduction of countrywide tariff agreements for each industry. Concluded through negotiations rather than imposed by fiat, as before, agreements were drafted on the basis of similar legislation adopted in Germany, the United States, and even the Soviet Union during the reformist New Economic Policy of the early 1920s. In October 1990 we formally established the new union and endorsed a draft tariff agreement to be submitted to the Soviet government.

In 1991 we took part in a largely political strike to secure bargaining rights, and we won. The Soviet government had signed a tariff agreement and, although it was not with us but with the old unions, the precedent had been established. Thereafter, the government had to negotiate with the unions as partners and jointly sign framework agreements covering labor safety and social benefits. In a country where Party decrees regulated all aspects of labor and social life, we had never seen anything like that.

Using our union agreements as a model, independent unions emerged in many other industries, including those representing railway workers, air-traffic controllers, and merchant-marine sailors. This period, between 1991 and 1993, was a time of great expectations and idealism everywhere. However, disappointed by the results of economic reforms and by the dirty political infighting going on at the time, many Russians withdrew from activism.

Earlier, in the 1980s, the KGB had foreseen a surge in political activism and had moved to preempt it by establishing two organizations that still play a role on the political scene. The first was Vladimir Zhirinovskii's ultranationalist Liberal Democratic Party (LDPR), designed to channel public frustration and extremist tendencies. The second was a puppet, quasi-alternative union, the so-called Socialist Labor Unions, which proclaims that it is a truly independent labor organization and loudly criticizes the old labor unions represented by the Federation of Independent Labor Unions of Russia (FNPR). Although advocating legal methods to advance workers' interests, the FNPR plays the same role in labor affairs as the LDPR does in politics. In fact, the organization prevents workers from creating a single effective center of independent labor activity.

Record of Accomplishment

Two of our major accomplishment were to have established a precedent for negotiations between the government and the workers, and to have introduced and put into practice an industrywide tariff agreement. We helped create the Tripartite Commission on Social Partnership, which brought together representatives of government, management, and labor. We broke the monopoly that the old unions had exercised over the distribution of social benefits when we successfully lobbied the government to allow independent unions to take part in the process.

In the early 1990s we pushed through what were for those times groundbreaking laws on collective bargaining. In 1995 we secured an amendment to the federal Criminal Code that made it a criminal offence for an employer not to pay employees' salaries. These laws were adopted by the old Supreme Soviet, where we had sixteen of our own deputies. Since then, however, the State Duma annulled all these legislative accomplishments.

Beginning in late 1995, the momentum of democratization and liberalization in the labor movement began to flag, and the bureaucracy recaptured lost ground. Between 1995 and 1999, the bureaucracy took its revenge: The government began devising a state monopolistic variant of capitalism. As a result, the labor movement suffered enormous setbacks, although we have managed to retain some key accomplishments.

Innovative Approaches to
Serving Emboldened New Constituents

In the early activist days, we worked with a number of scholars who specialized in developing and applying game theory methods so that organizations could realize their potential, develop mission statements, and set specific goals. With their help, we organized seminars to focus on these issues. For example, the main goal of our labor union, as formulated during these exercises, was not to protect workers' interests at the outset but first to identify those interests, articulate them, lobby for them, and if necessary strike to attain them. Only then would we try to protect the interests. The first priority, we realized, was to find out what our constituents wanted, instead of inventing artificial goals.

Under the Soviet system, many miners were rejected from union membership because of their political convictions. Although I have an advanced engineering degree, I chose to work as a simple miner because I could not work under the old system. On my team I had a mathematics teacher and a military helicopter pilot. Very few of my team members had only a high school education; most were well educated, but they too could not work at a higher level for a system whose values they rejected. Because they refused to fight the system actively in their professional fields, they chose to opt out and resort to simple manual labor. Just as in Moscow many dissidents worked as cleaning staff and stokers, so in the provinces the same kinds of people chose to do manual labor, which brought in good money and provided relative freedom without forcing them to betray their values. When Gorbachev opened up the system a little, all these progressive thinkers came out in the open and voiced their opinions. All along, it appeared, many miners had within them a hidden potential for political action; they proved very receptive to the new methods of political activism.

Bureaucracy Resurgent, Public Trust Diminished

The main obstacle, which we have thus far been unable to surmount, is the former Soviet bureaucracy, which now prevails everywhere. This problem does not apply to our organization, since we have built it from scratch. I refer to the federal government itself. Those in power have failed to create a responsive government system reflecting the vibrant structures of a civil society. Instead, they chose to adopt the macroeconomic policy of selling off state property as a means of facilitating the transition from a command to a market economy. Although this strategy worked well in eastern Europe, where both the memory and the experience of private ownership were relatively fresh, where only one generation had lived under communism, it was unsuited to Russia, where several generations had lived under totalitarian rule. Also, we have a huge territory and a large population. The Communist Party once had 16 million members, of whom about 10 million held administrative positions. These people did not go anywhere after the fall of communism. The reformers decided not to enlist the help of the broad public, although most people supported them. Instead, they decided to work with the midlevel bureaucracy, assuming that it would be receptive to reformist ideas. And the reforms were halted precisely there.

Bureaucrats were indifferent as to which group they should service: the old Soviet regime or the new Yeltsin regime. They began providing support for the Yeltsin regime, using the only methods they had ever known—political and economic coercion. The result was a rift between the public and the reformers in government that is unbridgeable. I find it particularly frustrating that the reformers do not want to take responsibility for their actions. Instead, they blame the Communists for not having repented for seventy years of repression. In fact, the reformers often try to instigate anticommunist hysteria among the population, including our union membership, in order to promote their own political careers.

Dealing with Owners, Large and Small

Our union works with the federal government, which still owns part of the mining industry; private managers, who may also run other enterprises; and large industrial holding groups, many of which own shares of some mines. We have found our work to be most effective with the large corporate owners, mainly because they depend on interrelated links within their financial empires. If they supply nickel to Western markets, for example, we could call a well-prepared strike and sabotage the entire supply chain—an important bargaining chip. The smaller owners who privately own and run mines have much more limited financial resources and less exposure, factors that minimize their susceptibility to union pressure. Smaller owners, moreover, often have ties to local criminal structures, frequently resulting in assassination attempts on our activists by privately hired thugs. Finally, the government more often than not appoints a bureaucrat to run a government-owned enterprise, but does not check to see how profitably or efficiently he is running it. Often these officials are corrupt, a fact which sometimes gives us leverage in blackmailing them.

At one point, there was an attempt to create so-called social partnership commissions, which would bring together representatives of management, labor, and government to work out labor problems. However, like every other reform effort in Russia, this was done in a haphazard way. Indeed, these are only pseudocommissions, in large part because employers have not identified their own interests or or-

ganized among themselves. Although we have a law on social partnership commissions and a law on labor unions, we have no federal
legal framework allowing employers to organize. Sverdlovsk oblast
alone has such a law, although it does not stipulate that an employers' union should negotiate with labor on social disputes. A model
has been created on paper, but in reality it does not work. At the
same time, the independent labor movement must share the blame.
We are still embryonic in our development—and the old unions do
not want to reform at all.

We do not believe that owners of enterprises automatically have
the best interests of labor at heart, as the highly ideologized market
reformers would have us believe. The owners need to be taught and
conditioned to treat workers with dignity. Take Norilsk Nickel as an
example. Oneksimbank bought the controlling shares from the
plant's "red director" and came in as owners, bringing all their bean
counters from Moscow. Half a year later, they were facing workers'
wage arrears that were greater than before. They were thinking of
restructuring and expansion, but did not share this information with
the workers or the union leadership. Naturally, we wanted to know
how management planned to spend its money, especially when employees had not been paid in a long time. We tried to warn them, but
they would not listen. We threatened to strike; they told us to go
right ahead. We could not afford to have the entire staff of 80,000
people go on strike, since we did not have enough money in our
strike reserve fund to help people survive. However, we did stop all
work at the port that ships out the final product, thus preventing the
company from selling its output and forcing it to lose money in the
process. At that point, management understood the real threat and
the ramifications of a strike. They sat down at the negotiating table
and began talking to us.

Restructuring the Industry, Retraining the Miners

A special division in our union helps members find new jobs or learn
new skills in case of layoffs. However, only the government has the
resources to make a real impact in this area. Therefore, we see our
main goal as lobbying the government to approve budget funds for
these ends. In the past, money from the federal budget allocated for
retraining disappeared through corruption; workers never saw any
of it. The coal industry is currently undergoing major restructuring,

with the help of international credits. We were able to create supervisory boards on the ground involving representatives of labor, local governments, and employers. These boards decide how to use the restructuring money allocated to a particular town or enterprise. In Rostov, under a pilot project, we were able to secure monetary compensation for all miners who had been laid off because of coal mine closures; the miners could then reinvest these payments in retraining or starting a business.

Another idea currently under consideration is to pay miners with housing vouchers, like the ones received by retired military officers and people resettled from the Far North. These government-backed vouchers could be used to purchase housing from realtors, who could then claim the monetary value of the vouchers from the state. We also plan to establish a nonprofit foundation to raise financial capital, and we will lobby the government to have this foundation distribute budgetary funds allocated for retraining.

Although most regional officials understand that restructuring the mining industry has a great impact on social conditions, many still depend on federal subsidies rather than taking the initiative themselves. Often they seek our help in pressuring Moscow for more money, but if we agree, they want to distribute the subsidies. We tell them: "We will help you, but let's distribute it together." Officials who accept our terms make cooperative partners; the others do not. Occasionally, to be sure, we do have to make temporary alliances with obstreperous governors.

Russia's Economic Integration: Does the West Really Want It?

The most painful question right now involves buttressing Russia's competitive advantage in world markets. We have relatively cheap labor. In addition to natural resources, we have advanced technologies. But when Russia tried to integrate with the world markets, we faced the problem of competition from Western companies, which consider Russia as a threat and would rather not see Russia integrate. After all, cheap labor combined with high technology makes for serious competition.

Additionally, during the Cold War period, when two global economic systems were competing, we had a certain level of integration with other countries of the communist camp. I often meet with representatives of labor unions in Bulgaria, Hungary, and Poland. They now have the problem that their products are barred from entering western European markets. In the past, they would work for the Soviet Union's market. One of the strategic questions right now is reintegration among the former socialist countries, as well as Russia's integration with the Western economy.

Two years ago I met with several high-ranking U.S. officials, including staff members of the National Security Council, the official responsible for aid distribution to Russia, and officials from the U.S. Agency for International Development (USAID), as well as with Republican and Democratic members of the Senate. They asked me: "Why does Russia trade with Iran?" I told them: "Our military-industrial complex has high technologies developed during the Cold War, and we have rare metals as well. If you do not allow us to compete in your markets, what does our industry have to do to survive?" Russia's enterprise directors, backed by millions of workers employed in the military-industrial complex, constantly pressure the government to find new markets for their products, irrespective of any political motivations. The question of Russia's integration with the world economy is a question of acknowledging Russia's interests and needs.

Consider the coal mining industry. We had a serious conflict with the German miners' union. Our union supported the comprehensive restructuring of Russia's coal industry. The German miners' union, however, which belongs (as we do) to the International Union of Coal, Chemical, and Energy Workers, supported the position of our rival, the coal mining union affiliated with the FNPR, the heir to the old Soviet labor unions. This rival miners' union opposed restructuring. That was understandable. Today, the federal government subsidizes Russia's coal industry with 1.5 percent of the national budget. If we could make our coal mines competitive and reduce production costs, that would force German mines out of business, because our coal is of superior quality. The lessons? On the one hand, fellow labor unions should show solidarity and support each other. On the other hand, market forces align us on opposing sides of issues.

I see the future following this general direction: Russia has its own proprietary technologies, which should remain under government purview, ensuring the nation's competitive advantage. Let us use these technologies to make things that we build well. We are not good at making cars, so let us welcome Ford, BMW, and Daimler-

Benz to build assembly plants, use our cheap, educated workforce for production, and develop our huge consumer market. We also must keep in mind the special Russian mentality: After all, we used to be a great country, respected throughout the world, but today everybody orders us around. It's ridiculous for a great power to have a $20 billion budget.

I have also met many times with officials from the International Monetary Fund and the World Bank. Take the "greenhouse effect," which was discussed with them at meetings in Kyoto and Buenos Aires. Participants concluded that countries need to limit their carbon dioxide emissions, so they established country quotas of 25 billion tons of carbon dioxide. However, it is not realistic to expect our coal-based electric power industry to stay within these quotas. A main priority for global financial institutions should be to invest in restructuring the energy-producing sector, not in implementing macroeconomic reforms.

Premature Conclusions About
Civil Society Formation

In general, I think that at first there was much euphoria between Russia and the West, both within the governments and among civil organizations, including labor unions. Western unions actively worked with us, partly out of solidarity, partly to get U.S. government grants designed to support civil society development in Russia. Several years later, however, some people in the West decided that democratic transformation had taken strong root in Russia and that no further help was required. Everything would develop on its own. However, they were judging Russia's level of democracy and economic freedom using very superficial factors: privatization, emergence of a class of owners, several successful elections for the parliament and the presidency, freedom of the press. If all the elements of democracy and the free market are in place, they argued, there is no need to support the development of civil society, because it should be able to develop on its own.

I have spoken about this with U.S. and European government funding agencies. I told them that today we are seeing a dramatic increase in nationalist outbursts and wide popular support for the ultranationalist Vladimir Zhirinovskii. All because civil society in our country lacks structure. There is now great danger that Russia will develop not along the route envisioned by our leaders but along some much more menacing path.

Western labor unions are still working with us, although the nature of their work has changed. They tend to focus on specific problems, realizing that Western capital is penetrating the Russian market. Although western European labor unions do not make a clear distinction between truly independent unions, like ours, and the unreformed FNPR, American labor unions are much more aware of the challenges facing Russia's labor movement. They actively try to educate us on methods and technologies used in modern labor-management relations, for example collective bargaining. Their guiding principle: we should work on building unity and labor solidarity. In contrast, western European labor unions think that the reforms are over and that there is a kind of status quo in the Russian labor movement today.

At the same time, as a result of the devastating impact of the reforms in Russia, the West and the very concept of democracy have been largely discredited in the eyes of the Russian public, a feeling perpetuated by the Communist press. Naturally, many Russians tend to view any kind of American attempt to help with suspicion. However, those who have overcome such suspicions and have worked with American labor leaders see how useful and beneficial the practices they teach us are. For instance, the Moscow center of the AFL-CIO does excellent work in providing legal analysis and counsel. Other Western organizations that are helping Russian labor unions include Freedom House, the Friedrich Ebert Foundation (Germany), and the European Union's TACIS (mostly in the regions). Western investors have little contact with Russian labor unions because they work mostly through national and regional governments. However, they should work with us directly as well.

Surveying the Future:
Dangers and Opportunities in Abundance

Looking to the future, we must realize that our number one priority is organizational work. Unions in general face a tough future in Russia: Private owners of enterprises are now less susceptible to lobbying and less receptive to change. Moreover, most workers still belong to the old, unreformed unions and are too docile to join a truly independent union. Our union tends to attract the most activist workers.

Another important factor in our future development is forming a co-herent political identity; that is now only in an embryonic stage. At this point, it seems that Russia is most likely to take the social-demo-cratic route. We anticipate face-offs with the criminal elements, which no doubt will try to take control of our union if and when they assume ownership of individual enterprises.

In the near future, three main centers of the labor movement will emerge in Russia: the Federation of Independent Labor Unions of Russia, the All-Russian Confederation of Labor, and the Socialist Labor Unions (created by the Soviet KGB and still maintained with tacit government support). In some twenty years, though, only two organizations, in my view, will remain on the scene.

Much will depend on how Russia's overall economy develops. In one scenario, Russia will continue along the route of monopolistic capitalism; in this case, owners might be able to simply buy out the unions. Or, Russian capitalism will develop along lines of greater so-cial equality—but for that to happen, we would have to see domestic capital assets flow back into the economy from abroad. Naturally, much rides on the new president and on the team that will run the governmental apparatus.

Two big questions for the post-Yeltsin era remain: Will the bu-reaucracy overtake and solidify its grip on politics and the economy? Or will civil society and the private sector resist this force success-fully? Unions today must organize politically and take an active role to make sure that workers are not left out of the transition process.

There is a key difference between us and, say, the Socialist Labor Unions. They think that the main goal of a workers' movement is collectively to "sell" labor to employers. We believe that the main goal of labor unions is to help form a civil society. Indeed, a well-or-ganized union in a small town could be a powerful force to make en-terprise directors comply with the law, to ensure administrative transparency from local authorities, and to make the courts and the police follow legal guidelines instead of taking bribes. In other words, labor unions can be agents of positive change for the country as a whole, extending their reach far beyond the narrow interests of workers alone.

9

TRANSFORMING RUSSIAN POLITICAL MORES

The Key to Economic Evolution

Aleksandr Auzan

It is common knowledge that societies undertake radical reforms when various societal groups come to a new understanding of the world. Anchoring the effects of these reforms and forming new societal structures, however, become possible only when the general population changes its behavior, standards, laws, and mores. The most striking changes in behavioral norms involving many millions of people in Russia may have occurred in the consumer market in the 1990s. It is readily apparent that the rules that once governed the old deficit economy have nothing to do with the present-day Russian economy. In those days, personal connections served as the basis for attaining personal wealth; rumors were the major—and practically the only—source of information, not so much about the quality of goods but about their availability; and consumer problems (which could hardly have been called contractual disputes in the context of

Born in 1954, **Aleksandr Aleksandrovich Auzan** studied and taught economics at Moscow State University. He has written many articles and books about organizing consumers to protect their rights. Since 1992, Auzan has headed the International Confederation of Consumer Organizations (KonfOP).

He serves on the boards of numerous organizations, including the Russian branch of the Open Society Institute and several research institutes. Translated by Anna Kucharev.

Soviet life) were resolved through written complaints to newspapers or Party organs. In the early 1990s, this entire system ceased operating and executing the functions to which virtually everyone in the nation had become accustomed.

Two circumstances pressed the urgency of behavioral change among the general population: first, the collapse of the customary way of life, and second, the emergence of a radically new economic situation. Shock-therapy reforms in late 1991 and early 1992 brought about an unusual situation—an abundance of goods and a deficit of money. Brought up under the Soviet system, where the reverse problem prevailed, Russians had no previous experience of how to act under such conditions. And changes in conventional behavior did not come about as they usually do in countries where market economies have developed through a process of evolution. In the developed countries, standards come first, are then secured by laws, and subsequently crystallize into the appropriate administrative mechanisms. In Russia, under conditions of radical economic reform, the reverse was true. In the USSR in 1991 and in Russia in 1992, the Consumer Rights Protection Law was passed, but it was not based on people's habits or skills in using the law as a practical instrument. The experience, knowledge, and understanding of how to live in the new circumstances and take advantage of these new mechanisms were gained only later. At the end of the 1990s, one can authoritatively state that the overwhelming majority of Russians have learned how to resolve contractual disputes through legal means and how to make use of information before transacting business. In Russia, the first sphere of life in which the new standards gained a foothold and developed most rapidly may have been the consumer market.

The critical results in this sphere did not occur spontaneously but were achieved through the energetic activity of small groups of people whose objective was the establishment of new civil relationships in the consumer market. These people worked both within the state apparatus and outside it.

At first, the most formidable challenge seemed to be getting the new laws passed and translated into a legal code for Russian society, but this turned out to be one of the easiest problems to solve. The Consumer Rights Protection Law encourages direct action. People can read and understand its text without a lawyer and can put it into action directly, because the consumer has the advantage in disputes with entrepreneurs or with federal or municipal agencies delivering paid services. Under this law, the judicial process was greatly simplified: In order to start legal proceedings, anyone can file a complaint locally without paying any fees and can sue either the vendor or the manufacturer, whomever he prefers.

The next problem that arose was convincing consumers to use this convenient tool. To be sure, certain rules protecting consumer interests had existed since the early 1980s—and even then it was clear that the biggest obstacle to their use was not legal but psychological. The first clients whom we urged to defend their own interests legally were visibly afraid of using the courts. We would literally grab a dissatisfied consumer by the hand and bring him to the courtroom where his right to have his substandard refrigerator replaced was being defended, and he would ask, "But what if they should sentence *me*?" Overcoming this psychological barrier was a difficult process, but it was essential if the whole new system of legal defense was to function at all.

And this is how it was accomplished. In the early 1990s, legal precedents were established through the actions of lawyers representing consumer associations. Every few months the courts would hand down a ruling that previously would have been unthinkable. For instance, in January 1992 a court for the first time awarded compensation for "mental distress" suffered by a consumer who had purchased a defective microwave oven. Initially the awards paid out for mental distress were not large—about 50 percent of the price of the merchandise—but they began to increase with every passing month, and by the mid-1990s they had become fairly substantial sums. Publicizing the outcomes of lawsuits played a large part in the rapid shift of public awareness in the area of consumer behavior. We knew that a skeptical attitude toward using the law is characteristic of the Russian mentality. A number of Russian sayings (such as "The law is a sieve, it leaks whichever way you turn it") are evidence that legal nihilism has been the prevailing attitude in our society for centuries, because the law was nearly always used against the individual.

Therefore, encouraging the public to accept the opportunities afforded by the new law was futile. It only made sense to publicize the practical results attained by specific individuals. If a Russian were told that the Consumer Rights Protection Law guaranteed him certain rights, he would not believe that it was possible to get justice in any government office, least of all in court. However, if he heard over the radio that a Mr. Ivanov had been awarded 4 million rubles compensation for material and psychological damages resulting from the substandard car he had purchased, he would clap his hands, recalling that he had been in exactly the same situation but got nothing: "That Ivanov got his money, but I didn't get any. Next time, I'll get mine."

The years 1992 to 1995 witnessed a triumphal procession of consumers through the courts. It became fashionable to file lawsuits. All the media were writing about consumers' victories, and 99 percent of the disputes in courts really were resolved in consumers' favor. One of the factors contributing to this was the attitude of the judges themselves; their incomes and living standards at the time were just like those of the claimants in their courts, so they sympathized with the consumers. Let me immediately add that now, at the end of the 1990s, circumstances have changed radically. I will discuss this in greater detail below.

New standards are developing in the individual's attitude to the courts, the courts' attitude to consumer affairs, and the attitude of businesspeople to court decisions (from total disregard of laws and courts in the early 1990s to an acknowledgment that improper business conduct could have serious consequences for them).

Consumer-business relations are also changing. A new culture of contractual relations between consumers and businesses presumes that a consumer will familiarize himself with the text of an agreement, enter into negotiations to modify any of its conditions, and conduct business in a way that protects his interests in the future, including resorting to the court system when necessary. It was not enough to talk about the standards stipulated by the law to convince entrepreneurs and consumers to adopt such a culture: Action was required. In my opinion, the campaigns that consumer associations waged during the 1990s played a key role. Three campaigns in particular had a tremendous impact on the way business in Russia is conducted.

The first campaign began in late 1991 and continued until the summer of 1993. In the autumn of 1991, Luks, a joint stock company and one of Russia's first private trading companies, sold 20,000 pairs of jeans, which were advertised as Levi's and had Levi's labels on them but were actually knockoffs. As a result, consumers were cheated, although it should be noted that they paid a lower price for the knockoffs than they would have paid for a pair of real Levi's. The consumer associations filed a complaint with a recently created antimonopoly organization. The case was heard in the Arbitration Court of Russia and even reached the country's Supreme Arbitration Court. The associations sought to force Luks to admit that it had sold goods of inferior quality, to inform consumers through the mass media that they had been cheated and were entitled to compensation, and, ultimately, to pay the stipulated fine for violating the Consumer Rights Protection Law. It should be noted that, out of 20,000 consumers who had been misled by the company, only 600 pursued their interests all the way through the courts, working with the consumer associations. These 600 people received monetary compensation in 1993. But the significance of this first campaign went far beyond the experience of the 20,000 people who had purchased fake Levi's. What in fact occurred can be called a "receipt revolution."

The basic concept that consumers should obtain a receipt when making a purchase in order to protect their rights and be eligible for compensation should the merchandise prove inferior was articulated thousands of times during the mass media's truth-in-advertising crusade against the Luks company. From 1993 on, greater numbers of consumers began demanding receipts when buying expensive merchandise. A certain formalization of transactions developed.

A few years later (1995–1996), a major information campaign influenced the development of another important aspect of contractual culture. In March 1995, the International Confederation of Consumer Organizations (KonfOP) filed lawsuits and launched an informational campaign against three major transnational electronics manufacturers—Sony, Samsung, and Matsushita Electric (whose trademark is Panasonic)—for violating consumers' rights to guaranteed service. Contrary to the Consumer Rights Protection Law, these companies did not guarantee consumers the right to exchange a defective product or to receive a refund. Instead, the warranties required consumers to go to company service centers for any warranty repairs. This was a blatant violation of the law, but the companies did not consider themselves bound to conform their warranties to Russian law—they found it more convenient to apply the warranty language used in other countries. The companies chose to ignore certain specific requirements of the Russian law, although the Russian market was already becoming important to them (by the mid-1990s, electronics sales in Russia were growing exponentially). The publicity campaign lasted several months. In the end, all three companies amended their warranties and agreed to fund compensation programs for consumers. By March 1996, as a result of the publicity and the sales losses they had sustained, nearly all the transnational companies operating in Russia had brought their warranties into conformity with legal requirements, offering consumers who purchased substandard merchandise the right to choose between repair, exchange, or voiding the transaction and obtaining a refund.

The third campaign, conducted in 1995–1996, concerned Russian financial institutions. Depositors had suffered enormous losses when nonbanking financial entities began collapsing in 1994–1995 and major banks, such as Chara and Natsional'nyi Kredit, followed suit. The general principle we tried to establish after the wreckage of the old financial institutions can be summed up in a saying that was very popular in our organization: "When reading any financial services contract, look at the fine print as well as the numbers."

By the second half of the 1990s, although many old problems remained and new ones involving the quality of goods and services as well as corporate ethics had arisen, the vast majority of Russians were already paying attention to how business is transacted.

The third area of change in the norms of consumer behavior and societal relationships that the consumer associations stimulated was consumer-government relations. In the early 1990s, filing lawsuits against the government would have been unthinkable. No one would have believed that the government would retreat, much less make concessions, in defending itself against lawsuits and public campaigns. KonfOP brought its first suit against the government in 1993, challenging a federal statute that prohibited the use of right-hand drive cars in Russia. These inexpensive foreign cars, purchased mainly in the Far East, were used all over the country; they made it possible to begin to "automobilize" areas east of the Urals in the post-Soviet period. The Russian government was stunned by that lawsuit. When government lawyers concluded that the state was bound to lose the case in court, the president of the Russian Federation revoked the statute or, more precisely, postponed its coming into effect for ten years. I doubt that the Russian government will remember in 2003 that this law ever existed. Even should it try to implement this law, the issue will once again have to be resolved in court, a head-on confrontation that was avoided in 1993.

A confrontation with the government did take place in 1996–1997, not with the federal authorities but with the Moscow city authorities—who were no less influential, especially in Moscow, than the national government itself. In 1995 the city of Moscow introduced the practice of towing cars parked illegally, but its system differed radically from the methods used in developed countries. In the first place, towing rights were awarded to private companies that had been established with the assistance of the Moscow city government itself. Then, drivers were not notified that their vehicles had been towed; and when they did manage to locate their vehicles at one of the impoundment lots, they were faced with exorbitant bills. In fact, the system devised by the municipal government was a way of granting private firms a license to provide unsolicited "services" at unregulated prices. It was a consumer-fleecing venture operated jointly by municipal authorities and a few private firms backed by the Moscow city government. Attempts to convince city officials to revoke this decree and switch to a normal towing procedure proved unsuccessful. Other large cities in Russia, moreover, began imitating Moscow's procedure.

Given this situation, consumer associations decided to risk taking the Moscow city government to court. The lawsuit eventually reached the Supreme Court of Russia. The mayor tried to defend his position at every stage. He even sent a letter to the members of the Supreme Court requesting that they reject the case. Nevertheless, in the summer of 1997 the Supreme Court decided the case in favor of the consumer associations. Soon thereafter the State Duma amended the Administrative Code to prohibit the introduction of similar practices. The case was a major victory for public consciousness and societal standards over the arbitrary exercise of political power, in this instance an attempt to create an illegal but profitable system of replenishing off-line municipal budget funds while feeding the appetites of city-hall cronies.

Now, at the end of the 1990s, Russian citizens do not find it unusual to seek concessions from federal or municipal governments using legal and informational weapons. Nowadays one hardly ever hears statements such as: "The issue is beyond discussion. This decree has been signed by the prime minister, and it will go into effect," words that we frequently heard from the supporters of illegal government decisions in the mid-1990s. The point finally arrived when we stood our ground and firmly insisted that the prime minister repeal the decree in question.

These days, many Russians know that compensatory actions are possible. What they do not yet know is what mechanisms they can use to counteract illegal government measures. In order for such mechanisms to function, there must be individuals in society capable of exerting pressure through the judicial system and ready to provide information to the media. It is vital that such individuals enjoy the trust of the population. In connection with this, I'd like to say a few words about consumer associations and how they are organized in Russia.

Consumer associations sprang up in the late 1980s in major Russian cities as a result of the efforts of intellectuals (economists, lawyers, and journalists) who had recognized the need for such organizations in the early 1980s, joined by activists of the so-called black waiting lists. (During the deficit economy, to acquire an item in short supply one had to register, spend years on waiting lists, and show up at certain intervals to ensure one's place in the line as it moved forward. Some entrepreneurs organized "black" waiting lists; for a fee, they assured consumers of their place in line.) Neither the intellectuals nor the activists had business or government support, and thus they were compelled to combine forces. In 1989 these groups, myself among them, founded a single, unified organization, now functioning in seven countries of the former Soviet Union, which since 1992 has been known as the International Confederation of Consumer Organizations (KonfOP). The group's mission is to provide professional help to consumers, on the premise that the consumer is always a nonprofessional who, as a rule, must confront official or commercial agencies that have all the requisite professional staff and experience. Accordingly, our objective is to provide the consumer with lawyers, economists, financial specialists, and journalists who can support him with their professional and intellectual resources. Consumer associations have their own publications, TV and radio programs, and (since 1997) Internet web sites. Using these assets, they have been able to take the lead in initiating the campaigns and lawsuits that have transformed the standards and relationships affecting the consumer market.

KonfOP has helped solve problems of national importance. The financial crisis of August 1998 was not merely financial in nature. For us, the most frightening consequence of the August events was the government's default on its debts. This was a terrible blow to the legal system that had been functioning in the country for several years. The refusal of the government to fulfill its obligations and negotiate with its creditors was dangerous, chiefly because it destroyed longstanding legal relationships. And the decision to default was taken by the government of the Russian Federation, whose primary responsibility, under the judicial system, should have been to maintain such relationships.

The financial dimension of the default drama, of course, should not be underestimated: It had a direct effect on consumers. The relatively small number of people who held the obligations that the government refused to honor suffered, but losses on a far greater scale were borne by those covered under mandatory health insurance funds and nongovernmental pension funds, which held government securities as the law required. Down payments made to construction companies and prepaid subscription fees were often invested in these securities.

The August crisis disclosed another trouble spot, associated with the collapse of the banking system, and these two areas overlapped to a greater degree than is usually recognized. In our view, the default was an attempt to cover up the bank crisis and help out certain banks held by Russia's oligarchs. Naturally, the banks denied this, contending that the crisis was a result of the government's refusal to meet its obligations. As early as August 17, KonfOP announced that it did not recognize the actions of the Russian government as legal and would contest them in court. In early September, the confederation filed a lawsuit in the Supreme Court declaring the government default illegal and demanding that it meet its responsibility to pay its debts.

We realized, of course, that the government would not be able to pay all its debts, but we felt certain that the issue should be resolved through negotiations with creditors instead of through the executive branch's unilateral illegal actions. KonfOP contacted like-minded business associations, namely the All-Russian Union of Insurers, the Nongovernmental League of Pension Funds, two associations of money market participants, and the board of directors of Share Investment Funds. In early November our six organizations announced the creation of the Moscow Creditors' Club (MCC). Our immediate and primary goal was to negotiate a structure for the repayment of defaulted government obligations that took into account the interests of both sides. To our surprise, the government recognized the MCC as a party to the negotiations on November 9.

The negotiations began on November 11. On November 24, after two weeks of exhausting meetings, we reached an agreement that, in my view, essentially determined the resolution of the default. First, the default would henceforth be governed by legal procedures. On December 12, the prime minister signed an order, agreed to by the MCC, that required the Ministry of Finance to make new proposals to creditors, who would then be entitled either to accept or reject them. Second, the government agreed to make financial concessions, including reimbursement in full for losses incurred by the mandatory health insurance funds, by nongovernmental organizations' funds, and by subscribers to publications. Although only 30 percent of the nongovernmental pension funds was returned, a number we considered insufficient, the concessions meant that some real debt restructuring had been accomplished.

At the same time, KonfOP had to negotiate with the major banks. To this day we are still engaged in this task. I fear that in some cases, especially where refunds will necessitate bankruptcy procedures, the process may take one or two years. In August and September 1998, with mediation from the Central Bank, KonfOP conducted virtually nonstop negotiations with five of the largest banks in Russia. Because of the general panic at that time, the first round of negotiations dealt with normalizing relations between the banks and their investors. We fought for the acceptance and registration of investors' claims. We demanded that hotlines be set up and money be paid to those in extreme need—for example, in cases of illness or death, or when people needed to pay for surgery or education. KonfOP managed to reach agreements with four major banks. Nevertheless, we began a legal battle at the end of September with all the banks over the deposits that they were refusing to return. The banks tried to interfere with the process of our filing claims with the courts, as well as with the trials themselves. Legal rulings were ultimately made in favor of investors, but the banks nevertheless refused to accept them.

The front line then shifted. More and more governmental bodies became involved in the struggle. In late December 1998, for example, the major banks persuaded the Central Bank to adopt an illegal measure that virtually halted implementation of court rulings made in favor of the investors. With the help of the Ministry of Justice and the Prosecutor General's Office, we fought the Central Bank to rescind this measure and reinstate the implementation of the rulings. A full account of our war with the banks would warrant an entire book. The foregoing brief description of the conflicts over consumer rights, however, allows me to single out the obstacles to the development of normal civil institutions in Russian society.

There are three major obstacles: the condition of the legal system, the social passivity of business, and the virtual absence of self-governing organizations at the municipal level. Let us begin with the legal system. It played a very positive role in the establishment of legal customs in society during the first half of the 1990s. Thereafter, however, the legal system suffered a severe crisis. According to available statistical data, there were thousands of consumer protection lawsuits in 1992 and millions in 1995; the courts virtually drowned under the pressure of these lawsuits. The legal system inherited from Soviet times dealt with only two kinds of civil cases: divorce and the accompanying division of property, and inheritance. When contractual disputes between vendors and consumers and, especially, between banks and investors flooded the courts, the legal system ground to a halt. Against this backdrop, judges at all levels have changed their positions with respect to contractual disputes in the consumer market. The State Duma has been very slow in passing legal reform bills; the legal system has not expanded or become more effective; and the Supreme Court has begun devising legal and illegal constraints on litigation over consumer protection issues, aiming to limit extensive resort to the courts.

In my view, this is a dangerous trend. Some changes, such as charging fees for filing lawsuits involving expensive consumer goods and financial services, are probably worthwhile. However, reducing awards for aggravated pain and suffering and penalties for breach of contract is absolutely out of the question. This is exactly what the Supreme Court is doing, however, and judges in the courts of original jurisdiction are eagerly following suit.

The second obstacle is the social passivity of business. Some would view such a disjointed adversary as an advantage to consumer organizations. In reality, the opposite has proved true: Under existing circumstances, we cannot solve our problems through direct dialogue with the business community either in specific areas or at a general level where multiple spheres intersect. Nor have we been able to solve many problems by introducing ethical standards. Frankly, I hope that the events of August 1998 that brought entrepreneurs to the brink of disaster have encouraged more social activism from business. Actually, in the autumn of 1998 many new business associations began to form, and the process of unification has begun. I hope that this trend will develop to the point where we will have partners for a dialogue fostering ethical self-regulation and advocating mediation procedures conducive to out-of court settlements of contractual disputes.

The third and perhaps the most dangerous obstacle is the absence of local self-government. I should note here that the legal documents adopted by the Russian Federation mislead Russians and foreign observers alike in making frequent mention of a system of self-government. Laws on local self-government create the impression that such a system actually exists. In fact, what is referred to in Russia as self-government is nothing more than the nearly unlimited power of mayors. Almost entirely lacking are mechanisms at the community level that could tackle such problems as negotiating and signing leases and service contracts and protecting the rights of tenants and landlords. Such bodies do not exist in Russia. Instead, municipalities are ruled by bosses who are far less restricted in the exercise of authoritarian powers than are representatives of federal agencies.

What factors work in favor of a new civil society? First, the high learning ability of the population in general, and consumers in particular, as well as the trust that consumers have developed in public organizations. Second, the cooperation that has developed between the media and public organizations. Third, the noninstitutionalized but strong cooperation among professionals representing public organizations, government agencies, and certain commercial enterprises.

A high capacity for learning is one of the characteristic traits of Russians, who have always had to solve problems of survival independently, and adapt both to changing power configurations and to utterly new and often unpredictable political twists and turns. On occasions I have been surprised by the speed with which people mastered certain elements of financial analysis or the legal and analytical tools of money markets, banking, and insurance—fields that were entirely new to them. When I was dealing with groups of defrauded investors, I marveled at how easily they figured out how to influence elected officials, how to manage assets wisely, or how to launch arbitration proceedings.

Making businesspeople more socially responsible and municipal
self-government more effective are in my view the most important issues for the next decade.

Implementing large-scale changes during the new stage of civil society development in Russia will require the following plan of action. First, a number of large and influential citizens' organizations,
which mostly defend civil rights, have formed in Russia. Although
these organizations are in contact with one another and share many
views on current events, they have not yet combined forces to influence the political authorities and public opinion. These citizens' associations must develop closer ties with one another. Because the
most powerful and influential citizens' organizations do not aspire
to political power and do not convert the people's trust into
deputies' mandates and ministerial seats, they could constitute a nucleus for influencing the ethics of government officials as well as that
of the political opposition. If we succeed in creating permanent contacts and sustaining a large citizens' center for exerting influence, we
will have gone a long way toward institutionalizing citizen activism
in Russian society and governance.

The second feature of such an action plan involves the social organization of business and envisages the creation of business social
centers. Business associations today are either intrabusiness structures engaged in political lobbying or extrabusiness associations
such as the Round Table of Russian Business that hibernate between
elections and are only active during election campaigns to select pro-
business candidates. But I see a different and more promising future
for such business associations: A connection with organizations promoting business self-management, which have formed in the past
five years. These organizations direct their activities toward representing and advocating business interests, particularly toward creating their own business standards, managing their relationships with
clients, and introducing corporate insurance, ethical norms, and operating standards. Such management organizations operate in the
money market, the real estate market, and the tourist industry, as
well as among electronics and other technical companies. If the efforts of the existing self-management organizations were united,
their programs expanded, and the links among pro-business lobbying centers, citizens' organizations, and the media strengthened, this
would have a salutary effect on municipal organization, legal reform, and protection of shareholders' rights.

In 1998, the Social Contract Foundation was established expressly to support such trends. The board of trustees includes such renowned figures as TV anchor Vladimir Pozner; economist Vitaly Naishul; Natal'ia Fonareva, deputy minister for antimonopoly policy; and Anton Danilov-Danilyan, head of the Economic Department of the president's administration.

I am also a member of the board of trustees of this foundation. Other participants include business leaders who support more effective business management. I hope the establishment of the foundation is the first step toward realizing our further goals.

I do not wish to address Russia's need for foreign aid in any detail because I don't think this is an issue of primary importance in the development of Russian society. Foreign aid, specifically aid to various nonprofit citizen initiatives, played a great role in the early and mid-1990s. But perhaps precisely because these programs were so successful, the question of foreign aid from Western countries should be formulated in an entirely different way.

In the first place, it seems to me important to understand why a civil society exists in Russia. It did not exist in the early 1990s, but we do have such a society nearly a decade later; that is why this aid should be managed entirely differently. Russian citizens' organizations should be authorized to handle this aid—not in the sense of using it for their own programs, but because these new institutions are better suited than Western philanthropic foundations to decide for what purposes and through which mechanisms aid should be channeled and used in Russia.

Second, it seems to me that those who intend to initiate or develop existing aid projects for Russian society are not always aware that Russia no longer needs help, say, in creating a legislature (which for the most part has already been created). Instead, we need help in establishing customs and institutions that are necessary if a truly modern legislature is to do its job. Inertia leads one to talk on and on about legislative guarantees and legal conditions. But they are not the main problems. The main problem is knowing which informal rules are in effect and which voluntary institutions, agreements, and associations can activate and maintain existing legal norms.

As for the crisis in the legal system, Western experience in the use of out-of-court settlements and various forms of mediation, ombudsmanship, and organized business management may be as important as the reforms themselves. Ethical behavior toward business competitors, clients, and the government; informational and ethical standards that should serve as media guidelines—these are fields that have not yet been seeded in Russia. Self-regulation in advertising and television is another critical standard for Russia to master.

In my view, the lack of ethical standards (and they are practically absent) in business and government creates a sense of impending disaster as a permanent condition of public consciousness, a catastrophic perception of the present, and a pessimistic expectation of failure from reckless leaders involved in risky projects. And so I believe that honest borrowing practices, high standards of ethical self-control, and the dissemination of pertinent information through the media, the government, business, and individuals will create a solid barrier to such explosive scenarios.

With respect to Russia's prospects for economic growth, I would like to describe a point of view that some might consider surprising. Russia's possibilities for economic growth are usually examined from the standpoint of the traditional approach to economics, determining what resources, foreign as well as domestic, a country can attract and how it can best utilize them. Economic growth in Russia is not hindered by a lack of technology. Russia has produced its own major technological achievements, and it is capable of mastering the new Western technologies. If the volume of capital belonging to Russian companies and kept abroad is taken into account, the monetary resources of the Russian economy are much greater than the West believes. The problem lies in the system of operative rules. As long as the public considers that thievery is admissible at different levels of society and does not regard the act of theft as sufficient grounds for a politician or business executive to be excluded from certain activities; as long as public mores allow virulent envy and intolerance toward the acquisition of wealth; and as long as people assume that the government should take care of the individual and in exchange should receive carte blanche to do whatever it wants with that individual (and such attitudes are still widespread in Russia)— no market-based growth in the Russian economy, in my opinion, is possible.

I am fully aware that changing these mores will be a long and slow process. Again, one has to differentiate between the ability of the Russian population to master new tools quickly, as demonstrated by the experience of the 1990s, and their more limited capacity to transform certain deep-seated views and habits that have been

formed over the centuries and passed on from generation to generation. I believe that the road to economic growth will be one of gradual, long-term changes in rules and mores, not at the national level
but in the daily lives of people and social groups.

We are talking about the creation of a new social contract in Russia, a new type of agreement between societal groups and the state.
In the next decade, the best type of economic development for Russia, among those that are realistically possible, will be a process of
slow incremental growth accompanied by gradual changes both in
mores and in production results. In ten or fifteen years, I should like
to see a country that has acquired new mores, standards, institutions, and organizations, like new rings on a growing tree—the kind
of growth that will facilitate the falling away of traditional standards, notions about life, and attitudes toward one's kin, one's
neighbors, and the government. It is these traditional standards and
attitudes that are dangerous to the Russian people.

As to my own role in the future process of change, by no means do
I see myself involved in national politics. I do not think participation
in politics is effective. Generally speaking, politics has a very low efficiency coefficient. Many capable and talented people in Russia
have been involved in politics during the 1990s, or to be more exact,
starting in the mid-1980s. Politics is, in a sense, overly saturated
with people. I fear that Russia has lost more than it has gained from
this mass involvement in politics. Many persons who might have
done much good in economics, business, or social or civic life
wound up in the maelstrom of political passions and now are practically useless to society. I deliberately avoid this kind of activity and
on several occasions have declined offers to take part in Russian
governments.

I see my own future prospects specifically in helping form a central
civil association with the power to impose ethical constraints on
business, government, and the political opposition, and introduce
new behavioral patterns there as well as among the broader public.
Here is how I see the problem. If the ideas I consider essential can be
realized only through the acquisition of political power, that would
indicate that we are incapable of persuading the majority of the people in our society that these ideas are valid. It would mean that these
ideas can be implemented only with the help of an "Uncle Policeman" who has been ordered by those smart lads in the government
to force people to behave in this way or that. Coercive activity of

this kind is unacceptable to me. It seems to me that the trust that certain people or certain ideas can evoke in Russia's population, its citizens, can best be manifested through the power of authority rather than the authority of power. That is exactly how I envision the meaning of the citizens' center of influence that I intend to help build.

Part Three

STRIVING TOWARD RULE OF LAW

10

THE LEGAL PROFESSION AND CIVIL SOCIETY IN RUSSIA

Problems and Prospects

Vladislav Grib

All legal reforms in Russia today, whether already enacted or under active consideration, hinge upon the passage of the Constitution in December 1993, for this basic law reinforced and undergirded the most important principles and institutions of our country's social, cultural, economic, and political development.

By no means have all of Russia's many laws and regulations been brought into conformity with the Constitution, as will be discussed below, but what has been accomplished represents important work of both the executive and legislative branches, acting separately or jointly. The president signed two edicts, that of December 24, 1993, specifying measures to bring existing laws into conformity with the Constitution; and that of July 6, 1995, elaborating the concept of le-

Vladislav Valer'evich Grib holds a *kandidat* degree in law and is the dean of Moscow State University Law School.

He is the founding president of the Union of Young Lawyers of the Russian Federation. He is also editor in chief of the Jurist publishing group, which produces more than twenty legal journals targeted at every specialty within the legal profession (for example, judges, prosecutors, investigators, defense attorneys, public notaries, and the like). Grib also serves as chair of the executive committee of the Russian Academy of Legal Sciences and directs a number of federal programs and projects in the area of legal reform in the Russian Federation. Translated by Marian Schwartz.

gal reform in the federation. For its part, the State Duma, between 1994 and 1997, approved the Civil Code (Parts I and II), the Criminal Code, the Family Code, the Tax Code (general section), and the Arbitration and Procedural Code. Other codification legislation under active consideration includes deliberations on civil procedure, criminal procedure, and labor. All this legislation has great significance for the formation of Russia's new legal profession: It defines new approaches, procedures, and operational principles for lawyers practicing in different spheres of social relations.

At first glance, it might appear that judicial and legal reform in Russia is in full swing. Unfortunately, this is far from the truth. The country's political and economic instability, of course, has not created ideal conditions for the further development and deepening of legal reform. Moreover, the historical, social, ethnic, psychological, and political characteristics of the Russian people and government have not been propitious—a point I shall pursue below. When examining recent reforms in Russia, Western observers usually point to the "two Russian miracles—the free press and the independent system of justice." Indeed, the judiciary has come a long way from being an instrument of the totalitarian regime. Legal and procedural changes have strengthened the guarantees of judges' independence; raised the status of the judiciary; reformed the system of arbitration courts, general jurisdiction courts, and military courts; and introduced the institution of the Justice of the Peace. Nonjudicial organs, such as "comrade courts" and trade union committees, which in the Soviet era used to adjudge many labor and other disputes, have been virtually eliminated. As a result of the government's ratification of the European Conference on the Defense of Human Rights and Basic Freedoms, Russian citizens now have the right to appeal to the European Court of Human Rights if they consider that their rights have been violated or that they have been denied adequate protection under domestic legislation and in the national courts.

At the same time, the restructuring of the judicial system has entailed significant complications. In its present form, at least, Russian federalism clearly does not favor an independent judicial system. For example, a number of regional leaders—governors, heads of administrations, and presidents of republics—are trying to resubordinate the judiciary to themselves and win the right to appoint judges within their regions. (In Russia, judges are appointed for life by the president.) With each passing year, federal authority has a harder time restraining these attempts. In early 1999, a special law was passed on financing the courts; although this eased some of the problems of financing the judicial system, budget shortfalls continue to undermine the judiciary's independence and efficiency. Legislative changes have often been insufficiently thought through and remain incomplete.

Nonetheless, we are reforming the judiciary and legal procedure and creating a new judicial community—not altogether smoothly, but actively and successfully. Judicial reform is indissolubly linked with reforming the bar association and the notarial system as well as the agencies of justice themselves.

If the constitutional principle proclaiming the Russian Federation a rule-of-law state is to be implemented, it is the Ministry of Justice that must formulate legal policy and oversee its execution. The Ministry of Justice has been transformed from an agency of the second rank into one of the most important agencies in Russia, exercising substantial rights and authority, including administrative oversight of legislation, legal policy implementation, intellectual property law, judicial decisions, and the activities of political parties, public and religious associations, and correctional institutions. President Boris Yeltsin made the Ministry of Justice report directly to him, thus confirming the agency's authoritative standing within the executive branch. Nonetheless, the ministry's authority has not been undergirded with administrative and personnel resources, especially in the regions. Even so, the Ministry of Justice is coming into its own as the executive branch's lead agency for legal and legislative reform, coordinating the work of all other agencies. The authority and standing of all law enforcement officials, including those specializing in new functions, such as bailiffs and registrars of state property rights, have increased accordingly.

Like many other institutions in our recent past, the Russian bar association hardly qualifies as an institution of civil society in the full sense. Since the Soviet state had no real system of justice, there was no prospect that a bar association could ever defend the interests of civil society. Lawyers were not even allowed to engage in professional activity. If the courts were not needed, a real bar association was needed even less.

Today we must structure a new, totally independent bar association—not an easy job because the principal obstacle to reform is not our imperfect laws but the imperfect sense of the law among the

Russian legal profession itself. Our Soviet-era legal culture and professional mindsets are the very elements that cannot soon be reformed. We must admit that Russian lawyers, especially those of the older generation, unwittingly bear the burden of the past: pseudoprofessional thinking, a rigid pseudosystem of administering justice, pseudodefense, and pseudoprosecution.

In the early 1990s, the problem of drafting legislation affecting the bar association became acute. As the first draft laws appeared, we had illusions that the legislation would be enacted swiftly, but it was not. Although legislation on the police, investigative operations, and the Prosecutor General's Office exists, there is still no law on the bar association.

The bar association of Russia differs from that in the United States. America is a country of lawyers (according to statistics, about 60 percent of all the lawyers in all the countries of the world live and work in the United States), where issues of access to legal counsel and legal practice are well regulated. Russia, on the other hand, is in the midst of the complicated and difficult process of regulating legal practice and access to it. Various groups of Russian lawyers frequently lobby for diametrically opposed concepts of determining bills for legal services. The most authoritative of these bodies are the Guild of Russian Lawyers and the Federal Union of Lawyers. The former group supports a single association of lawyers as a very manageable arrangement. Critics note, however, that Soviet and Russian lawyers have suffered severely in recent decades from the dictates of Party and state. That is why representatives of the Federal Union of Lawyers, for their part, regard a cohesive lawyers' community not as a monopoly but as a civilized form of organization for the legal community comparable to those elsewhere in the world.

In spite of the legal problems in developing the Russian bar association, the legal profession has become one of the most respected. Moreover, among public and entrepreneurial circles, trust in lawyers has increased, while media coverage has intensified. Although de jure the bar association lives by the Soviet laws that still regulate its activities, de facto it has become a civilized legal institution by the use of procedural and administrative measures. Only one final obstacle remains: enactment of new legislation on the bar association.

The institution of the notary public has undergone even greater changes. During the Soviet period, from 1917 until 1993, notaries were incorporated completely within the Party and governmental system. (For this reason, our country never jointed the Latin notary system, which includes only independent notaries.) Notaries were either a part of the court system and subordinated to oblast-level courts or were components of law enforcement agencies.

With the passage on February 11, 1993, of the Russian Federation's basic legislation on notaries, however, notaries acquired the right to perform public legal functions under conditions that approximated world standards, acting as independent legal professionals bearing full responsibility for their actions. At present, notaries do not belong to the executive branch and are neither government officials, nor public sector or municipal employees. They are understood to be officials executing the law and performing and attesting to legal acts in the name of the government. Before 1993, the notarial profession had the bleakest of futures. Extremely low prestige (notaries needed only the lowest level of legal education), low wages, monotonous work, and bad working conditions placed the profession at the very bottom of legal specializations.

But after 1993, all this turned around. The 1993 law on the notary profession made it possible for notaries to earn a good and stable salary. Their authority and prestige rose sharply. Highly qualified legal professionals, who had gone through rigorous competitive selection, entered the profession. Working conditions for notaries as well as their organizational and technical support improved noticeably. Lines waiting in front of notary offices disappeared as notarial services became more widespread.

Today, notaries are the only representatives of the legal profession who are required to take out insurance for their activities and who bear responsibility for their professional and other errors. Thus, from a ranking at the bottom of the legal profession, the notary has taken a big leap into the top echelon, especially because he has an opportunity to earn a high and stable income (the number of notaries is limited, as a rule, to one notary for every 25,000 persons).

Unfortunately, though, this propitious change did not last long. Not all governments officials and legislators recognized how useful the profession was, in economic as well as strictly legal terms. The 1993 legislation governing the notary system proved to be incomplete and contradictory, and an amended law could not pass the Duma. Moreover, with passage of the new Civil Code in October 1994, notaries lost their main source of income, certification of real estate transactions. Then fees for notary certification were lowered, the list of transactions requiring notarization was shortened, and income taxes on notaries were raised. Today, all one can say is that the Russian notary is not going through the best of times. The heyday of the new notarial profession has passed, although its utility and necessity remain incontestable.

We should bear in mind that substantial savings are made possible when the courts are freed from handling uncontested cases that can be resolved within the notary system and when a vigorous notary profession can reduce the number of legal disputes. In the Anglo-Saxon legal system, particularly in the United States, where the notarial profession is relatively undeveloped, expenditures in support of the legal system are approximately three to seven times higher than those in European civil legal systems.

By the same token, the development of the notary system in Russia would facilitate the preliminary monitoring of the legality of actions involved in civil litigation and would lower the number of disputes on the court docket, thus reducing the budgetary allocations needed to implement judicial reform.

At present, many Russian legal professionals are working in the law enforcement agencies (the Ministry of Internal Affairs, the Prosecutor General's Office, the Federal Security Service, the Federal Tax Policy Service, and others).

Russia's law enforcement system is going through a period of active reform. For both objective and subjective reasons, however, this reform is not going smoothly. On the positive side, the law enforcement system is shedding Soviet stereotypes and operational habits. Legislative reforms are proceeding actively and productively. Investigators, investigative agencies, and the prosecutor's office are becoming increasingly independent as their role and place in the legal and judicial system are defined more precisely. The system of training qualified law enforcement personnel is being reformed. New specialties have appeared, for example the tax police. Space does not allow me to describe to a sufficient extent the more negative trends and problems characterizing Russian law enforcement today. Briefly, they are the following.

First, low salaries give rise to dissatisfaction and to a low moral and psychological climate in the law enforcement ranks. Second, the frequent reshuffling of senior officials in the federal prosecutor's office, the police, and the security services leads to a kind of staff fever within the departments, which naturally cannot have a positive effect on performance.

Unfortunately, both federal and regional leaders attempt to take advantage of law enforcement agencies. Nonetheless, every year they become more efficient, especially in the fight against corruption, organized crime, and new types of economic crimes. Every year the number of legal professionals in the law enforcement system increases; this in itself improves the quality of overall performance and facilitates changing the guiding administrative principles inherited from the Soviet era. In particular, we are shifting from the defense of class and government interests to the defense of the rights of the Russian citizen and private property.

In discussing the development of the legal profession in our country, we must not ignore traditional notions of law, rights, and justice in Russia. Many Russian lawyers feel that we have to create a normal sense of justice so that lawyers themselves do not doubt the importance of the law. To Russia's misfortune, it has generally been considered more correct to focus only on one's personal sense of justice rather than on what were considered dry laws. Often the Russian public has perceived this proclivity as a victory of natural law over positive law, contending that strictly logical conclusions can follow from applying the basic principles of natural law and thus can resolve legal disputes. In "the very nature of things," the public tends to believe, there are indications relevant to the legal canon governing interpersonal relations. On this view, a subjective sense of justice is a reliable guide to the law. As the Russian lawyer Karl R. Kacharovsky observed, the Russian sense of justice "pays principal attention to the very essence of the given legal relation, to the factual state of affairs; it is guided by established [legal] form only when that does not contradict the essence and content of the given phenomenon of the social environment."

Another characteristic of the Russian sense of justice draws upon elements altogether outside a legal framework, including morality, religion, and social goals. Legal scholars stress the religious dimension of the Russian sense of justice: A law existing outside a moral framework and based on nonreligious principles is not considered binding. It is the collapse of religious ideals in Russia, these specialist argue, that has brought about the crisis in the sense of justice. Probably no Russian legal scholar has paid more attention to the correlation between the sense of justice and religion that Ivan A. Il'in. "Legal consciousness and the Kingdom of God live together as part of one and the same emotional fabric. They find their expression in one and the same spiritual milieu," Il'in wrote. He notes that at the present time Russia does not enjoy that unity between religion and the sense of justice. Il'in does not simply argue that the large gap between the sense of justice and religion led the country to catastrophe (he means the Revolution); he does not simply describe how over the course of many decades the spiritual principle had dimmed and vanished in people's souls, how Russians had ceased to be guided by the spiritual authorities, to the point where their sense of justice had become barren and sere. More than that, Il'in exhorted his fellow citizens to come to their senses and realize that only a religious sense of justice could help lead the country out of its crisis.

A third feature of the popular sense of justice is a utilitarian or expedient approach. If certain actions are considered useful to society, then people will ignore the government's prohibitions. Occasionally a community that considers it useful to do so may make decisions that, from the standpoint of ensuring legal guarantees for the individual, are plainly immoral.

Research conducted recently at Russia's leading law school, Moscow State University Law School, attests to the persistence even among the new generation of lawyers of all three features of the Russian sense of justice. One in every four students at the law school stated that he was prepared to commit a crime deliberately, the most common motive being the poverty of their loved ones, considered an involuntary reason for criminal conduct. More rarely cited is the desire for personal enrichment or a commercial career. One in every three future lawyers believed that the law, in principle, affords an opportunity to defend one's rights, and 42 percent thought that the law must be observed, whether it is good or bad. At the same time, 45 percent considered it justifiable to break the law under specific conditions. The proportion of those who hold extremely negative attitudes toward observing the law was high: 41 percent of those surveyed hold the view that an intelligent person will always find a way to circumvent the law if it hampers him, while 28 percent thought that surviving in the current situation in the country without breaking the law is virtually impossible.

As a result, we have the following picture. Priorities are equally divided along three basic lines: unconditional observance of the law

(34.4 percent); provoked nonobservance of the law (30 percent); and unconditional violation of the law (35.6 percent). Thus two-thirds of law school students fall into one or another group of individuals oriented toward breaking the law, and only one in three lean toward its unconditional observance.

The conclusion: The level of education for future lawyers does not meet the high moral and ethical requirements necessary for representatives of the legal profession. Educators unjustifiably stress the acquisition of primarily legal knowledge, overlooking the fact that creating a sense of morality and justice, a personal legal discipline, and a code of professional ethics cannot be achieved by a narrowly legal curriculum, especially considering that law school graduates will be working in the most diverse spheres: jurisprudence, economics, and administration.

Legal education needs to receive special attention from the government and society. During the Soviet period, legal education was a relatively autonomous and closed system reflecting all the contradictions of the political order. From today's vantage point, Soviet legal education was plagued by loss of historical continuity, a unilaterally ideologized context, excessive harshness and administrative centralization, a focus on training practicing lawyers (rather than scholars), the criminological bent in its training programs, and its divergence from foreign educational systems.

Today the situation has undergone a profound change. Russia is experiencing a boom in the legal profession, now popular among young people because of its newfound prestige. It has become profitable and prestigious for both government and nonstate institutions of higher education to open law schools. At one point, the government almost lost control of the process: Law schools were being established by institutions of higher education that lacked both technical resources and qualified instructors. Russia now has fifteen times more law schools than the Soviet Union had and many times more law students.

These statistics can be examined in different ways. On the one hand, the executive and legislative agencies, the judicial and law enforcement systems, finance and business, and the bar association need tens of thousands of legal professionals to meet the demands of a democratic, rule-of-law state with a market economy. On the other hand, the Russian educational system has proved itself unprepared for administering so many law schools, monitoring the training of legal personnel, and initiating a major reform in legal education. Strict control must be maintained over the quality of legal education so that it meets the requirements of modern jurisprudence.

Law-oriented nongovernmental organizations (NGOs) have had a significant influence on the development of civil society in Russia and the shaping of the legal profession. From the start of the current reforms, voluntary associations of active, altruistic citizens guided by the principles of humanism and justice have replaced the largely politicized public organizations that were under the direct guardianship of Party and government agencies. The NGOs arising in Russia in the late 1980s and early 1990s were designed to defend the rule of law and educate the broad public about the law. The historical role of NGOs in the rise of a rule-of-law state would be difficult to overestimate. They have stimulated this process from below, bringing to social relations new elements of self-government, emphasizing the primacy of legal values, and creating confidence among citizens that they have equal status with the government and public institutions. This is a difficult but important step in divesting the public of the ideological mindset the former authoritarian state had imposed.

Today, Russia's NGOs are called upon to:

- introduce a fundamental shift in citizens' consciousness from the values of authority (power) to the values of equality before the law;
- prod government agencies to reject administration by directive, improve lawmaking, and divide the functions of executive power and legal institutions;
- help organizations and citizens reject informal and often contradictory legal standards in resolving disputes and appealing to the courts for remedy;
- educate citizens about their legal relationship with the government and the importance of observing human rights;
- assist in making legal values of primary importance in relations among citizens, especially now that private property is developing in Russia and the number of property disputes is increasing; and
- help engender a sense of mutual legal responsibility among citizens for protecting the natural environment, closely interweaving legal and ecological education.

What are Russian NGOs today? How and under what conditions are they fulfilling their mission to reshape the public's sense of law and legal culture? Nowadays, nongovernmental organizations that have little technical potential and few human resources, but that are mobile and can work to meet the most urgent demands of Russian society, predominate. Over 86 percent of noncommercial public law organizations functioning in Russia were established between 1989 and 1998; the average organization has been active for seven and a half years.

The formation of NGOs in response to the growing demand of Russia's population for legal protection during the economic and political crisis falls into two periods: 1991 to 1993, during which 29 percent of them were formed; and 1996 to 1997, during which 29.1 percent of the currently functioning NGOs emerged. The former was the period of economic crisis provoked by the breakup of the Soviet Union and the start of the fundamental reform of production relations in Russia; the latter was the beginning of the collapse of the financial pyramids and the profound financial crisis in the country. During these periods, the demand for legal protection was particularly acute.

Among Russia's public initiative organizations today, the most numerous are the legal defense NGOs, together with those implementing multilevel legal initiatives. This is natural in a conflict-ridden society. According to our estimates, based on research conducted in January and February 1999, Russia today has more than 2,500 nongovernmental public organizations engaged in legal defense and legal education for various groups of the population, or in the implementation of various legal programs.

Unfortunately, though, the noncommercial public organizations active in the legal sphere are by no means all authoritative. Many have projects and programs intended to address a broad spectrum of legal problems rather than to meet the needs of specific regions or population groups. One of the most authoritative, dynamically developing, and promising organizations is the Union of Young Lawyers of the Russian Federation (MSIu RF). Unlike other organizations, the initiative for its founding in September 1993 came from the law students themselves. The MSIu RF has become Russia's largest association of legal professionals, bringing together thousands of attorneys, law professors, investigators, judges, legal consultants, graduate students, and law school students. A financially and politically independent public organization, the MSIu RF has the goal of promoting an entirely new status for Russian legal professionals that meets the demands of a democratic, rule-of-law state.

From the start, the creation of such an organization evoked much interest in Russian society, especially in legal circles. In presenting the MSIu RF certificate of registration, the minister of justice wished the young lawyers success in their principal goal: creating a new generation of legal professionals free of Communist and Soviet legal dogma. Since its inception, the MSIu RF has organized and offered pro bono legal consultations for the public throughout the Russian Federation, from Vladivostok to Kaliningrad. For law students, this work has been a test of their civic and professional maturity. In 1996, an MSIu RF initiative, a legal support program for regional legislatures, provided each deputy with a legal aide chosen from among the most talented upper-class law students. Legislatures in the oblasts and republics of Russia have endorsed the program, which is being successfully implemented in Moscow, Volgograd, Rostov on Don, and other cities. For the first time in the history of Soviet and post-Soviet Russia, legislative drafting has been done not only by legal scholars and government officials but also by regional associations of young lawyers. In 1997, the State Committee on Youth Affairs instructed the MSIu RF to draft a federal law, "On the Foundations of State Youth Policy in the Russian Federation."

With the assistance of the MSIu RF, twenty-two law journals and one newspaper covering military law, *The Law and the Army,* have appeared. The Supreme Court, the Higher Arbitration Court, the Ministry of Internal Affairs, the Prosecutor General's Office, and a number of other government departments have sponsored such publications as *The Lawyer, The Russian Judge, The Russian Investigator, The Notary,* and *Legal Education and Science.*

One of the most interesting programs of the MSIu RF is the Corporation of Russian Lawyers. We know that in the United States and other countries with a developed legal system there are dozens of the most varied associations of lawyers, depending on their legal or professional specialization. In Russia, we are only starting to see this trend, although there is an urgent need to defend the rights of all kinds of legal professionals. In December 1996, the MSIu RF organized and founded the Russian Association of Licensed Legal Professionals. (In 1996, more than 10,000 licensed legal professionals in

Russia held official licenses but had no right to participate in preliminary criminal investigations and, unlike attorneys, had no right to tax benefits.) The association's goal: to extend the professional rights of licensed legal professionals and to develop the law profession in Russia.

In March 1999, the MSIu RF was one of the organizers of the Russian Academy of Juridical Sciences, which brought together legal scholars and law professors from hundreds of law schools in fifty regions of Russia.

A number of MSIu RF programs and initiatives are being carried out with the support of foreign partners, including the Charles Stewart Mott Foundation, the Ford Foundation, and the Open Society Institute. Pro bono legal counseling has risen to a higher level, especially in Moscow, and in a special resolution the Moscow municipality supported the opening of MSIu RF consultations in district offices, where young lawyers assist not only needy citizens but also advisers of the district legislatures.

A top priority for the MSIu RF in 1998 and 1999 has been the fight against corruption. With the support of the Soros Foundation, the Eurasia Foundation, and the federal government, these programs assess measures to fight corruption. Especially interesting in this connection is the collaboration between the MSIu RF and the Soros Foundation on a project entitled "Future Without Corruption," which supports competitions, summer schools, and research involving young lawyers.

An important MSIu RF partner is the Russian Legal Reforms Fund, a Russian government agency that allocates budgetary funds as well as funds from World Bank loans earmarked for legal reform in Russia.

The MSIu RF has helped organize and found dozens of federal and regional public youth associations. For example, the MSIu RF president is the deputy to the president of the National Council of Children's and Young People's Associations (which brings together most federal and interregional associations). Many of yesterday's and today's leaders of Russia's federal departments in the areas of education and youth policy were or are members of the board of this council.

In six years, the MSIu RF has seen its leaders grow in professional stature. Fourth- and fifth-year law students in 1993 had by 1999 become directors of law firms and attorney's offices, deputies in municipal and regional legislatures, law instructors, entrepreneurs, government officials, judges, and investigators. Its members have helped implement hundreds of legal initiatives, programs, and projects; write dozens of laws; and organize new professional associations of legal professionals and legal publications. They have provided free legal assistance to thousands of Russian citizens and hundreds of noncommercial public youth associations.

Participation in MSIu RF activity, one can't help but think, is a kind of school of professional experience and education in civic responsibility; after young lawyers go through it, they become worthy citizens of our country.

Like most of my generation, who were born in the early 1970s and were taught in the Soviet educational system, I was a Pioneer and a Komsomol, a typical representative of my generation of young Soviet citizens. Everything that happened in the late 1980s and 1990s evokes in me, my friends, and my colleagues an ambivalent response. Constructing a democracy is inextricably linked with two major negative factors: the breakup of the Soviet Union and the socioeconomic and political instability in Russia. The United States won the Cold War. Thirty-year-olds, forty-year-olds, and older generations of Russians well remember the terminology of the Cold War: the "arms race," the "aggressive NATO bloc," "the United States, world policeman," and so forth.

Although years have passed since the end of communism in Russia, and many Soviet concepts now evoke only memories in our generation, one important aspect of our history should never be forgotten: the historical, cultural, and ethnic makeup of Russia. For example, the NATO bombing in Yugoslavia evoked negative emotions toward the United States among people of every generation, religion, and political affiliation. These emotions were evoked not only by the fact of the rocket and bomb attacks but by the fact that the United States did not consult with Russia or make the decision to bomb through the UN Security Council, where Russia has a veto. The NATO military operation was carried out in a region of the world and against a nation with which Russia has had long historical and cultural ties. All it would have taken was to have worked flexibly and closely with Russia on this problem, especially in light of the fact that the issue has now been resolved jointly.

It is no accident that I have dwelled on this problem. You can invest in a country's economy, render humanitarian assistance, administer philanthropy, and create a positive image of countries and corporations—and then, with one ill-considered political step, you can nullify so much.

As for cooperation with the West in the legal sphere, Russian lawyers are unquestionably interested in the experience and assistance of their foreign colleagues. The United States, for example, is the "legal superpower." The U.S. legal system has a rich history in the most diverse areas, including the legal profession, the justice system, legal education, and public associations of lawyers.

We have made use of many American ideas, especially the People's Law School project and pro bono legal consultation. We have received financial support from many American foundations. We work with the American Bar Association's South East Europe Legal Initiative. Such assistance could be even more effective, though, if it were not limited to financial support but encompassed information programs. We need not only Western foundations' grant programs for Russian organizations but closer ties between Russian and Western law schools, law firms, and associations of lawyers.

Russia still has to shape a legal profession with its own traditions, ethics, and professional concepts and principles. According to surveys, the legal profession is the most popular field among young people. However, as already noted, it has its problems, which can be briefly summarized as follows:

- the imperfect system of legal education;
- the lack of sufficient legislative regulation of the activities of attorneys, notaries, lawyers in private practice, and a number of other legal professionals;
- the ineffective system of self-organization among Russian lawyers; and
- the inadequate economic and financial base for the Russian justice system.

Until these problems are resolved, we cannot build a rule-of-law state. Russian lawyers have even tried to create their own political organization. In 1995, the Russian Association of Lawyers, a political movement, took part in the State Duma election, but it garnered less than 2 percent of the vote and thus failed to cross the 5 percent threshold. In 1998, the organization Lawyers for Human Rights and a Decent Life was created, but it too, unfortunately, failed to win representation in the Duma.

We have confidence, however. Today, as a new century begins, a new generation of lawyers is taking the place of the older generation. For our generation, the concept of democracy, a rule-of-law state, and freedom are not new words in the legal lexicon but principles of life. Our generation must make these principles comprehensible not only to legal scholars but to every Russian citizen who can appreciate their significance.

Much remains to be done. First, we must create more effective mechanisms for formulating and executing laws; the lack of such mechanisms constitutes a serious problem that undermines public trust in the law. Second, we must make sure that the law is not used as a political instrument if we are to ensure equality for all before the law and the primacy of the law in all spheres of life, for all public, political, and entrepreneurial organizations. Third, we must improve the legislative process and legal proceedings on the regional and local as well as the federal level. Fourth, we must raise the moral, ethical, and professional authority of the legal profession—judges, attorneys, prosecutors, and other legal specialists—as representatives of a profession without which a democratic, rule-of-law state cannot function. And finally, we must work to overcome the legal nihilism of the Russian people, their lack of faith in the law and in the institutions of governmental authority.

I am certain that in the next few years Russia will become an economically flourishing, democratically developed country. I base this certainty on Russia's rich historical, intellectual, spiritual, cultural, and economic potential, as well as on my own legal practice, in the course of which my colleagues and I are helping civil society develop in different corners of Russia.

Unquestionably, we will welcome assistance from the West in the legal field if this assistance is sincere and is rendered on a partnership basis. Western experience is useful to us, and we are grateful for the advice and recommendations of our foreign colleagues. Russia needs investments, but investments directed more to actual production of goods and services rather than to financial speculative undertakings. From the sad example of August 1998, we know where this latter activity can lead.

Russia has an interest in developing equal economic relations with the West and in securing equal conditions for transacting business in these countries. Russia will not accept the language of force in international affairs. Moreover, in its foreign policy, Russia has its own special position—and this too has to be taken into account. Our country must still define its own guidelines in international affairs. This does not just apply to relations with the West: Russia is a socioeconomic, cultural, and historical symbiosis of Europe and Asia. As such, Russia should expand and deepen its influence in Asia as well as in Europe. And it is in Asia that the most unexpected political and economic alliances could arise.

It seems to me that the tendency in the West to overlook Russia and deprecate its role in world politics is dangerous. I invite anyone who has fallen under the influence of that tendency to take a look at the map and leaf through economic and statistical references and history textbooks, while recalling the words of the French scholar and writer Blaise Pascal: "The past and the present are our means: only the future is our goal."

11

Freedom of Speech and the Rule of Law

Andrei Richter

This book is being published in the year 2000, ten years from 1990. And for the Russian press, it was the year 1990, not 1989 or 1991, that marked the real turning point toward freedom and independence.

It was in that year that the USSR Statute "On the Press and Other Mass Media" was adopted. Though short-lived (it died along with the Soviet Union one year later), this statute subsequently served as a model for legislators in all the former union republics. An elaborate document, containing some sections phrased in socialist rhetoric (for easier passage by the Supreme Soviet) and others studded with complex legal terminology (designed to undermine the Party's monopoly on the mass media), it has nonetheless defined the environment of the press in my country. The main objectives of its drafters—to confirm the ban on press censorship and create favorable conditions for the establishment of independent mass media—have been attained.

As a result, Russian newspapers and periodicals today are in many respects the freest in the world. I can read opinions from the entire

Born in 1959, **Andrei Georgievich Richter** studied English language and literature and for many years worked as a university instructor and interpreter for the Soviet government. He completed his doctorate in journalism from Moscow State University, where he remained to teach journalism. The author of numerous scholarly and journalistic publications in several languages, Richter has been a visiting scholar at Columbia University and a visiting professor at Belmont University, Tennessee. He is currently director of the Media Law and Policy Center and teaches journalism at Moscow State University. He serves on the boards of numerous professional organizations and journals. This chapter was written in English by the author.

political spectrum; Watergate-type scandals cry "Foul!" from newspaper pages almost on a weekly basis; and journalists are not fined, exiled, or sent to jail for expressing views that contradict Kremlin policies.

Moreover, the denizens of the press are free of many restrictions typical in Western societies: They often use language that would be inadmissible in civilized political debate, resort to mud-slinging as a common means of argument, and sacrifice so-called national interests for the benefit of political calculations or group interests.

The issue of dubious press ethics and its implications for public life is extremely acute. During the first Chechen war, to take one example, the Russian media showed the charred remains of Russian troops and naked Russian soldiers covered with battle wounds and on the point of death. Initial public shock turned to callousness toward suffering. . . .

Although aware of Western standards regarding the portrayal of violence and the graphic depiction of death, Russian media bosses believe that it is "absurd" to impose moral limits upon themselves. More than once Russian psychiatrists, worried by the increase of mental disorders, have warned of the dangers of television programs that "intensify feelings of fear, instability, and aggression." A striking example of a flagrantly irresponsible attitude to ethics was the television broadcast in September 1999—as part of the regular evening news program *Segodnia* (on NTV)—of the execution of a Russian hostage by beheading as well as the torturing of other Russians by Islamic terrorists. NTV aired the program despite its often proclaimed adherence to Western norms of humanism and decency.

While violence leads to callousness, does slander lead to lawsuits? In fact, libel suits are the most frequent media-related cases considered by Russian courts: In 1998 there were 4,158 of them, a sharp increase from 1,140 in 1990.[1] But most plaintiffs seem motivated more by the hope of fetching court judgments as high as 15 million rubles than by the aim of restoring their reputations.[2] In a September 1999 interview, Moscow mayor Yurii Luzhkov said that he had scored 40 to 0 in his libel suits against the media, all held in Moscow courts, of course. Does Luzhkov look cleaner today than, say, five years ago? I doubt it. Has his litigation stopped the anti-Luzhkov press from comparing him with Mussolini? Not in the least.

The liberated press has not only achieved the status of the "fourth power," the Russian equivalent of the "fourth estate"; the "watchdog" wants to be (and already is) a catalyst. The press has become an active second (if not the first) power: The press sets the agenda for the government and society, actively suggesting and even demanding ways that political issues should be resolved. The press creates politicians and destroys them. Take the case of General Aleksandr Lebed. Among the score of army commanders, who was known to the public in the early 1990s? None. But the commander of the Fourteenth Army was constantly in the limelight; his ideas on anything—from the advantages of Augusto Pinochet's dictatorship in Chile to the weak points of Kremlin politicians—were praised by uncritical journalists. And just when Lebed's career was about to take a sharp upturn, the press attacked him with dubious accusations of attempting to seize power . . . and sent him into political oblivion only hours after his dismissal from his post as secretary of the Security Council. But not for long. How many Siberian governors get a national audience today, the chance to present their views on everything? Governor-General Lebed, period.

A counterargument could naturally be that the government does not pay adequate attention to the investigative disclosures of corruption and other crimes committed by its own functionaries. That is true, though only in part. The government uses only those accusations that benefit the Kremlin at a particular moment. The long press campaign that implicated Defense Minister Pavel Grachev in corruption activities resulted in his resignation, when almost nobody thought that President Boris Yeltsin would sacrifice his old buddy. In early 1999, businessmen Boris Berezovskii and Anatolii Bykov were subpoenaed by the Prosecutor General's Office in the wake of press revelations about their illegal business schemes—but later, despite the continuing wave of journalists' investigations, the subpoenas were annulled.

The obvious lack of public reaction to press revelations is not the fault of government. It is rather the fault of society: While the public is in deep political apathy, it is all too easy to disregard public opinion (or is it non-opinion?).

The mass media have become instruments of a struggle between different industrial groups and political clans: Television newscasts and newspapers often target not the general public, but rather the audience at the top of the political hierarchy. The most vivid example is an extremely rare case of breaking news on NTV—and it was caused not by an illness to Boris Yeltsin or the crash of an airliner. It happened in June 1996, at about midnight, almost immediately after the arrest of two persons unknown to the public, pro-Yeltsin activists, who were detained by security officers while leaving government offices at the White House (with $500,000 in cash). Within hours—and much to the amazement of millions of Russians—the media inflated the case to help one group of politicians compromise another. As a result, leaders of the latter group lost their Kremlin jobs.

Of all the forms of mass media, television remains the key factor in Russia's changing politics. As in the West, the flagship of every national TV station is still its news program. The clear tendency here is to find ways to adapt the CNN style of broadcasting the news to the Byzantine world of Russian politics and to the traditional tastes of the audience. Because national news and current-affairs programs concentrate on what happens in Moscow, it is hard to grasp what goes on in Russia at large or to get news from the provinces (with the exception of natural disasters and dramatic political or military conflicts).

According to a recent study of national news reporting, the provinces are portrayed as a source of all kinds of dangers and threats. Life there is depicted as not only hard, but without prospects, sometimes even fearful and horrible. Provincials are unpredictable, their behavior is bizarre; they do not live, they exist. When interviewed in newscasts, provincials typically ask or demand something, they complain about different things, they suffer, but they seldom do anything constructive. As Moscow TV would have it, the provinces are hostile to the capital city, considering it the main source of their hardships and their principal exploiter. At the same time, they still hope that salvation will come from "the Center," from the national government. Such newscasts ignore any feelings Russians may have that they share a common life and destiny; instead they stress a distinct theme: The struggle of everyone with everyone. This kind of coverage leads to the alienation of Moscow from the rest of the country. That is only one example of how there is no programming policy in the public interest. The media's goals of promoting stability and prosperity, which have been proclaimed many times in presidential decrees as well as in declarations of media moguls, turn out to be false.

Media coverage of local news, to the extent that it exists at all, is of poor quality and tends to editorialize on current affairs either from the points of view of provincial administrators (in the case of state-run TV) or of owners of private media holdings. When they do not editorialize, the news media sensationalize the local criminal scene, natural disasters, and major accidents.

Media coverage of military conflicts like the war in Chechnya has led to a split in the Russian national identity, the public acceptance of violence, and a widespread distrust of all politicians. Russian society was so shaken by the Chechen war coverage that it had little left to believe in. Such a degree of public despair and cynicism could result in anarchy. Social conflicts, such as strikes, labor unrest, and demonstrations, do receive media coverage, but the emphasis here is: There is no way out for the protesters, no future and no exit. The damaging effects such conflicts have for the economy and the well-being of the general public dominate the coverage; the actual grievances of the protesters are downplayed.

Media coverage of political debate typically reinforces the "enemy" image of the Communists and their allies in the national parliament, instead of the need for compromise and consolidation. Mud slinging and cynicism are the principal methods used. As elsewhere in the world, television dominates Russia's election campaigns and has become an important and sophisticated image-making instrument. Despite a declared commitment to balance different political views, the *Vremya* news program (on state-run Channel 1) strongly favored Yeltsin during the presidential campaign of 1996 (the same was true of other national broadcasters).[3] Along with a lack of balance in the quantity and quality of coverage of favored candidates is a bias against the opposition. Information broadcast about political opponents or competitors can never be regarded as a presentation of hard news. To quote a respected source, "Businessmen invest in television as an industry, but even more as a condition for the existence of their own businesses."[4] Whenever private businesses cannot directly influence the content of information carried on television, they sponsor public-affairs programs that provide such influence indirectly.

Ratings and profits have become the new passwords in television. About 800 TV broadcasters have licenses to operate in Russia, and most of them aim to entertain. Most do not air news, current-affairs programs, educational programs for children and adults, or documentaries. Their listings resemble menus of cheap American B-movies, cartoons, and video pop-charts. In 1996, as a reward for assistance in conducting a pro-Yeltsin election campaign, the private NTV company completely took over the only national educational and cultural television channel, *Rossyiskie universitety* (Russian universities). As a result, except for the *Kultura* station described below, there are no educational programs on state-run national TV. Expanded commercial opportunities have led to an increase in imported entertainment programs: soap operas, imitations of American entertainment shows (such as *Pole chudes,* like *Wheel of Fortune,* and *Dobryi vecher,* like *The Late Night Show*), and packages of Western movies.

More and more, it appears that television does not support the development of Russian national identity or culture, but serves the narrow interests of corporations. Such corporations are a natural product of the profound social, political, and economic changes associated with the introduction of the market economy in the late 1980s. Despite a strong Russian flavor, the market economy is seen by many as an introduction to modernization, American-style. Among other things, that means a change in the hierarchy of values and cultural symbols. A perverse interpretation of these values by broadcasters has led to a hostile attitude of the public to the Western way of life, and has prolonged the transition period characterizing my country over the past decade for an indefinitely extended period of time.

In these ten years, several private banks and companies have shown an interest in controlling the mass media. Those companies passed the short distance from rivalry to cooperation, at least in order to achieve some political stability, in 1996–1998, and then back to rivalry in 1999. Political stability is the only chance for Russia to emerge from its current economic crisis, receive foreign credits, and revive domestic industry. And if the mass media help to promote this goal and do not take the authorities too much to task for their mistakes, then perhaps this is all to the good.

But herein lies the danger. When millions of people suffer from wage arrears, corruption is rampant on all levels, thousands are killed in ethnic conflicts and terrorist bombings, the president is sick, and the opposition is strong—and when the mass media (above all, the major TV channels) show unshakable unanimity in their desire to preserve the status quo—then there is something wrong in the way the principles of democracy are applied to the media.

Of course, in no country are broadcasters entirely independent from the political establishment or big business. But in Russia, their lack of independence is aggravated by such factors as the small number of television channels, the high cost of print media, the undeveloped market economy, the lack of paid-subscription TV, and the clannish relationship between business and the government. The boundaries between free and politically engaged media, and between private and state media, are still too fragile. And there is no doubt that it is dangerous for the future of both the mass media and the nation if these circumstances do not change.

Only when the stability of society is seen not from a partisan but from a national standpoint will it be possible to move toward the ideal of media programming for the sake of a fruitful public and political life. The president's decision to establish in 1996 the national TV program *Kultura* (Culture), designed to promote national cultural values and educational programs, is a rare positive step that hopefully others will follow.

In 1990 and the years immediately thereafter, the Russian press gained a level of freedom unprecedented in almost three centuries. Some even call the perestroika years the golden age of Russian print media. Since then, though, the condition of the press has deteriorated as a result of the economic crisis of 1998 and its growing dependence on government subsidies. By now, only a handful of publications have retained their financial independence, either from the state or from politically biased groups that view them (in the hallowed Russian tradition) as their pipelines to the public and their instruments of political control. Constructing and strengthening a democratic society, the prerequisite of the nation's real and lasting freedom, is a more responsible and consequential task than destroying the Communist machine. This is the biggest challenge for Russian journalists. Whether we will be as proud of our press a year or two hence as we were until recently, only time will tell.

I began this essay by referring to the adoption of the mass media statute in 1990. And I should like to conclude by referring once again to the law. Is a press law so important? Yes. What we see today in Russia is what will shape our society in five or ten years. The all-too-familiar power-hungry young politicians (and those not so young) will secure their places in the social-science textbooks. Tired of under-the-table fighting, they will start to resolve their problems in the parliament and at political conventions. Industrial moguls, now obsessed with their security, will settle scores, not in Chicago-style shootouts but in the courts of justice. Common citizens will stop thinking about empty food baskets and unpaid wages and will voice their concerns about the education of their children, environmental issues, and other matters affecting their interests. That may sound like a dream, but what other scenario could we wish for our homeland? What else is worth living for?

That entire future will evolve around the laws of the country. Most of these laws are already there, on the books. Most of them will fit the civilized Russia of the future, there can be no doubt about that. The future of the mass media will evolve around the laws as well. Today we view these laws—and with good reason—as empty words. But they are not empty promises. If society itself is ruled by law, there will be no other choice for the press but to be law abiding. True, a long road lies ahead. A market society is not yet here; real democracy is still over the horizon. Getting used to the spirit of justice, educating ourselves about the need to follow the letter of the law, is a way to approach the twenty-first century without encountering new shocks and revolutions along the road.

We should also focus on fighting for the embodiment of democratic principles in legislation. Although the original mass media statute has passed the test, other laws fail, either in part or as a whole. Only now are new laws being drafted to fill the tremendous gaps in media legislation. The universe of broadcasting remains unregulated: Issues of licensing, public control, foreign ownership, and advertising are subject to lobbying by businesses, government officials, and parliamentary factions—although, unfortunately, not by our public organizations. Freedom of information will be governed by another bill now under consideration by the Duma. These and other laws are of great importance not just for the freedom of speech and of the press in Russia; they are crucial for the future of our society. It is time for the public, at least for its most responsible and active elements, to become aware of this and have a say in what seems to be the empty practice of lawmaking.

Notes

1. Lawsuits actually adjudged by the courts are much fewer in number, 435 and 1,571, respectively, in 1990 and 1998.

2. As in the case of *Aleksandr Lyubimov v. Izvestia*. Judges, however, are usually sympathetic with journalists and, if they feel it necessary to satisfy the plaintiffs, award much lesser sums.

3. For example, during a sample period from March 22 to April 10, 1996, Yelstin's name was mentioned 103 times in the *Vremya* news program, while candidate number two, Communist Gennadii Zyuganov, who was at that time ahead of Yeltsin in the public polls, was mentioned fewer than 10 times.

4. *Zakonodatelstvo i praktika sredstv massovoi informatsii* (Media law and policy bulletin) (Moscow Media Law and Policy Center), no. 3 (1997): p. 31.

12

WHERE SOCIETY MUST
REIN IN GOVERNMENT

Restorative Justice and
Preservation of the Community

Rustem Maksudov

Judicial Reform: An Elusive Ideal

Professional attitudes toward the judicial reforms implemented from 1991 to 1995 in Russia generally fall into three points of view. The first is that judicial reform is under way, although attended by great difficulties. That is the view most frequently espoused by progressive jurists in the educational system.[1] The second is that judicial reform is complete because there is no longer a government agency charged with implementing the basic policy document, *The Conception of Judicial Reform in the Russian Federation*.[2] The third point of view is that held most often among the higher echelons of the Ministry of the Interior and the Prosecutor General's Office: The steps taken in judicial reform have been a series of ill-considered actions all violating the normal operation of law enforcement agencies and encouraging crime.[3] But one

Born in 1959 in Tatarstan, **Rustem Ramzievich Maksudov** studied history at Kazan State University, where he worked for ten years as a researcher. After becoming an activist in the area of criminal justice reform, Maksudov trained in Western mediation techniques, which he has applied in numerous projects as an expert and facilitator. He works with juvenile delinquents, has published numerous articles, and teaches civil rights at the Sakharov Center in Moscow. Translated by Antonina W. Bouis.

rarely finds in any of these viewpoints an analysis of judicial reform activity that addresses the ideal of justice that is inherent in the basic policy document, or the problems associated with making this ideal a reality under the conditions prevailing in Russia today.

In analyzing *The Conception of Judicial Reform in the Russian Federation,* we can distinguish between the goals set for transforming the law enforcement system (internal goals) and those set externally for the government and society. The following passage succinctly expresses the external goals: "Into the arena of public life there comes an independent court that is free of selfish interests, political sympathies, and ideological prejudices, appearing as the guarantor of legality and fairness, and summoned to play the same role in society as conscience does among people."[4] In fact, the document aims to introduce Western judicial practices to Russia. According to the reformers' thinking, Party and administrative controls must give way to legal regulations. Western judicial practices, however, exist in the context of the rule of law and in the light of their own legal, social, and cultural traditions.

Reformers working to implement the policy document have encountered the absence of the rule of law in:

- the structure of governmental agencies;
- the functioning of law enforcement agencies;
- the decisionmaking processes of governmental agencies; and
- the conditions in which the Russian population lives.

It is the last factor, in my opinion, that is the main brake on judicial reform (along with the absence of a new Alexander II). As the legal scholar V. Pastukhov notes,

> The search for justice in the West is the search for decisions grounded in law. And that means a definite respect for both form and formality. A consequence of that is the undeviating observance of rules and procedures and on the whole a reverential attitude toward procedural issues. In the consciousness of the Russian people as a whole and in the professional consciousness of the Russian legal caste, in particular, the identification of law and justice has not been made.[5]

For Pastukhov, the way out of this dilemma is to work on reshaping the rule-of-law values that are held by judges and the population alike. This approach, however, rules out developing an alternative approach to legal reform that includes an analysis of patterns in the evolution of the Western legal tradition and reflects the traditions of Russian life as well. Stressing the need to form public awareness of the rule of law overlooks the fact that this awareness occurred in the West not because it was "formed," but because it resulted from a long historical evolution; it was not something that mass media specialists could artificially impose. In Russia, we will never build a state based on the rule of law in the Western sense, not because we are uncivilized, but because it is impossible to retrace someone else's historical path. At the same time, while rejecting any direct transplanting of historical experience, we should:

- restore the operation of the legal system in our society and develop significant social and cultural forms for making it work;
- analyze the effectiveness of the judicial system as now organized; and
- describe the organizational structures needed.

Legal systems offer citizens a choice of civilized methods for settling social conflicts. In that sense, the right to oppose coercive and uncivilized forms of pressure (bribes, blackmail, manipulation through mass media) is a means of social control. But the Western rule of law as it is now organized judicially, at least in the opinion of some legal theorists and criminologists, is undergoing a crisis.

The most important change, as described by Professor Harold Berman of Emory University, is the introduction of all-pervasive government control over basic aspects of citizens' economic and social life, and the legal consolidation of that control.[6] In Berman's view, these changes "endanger the objectivity of the law, since they make the state an invisible party to most legal actions among citizens and juridical persons."[7] The crisis of the Western legal system is manifested in:

- the perception that contemporary law in theory and in practice is less an integrated entity of codes, an organism, a *corpus juris,* than a hodgepodge of short-term decisions and contradictory regulations, connected only by general methods and techniques;
- the perception that law does not have its own history;

- the perception that changes in the law occur only in response to external pressures;
- the perception that law is increasingly an instrument of the state; and
- the tendency, widely observed, to subordinate many separate jurisdictions and systems to a single central program of legislative and administrative regulation.[8]

The most important problem of all is that justified methods of state control and their technical inclusion in bodies of existing law[9] lead to consequences destructive to human collectivity.[10] As legal scholar Nils Christie observes, "Contemporary systems of controlling crime illustrate a lost opportunity to include citizens in solving problems that are of direct importance to them. Our society is a society of monopolists in problem-solving."[11] In almost every Western country there is a tendency toward the growth of an enormous army of specialists, whose role consists of overseeing and correcting human behavior.[12] These specialists *know* how to solve problems, and they often solve them in an authoritarian way. Depriving people of the chance to participate in finding ways to solve conflicts and reduce criminal behavior, however, destroys basic social connections and relationships.

How does contemporary justice work toward the destruction of human collectivity? The analysis of Howard Zehr focuses not on the internal procedures of justice but on its functions in society.[13] For instance, when most people characterize the Western legal tradition, they speak of judicial procedures. For Zehr, however, the most important aspect of justice is its social and cultural significance. The role of modern criminal justice is to punish the individual who violates the law, in a system of punitive justice.

Crime in the existing justice system is understood as activity forbidden by law. Violation of a specific law leads to a punishment. The process of justice focuses on establishing innocence. Determining whether a person is guilty or innocent is accomplished with the help of appropriate legal procedures. If commission of a crime is proved, punishment is meted out, the severity of which is also determined by law. The most important role in this process is played by specialists—investigator, judge, prosecutor, and defense attorney. The real feelings of people, their desire to find their own solutions, and the impact of the criminal process on relationships remain in the shadows. Only if such considerations help solve the tasks at hand (establishing guilt and imposing punishment) are they of interest to the justice professionals. The direct participants are in fact "extras" in a professional competition. The existing system of justice, with its competitive procedures, deepens conflicts between people and leads to an escalation of cruelty in society. Added to this are the consequences of having very large numbers of people in prisons, where they learn criminal behavior.

The lobbying efforts of law enforcement agencies and corporations that profit from expanding the "war on crime," as well as the rhetoric of politicians and the mass media, depict this situation as normal.[14] Gradually, a significant part of the population begins to support efforts directed toward increasing criminal sentences, expanding the staff of law enforcement agencies and the courts, and constructing new prisons. A vicious circle is created and exploited by certain politicians and representatives of law enforcement agencies who maintain that their efforts are in response to public opinion.[15]

The Crisis of Collectivity: A Starting Point for Transforming Russia's Judicial System

In considering judicial structures for resolving social conflicts that would *not* lead to the destruction of social ties, we can learn from the methods used in Russia's prerevolutionary *obshchina,* or communes. Formal judicial conflict resolution never did take hold in Russia as a historically significant principle. Even the rural district courts that appeared after the emancipation of the serfs in 1861 did not become the principal forums for conflict resolution. In the opinion of Nikolai Pavlov-Sil'vanskii, "In establishing the regional courts, the law chose a unit that was too large; therefore the regional court did not satisfy the needs of life, and the village *obshchina* court continued to exist side by side with it."[16]

What models were used to resolve conflicts in the *obshchina?* One example relates to the life of the Russian peasantry in the late nineteenth and early twentieth centuries. At the start of the century, on instructions from the Russian Senate, young barristers were sent to rural areas to learn what was happening in villages with regard to legal decisions affecting the majority of the population. One of the lawyers described the following event:

The elders judged the case of two peasants who had an argument over a piece of land. As a result, the following decision was taken: "A is right, and B is not right. Therefore A will get two-thirds and B only one-third of the parcel of land." To which the young lawyer said, "If A is right, he should get all the land, and if he's not, then he shouldn't get any land at all. How can you make such a decision?" The elder replied, "Land is only land, but they have to live in the same village to the end of their days."[17]

The elders in prerevolutionary Russia resolved conflicts by considering collective life as an unconditional value. Communal methods of conflict resolution existed side by side with the work of official justice, limiting the sphere where punitive measures applied. The Bolshevik Revolution destroyed this mechanism of preserving collectivity. The Communist collective expressed first and foremost the supremacy of communal relations.[18] Under communism, communities organized along true collective lines became obsolete. The basic form of life became the communal nucleus, where mutual hostility, denunciations, the desire to survive at the expense of others, and the basest of human instincts reigned supreme.

After the revolution, Party committees at various levels took over the functions of the organs that had resolved conflicts before (especially in the cities). Administrative and repressive measures linked to the pursuit of political and economic goals were the principal method for regulating conflicts and combating crime. In the USSR, the courts were only one of many mechanisms for executing Party decisions.[19] The judicial reforms of the 1960s, reflected in the Criminal Code of the RSFSR, sought to strengthen the integrity of investigations and to eliminate the Stalinist habit of falsifying cases. But even in the post-Stalinist period, the functions of the courts remained essentially the same. Suffice to say that right up until 1989 a people's judge in Russia was not allowed to have a legal education.

In the early 1990s, the Soviet system of Party control collapsed, and with it the established methods for regulating conflicts.[20] And economic reforms gave rise to many new kinds of conflicts. Today we can see the ubiquitous destruction of normal human ties and convivial contacts. The absence of effective methods for resolving conflicts, such as methods cultivated in prerevolutionary Russia, has led to the decline of significant social innovation, the atomization of society, and the absence of adult role models for future generations.

The government's attempts to re-create a system of social control through force have only made matters worse and led to serious consequences for the state and society.[21]

*   *   *

Although today there is no hope of reestablishing the *obshchina* (especially in urban centers), I believe that the experience of communal methods of conflict resolution helps to define the social and cultural goals of any transformation in the judicial system. These are, first and foremost:

- the restoration of social relations that may have been violated in consequence of a crime;
- the mobilization and use of local community resources in resolving criminal situations and adopting measures of prevention and rehabilitation; and
- the limitation of punitive measures.

"Restorative Justice" in Russia: The Idea and the Methodology

Even in the West, there has been an increase in the application of conciliatory and peacemaking procedures designed to resolve conflicts without recourse to the courts. Throughout the world, the ideas and methodology of "restorative justice" (reconciliation programs, family counseling, counseling between victim and offender) are spreading and helping to restore the broken tissues of human relations.

Restorative justice is based on a completely different understanding of crime.[22] A crime is first and foremost an act of violence affecting people and their relationships. Those who suffered from a crime as well as those who perpetrated it should participate in the judicial process. In prerevolutionary Russia, as noted above, both the creation and the defense of collective values took place in collective bodies—councils, circles, and the peasant *mir*, or council. In my opinion, it is this aspect of the methodology of restorative justice that is important today. Placing the offender into a relationship with the participants in a meeting gives him a positive impetus to change, and encourages the other participants in the meeting to assume responsibility for bringing that impulse to life.

Following are three elements that set this methodology in motion. *First,* there must be group understanding of the criminal act.

- A criminal case can involve the parties concerned (offender, victim, their social circle) when the police and courts limit their actions to apprehending the offender and sending the case to restorative justice programs. For the offender, the victim, and the victim's family and friends, participation in these programs results from a free and conscious choice. If they choose not to participate, they can go through the usual judicial procedures.
- A special meeting of the participants with a group leader can often achieve positive results. The leader stimulates an exchange of opinions about the criminal act that would ultimately lead to a picture of its consequences acceptable to all participants. This is the first element of comprehending the situation from a collective viewpoint.

In the course of the discussion, the *second* element occurs: The offender proposes a resolution to the matter, to be discussed and accepted by all participants.

The *third* element is a discussion among all participants on how to change the offender's behavior, for example, by his getting a job or undergoing a specific rehabilitation program. This dialogue creates the conditions for *changing the behavior of the offender.* Whether there will be a real change or not depends on the individual himself, of course, but restorative justice programs give a better chance for that change to take place than do juvenile detention colonies and prisons.

The traditions of repentance, charity, and forgiveness have not vanished from Russian life. The accused person often repents and performs actions to compensate for the damage he caused. For victims struggling with psychological trauma, the attitude of the accused toward what he did and the prospect of receiving compensation for damages are important. And many victims are not determined to impose punishment. Without the restorative justice that takes place today, even in a truncated and fragmented way, the existing judicial system and the law enforcement agencies could not function.

At the same time, the focus on reconciliation often is elusive: Meetings and counseling often cannot be arranged, owing perhaps to mutual distrust or fear of pressure. When some aspect of reconciliation does take place (for instance, compensation for damages), it is rarely seen as completing the administration of justice. Sometimes the victim cannot get answers to questions that would help relieve a stressful situation, or the offender fails to understand the real consequences of his actions and does not utilize special rehabilitation programs.

To overcome these problems, special programs for reconciling victims and offenders have been created. Victim and Offender Reconciliation Programs have been proliferating worldwide for the past twenty-five years. In Europe, these programs are most prevalent in Austria, Belgium, Great Britain, Germany, Norway, Finland, and France. In Poland and the Czech Republic, after the success of experimental reconciliation programs, legislatures have endorsed their expansion.

Since the summer of 1997, I have been working with Mikhail Fliamer to promote and implement the idea of restorative justice in Russia. At the present time, we are working on the creation and testing of reconciliation techniques in cases involving minors, in accordance with Russian law. Below is a brief description of the elements of this technique and the first steps in its implementation in Russia:[23]

Obtaining Case Materials. In the reconciliation program under way in the Tagansky District of Moscow, the investigator in cases involving minors sends notification of the possibility of using a reconciliation program to agency tasked with preventing juvenile crime. The notification includes file data as well as the addresses of victim and defendant. The notification is sent after the evidence of the charges has been compiled and the victim has been questioned. It is necessary that the defendant admit guilt, and that he not be under arrest for the given action.

Having Preliminary Meetings. After the person in charge of the case at the reconciliation program receives the materials, he speaks with the offender and the victim separately. First, he determines their readiness to participate in the reconciliation procedure, their attitude toward the crime, and their willingness to compensate and accept compensation for damages. In the cases of minors, this applies to their legal representatives as well. At these meetings, the reconciliation leader hears out each side's version of the incident. Even at this stage, the reconciliation process differs significantly from criminal procedures. The leader begins to create beneficial conditions for a future dialogue between the victim and the offender. He is interested in the feelings and needs of the victim and the offender, and their attitudes toward the situation. With the victim, the leader discusses the consequences of the violation, the problems that have resulted, and the capabilities of the reconciliation program to solve them. Dealing with the offender, the leader refrains from making value judgments on his actions. The goal of reconciliation is to recognize the unfairness of the incident and to compensate for the damages caused by the crime, not to condemn the offender for his actions. Only by dealing with the offender as a responsible adult can one expect him to behave as such.

One of the most important social and psychological results of reconciliation programs is overcoming the labeling of victims and offenders. After the preliminary meetings, the leader prepares the victim and the offender to play roles in which they themselves will propose a solution. In this way, the leader, unlike an attorney, does not defend the specific interest of anyone in the process. Both sides may reject reconciliation simply because the process is unfamiliar. They may prefer "not to face the problem." The leader then explains the process of reconciliation and its advantages. If the leader reaches the conclusion that both sides are ready and secures their consent, he brings them together.

Holding the Meeting.   The next stage involves holding a meeting between the two sides in the presence of the leader, and arriving at a binding conciliation agreement that is acceptable to both sides. After introducing the participants, the leader must explain the procedure and his role as a neutral facilitator. He states the rules of the dialogue, for instance no interrupting the speaker and no swearing. One important rule is preserving the confidentiality of the profoundly personal aspects of the meetings.

After the leader's introductory statement, the crime victim recounts her version of the event, focusing not so much on *what* happened as on *how* it affected her life. This emphasis is most important; it differs from the emphasis of a criminal investigation, which seeks to find out every detail of what happened. If the offender tries to whitewash himself, the leader explains that the proceedings are neither an investigation nor a court hearing to determine who is guilty, and that it is important to learn how the criminal incident affected the victim.

Then the offender has the opportunity to explain his actions: why he committed the crime, what prompted him. In these kinds of sessions, the offender often apologizes. As a rule, however, the victim is not ready to forgive. The participants can ask each other further questions. The leader gives them the opportunity to communicate as naturally as possible, interfering only when necessary. When both sides have formulated a common picture of the incident, the leader brings up the questions of compensation. He asks the victim what the offender can do to make up for his action: pay money or perform some work. After a general discussion, the sides make a decision on the method of compensation. The next topic examines the offender's future life: what is to be done to prevent him from repeating his crime. The offender could be asked, for instance, to take treatment for alcoholism or drug addiction, to get a job, and so on. A written agreement is then drawn up and signed by all the participants.

Composing the Reconciliation Agreement.   The meeting (or, in complicated cases, meetings) is considered to be concluded successfully if the victim and offender manage to move beyond their emotional responses to the drafting and signing of a reconciliation agreement. This agreement has the following sections:

- a description of how the situation is perceived by victim and offender;
- specification of the compensation due to the victim for material damages;
- special requirements relating to the future behavior and regime of the offender, including undergoing addiction treatment, counseling, or therapy; and
- procedures to monitor the execution of the agreement.

Sending the Reconciliation Agreement to Court.   At the court session, the victim requests that the reconciliation agreement be appended to the case dossier. The judge decides the issue in consultation with the two sides.

Checking on the Execution of the Agreement's Terms.   Reconciliation is not considered to have been achieved until all the terms of the agreement have been fulfilled. In our technique, we prefer to arrange additional meetings in order to evaluate the execution of the agreement's terms and conditions.

Ensuring Judicial Regulation of the Reconciliation.   Reconciliation requires an official statement from the victim dropping charges against the person who committed the crime (Article 76 of the Criminal Code). For instance, the statement might drop the request to have the accused brought to criminal responsibility (if the case has not yet been started), or it might halt a case instigated by the victim. And for the reconciliation to have legal effect, it must be preceded by measures to compensate for damages suffered by the victim. Such measure could include compensation in financial or other forms for property damage, elimination of material damage through the offender's own efforts, financial compensation for moral damages, or guarantees for compensation to be made within a certain time period. In criminal cases of lesser gravity, the results of reconciliation procedures could be a sufficient basis for dropping the case, whereas in graver crimes a reduction in sentence might ensue.

Who Can Act As Leader in Reconciliation Procedures?   Properly trained representatives of social and public organizations can act as leaders in reconciliation procedures and can operate within the framework of social and legal defense for the least protected groups of the population (women, adolescents, refugees, and so on) who fall into the orbit of criminal justice.

In Russia, criminal justice, with the exception of jury trials, operates with the public interest often being replaced by government interests (and most frequently by the interests of the most influential executive branch agencies). As Dimitrina Petrova writes about the Communist ideological context, "It was assumed that part of the public, even if it could speak about having its own interests, would have to sacrifice them for the sake of state interests, just as personal interests had to be subsumed voluntarily to the interests of the group and, in the final analysis, to the interests of the state."[24] It was assumed that in the Soviet system of law and order, the public interest was expressed first by the law enforcement agencies themselves and the "social" structures they sanctioned (people's militias, "comrade" courts, and so on). This assumption, natural enough in the context of Communist practice and ideology, is today an extremely persistent and dangerous anachronism.

Another anachronism is the bias of many legal scholars against public human and civil rights organizations. Jurists as a whole expect nothing constructive to come from these organizations. One lawyer expressed it in a colorful way: "Filthy, ragged civil-rights activists, who understand nothing in jurisprudence, are getting in the way of justice." What is behind this? At best, the desire of professional lawyers to have a monopoly on justice.

What prompts social workers and other members of public organizations to work in the field of criminal justice? They are moved by the tragedies of thousands caught in the maw of the criminal justice system and by the fact that the existing system does not defend the rights of the poor or prevent torture in police precincts and investigation isolation cells.[25] Many judges still accept the tasks given them by the executive branch without caring about the social consequences of their decisions; they merely repeat old slogans about stepping up the war on crime and so on. This attitude re-creates former political conditions, where justice was a leash to keep people in line.[26]

At the same time, we do not reject the possibility of representatives from law enforcement agencies taking part in the reconciliation process. The orientation toward increasing punitive practice, however, keeps these structures from redirecting their activity in a way that would combine criminal procedural aspects with social rehabilitation aspects, thereby drawing upon the expertise of professionals in the humanities.

The institution of reconciliation as a form of restorative justice can effectively defend the public interest in criminal cases. In my opinion, the main obstacle to the development of this institution in Russia is the prevalence of the principle of statism[27] in law enforcement agencies and the courts. And even if jurists were to reject that principle, a further obstacle is the lack of preparation of social workers themselves to deal constructively with the new opportunity to cooperate. Representatives of social organizations will have to learn how to apply new techniques.[28] The issues that arise within the framework of reconciliation (growth of awareness of rule of law among the population, the organization of compensation for damages, help in rehabilitating both offender and victim, and so on) can be resolved only on the basis of cooperation between social workers and jurists (advocates, investigators, prosecutors, and judges). The institution of reconciliation must, therefore, bear a mixed state and public character. Expanding opportunities for conducting reconciliation programs within the practice of Russian jurisprudence is the first step in the transformation of jurisprudence itself.

The First Reconciliation Meetings:
Impact and Problems

The opportunity to express feelings, speak out, and get answers has been the most important element of the reconciliation meetings and has led in all cases to positive results.

Reconciliation meetings have had socializing, rehabilitating, and psychotherapeutic effects. Such meetings helped restore an eleven-year-old mugging victim's sense of personal security; the boy had suffered great anxiety before the meeting. After expressing their emotions and feelings, many victims were no longer angry; their hatred had become a desire to participate in improving the lot of the offender. The meetings led some adolescents and their parents to a profound recognition of their own problems—an important basis for complete rehabilitation.

The meetings have also helped establish the social skills that must be learned by the offenders in order to handle situations in a noncriminal way. These skills include "putting yourself in another's place," "solving interpersonal problems without violence," "self-control," "relationship building with peers and other people," "creating your future," and "being autonomous and not depending on the actions of others."[29] Families in which adolescents did not learn these skills are fertile soil for the growth of criminal behavior.

The absence of these skills in adults and corresponding gaps in the socialization of children lead to incessant family conflicts (which often have a criminal aspect—children stealing from parents, parents abusing children, and so on). A promising direction for reconciliation programs is holding such meetings in families and school groups.

Cooperation between the program leaders and representatives of various rehabilitation services and programs is also important. More representatives of state organs should be included in the management of this process. This inclusive approach requires working to change the mindset that reigns in law enforcement agencies and courts, and gaining a broader understanding of reconciliation programs in the criminal justice system and within executive branch agencies.

Supporting New Social Initiatives in Criminal Jurisprudence

As far as many charitable foundations are concerned, the role of society and the public in administering criminal justice is restricted primarily to human rights organizations and their networks. For these foundations, the sphere of criminal justice itself is highly politicized, is repressive in nature, and poses a danger to those who want to make positive changes.

At the same time, without public participation, we will not be able to stop arbitrary behavior by law enforcement agencies and judges, or a punitive approach in administrative decisions regarding deviant and criminal behaviors, an approach that is particularly intolerant of crimes committed by adolescents.

Although the human rights movement has focused on the first of these two problems, there is still no general public movement or appropriate social initiatives to deal with the second. This fact, combined with the government's repressive policies on crime, is the most important reason for the terrible conditions in investigation isolation cells and youth colonies and for the enormous prison population in Russia.

An important condition for making progress is an analysis of how society can most effectively play a role in criminal justice, as well as the creation of programs to support existing associations and initiatives (training and educational programs, methodological work, and orientation seminars).

Representatives of law enforcement agencies cannot function without allowing greater involvement of public and social workers in the criminal justice system. Repressive measures can be used to control society only in a totalitarian state. Today in Moscow, two public organizations are dedicated to including reconciliation and rehabilitation programs in their work with juvenile offenders and children at risk (the Court and Judicial Reform Public Center and the No to Alcoholism and Drug Addiction foundation). We have observed a positive shift in attitudes with regard to this issue among many public organizations in Russia. To a certain extent, this work is supported by representatives of the Prosecutor General's Office, the Moscow Prosecutor's Office, the Criminal Investigation Department of the Moscow police, and law enforcement agencies in various regions (Kazan, Petrozavodsk, Tomsk, and others). Significant work is also being done in St. Petersburg, initiated by the municipal court.

This is heartening evidence that government agencies are interested in collaborating with public organizations. Today it is particularly important to develop techniques, on the basis of the ideas and programs of restorative justice, for further joint action by public organizations and government agencies that will make Russia's judicial system more responsive to society's needs and more effective in satisfying them.

Notes

1. Interestingly, in opposition to this viewpoint, Chairman of the Supreme Court Vyacheslav M. Lebedev today prefers to speak not of judicial reform but of the creation of an independent court system and the establishment of judicial authority. See Vyacheslav M. Lebedev, *Sudebnaia reforma: itogi, prioritety, perspektivy. Materialy konferentsii* (Judicial reform: achievements, priorities, prospects. Conference materials) (Moscow: n.p., 1997), pp. 7–20.

2. The Department of Judicial Reform and Courts within the State Legal Department subordinated to the President of the Russian Federation, headed by Sergei A. Pashin, was disbanded in 1995.

3. According to the Scientific Research Institute on the Problems of Strengthening Law and Order within the Prosecutor General's Office of the Russian Federation, many steps taken in the sphere of criminal justice in accordance with this document have actually generated crime. See *Osnovy gosudarstvennoi politiki bor'by s prestupnost'iu v Rossii: Teoreticheskaia model'* (Bases of the state policy of war on crime in Russia: A theoretical model) (Moscow: Norma, 1997), p. 17.

4. *Kontsepsiia sudebnoi reformy v Rossiiskoi Federatsii* (Conception of judicial reform in the Russian Federation) (Moscow: Respublika, 1992), p. 6.

5. V. Pastukhov, "Rossiiskoe pravosudie: vzgliad izvne i iznutri (Tezisy doklada)" (Russian jurisprudence: A look from outside and from inside [outline of a report]) (paper presented at the roundtable meeting "Monitoring Judicial Reform in the Russian Federation," Center for Constitutional Research, Moscow, May 29, 1988).

6. This state of affairs prompted Giles Delese to call modern society the "society of control." Giles Delese, "The Society of Control (Postscriptum): Elements," *Eurasian Review,* no. 9 (1999).

7. Harold Berman, *Zapadnaia traditsiia prava: epokha formirovaniia* (Western tradition of law: The era of formation) (Moscow: MGU, 1994), p. 51.

8. Ibid., pp. 52–53.

9. When I speak of justice in this article, I mean criminal justice.

10. I use the term "collectiveness" in the sense of Ferdinand Toennies's *Gemeinschaft.* "According to Toennies, *Gemeinschaft* is the bearer of qualities that are highly esteemed both by the ordinary consciousness and by many moral systems: they include first of all human closeness, readiness to help . . . A social system based on *Gemeinschaft* does not have 'accounts,' and those who are included in it feel secure, protected, but at the same time connected by moral responsibilities to the individual members and the entire group." A. N. Malinkin, "O zhizni i tvorchestve Ferdinanda Tennisa" (The life and work of Ferdinand Toennies), *Sotsiologicheskii zhurnal,* nos. 3-4 (1998), p. 205.

11. Nils Christie, "Konflikt kak sobstvennost'" (Conflict as property), *Pravosudie po delam nesovershennoletnikh: Perspektivy razvitiia,* no. 1 (Moscow: Sudebno-pravovaia reforma, 1999).

12. "It is quite obvious that a high level of crime and other manifestations of antisocial behavior serve as indices of a lack of order: it is much less accepted that a large number of police, financial inspectors, and auditors is also an index of the fall of morality, even if the manifestations of antisocial behavior are limited." Amitai Etzioni, "Novoe zolotoe pravilo: Soobschestvo i nravstvennost' v demokraticheskom obshchestve" (The new golden rule: Community and morality in democratic society), in *Novaia postindustrial'naia volna na Zapade: Antologiia* (The new postindustrial wave in the West: An anthology) (Moscow: Akademiia, n.d.), p. 323.

13. Howard Zehr, *Changing Lenses: A New Focus for Crime and Justice* (Herald Press, 1990). Published in Russian as *Vosstanovitel'noe pravosudie: novyi vzgliad na prestuplenie i nakazanie* (Moscow: Sudebno-pravovaia reforma, 1998).

14. The situation in the United States in this regard is examined in Nils Christie, *Crime Control As Industry: Toward GULAGS, Western Type?* (London and New York: Routledge, 1993).

15. The reach of the mass media today is so all-encompassing that some human-rights activists maintain that it is necessary to create a new generation of human rights—the right to protection from information.

16. Nikolai Pavlov-Sil'vanskii, *Feodalizm v Rossii* (Feudalism in Russia) (Moscow: Nauka, 1988), p. 194.

17. Cited from Theodor Shanin, *Kuda idet Rossiia?* (Whither Russia?) (Moscow: Aspect Press, 1996), p. 170.

18. Aleksandr A. Zinov'ev, *Kommunizm kak real'nost'* (Communism as reality) (Moscow: Tsentrpoligraf, 1994).

19. Sergei A. Pashin describes the functions of the judicial system in Soviet society as follows: "First of all, the usual attitude, which remains prevalent today, sees the court as an appendage of executive power and as an organ that must 'produce,' must decide a political or an economic issue. When construction sites, steel mills, and chemical factories were empty, the courts had to send manpower there. And

when there is a greater perceived problem with crime, or rather with that variety of crime that is on the tongues of the authorities and the population alike, the courts have to fight against it.

"Over the years the courts combated theft of wheat from the fields, lateness for work, speculation, hooliganism, and the practice of lathe operators and taxi drivers of accepting tips. This perception of the courts' job is so strong that some judges, whom I have the honor of teaching evidentiary law at the Russian Law Academy, often exclaim in bewilderment: 'Probably everything you tell us is correct, but in this crime wave how can we keep to the formalities! Because of some trifling mistake in gathering evidence, a criminal might get away with the crime, and that cannot be permitted!' These colleagues do not perceive themselves as protecting the interests of the law but as servants of an interest outside the justice system—in this case, the goal set for the law enforcement agencies of stopping crime."

Sergei A. Pashin, *Mekhanizmy reformy i kontrreformy, Sudebnaia reforma: problemy analiza i osveshcheniia* (Mechanisms of reform and counterreform, judicial reform: Problems of analysis and interpretation) (Moscow: n.p., 1996), p. 40.

20. I do not want to be seen as supporting the re-creation of structures analogous to Party ones. I share the opinion that these structures are totalitarian and inhumane.

21. In connection with this tendency, the defense of individuals from justice and law enforcement agencies acting as instruments of irrational state policy has taken on greater urgency in Russia. The idea of presenting law as an indivisible part of human rights teaches that law is a defense against repressive state instruments—including police, courts, and prosecutors. Rights protection, specifically methods for protecting individual rights against police actions and in court, is becoming a more popular topic in law education. But the idea of human rights, so vitally important for many people, does not lead to an understanding of the *sociocultural* functions of law systems in society and their place in the *mechanisms of supporting the wholeness of society*.

22. A more detailed look at the philosophy of restorative justice can be found in Zehr, *Changing Lenses*.

23. This description was prepared jointly with Mikhail G. Fliamer. See Rustem Maksudov and Mikhail G. Fliamer, *Programmy primireniia po delam nesovershennoletnikh: po puti prakticheskoi realizatsii idei vosstanovitel'nogo pravosudiia v Rossii* (Reconciliation programs in juvenile cases: On the path to a practical realization of the ideas of restorative justice in Russia), *Pravosudie po delam nesovershennoletnikh: Perspektivy razvitiia*, no. 1 (Moscow: Sudebno-pravovaia reforma, 1999); and Rustem Maksudov and Mikhail G. Fliamer, *Primirenie v ugolovnom pravosudii Rossii* (Reconciliation in criminal justice in Russia) (forthcoming).

24. Dimitrina Petrova, *Politicheskie i pravovye prepyatstviia na puti razvitiia prava obshchestvennykh interesov* (Political and legal obstacles on the path of the development of a law of public interests), *East European Constitutional Review*, vol. 1, no. 18 (1997): 25.

25. Lately, this fact has been admitted by the leadership of the Ministry of Internal Affairs and the Prosecutor General's Office. In the near future, a draft of the federal program for stopping torture in law enforcement organs will be brought into

compliance with the European Convention on Stopping Torture and Inhumane or Humiliating Treatment or Punishment, ratified by the Russian Federation.

26. As Sergei Pashin notes, the phenomenon of "people being mauled by the 'law-enforcement mechanism' today is inevitable, not because we lack democratic laws or because Stalinists, Partycrats, and hard-liners are at the helm of that huge machine, but because government repression of people is not an excess of zeal but a normal production technique." Sergei A. Pashin, *Sudebnyi kontrol' za pravil'nost'iu arestov* (Court control over correctness of arrests), *Pravozashchitnik,* vol. 1, no. 3 (1995) p. 53.

27. *Statism* (from the French *état*) is defined as the system of political thought that sees the state as the highest result and goal of social development (*Great Soviet Encyclopedia,* vol. 30, p. 289).

28. Marina Liborakina, Mikhail G. Fliamer, and Vladimir N. Iakimets, *Sotsial'-noe partnerstvo* (Social partnership) (Moscow: Shkola kul'turnoi politiki, 1996), p. 114.

29. See Friedrich Lesel, *Vospitanie-nakazanie-pomoshch: v chem nuzhdaiutsia molodye narushiteli? Deti i iunoshi v konflikte s zakonom* (Education, punishment, help: What do young offenders need? Children and adolescents in conflict with the law) (paper presented at a regional seminar in the Baltic republics, Jurmala, Latvia, May 30–June 2, 1994). Published Geneva: ICCB.

Part Four

CIVIL SOCIETY BUILDING BLOCKS

13

NONGOVERNMENTAL ORGANIZATIONS

Building Blocks for Russia's Civil Society

Andrei Topolev and Elena Topoleva

Freedom of speech is one of the most important and notable accomplishments of Mikhail Gorbachev's perestroika. The free exchange of information and ideas created the torrent that swept aside the Iron Curtain, and then the Berlin Wall as well. Transforming Russia's economy and introducing a market economy have always encountered resistance from a significant part of our population, whose views are reflected primarily by the left-wing parties. Nonetheless, the general concept of human rights and freedoms finds support among virtually every element of society. The efforts undertaken by the international community to make these concepts a reality in Russia must be properly appreciated as well.

Born in 1959, **Elena Andreevna Topoleva** met her future husband, **Andrei Viktorovich Topolev** (born in 1954), in high school, where both were active members of an unofficial student organization. Andrei earned his degree in history and philology at the Patrice Lumumba University of People's Friendship in Moscow. After studying Russian philology at Moscow State University, Elena followed her husband to Africa, where he taught Russian and worked as a translator. After returning to Russia, Andrei pursued a research career. In 1993 they both began working at Postfactum, a news agency, until they cofounded the Agency for Social Information in 1994, which both still lead. Translated by Marian Schwartz.

In the wake of the new ideas, a stream of Western loans, investments, and grants flooded into Russia. This assistance, we believe, had its most significant result in shaping the third, nongovernmental, sector. Programs supporting business fared less well: The new entrepreneurs were unable at the outset to apply foreign experience to Russia's specific conditions, and although the government verbally welcomed small and midsize business initiatives, it in fact choked them with unreasonable taxes and bureaucratic tyranny. But the third sector—the nongovernmental, nonprofit organizations (NGOs), which received significant organizational and financial support from abroad—developed in relatively more favorable conditions. These organizations, virtually unmonitored by government officials, depended for their success wholly on the fact that people were trying to protect the rights and freedoms of their fellow citizens through philanthropy, charity, and volunteerism at the grass roots. It is important to note, however, that these ideas were by no means new for Russia, nor were they imported solely from the West.

The first public organizations appeared in our country as early as the eighteenth century. To be sure, public organizations were never numerous, and in the Soviet era they were almost wholly subordinated to the state machine. Nonetheless, civic associations have long existed in Russia. The same can be said about volunteerism. Even in Soviet times, voluntary labor existed not only in the form of the "mandatory voluntary" Saturday workdays *(subbotniki)* but also in less distorted manifestations. Teams of enthusiasts would sally forth on Sundays to restore historical and cultural monuments—churches, noblemen's estates, and private homes. Many state agencies took children's homes and boarding schools under their wing. State employees helped the children during their free time on their own initiative. The "Timur Teams" of teenage volunteers (so named after the Young Pioneer hero of a novel by Arkady Gaidar) assisted helpless and lonely old people. We could cite many such examples. Traditions of patronage and philanthropy also have a centuries-old history in our country. Russian merchants and entrepreneurs always considered it their charitable duty to help their neighbor. They contributed huge sums of money to support culture and art and to build churches and hospitals.

The foreign seeds that NGOs brought to Russia during the 1980s therefore fell on fertile soil. Generously "fertilized and watered" with Western money and cultivated with the best American and western European technology, these seeds quickly yielded good shoots. The leaders of the new wave of public organizations, moreover, for the most part were more educated, had more initiative, and were more honest. Many of this generation, now between thirty-eight and forty-five years of age, were "cast overboard" after perestroika, no longer needed by the state and unable to organize their own businesses under conditions of "wild" capitalism. They willingly studied Western experience, not simply mastering it but creatively adapting it to Russian conditions. In the early 1990s, dozens of experts and trainers came to Russia from the United States, Great Britain, and Germany. By the mid-1990s, teams of Russian specialists had emerged and began to teach their colleagues, compatriots, and representatives of NGOs from other countries of the former Soviet Union. Accordingly, the demand for foreign specialists in the third sector quickly declined.

Take the case of Evgenia Alekseeva, the codirector of Focus, a nonprofit organization in Moscow. Evgenia recently turned forty-five, but you would undoubtedly include her among Russia's modern young leaders: She is full of energy, looks marvelous, and "feels like twenty-five." At one time she studied medicine and worked as a pediatrician in a hospital. On her miserable salary, she had to accept an unmanageable workload and in addition do all her own housework—she was raising two daughters. Then an encounter with Americans and America completely turned her life around. This happened after perestroika, when the frontier had opened and contacts with the mysterious West became possible. Evgenia discovered a new world and new possibilities for herself. In a short time, almost from scratch, she learned English, read a mountain of books, and attended training seminars. What influenced her the most, though, was her personal acquaintance and close contact with Americans, some of whom later became her close friends. She came to see the world and her place in it differently. She realized how much depended on her and how she could completely change her life.

And that is what she did. She cut her medical career short and together with friends from Russia and the United States founded Golubka, a public organization that fights for peace and democracy, advocating nonviolent methods. She even made adjustments to her personal life. Now she no longer bears all the domestic chores alone; all family members share them equally. Evgenia has become a highly professional manager; she directs very important social projects and without exaggeration can be called one of Russia's best NGO trainers and consultants. She has conducted hundreds of seminars on organizational development and strategic planning, social marketing, and conflict resolution. Her special subject of interest is empowerment seminars for women. Evgenia was able to rid herself of the dependency syndrome, building her life anew and making it vivid and interesting—and this is what she tries to teach others.

As for Western financial assistance to the third sector, it has proven fairly effective. If you compare the funds the West puts into supporting Russian NGOs with those directed to governmental agencies or invested in business, it is obvious that relatively small investments in civil-society undertakings have yielded incomparably greater results. Thanks to assistance from the West, many Russian public organizations representing the third sector have become well known both in our country and abroad (for example, the Glasnost Defense Foundation, the Committees of Soldiers' Mothers, and the Rainbow Keepers) for their professional and effective work. At the same time, most of the small, grassroots organizations operating primarily at the local or regional level often have not received a piece of the grant "pie." In recent years, however, even these have become noticeably stronger and more visible, in the final analysis also thanks to Western assistance, in the form of seminars organized by Russian specialists who themselves were taught by Americans or western European experts. In recent years, the system of administering aid by making subgrants to grassroots NGOs has become more widespread. Russian umbrella organizations allocate project funds based on a system of competitions, evaluations, and monitoring.

According to the latest research, the principal funding source for NGOs is Russian business, as well as in-kind support from local authorities, typically in the form of office space and discounts for utility services. Nonetheless, the large and well-known organizations, such as those mentioned above, continue to survive only on Western money, a situation that seems unlikely to change soon. It is on these umbrella organizations that the third sector critically depends. They train grassroots NGOs, prepare legislation, lobby state agencies, supply information, and publish textbooks and technical manuals. They make an invaluable contribution to the development of a professional community of third-sector organizations.

By "NGO community" we mean those organizations that not only exist on paper but function actively and see themselves as part of

Russia's third sector. They include human-rights defenders, ecologists, participants in the women's movement, philanthropic foundations helping various categories of the needy, associations of scholars and specialists, youth- and children-oriented NGOs, and recreation clubs. According to various experts, there are 50,000–60,000 such organizations in Russia. Ten years ago, many of them did not even exist, and those that did knew nothing about one another. Today, this is a real community united by common tasks and interests, with recognized leaders and even a professional jargon that outsiders cannot understand.

Herein lies both the strength and the weakness of the nonprofit sector. On the one hand, thanks to Western assistance, an NGO community has taken shape that has clearly recognized its own role and positioned itself in society. On the other hand, this community is becoming increasingly self-sufficient; rather than advancing genuine social change, it often concerns itself with the tactics of self-perpetuation. Moreover, a broad stratum of the population does not understand what the terms "third sector" and "nonprofit organization" mean. Many of these organizations themselves pay little attention to involving citizens in their work. They do not work systematically with volunteers and seldom engage in collecting private donations. To be sure, one can understand their dilemma. Just try to convince someone who is crushed by need and no longer believes in anything good to help out a public organization! On the other hand, however, an NGO in Russia will never become a real social force if it does not rely on citizens.

Of course, it will take years, perhaps decades, to change the consciousness of a people who for seventy years were told that public conduct should chiefly mean obedience to the regime. Russians have forgotten how to make decisions, to think through their own individual opinions, to say nothing of standing up for those opinions. But until people's consciousness changes and people accept personal responsibility, especially for ther own lives and those of their families but also for the society in which they live, we believe that serious economic growth will not begin in Russia.

In order to loosen the residual chains of post-Soviet thinking in Russia and encourage personal initiative and a sense of civic responsibility, we must involve the third sector more deeply. Here, Western assistance could play an invaluable role. Allocating funds for NGO projects designed to involve citizens in community problems can help, but new approaches are also needed. The time has come for other kinds of experts and technologies. Today, the Russian third sector no longer needs Western trainers for organizational development and strategic planning; by now these NGOs are fairly well developed and know how to plan their activities themselves. A new, but no less important, task is to involve citizens directly and work with them. We recognize and articulate this task more often now, but we are still unclear about how to do it.

At least one of the Russian third sector's accomplishments is clear: the formation of our own information space. Thanks to Western assistance, nonprofit organizations in our country pioneered the use of e-mail and then the Internet. Now hundreds of organizations scattered across our enormous country can gain access to information and have an inexpensive means of contacting each other. Today our information networks link women's and educational advocates, environmentalists, and human-rights activists. They exchange data and help shape public opinion. Witness, for example, the public campaigns led by human-rights activists and environmentalists in defense of the military journalist Gregorii Pasko, who was accused of espionage for having disseminated accurate information about radioactive waste contamination of the Pacific coast. Witness, too, the public campaign to change the tax code and help make NGOs more stable financially. Although relatively few NGO organizations have access to the Internet, the importance of this information resource cannot be underestimated.

The Social Information Agency (ASI), which we established in 1994, was expressly designed to inform the Russian public about successful initiatives taken by their fellow citizens. Elena describes the change in our lives in these words:

After perestroika began and life around me began to change in a decisive way, I felt the desire to undertake something serious myself, to stop being a cog in the political machine, a rank-and-file employee of a state organization. The first step I took was to resign from a large state publishing house, Russky Yazyk (Russian Language), and start working in the publishing department of Amstron, a joint Russian-American enterprise. This was an amusing period in my professional career. During those times of "wild" capitalism, Amstron was quite typical. It did everything from selling shoes to publishing books. There were two of us in the publishing department, and we had many plans, but we only managed to publish one pamphlet, *The Prophesies of Nostradamus*. What was most important for me was that I stopped being just an editor and independently learned all the stages of the book publishing business: editing, designing, printing, and distributing. It was unfamiliar and difficult, but incredibly exciting.

Later there were other jobs and other activities, for instance setting up a private business designing presentation materials and typesetting books. At the time, hardly anyone knew how to do this on the computer, so I had plenty of orders, and my husband Andrei and I, having begun working together for the first time, made a success of it.

For two years we both worked at the Postfactum information agency, where there was an unusual atmosphere of creativity and an extraordinary team of talented, intelligent, and bold journalists, editors, and managers. Together with the Interlegal philanthropic foundation, Postfactum published bulletins that discussed various areas of public life in Russia. I began editing one of them, *Philanthropy and Humanitarian Aid*. And so, for the first time, I came in contact with the world of nongovernmental organizations, without even being completely aware of what they were. Later, Interlegal consolidated all the bulletins into one publication called *The Third Sector*, which I was responsible for producing. Until then my work was essentially to select and summarize existing materials from the Postfactum information base. But now I had nothing ready-made; I had to figure out this third sector for myself and understand the real-life organizations that represented it.

This is where my fate was decided. The people I met along the way—the leaders of the most vital and active nonprofit organizations—turned my life around. I discovered for myself a completely new world that was inhabited by unusually interesting and passionate people who were excited about what they were doing. At the time it seemed to me that even outwardly they differed from others—they were so colorful and attractive, albeit quite varied. I immediately wanted to become part of this world and understand what brought these remarkable individuals together. Thus editing *The Third Sector* became a serious avocation and later my vocation.

After plunging into the world of Moscow NGOs and getting to know the foreign organizations then working in the capital, I finally made my choice—in favor of the third sector. I didn't want to be the only one to discover it; I wanted my fellow citizens, most of whom certainly had no suspicion of its existence, to find out as well. I got the idea of creating a specialized information agency (similar to Postfactum) that would inform the population through the press about the activities of Russian NGOs. Evidently the idea was timely, because some of my new colleagues were simultaneously thinking along the same lines, and the leaders I had met the year before backed it eagerly. From the very beginning, my husband Andrei also took an active part in the creation of what became ASI, the Social Information Agency. The directors of Postfactum at the time had no objections to creating ASI, using the Postfactum premises for office space, and in the fall of 1994 we began publishing weekly information bulletins and sending them out to the newspapers, television, and radio.

In October of that year ASI was officially registered as a nonprofit organization and I became its director; Andrei became codirector. Six months later we left the now moribund Postfactum and began our own separate existence. Today, ASI provides a weekly compilation of news and announcements for the media, weekly check-lists of issues for NGOs, information and analytical bulletins on acute social topics, coverage of regular public activities for journalists and activists in the third sector, and roundtables and press conferences. ASI works with its fifteen branches in the regions of Russia and maintains contacts with partners in Russian cities and abroad.

ASI's principal means of disseminating news is e-mail and the Internet. Strange as it may seem, the new media still relies on old-fashioned radio for disseminating information. Many surveys, especially in the provinces, show that because of price increases for print media, radio is becoming an increasingly popular source of information, and not only for the socially vulnerable strata of the population. In this regard television is less important, since TV news programs focus on major political and economic events, while the broadcast networks feature entertainment. Taking these factors into account, ASI recently took part in two projects aimed at radio listeners. The first, conducted jointly with Radio Russia, envisages a series of radio broadcasts on the defense of human rights. The second, produced together with the BBC, is a cycle of radio shows involving representatives of regional NGOs and professional journalists.

*   *   *

ASI reports on initiatives and how nonprofit organizations are putting them into practice. What is a civil society? Very simple. It is a society of *citizens*—people who take an active public stance, defend their rights, have their own position and articulate it, and monitor the actions of those in positions of power. We feel that a civil society will take shape in Russia only when there are a critical number of such Russians. The nonprofit organizations must help achieve this goal. At the moment there are only individuals, many of whom are in fact leaders of NGOs—but they are not transmitting their activism to others; they are not attracting and training people who share their ideas.

It is our deep conviction that the main public function of an NGO is to educate citizens, to assist them in formulating and defending their rights and bringing their demands before the authorities, and to render the most effective assistance to people in need by mobilizing human resources. Unfortunately, the third sector in Russia today is fulfilling this function to only a very limited extent. In part, this is the reason for the absence of a civil society.

Everyone now realizes that a return to the totalitarian past is impossible. Slowly but surely, the Russian ship of state is changing course in order to follow the same direction that all civilized countries are following. However, the absence of democratic traditions that characterizes Russia's history (and not just its recent past) will long be a brake on progress. In order to provide for a better future, it is not enough to elect a government that enjoys the trust and support of the majority in society. Mechanisms for the smooth transition of presidential and governmental administrations, and for effective civil oversight over the functioning of government, must be worked out precisely. In addition, in a country where there have always been too many good laws that were never executed, new generations of citizens must come to respect the law and guard democratic values as the natural basis for civil life. And in this process, the third sector will play a decisive role.

14

ON THE PATH TO
A NEW RUSSIA

The Youth Movement

Nadia Seriakova

Russia. The end of the twentieth century. What names will historians eventually find to designate this period!

Every society has a set of accepted or inherited basic ideas that determine public morality, relations among people, and the government's policy toward other states. When linked to a propaganda system, these basic ideas become an ideology.

The basic idea that determined the path of the Russian people for almost 150 years was the idea of revolutionary violence. Today new ideas are gradually germinating, and the soil is being prepared so that they can bear fruit.

Russia's young people define current times as an era of contrasts.

Democracy in Russia "happened" suddenly, as did so much else in the past decade. The people who had lived for many years in a Com-

After graduating from Culture University with a degree in arts administration in 1990, **Nadezhda (Nadia) Aleksandrovna Seriakova** worked in the Soviet Ministry of Culture. In 1993 she became a program manager in the Moscow office of the International Republican Institute, an American organization, and eventually became its executive director. In 1995 Seriakova founded the New Perspectives Foundation, which she now heads. She also works with the International Foundation for Electoral Systems, a group providing technical assistance to countries organizing democratic elections. Translated by Antonina W. Bouis.

munist space awoke one day to find that they had been duped. The West believes that everyone in the Soviet Union had a hand in building communism. But every day, normal life went on in the Soviet Union, with all its joys and sorrows. It was the usual routine. The average Soviet citizen, whatever position he held, would not wake up in the morning and say to himself, "Good morning! I'm off to build communism."

I consider myself part of the generation of Russians who managed to grow up under two different systems. What did I get from my "Communist past?" My childhood Pioneer Youth organization provided good training for life, strangely enough. I believed in what I did, but there wasn't a word of Communist propaganda in it. The Pioneer organization in my school, which I headed, did honor the memory of the heroes who had died in the Great Patriotic War, and our various subgroups were named for them. But there wasn't anything Communist about it. We helped old people, cleaned streets, learned to sing, read poems, and wrote poems of our own. Does it all seem so rosy because it's part of my childhood?

When I grew older, my friends and I pondered changing the course of our lives. Since we had no other historical experience, we dreamed of a revolution that would bring us something new. What bothered us most was the absolute predictability of life in our country. We all knew what would happen after graduation, where we would work, and even what our salaries would be.

We didn't have a serious understanding of what democracy was. The world was divided into two unequal parts: our socialist part and the capitalist remainder. We couldn't imagine that life could be worthier in that other world, solidly hidden by the heavy, creaking curtain.

Perestroika meant so much—and yet there was nothing comprehensible about it. "Freedom" was bandied about in every square. From whom or for what? We weren't slaves. The only thing I remembered during all those years from my early childhood was my parents listening at night to the Voice of America and secretly talking about Andrei Sakharov. They asked me never to tell anyone about those conversations. I didn't even understand them.

Young people felt the avalanche of democracy with even greater force. Just imagine the situation. A growing child, living in a family, loving her parents. One fine day she's told the truth, that she's not related, that these are not her parents at all. For a start, they suggest changing her surname. What happens to such a child? What feelings should she have? At best, hatred and anger, emotions that make her apathetic and incapable of trust for a long time. This is what happened to our youth. The homeland we loved became alien to us overnight. To trust and love a new homeland—can that be possible in such a short time?

The seeds of democracy fell on infertile soil. It's like sowing wheat in the winter in the snow. Of course, the seeds will germinate sometime, but they won't be as well tended or evenly planted as expected. I am absolutely certain that this eminently just idea of democracy was doomed from the start in Russia, for one simple reason—people had never known anything about it. (I don't mean democracy in the philosophic sense.) It will take time, perhaps several more years, for the idea to be accepted in our country, for people to see for themselves, to listen and read about the possibilities inherent in democracy, to understand its reality.

But instead, we had what we had. "Everything was upside down in the Oblonsky household . . ." Truth turned out to be brazen falsehood, freedom a free-for-all, and civic rights an expensive commodity. The talk was only of price. People quickly remembered the formulas like "commodity is money is commodity," and things got going. Now, the situation did not depend on a person's natural abilities (nor had it in the past, come to that). Everything could be bought, and just as easily sold.

Probably no other country in the world can explain so logically the concept of "selling air." A few months after the collapse of the Soviet Union, while looking for work, I took a job "selling air." It wasn't very profitable. I never saw the goods, the sellers, or the buyers; my job was to know who wanted to buy what and who owned it. I had constant calls from sellers: "There are several carloads of sugar at this price," and I would write the information down in a notebook, under the heading "Sugar." There were similar offers there already, and my task was to find the cheapest prices. Then buyers called who urgently needed metal. I didn't have a notebook heading like that, but I knew a lot of people who had information on those goods. And so on, till I got a headache. I'm still not sure if any of my sellers sold what they had, or if even one of the purchasers found what he needed. Or whether they had actually had what they wanted to sell.

Real Democracy

For me, real Democracy began in 1993, when quite accidentally I was asked to organize a seminar in Khabarovsk for the International Republican Institute of the United States. I had never been to Khabarovsk and I didn't know anyone there, but my organizational zeal performed miracles. The seminar didn't turn out that badly at all; there were six Americans and about forty local democrats. The seminar topic, how to organize political parties, had been explained to us earlier. The American consultants related their experiences and the Russian participants learned and adapted what they heard.

Thus I became a staff member of the Institute and later its executive director. The three years I worked there I recall with great warmth; I consider them the years in which I became a citizen of my new homeland—Russia.

In those years, American participation in these kinds of programs was welcomed. The opportunity to have contact, ask questions, and speak openly soaked down like moisture into parched soil. Of course, the American experience was not always appropriate to our conditions. But those who could hear, heard; and those who could accumulate ideas, did. The rest complained quietly that it was useless.

The many questions that I heard during those years at the seminars boiled down to one: "Why are you Americans coming to Russia and doing this?" Really, it wasn't that easy to understand why people would travel so far to help build democracy in Russia. Wasn't it easier to stay home in your big house, where there were no problems and you didn't have to risk your money or your reputation? One American friend told me about herself. In the bygone days of the Cold War, when Americans didn't even think about friendship with Russia, she had asked herself, "Who are these scary Russians? Can they really be so inhuman?" The Russian classic novels had astonished her with their humanity and profound philosophy. However, this only added to her incomprehension of the Russian soul. Then she decided to learn Russian. Neither her parents nor her teachers could understand this passion for all things Russian. It must have been an act of youthful protest, when adolescents act differently from everyone else and find meaning in their rebellion.

We met in Moscow, and I was stunned by her fluency in Russian and her ability to invent words. It was in the fall and we were traveling by train to a distant Siberian city. "This is my favorite time of year," I said, "except for the slush." The Russian word for slush ends like an infinitive verb, and she decided that it *was* a verb, which she then proceeded to conjugate most amusingly.

"When I am a grownup woman, and I have my own children and grandchildren, I will tell them who the Russians are. And for sure, neither I, nor my family, nor my descendants will ever live in such alienation from Russia." That was my friend's reply to the question, "Why do you do this?" This may be the simple answer that makes it possible to understand. If not, so be it.

Formation of Civil Society

Two years ago I returned to my university to write a dissertation on youth and its participation in civil society. My interests focused on the civil education of young people, which my foundation works on to this day. However, I was very surprised by the conclusion of a certain philosophy professor: that there was no such concept as "civil education" in Russia. This discouraged me greatly. What was I doing, then?

In fact, if you ask my peers, people on the street, older people, about civil society, you will hear a thousand different answers. And not because people are removed from the topic. The reason is the same. The Russian people have no basic concept of democracy.

It seems fairly obvious. There is a nation-state where people are organized into various societies; these societies have problems that someone has to solve; and these "someones" indeed exist. There's just one thing left to do: identify the people who can be entrusted with solving the problems. Easy enough to say.

In Russia, this stage has not yet been reached. Only one thing has been understood: It pays to be among the chosen. But no one, even among the chosen, is interested in actually solving problems. In this preelection era, and you can't call it anything else in Russia, people somehow got hooked by those who wanted to become parliamentary deputies. And those running for office even knew all the Western techniques of enticing voters. Everything seemed quite proper. Groups of potential voters were studied, their problems defined, dialogues between candidates and voters organized, promises made, and so on. On election day the deputy still remembered his voters, some even wrote thank-you notes, just in case they should run again. And then this delicate connection was severed.

But I would not rush to blame those who were elected to high office for the fragility of the connection. Everyone realizes that the problems that come along with high office, the level of responsibility that falls like a heavy burden on the shoulders of the newly elected official, do not allow him to think constantly about his electorate. He has to deal with much more important matters.

Democracy cannot be established on the basis of holding elections alone. There are quite a few examples in history of a dictatorship coming on the heels of an election. From the point of view of civil society, political freedom rests on the citizens' broad exercise of their social and civil freedoms and on the existence of deep-rooted values of freedom and self-confidence. For these values to be strong, people must be able to make a free choice and voluntarily take on responsibility, based on their social and civil priorities. Democracy flowers in those countries where the law effectively protects the right of citizens to enter into associations with each other in the name of common civil goals and to form groups that reflect their common opinions, values, and interests.

The civil society that my colleagues and I are building, and trying to protect, has itself not yet understood what it needs. I do not refer to the nongovernmental organizations (NGOs) working in our country today. They deserve to have monuments erected in praise of the work they have done, under incredibly severe conditions, just to exist, to defend the rights of a certain segment of society, and at the same time to defend democracy.

There are obvious difficulties in the development of civil society in Russia today. The main problems include:

- dependence on external financing, which compromises independent action and the responsibility of the organizations' members;
- inadequate dissemination of information and communications technologies, which hampers the development of networks;
- the low level of social capital necessary for effective operations by democratic NGOs; and
- insufficient guarantees of constitutional rights, such as freedom of speech, the press, assembly, and association, which hamper the activity of independent NGOs.

The last problem may seem farfetched, but only because the concept of freedom of speech in our country has been turned into the concept of "everything is permitted." Only the lazy do not berate the government, the parliament, and the president for being the cause of all of Russia's ills. Of course, there are plenty of problems, but blaming them all only on officials at the highest levels of government is not fair—if only because we elected them. That is the paradox of democracy that we stubbornly refuse to accept.

The rest of the problems are obvious. We depend on foreign sources of financing. It is absurd to try to explain to others how non-commercial structures survive in Russia. And one more thing. Everyone who works in a noncommercial organization comes to realize that what he does is needed by no one but himself. It was with that thought that I went to a meeting of partners in the International Youth Foundation in the Philippines in the fall of 1999, where I met many people working for the good of their civil societies. Nani, a young woman from India, had a simple answer to my moaning. "Fine, but it's very good that you are doing what you need to do. That means you are happy." Perhaps that is the truth. I am doing what I need to do, first and foremost, and I am happy.

On the Path to a New Russia

People are so made that they like to tie the most important events to certain dates. It is unlikely that you don't know anyone who hasn't said at least once, "On Monday I will stop smoking," or "On New Year's Day I will start a new life," or something like that. The new millennium is even more appropriate for new beginnings and resolutions. How lucky we are to be born at the cusp not only of two centuries but of two millennia! Naturally, we can't get by without a little drama.

Our organization decided to keep up with the epochal inspiration and organize something global. We deal with the civil education of youth; according to the rules of distribution of universal duties, we ought to be leading youth into the new millennium. We appointed ourselves in charge of that, because we needed to do it.

We called our undertaking "On the Path to a New Russia"—a symbolic transition of young people into a New Russia, the new millennium. For a start, we created a virtual "youth state," with all the attributes of a civilized government: its own seal and flag, constitution, government and parliament, and, naturally, president. We even had our own anthem and our own currency. And to convince ourselves even more, we gathered 150 young people from all over Russia and marched from Moscow to a city with the lovely name of Novorossiisk (or New Russia).

I must say that preparations for the march took several months. We had to study the route thoroughly, select the participants, send out letters, coordinate our presence with local authorities, buy tickets, make arrangements for hotels and food, and, most importantly, come up with the content of the program. For that, we convened the "new government," which included, besides the principal staffers of our foundation in Moscow, representatives from regional structures; in other words, young people from other cities. This was a very good opportunity to work together as a team. And the first thing we did together was to determine the ten most important problems of young people in Russia.

There are plenty of problems, but the most serious for young people are: crime, inadequate education, drugs, unemployment, lack of money, lack of recreational opportunities, poor health care, prostitution, a poor human rights record, and the lack of a clear national identity. This list includes problems that we inherited from the former regime as well as problems that have appeared quite recently. Crime continues to be seen as a suitable alternative to education, drugs stifle health, money is incompatible with unemployment, entertainment is too expensive, prostitution demands legalization, and the new homeland remains an alien place for most young people. Not the lightest of baggage.

In our youth state, it was clear, we would try to avoid the mistakes and errors we observed in Russia. Therefore, in devising the political structure of our state, we decided to free ourselves once and for all from any state-imposed priorities. We had to start somewhere, for instance by forming political parties that would propose their candidates for the parliament. But since we were starting from square one, and since our state had no history, we decided to let the computer do it.

Of the 150 participants in the march, the computer first selected three leaders who were tasked with organizing political parties. The leaders were given equal opportunities to contact the other participants, both through the media and directly, to persuade them to join their parties; to gather signatures; and to register their parties. And when this process ended with a division of all the citizens into three parties, we headed off on our route, first by plane from Moscow to Krasnodar, in the south of Russia. And then along the coast of the Black Sea to our dreamland: New Russia.

All sorts of things happened along the way. The youth state went through various stages. Every day we lived through several years. Our full schedule quickly cut the participants off from real life; after the first day, people began confusing reality with the game. At first it seemed part of the game that every young person received a loan from the state in the amount of one thousand "hopes" (the name of our currency). When the state tried to collect its first taxes, however, everyone thought of this as reality. It seemed funny at first that radio and television showed only youth news, but when the election battles started, the participants had no time for jokes; they had to fight for real candidates. They approved the constitution jokingly, too; but when the president was the first to violate it, the citizens protested in all seriousness.

The elected parliament started writing real laws, based on the real needs of the youth state. Behind this difficult game stood the harsh truth: We were presenting our demands to real politicians; they couldn't overlook our interests, blow off the country's youth, trick us with their sweet promises. We were different. The new times demanded that from us. Even though the capabilities of those we elected were fictional, we could not abandon our hopes for greater opportunities in the new millennium, in the New Russia.

You may ask, and what are those hopes? They probably involve Russia's mastery of democracy. At least to begin to understand it.

The Future

And what will the New Russia be like? What awaits us all in the future? We continue to be the same old dreamers, who link the "future" with the "beautiful." People can't give up their dreams. No matter how hard it may be today, no matter what suffering people must bear, they hope for something better.

Many years ago, I read in *Hour of the Bull,* by the great Russian science fiction writer Ivan Efremov, that the disciplines that will transmit basic values into the future will be mainly teaching and medicine. Medicine, because people will wish to be physically healthy; and teaching, because more attention will be paid to people's education and upbringing. I think that this time has already arrived. Today, more than ever, it is crucial for people to be harmonious. It is impossible to speak of a beautiful future if it is mutilated by poisonous flaws, whether physical or spiritual. Someone who is given the opportunity to witness the world, to create it, to enjoy it, simply to live, cannot continue to scorn his chances.

We truly are lucky. We are very lucky to be born in these times. Historians studying our age will write and rewrite history a thousand times, endowing our contemporaries with capabilities and flaws that will be understandable only to later generations. I am absolutely certain that among the many words that will be spoken about our times, there will be words that define us as people who had common sense and who strove for freedom and love. May that be so.

15

Empowering Russia's Women

Will Their Potential Be Tapped?

Nadezhda Azhgikhina

I recall very clearly my first conversation in Moscow with a University of Pittsburgh professor, Helena Goscilo. It was 1989. All intellectual Moscow was discussing the latest political sensation in the monthly journals *Ogonyok* and *Znamia*; a civil war in literature raged between the "westernizers" and the traditionalist "village prose" writers; and the air was charged with the desire for change and renewal. We talked of the new Russian women's prose. Helena was finishing a book on Russian women writers; and I had just written an article on new and interesting women authors. She asked about the prospects of the women's movement in Russia. I told her that I saw no future for it: Women had suffered as much as men under the totalitarian state; all the problems of my female peers would be solved with the coming of democracy and a free-market economy. I was utterly certain that I was right—just like

After completing studies for a doctorate in literature from Moscow State University, **Nadezhda Il'inichna Azhgikhina** worked as writer and editor for the national daily *Komsomol'skaya pravda* in the 1980s and for the weekly magazine *Ogonyok* in the early 1990s. Since 1996 she has been a correspondent for the daily *Nezavisimaya gazeta,* where she is editor of the women's issues column. Active in the international women's movement, Azhgikhina cofounded the Association of Women Journalists and has written numerous books and articles on Russian politics, culture, and society. Translated by Antonina W. Bouis.

most of my colleagues, friends, and peers. We did not simply *hope* that democratization would bring everyone happiness, we would not concede that it could be any other way. My new American acquaintance warned me, though, that when it came to equal rights between men and women, I should not overestimate what democracy could accomplish.

Thereafter I had many discussions with women in Russia and the United States, as well as at international conferences on women held in Cairo, Beijing, Delhi, and Toronto. In each debate, discussion, and chance encounter, I discovered new facets of the problem.

Today, I have to agree with my American friend: Even in a democratic state, much more work is required if the idea of equality of the sexes is to become a reality. It turns out that the transition to democracy in postcommunist states takes eccentric and unexpected forms; gender inequality can become even stronger, quite markedly so. For Russia, in particular, "the women's issue" is a litmus test of reforms.

Over the past decade in Russia an independent women's movement has emerged that joins in debates on the most important public policy issues and helps improve the lot of women. In 1998, according to Ministry of Justice data, there were more than 600 women's organizations registered in the country. Another statistic may be more telling: In 1998 alone, more than 40,000 public associations were registered in the Russian Federation. And according to experts, at least two-thirds of all nongovernmental organizations, even though they may not specifically call themselves women's NGOs, deal with issues relating to the lives of women and have memberships consisting primarily of women.

Today, every major Russian city has several dozen organizations drawing together hundreds and thousands of women of varying age, status, and education. Almost every region of the country, from the Baltic Sea to Vladivostok, has a well-developed network tied into the women's movement, itself a sign of a new democratic era in Russian society. This phenomenon has received (and still receives) very mixed reactions, ranging from the delight of its activist proponents and comrades-in-arms to the open skepticism of its adversaries, coupled with assertions that feminism in any form is alien to Russian soil and that the new movement is nothing more than an artificial Western graft.

In fact, however, an attentive look at Soviet and post-Soviet history in Russia shows that the women's movement, and "Russian feminism" as one component of it, have long traditions, are profoundly unique, and have great potential.

The Sources and Meaning of Russian Feminism

Works on the history of women in Russia are rare. One of the best is Richard Stite's study of women revolutionaries and nihilists of the nineteenth and early twentieth centuries, *The Women's Liberation Movement in Russia: Feminism, Nihilism, and Bolshevism*. The first Russian compendium on the topic (Svetlana Aivazova's *Russkie zhenshchiny v labirinte ravnopraviya* [Russian Women in the Labyrinth of Equality]) saw light only in 1999, while Mariia Ktovskaya's monograph on the place of women in Russian history is still in preparation. Although most scholars of the Soviet period paid little attention to the topic, almost all contemporary historical sources confirm that women have always played significant roles in Russia's public life. For example, Princess Olga, the first Russian ruler to embrace Christianity, left a vivid mark on Russian life and promulgated a series of wide-ranging reforms. Princesses and women boyars participated in the rule of principalities and the political struggles accompanying feudal internecine warfare. Some historians note that as Christianity took hold in ancient Rus', women gradually became recluses, isolated from social activity. Other historians stress that their isolation followed the establishment of the Tatar yoke: The *Domostroi* codified the submissive position of women and their separation from family property rights, also justifying the need to punish them should they disobey the head of the family. For several centuries, the phrase "the wife shall fear her husband" was an axiom. The *Domostroi* provided detailed descriptions of the punishments to be imposed upon disobedient wives. The tradition of being sequestered in the *terem,* the women's part of the house, continued until the reforms of Peter the Great. Among other radical innovations, Peter made mandatory the presence of noblemen's wives and daughters at court social occasions ("assemblies"). It was only later, during the reign of Catherine the Great, that the first school for young ladies of the nobility (known as the Smolny Institute for Noble Maidens) was opened in St. Petersburg, together with its counterpart school for daughters of the bourgeoisie.

That same period saw the first woman to be elected president of the Russian Academy of Sciences, Ekaterina Dashkova, one of the most illustrious representatives of the Russian enlightenment, the publisher of the best journal of the period, *Sobesednik liubitelei rossiiskogo slova* (Interlocutor for Lovers of Russian Writing), and a brilliant memoirist as well. Many aristocratic ladies of the era liked to wear male garb; others, like the empresses Anna Ioannovna, Elizaveta Petrovna, and Catherine the Great, liked to hunt. The historian Mariia Kotovskaia points out that the eighteenth century presented an image of women that combined social brilliance and ambitious mannishness. That century also gave rise to yet another image, that of the professional woman serving typically as a governess or actress.

Many scholars consider the true predecessors of Russian feminists to be the wives of the Decembrists (conspirators who in 1825 sought to limit the Russian monarchy). These women followed their husbands into exile and hard labor in Siberia; their selflessness inspired more than one generation of writers and researchers. However, it would be difficult to speak of a struggle for women's emancipation in the early or even the mid-nineteenth century. Society saw woman primarily as a helpmate for man, as mother and educator of children. All activity outside this stereotyped framework met with public condemnation. Even the creative work of women writers and artists elicited suspicion among intellectuals. Some specialists (for instance, Svetlana Aivazova) consider Alexander Pushkin, who praised free love in his narrative poem *Aleko,* a proponent of relative independence for women.

The question of women's emancipation came up on the agenda only during the political debates of the 1860s. The first bourgeois reforms were maturing in Russia; many minor estates of the nobility were going bankrupt; and young women from aristocratic families had to find jobs or professions, because working was the only way that many of these women could feed their families. Women's education and their right to work were the topics of the day. Almost every journal of literary and social commentary, as well as outstanding writers in every field, paid great attention to the status of women, the family, and family relations. The points of view expressed were extremely varied. Works of fiction depicted very different types, ranging from romantic heroines, model mothers, and passionate lovers prepared to share the torments of hell with their beloved, to independent, active women.

Interestingly, it was men who first defended women's equality in Russia. In 1860, *Sovremennik* magazine published an article by the critic Mikhailov entitled "Women: Their Education and Significance in the Family and Society," which for the first time formulated the concept of sexual equality. Dmitrii Pisarev and Nikolai Chernyshevskii, among others, took up the themes. Pisarev's phrase "A woman isn't guilty of anything" became popular. Chernyshevskii declared that women had the right not only to education and work but even to free love; he depicted a working women's commune as a prototype of the happy future.

Discussions about equality were a sign of the times. Major scholars like Botkin, Pirogov, and Sechenov defended the idea of education and professional activity for women.

Aivazova considers that the active participation of men was the most significant factor defining the importance of Russian feminism in the nineteenth century. Herein lay the fundamental difference between Russian feminism and European feminism, which was formed in the whirlwind of bourgeois revolutions. Aivazova writes:

> After the French Revolution, women found themselves stripped of those rights which men had won for themselves, and that gave the impetus to feminism in France. In the middle of the nineteenth century in Russia, by contrast, neither men nor women had bourgeois freedoms; men together with women fought for the right of women to education and work as the start of civil independence for everyone.

The first female students were enthusiastically welcomed by the democratic community. Periodicals conveyed a new image, that of a woman student who was notably modest in dress and in manner, serious, and focused. Of course, the idea had its opponents—the legislation of 1861 blocked women's access to the universities. But in 1870 the government gave permission to introduce advanced curricula for women in the main university cities. In 1878, thanks to the efforts of four selfless fighters for women's equality, Mariia Trubnikova, Anna Filosofova, Nadezhda Stasova, and Elena Beketova, the doors opened at the Besstuzhevskie Higher Women's Courses in St. Petersburg. It was here that Russia's first female teachers and doctors were educated.

Some women went to Europe to study. Among the first was Nadezhda Suslova, who received a diploma as a doctor of surgery and midwifery in Zurich. Others, like the mathematician Sofia Kovalevskaia, entered into fictitious marriages in order to continue their education abroad.

The idea of women's emancipation comported well with the revolutionary mood in the second half of the century. Many young women from bankrupt noble families became nihilists, workers in garment factories, members of the radical People's Will organization, or members of other revolutionary circles. The largest revolutionary organization, Land and Liberty, counted eighteen women among its members; in the 1870s women made up almost 20 percent of all revolutionaries and were represented in almost all the secret organizations. Sofia Perovskaia was the first woman to be executed in Russia on political charges; Vera Figner spent a twenty-year sentence in solitary confinement in the Shlisselburg Fortress; Vera Zasulich opened fire at the chief of the St. Petersburg police; and Mariia Spiridonova later headed the Social Revolutionary Party.

Their contemporaries remembered these women revolutionaries as obsessed, uncompromising, and fearless. They are probably the only activists demanding the full participation of women in society who were written about during Soviet times.

But there were other women of whom my peers knew nothing. Often these were profoundly pious women, high-ranking noblewomen, or women from wealthy merchant families. They were united by the desire to do charitable works and help their neighbors. Many women became well known as philanthropists and sisters of mercy, creating communities all over Russia, caring for the elderly and the sick, arranging shelter for single mothers, and helping fight epidemics.

By the time of the 1905 revolution, thousands of women were working in village schools, hospitals, factories, and other enterprises. Civil and political rights became part of women's agenda.

The First All-Russian Women's Congress convened over a thousand delegates from throughout the country in St. Petersburg in December 1908. Besides Anna Shabanova (a professional doctor and confirmed feminist), the other organizers included Olga Shapir, a popular author, and Anna Filosofova, a public activist and defender of women's rights. The congress delegates represented the entire political spectrum. They included Ariadna Tyrkova, a member of the Central Committee of the Constitutional Democratic Party; Mariia Spiridonova, the "Social Revolutionary Madonna"; and Alexandra

Kollontai, a Social Democrat. Hereditary noblewomen as well as simple laborers came to discuss the economic and civil condition of women and the functions of women's organizations. The main resolution under debate concerned equal voting rights for women. Passions ran so high that police observers at one point forbade further discussion. In any event, a unified position eluded the congress. The workers group headed by Kollontai walked out, claiming that it was impossible for the proletarian women to cooperate with members of the bourgeoisie.

The congress had enormous resonance. Politicians reacted with either delight or outrage. Contemporaries had to admit that "the public's opinion of women has changed." In 1910, another women's congress was convened in St. Petersburg, the First All-Russian Congress Against the Selling of Women. The First All-Russian Congress on Education for Women took place in that city in 1912. The Second All-Russian Women's Congress, planned for 1913, did not take place. In 1917, Anna Shabanova finally achieved the creation of a national woman's organization, the All-Russian Women's Council— but by then there was no time left for it to function. The last echo of the congress was heard on March 19, 1917, when 40,000 St. Petersburg women marched through the streets of their city (by then called Petrograd) demanding equal political rights. Among the organizers were the famous feminists Shabanova, Tyrkova, and Mariia Pokrovskaia, as well as Poliksena Shishkova-Iavein and Countess Sofia Panina of the All-Russian Equality League. These events led to the declaration by the Provisional Government of universal political emancipation without limitation as to gender.

The Grip of the Soviet Myth

As one of its first legislative acts upon taking power in 1917, the Soviet regime proclaimed the equality of men and women in all areas of economic, political, and cultural life. The regime sanctioned abortion in the early 1920s. Thousands of Russian women left the villages to work on construction sites set up for the Five Year Plans, enter universities, and train as activists and agitators for building a socialist society. Many women from western Europe and North America rushed to take part in the "great socialist experiment," inspired by the ideals of equality. However, the position of women under the first years of Soviet rule disclosed the flip side of revolutionary transformations: the yawning gap between declarations and reality, between promises and daily life, foreshadowing the basic political contradictions in Russia and later the USSR.

Soviet laws on equal rights and women's capabilities were probably the most progressive in the world in the 1920s. But mechanisms for guaranteeing equality were never developed. In fact, for many decades the Soviet woman had to bear a double burden. On the one hand, she was required to work, master men's professions, and participate in mandatory public political activities. On the other hand, once she returned home she had play the traditional role of wife and mother. Social experiments—communal kitchens, workers' dormitory communes, and other innovations of the 1920s—soon became history, as did the discussions of the 1920s on freedom of creativity, free love, and freedom in general. The state became more harsh and totalitarian. The government needed cheap labor, thus women working on construction sites served its interests.

At the same time, transmitting ideas on women's emancipation developed by the educated classes (whether liberal or revolutionary) to a population of millions of primarily illiterate peasants required a long period of planning and preparation. A law passed in the 1920s required nothing more from a husband than to mail a postcard to his wife in order to get divorced. Thousands of men then decided to divorce their wives, but no one had thought to prepare a social safety net for abandoned or pregnant women and their children. The law did not last long. In the 1930s, as a result of the "leveling" of Party leadership, political repressions, and the consolidation of dictatorship, a peasant patriarchal lifestyle began to take root. It was also in the 1930s that abortion was banned (until Stalin's death in 1953), on the grounds that population growth had declined. Soon thereafter, divorce became more difficult, and a citizen's personal life fell under the intense scrutiny of state and Party organs.

Nevertheless, Stalin's Constitution of 1937 declared that the total equality of men and women had been achieved. All the achievements of the prerevolutionary feminists disappeared from the history books, feminism was pronounced a bourgeois deviation, and the Party's policy became the only correct line. The politburo decreed that official women's departments be established in every region, replacing all other women's initiatives (no nongovernmental, public organizations were possible then, of course). In later Soviet years, these departments were reconstituted as divisions of the Union of

Soviet Women, designed (like the Young Pioneers and the Komsomol) as leashes to the government and schools for training female members of the nomenklatura. Actually, many of those who worked in the local women's departments (all on the state payroll, of course) did try to help women who applied for aid. But in general, the public regarded women's departments as another set of feeding troughs for the nomenklatura that grew to inordinate size during the Leonid Brezhnev years.

Opinions diverge about the meaning of Soviet policy on women's issues. Among the liberal intelligentsia of the Brezhnev period there was the feeling that the very idea of women's emancipation was a great mistake, a violation of a woman's "natural predestination." Unfortunately, many reformers of the post-Soviet period also held this view.

The first article on women's issues written in the perestroika spirit, characteristically entitled "How Are We Solving the Women's Issue?" appeared in the journal *Kommunist* in 1989. The authors, Natal'ia Rimashevskaya, Natal'ia Zakharova, and Anastasia Posadskaia, contended that all undertakings aimed at defining the position of Russian women were paternalistic in nature, by definition consigning women to passive, dependent roles. In their opinion, a Russian woman was doubly humiliated by a "postsocialist patriarchal renaissance," which had in turn been derived from an unjust division of gender roles during the Soviet period. Another scholar, Elena Zdravomyslova, is convinced that the Soviet regime had drawn up something like a secret pact with Russia's women: The woman in a family conflict was as a rule supported by society, and women received family benefits and quotas in representative bodies; whereas men in the social structure were regarded as second-class citizens, dependent at work on the boss and the Party representative, and at home on the all-powerful wife.

But I do not believe that it is just an issue of paternalism or some secret pact. The utopian experiment undertaken in the USSR over a lengthy period of time presupposed a fundamentally new type of relationship among people, between citizens and the state, between the ordinary man and local officials.

For decades, millions of Russian men and women believed sincerely—and sometimes fanatically—in the justice of what was happening to them and the people around them. This hardly could have

been possible without the unique chimera known as the Great Soviet Myth. In *How I Understand Philosophy,* the renowned philosopher Merab Mamardashvili describes the character of the Soviet citizen, yearning for "paternal" advice and fearing to make
independent decisions or engage in personal reflections. This special
psychological type was hewn out of the great purges of 1937–1938,
the cruelties of war, and the constant efforts of the best Soviet
artists and writers, directors, and journalists. The Great Soviet
Myth gave rise to another reality-replacing phenomenon—the
"word factory" that produced millions of books and other works,
and that penetrated everywhere. For example, the film *Cossacks of
the Kuban* depicted a land of abundance at the very time that postwar Russia was starving.

The Great Soviet Myth would not have been so powerful and
could not have supported the monstrous state machine if it had not
had at its heart the Myth of the Soviet Woman. It was she who
achieved supreme harmony by building a glorious future, she who
was free to accept or reject men, as Liubov' Orlova's heroine did in
the film *The Circus*. The most celebrated works of Soviet literature
fashioned new mythological interpretations: The "mother of a hero"
(Maxim Gorky's novel); the classical heroine who chooses duty over
love (Trenev's *Liubov' Iarovaia*); and the romantic girlfriend of the
dying protagonist fighting for a better life (Nikolai Ostrovsky's *How
the Steel Was Tempered*). Such works, and their innumerable, and
feebler, imitations, show how the traditional plot in Russian classical
literature, revolving around relationships between spouses or lovers,
is replaced by the daughter-father conflict—where the father can be
Comrade Stalin, the Soviet secret police, the army, or indeed the entire nation. Instead of promising his daughter a spectral and
ephemeral union with a man, the father offers her a chance to provide noble service on behalf of the grand endeavor to create paradise; moreover, he is prepared to adopt all Russia's children and
transform them into heroes.

Is it then surprising that thousands of women who endured difficult lives, who lost their husbands or never found them during the
years of political terror and war, believed in this myth—sacrificing
their strength for the restoration of the ruined economy, learning to
operate new equipment, and losing their hearing in factories and
mills? The myth served to mobilize people toward achieving the

state's goals. And in fact, it manipulated the consciousness and the lives of men no less than those of women. Only in a different way.

Some people feel that Soviet rule hurt women and gave them nothing good, that everything introduced by the Revolution was artificial and unimportant. This is not so. If we look at history with an unprejudiced eye, we see that Soviet legislation really was the most advanced and consistent in terms of declaring sexual equality. Women truly did receive significant quotas as elected officials—as many as 30 percent of parliamentarians were women. Women truly did hold management positions, received free education, and used the services of a wide network of children's day-care institutions (which, incidentally, like all similar institutions in the social sphere, had been established before the Revolution by Russian activists and feminists). Women in the Central Asian republics truly were freed from many centuries-old prejudices; they could remove their veils. Women truly had guaranteed vacations and social benefits, particularly in the final years of the Soviet period.

True, no woman ever headed the state in the Soviet Union, and only a few women served at the highest levels of government. It is also true that the 30 percent of parliamentarians who were women were just as obedient as the other 70 percent in the totalitarian system. And it is true that very few medieval traditions were abolished, and that our most educated women were paid very low salaries. The leaders of the perestroika era, had they been wise, could have analyzed social policy with respect to men and women and supported a creative reformulation of everything of value that had been done. But that did not happen. The leaders of the country, like the rest of its citizens, were hostages of the myth—they were turned inside out.

In one form or another, the Soviet myth lasted right up until perestroika. But then it cracked. Alternative images of men and women appeared in literature, movies, and the public consciousness. Young writers (Vasilii Aksenov, Anatolii Gladilin, Vladimir Voinovich, and others) created characters different from the usual activists, shock workers, and "girls with a temper" by introducing feminine and sexy girls who were interested not in politics but in clothes. The "village school" writers (including Valentin Rasputin, Vasilii Belov, and Viktor Astaf'ev) offered the ideal of a peasant woman bound to patriarchal society and living a natural life, like a tree or a cow, and having no interest in social life for its own sake. Both images sparked lively debate in the 1960s and 1970s, representing as they did opposite poles of the discourse on alternatives to the official female images created by Soviet iconography. Right up to the Mikhail Gorbachev period, the Party newspaper *Pravda* continued to describe women as "work units" or as "workers and mothers," after the fashion of Nadezhda Krupskaia and Alexandra Kollontai. Even liberal publications *(Literaturnaia gazeta; Iunost')* began conceding that "a woman must be a woman," not striving for a successful career but waiting for a good husband. The village-oriented conservative publications *(Moskva; Nash sovremennik)* propagandized the "bearer of the national moral source"—the peasant woman. None of these images, and I remember them well, had anything to do with the real life of Soviet women in the final Soviet years.

Stereotypes and Reality

In the mid-1960s, Aleksandr Tvardovsky's *Novyi mir,* the most progressive journal of the era, published a novella by Natal'ia Baranskaia, *A Week Like Any Other*. Although successful abroad, and studied today in many Russian literature classes, the novella went almost unnoticed by Russians. It deals with the ordinary life of a working woman who is torn between work, two children, and a sweet but useless husband, never finding enough time for all her chores. Although Western critics found it a good description of the daily hell of Soviet life, Soviet critics paid the work no attention: It was nothing special, this was the way everyone lived. The author herself did not intend to give a harsh appraisal of the husband or the situation—she was merely describing it.

And yet the novella had a certain effect in Russia. Magazines began printing more pieces describing people's personal lives, events that were no less significant to the characters than fulfilling a five-year plan was to the state. Official critics berated these authors, the men for creating such unheroic characters and the women for sticking to "minor themes" such as birth and abortion, sick children, and drunken husbands. And yet the curtain shielding the myth, the conspiracy of silence about women, began to crumble.

The first feminist breakthroughs in the Soviet period occurred in the legendary almanac *Zhenshchina i Rossiia* (Woman and Russia), published in 1980 by Tat'iana Mamonova, Natal'ia Malakhova, Tat'iana Goricheva, and Iul'ia Voznesenskaia, first in samizdat and then in the samizdat journal *Mariia*. The almanac published women's protests against the invasion of Afghanistan, accounts of abuses in maternity hospitals and humiliation of female prisoners, and many other original texts that could not have been printed elsewhere. Interestingly, the feminist authors were not warmly welcomed by the dissident community: The dissidents believed, along with the rest of society, that women's issues as such did not exist in Russia, and that as soon as the system and the regime were changed, everything would be all right.

Persecuted by the KGB, the four women who published *Zhenshchina i Rossiia* were forced to leave the USSR. The next samizdat magazine to come along, *Zhenskoe chtenie* (Women's Reading), edited by Olga Lipovskaia, did not appear until almost ten years later, once again in Leningrad. This magazine was the first to translate texts by Western authors and to attempt to understand what was happening to men and women in Russia, without watching the censors or the ideologues.

At approximately the same time, the late 1980s and early 1990s, groups began forming in Moscow, primarily at academic institutes and research laboratories; these included LOTOS and Sappho. The women members were interested in Western feminist texts and gender research, so they prepared translations and discussed philosophical and sociological questions. This activity coincided with the lifting—timid at first—of the Iron Curtain and the emergence of women's issues, not only in the dissident milieu (which had nurtured Olga Lipovskaia and her Leningrad predecessors) but among the respectable Soviet elite as well. These latter Russians knew foreign languages (this at first was a requirement, since there were no feminist texts in Russian) and held good jobs in academic institutes, assets that later allowed them to combine their growing interest in the topic with their professional work.

On the whole, however, women's issues never came up in discussions of perestroika. Women who had stood in the front ranks of demonstrations for democracy and demanded that the memory of the victims of Stalin's terror should be honored, or who had collected signatures on petitions to free Andrei Sakharov from internal exile and open Russia's borders—these women found themselves shoved aside by loud-voiced men. Dissident thought, which had captured people's minds, did not accept consideration of women. And women themselves followed the line taken by the democratic newspapers of the period: It was better for men to be in charge.

The discourse about political power gradually became dominated by men. Mikhail Gorbachev's role here is interesting. In many of his speeches, he articulated a thought popular among the intelligentsia: "Women must be freed and given the opportunity to spend more time at home." I am certain that he meant the right to choose whether to stay at home or pursue a career. But the democratic press, unaccustomed to pluralism, began a consistent campaign to promote the image of a pretty housewife, helpmate of man, unburdened by profession or work. Needless to say, there were almost no women like that in the USSR—because of forced employment and the low salaries of men. So a gender stereotype gradually replaced the ideological one—and once again real women were left outside the scope of discussion.

And in fact, there really wasn't any discussion. In all the years of perestroika, the best magazine of the era, *Ogonyok*, carried only one article specifically about women (not counting articles about prostitutes, drug addicts, or murderers—there were plenty of those). That article was published on the eve of International Women's Day, March 8, 1988, and the author's notion (a woman, by the way) was that the only problem Soviet women faced was their husbands' low salaries.

Alas, many women shared that conviction, not so much because they believed in the "natural predestination of women" but because they felt that anything that had been banned or discouraged in the dreary Soviet period had to be somehow worthwhile.

Political newspapers and magazines did not discuss the problems of women. Gradually, an ironic tone became acceptable when speaking of women's independence. Television stations began airing films about wealthy, indolent women and their husbands. Many men, who had suffered from inferiority complexes during Soviet times because of their low earning power and their inability to live up to their potential, found that the easiest way to appease themselves was to humiliate women simply because they were not men. Some politicians even made statements like, "It's not for women and children that we write laws." A famous film director announced publicly: "By nature the Asiatic man considers the woman a lower creature." And no one was outraged (at least in public) by manifestations of this new sexism.

The market—or rather, its first stages—brought to Russia the concept of a woman's looks as a consumer product (pictures of half-dressed women appeared not only in cheap publications but in what were once considered respectable ones), along with new images of heroes and heroines. A hero in Russia had to be a "superman, with money, girls, guns, and cars" (so wrote Aleksandr Kabakov, a prominent liberal author). The best women were deemed to be models or wives of businessmen. Working women were depicted as boring failures; the first businesswomen, it was said, were women who despaired of having a personal life. Thus the Soviet myth once again took its revenge, offering new stereotypes even further from reality than the previous poster images of the model Soviet citizen.

Sadly, political and social realities did little to counterbalance this image. The popular liberal point of view held by many young reformers (including Yegor Gaidar) did not anticipate establishing any social guarantees for the population undergoing transformation to a market economy: They did not want to "execute a social-democratic agenda." Hence the tragic situation that marks Russia today: impoverished people, a sharp decline in life expectancy, epidemics, orphans, a starving elderly class, and homelessness on a scale not seen since the Civil War.

This process began with a sharp decline in the status of women. The first official census of the unemployed found that over 74 percent were women, most of them well qualified, and that it was much harder for them than for men to find new jobs or start businesses. The stereotype of the wild Russian market economy was at work, with women being considered (unspoken) second-class citizens. Experts estimate that women's salaries in the Soviet period were about 70 percent of men's; in Russia today, women make only 45 percent as much as men do. Only 12 percent of women are able to take regular care of their health—the system of affordable health care has been destroyed. Kindergartens and day-care centers are too expensive and too few. Many women with children are unable to pay for expensive services and stay home instead. Children's benefits (enough to buy a kilogram of cheese a month) haven't been paid in years, and 42 percent of the country's children live below the poverty line. I could go on with the terrible statistics.

Cruelty in families is growing—more than 14,000 women die annually from domestic abuse, and there is still no appropriate law to curb such behavior. After a slight decline, abortions are on the rise again, and so is sexual harassment, especially among Russians making their living in the private sector.

There is an abundance of such evidence, but I will only add that there are still not enough women in public life and that women's abilities are not being used by Russian society.

All this has given impetus to the women's movement, which has awoken in the north and the south, east and west, in university towns and mining villages. It has primarily been a reaction to the changes going on in the country—a desire to counteract the negative consequences of reforms that appeared so quickly.

Vy i My As a Form of Dialogue Among Women

Processes analogous to those that took place in Russia after the disintegration of the USSR also took place in virtually every former Soviet republic. Women were pushed out of power structures and the labor market, and ideas were bandied about concerning "woman's natural place" and "real Latvian women," "real Armenian women," "real Uzbek women," and so forth. The social support network was destroyed; women joined the ranks of the poorest strata of society; and under the guise of resurrecting national culture in many newly independent states, religious fundamentalism grew stronger. In some of the newly independent states, young girls were forced to wear the veil, women's access to education was made harder, and discussion began introducing polygamy.

All these events, which began in 1991 and are ongoing today, lead one to conclude that in all the post-Soviet states, the old Soviet tradition continues: overcoming the difficulties of a transition period—this time the transition to a market economy and national independence—at the expense of women. That's how it happened during the early five-year plans, and it was the same during the reestablishment of the Soviet economy after World War II. And it is the same now in the transition to democracy—and this circumstance makes one seriously doubt the consistency of democratic development.

But it is also a fact that in all the newly independent states, the first independent women's organizations appeared in the early 1990s; in the ensuing years women formed networks, movements, and centers; and today they not only help the needy but also influence politics. These movements and organizations have not yet achieved unity, and they are in many ways self-sufficient and dissimilar. At the same time, they thirst to exchange information and contacts, harboring interest in the work of women in neighboring states and in the international women's movement as well.

This process began in the early 1990s and underwent several stages. Svetlana Aivazova, Natal'ia Abubikirova, Marina Regentova, and Elena Kochkina, researchers of the Russian and post-Soviet women's movement, have identified three distinct periods: 1990–1993, 1993–1995, and 1995 to the present. This division seems appropriate, reflecting the development of the women's movement and women's sociopolitical status in the Russian Federation. Every period has its characteristic traits, contradictions, and hidden wellsprings, as well as special forms of dialogue between women's associations and the regime, among women's groups, and between Russian feminists and Western activists.

The first period (1990–1993) was marked by the disintegration of the USSR—the beginning of market reforms, a shortage of goods and services, the first wave of unemployment, and other acute social consequences of the economic restructuring of society. The interrelationship between women and the regime was extremely insignificant (as already mentioned, in 1991 only 5 percent of women were in governmental organizations). The idea of "woman's place" reigned, and Western and Russian pornography began expanding into the magazine and film markets. There were three groups of women's organizations in the country. The first consisted of activists from regional branches of the Union of Women of Russia (the former Committee of Soviet Women), trying to find a place in the changing structures of society and bureaucracy. Preserving strong Soviet echoes in their rhetoric, they did not reveal any familiarity with Western feminist texts, although they did retain the traditional Soviet ties with representatives of the international women's movement (even though only committee members had the opportunity to participate in international conferences until the 1990s).

The second group consisted of adherents of the Women's League and organizations close to it—women who had started their own businesses or worked in business or administration, who were relatively well off and sought a new niche in life. They wanted to make contacts with Western colleagues, primarily in business; feminism interested them, but it was not a way of life.

The third—and most interesting—group consisted of organizations linked to the First and Second Independent Women's Forums, which took place in 1991 and 1992 in the city of Dubna, near

Moscow. More than 200 women attended the first forum, and around 1,000 women attended the second, coming from many regions of Russia, countries of the former Soviet Union, Europe, and North America. A prominent role in the leadership of the organizing committee was played by members of the new Moscow Center for Gender Studies (of the Institute of Socioeconomic Problems of the Population, under the Russian Academy of Sciences), leaders of the education organization Falta, and women cinematographers. The attendees were varied in age, education, and interests. Severe workers from defense industry enterprises and relaxed young artists, Ph.D. candidates and policewomen, former Komsomol activists and dissidents—all were united by the desire to understand what was happening to women in a changing world.

This was the first meeting between Russian women and Western feminists. The word "feminism" was out of favor in Russia; not everyone understood what it meant, and the dialogue did not move easily. But it did take place! The result was the start of a women's network, the appearance of new groups, new friendships abroad, and new ideas and plans. The forum's motto, "Democracy Without Women Is No Democracy," became integral to Russian women's subsequent efforts.

One of the results of the meeting was the inauguration of the magazine *Vy i My*, dedicated to dialogue between Russian and American women; the publication was the idea of Colette Shulman and Katrina van den Heuvel, American journalists who had come to Russia. The magazine was published in Russian in the United States and brought to Russia, where it was distributed to women's organizations. At the time, it was the only true feminist magazine printed in Russian and thus accessible to a Russian audience; it expanded the horizons of Russian readers and offered fresh information on the women's movement in America and how various issues of concern to women were being solved.

Vy i My's contribution to the development of the Russian-American women's dialogue is incalculable. It became a forum where opinions and issues meshed and often clashed, where a genuine dialogue that had never before existed was first pursued. The early 1990s completely destroyed the barriers of the Cold War, destroyed the image of the enemy in the eyes of Russians and Americans, and laid the tracks for people's diplomacy. The women's dialogue added an important and essential note to the process.

The 1990–1993 period saw the start of personal contacts among specialists from various countries, the discovery of foreign literature, and the first translated articles on feminism in Russia. Russian researchers started taking part in international conferences, planning joint projects with Western colleagues, and mastering the new methodology. This was important in the social sciences—particularly in gender studies, about which little was known in Russia. During this period the first research was conducted on the place of women in the labor market and on gender relations and political power in Russia. The first anthology of essays on this topic was published. Unfortunately, these materials were known only to a narrow circle of interested specialists in Russia and had no public resonance.

Journalists were only beginning to show an interest in gender issues. Women as a topic for research concerned only a narrow group of Moscow writers, who met for seminars and discussions at the Foreign Policy Association or at *Ogonyok*'s offices. That group was the inception of the future Association of Women Journalists. Women active in cinematography and the arts also started meeting. They invited Western colleagues to speak, and they argued, but only within their small circles. They were accumulating experience.

In the early 1990s, Western foundations began to show an interest in gender issues in Russia. The Soros Foundation sponsored a meeting of Russian and American women writers in New York; the MacArthur Foundation provided the first grant to the Moscow Center for Gender Studies and then added women's issues to its priority areas for support in Russia and the former Soviet Union.

The next stage (1993–1995) was marked by a deeper inculcation of market reforms, the westernization of many people's way of life, and new national elections. It was then that the Women of Russia group, formed by the Union of Women of Russia, Union of Women of the Navy, and Union of Women Entrepreneurs, began campaigning. Politically centrist (not a recognized position in those years), the group formulated no clear economic or political platforms, but it did vigorously press for social security and the improvement of women's status. The group passed the mandatory 5 percent barrier and entered the State Duma.

This parliamentary faction managed to secure passage of a new family code and numerous laws on the family, but it did not finish its work on family planning and domestic violence legislation. At the start of the military intervention in Chechnya, the faction was too slow in making contact with the Mothers of Soldiers of Russia movement, which spoke out forcefully against the war, and the faction began losing popularity. It also ignored the initiatives of many independent women's organizations. Internal conflicts within the faction led to its defeat in the following elections and the loss of its presence in the Duma.

The work of the Women of Russia group should not be underestimated, however. It was the first time that women had appeared in politics as a distinct group pushing their own interests (they represented 13 percent of all deputies, including other political blocs), and their very standing as deputies led to discussions of women's position in society. In any case, women journalists raised the issue of domestic violence in stark terms and managed to change public opinion, persuading people that this was no private matter but shameful behavior that required state intervention.

At the same time, the women's movement revealed more clearly the differentiation among its members. The elitist Moscow and St. Petersburg groups today comprise highly educated women, most of them researchers with a knowledge of foreign languages who receive grants and travel around the world. Women's groups in the outlying regions of Russia, which started as self-help groups, include the formerly unemployed, single mothers or mothers of several children, mothers of soldiers, and physically disabled women. These associations exist in great numbers all over the country. In addition, there are the large regional organizations with thousands of members, for instance the Union of Women of the Don, the Congress of Women of the Kola Peninsula, and the Confederation of Businesswomen of the Urals. These organizations had no support from abroad and lacked literature and even knowledge of gender studies, women's rights, and human rights.

Contacts between these two different kinds of women's associations were not always smooth; mutual misunderstandings arose. The elitist groups began competing among themselves. An attempt to create a single umbrella group, an independent organization (a kind of alternative faction in the State Duma) proved unsuccessful. There was not a single bridging dialogue among women; rather, they constituted a series of embattled islands that rarely connected. This was partly because most of those involved in the new independent women's movement lacked public and organizational experience. Moreover, the culture of civilized discourse in Russian society was not developed; people had not yet learned, during the few years of democracy, how to argue without insulting one another.

The influential Association of Women Journalists, for its part, felt that the forum for debate, the platform where opponents could meet and perhaps find points of constructive cooperation, should be the press. Numerous discussions, roundtables, and open conversations—regional, national, and international—on various topics dealing with the life of women characterized that period. There was much truth seeking, and there were intense arguments ultimately leading to paths of cooperation. The journalists took part in these sessions as well, whether they were in Moscow, Sergiev Posad, Naberezhnye Chelny, Irkutsk, Murmansk, or other cities.

Vy i My participated in this dialogue with redoubled resolve, explaining many crucial issues: reproductive health, child rearing, family planning, the struggles of notable feminists, the lives of ordinary American and Russian women. The magazine did not come out often, but every issue that arrived in packages and boxes at women's organizations all over Russia was read until it literally fell apart, passing from hand to hand. A new magazine, *Zhenshchina+*, appeared, published by a Russian-German women's group; an Internet web site, Women's Network East-West, was established; and the women's informational network expanded in the newly independent states.

An enormous role in building this coalition was played by Western colleagues and friends who had experience and knew how to use modern technology. Many of them, like Sara Harder (of the Peace Foundation) and Martina Vandenberg (of the Consortium of Women's Nongovernmental Organizations of the CIS-USA), traveled around the country giving training sessions, teaching women leadership techniques, creating crisis centers and hotlines, and sharing their experience and know-how. Many volunteers worked at the hotlines, helping Russian researchers and the unemployed. Western colleagues helped Russian women better understand themselves; they supported the creation of libraries and arranged translations. *Our Bodies Ourselves for the New Century* (Boston Women's Health Book Collective) and *The Feminine Mystique* by Betty Friedan were published in Russian translation, and many related articles were also translated.

The period from 1995 to the present has brought a change. There is no women's faction in the parliament: The women deputies are not united, but support their parties first and foremost; they compete with one another; and their number (11 percent) does not suffice to influence decisions on improving the lot of women. The leaders of the former women's bloc have gone their separate ways, creating two competing organizations, one of which joined the new Fatherland election bloc in 1999 and the other creating an independent association only in September 1999, too late for a serious chance at success in the December 1999 parliamentary elections. The lists of candidates from the other blocs and parties show a significant decline in numbers of women compared to 1995. Party programs say almost nothing about women, even though their situation remains dire.

The women's movement itself has undergone changes. Today there isn't a single organization in Russia representing women's intellectual, creative, and political potential that is capable of influencing the government. Nor is there a charismatic leader who could encourage others to follow her—even though there are striking personalities in every region who have come up through the public women's movement. The movement resembles a series of coalitions that do have *some* influence on specific goals—but regretfully not political ones. Women's voices are heard more vociferously on TV and in the press, however, and women in general are being heard, which is a positive sign.

Nevertheless, an analysis performed by the Association of Women Journalists showed that in 1998 only 1.5 percent of all newspaper space was devoted specifically to women and their problems (in 1995 it was even less, at 1 percent). However, new and realistic images of women have appeared in the press, on radio, and on TV—images of women who work, create, and can change life in Russia. You can hear them on Radio Nadezhda, you can read about them in the "Women" column that has appeared regularly for the past three years in *Nezavisimaya gazeta*.

Today, Russian feminists no longer regard the West as the only true model, or Western women as missionaries. On the contrary, the Russian women's movement is looking for its own paths, its own solutions, while working creatively with the international experience it has gained. The All-Russian Women's Conference held in 1998, dedicated to the ninetieth anniversary of the women's movement in Russia, represented an important step along this path.

The nature of the relationship with the West has changed. Today, many regional organizations receive support from Western foundations—the Open Society Institute, the Eurasia Foundation, the MacArthur Foundation, the Ford Foundation, the Böll Foundation, and others—and many regional leaders have joined the coordinating boards of international women's organizations. After the UN Conference on Women in Beijing in 1995 (attended by more than 200 Russian women), thousands of Russian women have articulated their country's problems at international forums and brought back possible solutions to activists back home. Women's rights groups, crisis centers, and other forms of protecting women's interests have greatly increased in number. There are gender studies centers in St. Petersburg, Naberezhnye Chelny, Arkhangelsk, Ivanovo, Kareliia, and other places; gender courses are becoming part of university curricula, and there have been three summer schools on gender studies.

The independent women's press is expanding. *Vy i My* has been transformed from a forum for Russian-American dialogue into a forum for dialogue among women from all countries. It is now published in Russia with a circulation of 5,000 and is called *WE/MY*. Besides articles on topical issues (globalization, health, feminism, aging, the stages of a woman's life), it carries reports on Russia's regions and on women's movements in other countries. Other pertinent publications include *Devochki prosiat vnimaniia* (Attention to Girls; published in Naberezhnye Chelny); *Posidelki* (St. Petersburg); *Chego khochet zhenshchina* (What a Woman Wants; Murmansk); *Zhenshchina+* (Woman Plus) and *Aksin'ia* (Rostov); *Vera, Nadezhda, Liubov'* (Faith, Hope, Love; Novgorod); and *Pskovitianka* (Pskov Woman). There are women's electronic networks. The number of feminist periodicals in the newly independent states that are available to the Russian reader is expanding.

In all these ways, Russian women continue to enrich their experiences and seek new ways to realize their power and their capabilities. And these women have not lost hope that their potential will be needed in a democratic Russia.

16

REVIVING THE RUSSIAN ORTHODOX CHURCH

A Task Both Theological and Secular

Hilarion Alfeev

Personal History

I was born in 1966, when Russia was an atheistic country, and I was educated in a Soviet atheist school. One by one my relatives came to God and religion, although their conversions started with the younger generation and progressed to the older generations. For instance, one of my grandmothers was an avid Communist Party activist. My father was a scientist and an agnostic. My mother became religious in the late 1970s. In their own ways, all my cousins found the path to faith. By the early 1980s, only my grandmother remained an atheist. Family history totally contradicted the myth that the Church was just a refuge for *babushki*. The return to the Church by the youth and the intelligentsia started much earlier than the

Born in 1966, **Hieromonk Hilarion** (**Alfeev**) studied violin, piano, and composition in pursuit of a career in music, but decided to become a priest in 1987. Educated at the Moscow Theological Academy and holding a doctorate in divinity from Oxford University, Father Hilarion has taught many courses in seminaries and written extensively for Russian and foreign publications. He is presently executive director of the Secretariat for Inter-Christian Affairs, Department for External Church Relations, the Moscow Patriarchate, in which capacity he travels widely and works with a wide range of interdenominational organizations. Interview recorded and translated by Natan M. Shklyar.

Interview: June 4, 1999, Danilovskii Monastery, Moscow

1990s. Even in the 1970s and 1980s, young people manifested growing interest toward the Church.

I studied music (violin, piano, and composition) in school and later in the Moscow Conservatory. For several years I was faced with a choice: music or Church service? When I decided to pick the Church over music and told my conservatory's dean, he said that he could not "allow such a musical talent to go to waste." He tried to convince me that he could explain the deceitful nature of the Church. He thought that I was seduced by the Church. But he did not manage to convince me.

I became a priest at twenty years of age—but without any theological education. In Soviet days there were only three seminaries in the whole country (now there are more than fifty), so sometimes the Church was forced to ordain priests before they had any formal theological training or before they had educated themselves. I decided to complete my education by correspondence after I was ordained.

For several years I served in Lithuania, including two years as the dean of the Kaunas Cathedral. In January 1991, the Soviet army intervened in Lithuania and occupied the TV station in Vilnius. For several days the country was split between the Soviet-controlled part and the free, anti-Soviet part that was centered around the Kaunas TV station. Most of my parishioners were ethnic Russians, and I also frequently visited the local military garrison, talking to Russian soldiers and baptizing some of them. I personally knew all the military personnel at the garrison. When the Soviet forces invaded, I went on Kaunas TV and addressed the soldiers, asking them not to shoot at civilians even if ordered to do so by their superiors. This was a risky step, but I felt it was my duty to steer our Russian boys away from this action. Kaunas TV broadcast my speech every hour for the next several days. There were instances when Russian soldiers refused to take up arms. In the end, nobody from the Kaunas garrison took part in the operation, and the Kaunas TV station was never taken over.

After that I became something of a hero to the Lithuanian people, although some of my Russian parishioners thought that I had betrayed them. I always felt, though, that this was not a Russian-Lithuanian conflict but a military intervention of Soviet forces against native people, Russians as well as Lithuanians. Soon I began receiving threatening phone calls and had to go into hiding. My life in Lithuania became very turbulent.

By that time I had completed my correspondence degree with the Moscow Theological Academy, and the academy offered me a teaching position. I taught there from 1991 to 1993, including courses in theology, the New Testament, Byzantine Greek, and homiletics (the art of preaching). In 1993 I attended Oxford University and wrote my doctoral thesis, entitled "St. Simeon the New Theologian and the Orthodox Tradition." (St. Simeon was an eleventh-century Byzantine mystical writer.) After I graduated from Oxford in 1995, I wanted to return to teaching at the Moscow Theological Academy. However, I was told that because my education in Oxford had not been an Orthodox one, the Academy's leadership was not sure if I would be fit to teach in an Orthodox institution.

At that time I found myself under the wing of Metropolitan Kirill, the head of the Church's external relations department. In my view, Kirill is one of the most prominent leaders of our Church. Since then I have been working with him, and since 1997 I have been directing the secretariat that handles relations with other Christian confessions.

The Church As an Element of Civil Society in Russia

In Soviet days, the Russian Orthodox Church experienced continual repression in one form or another. The repression was most brutal in the 1920s and 1930s, when many priests were killed or imprisoned, monasteries and seminaries were closed, and many churches were destroyed. The situation improved a little during Stalin's late years, but once again deteriorated under Nikita Khrushchev. During Leonid Brezhnev's rule, while the country underwent a period of stagnation, the Church was less affected, in part because it had managed to lead an autonomous existence and even experienced an influx of young people. Overall, however, until 1988 the Church existed outside of society, in a kind of ghetto, and the separation between the church and society was strictly enforced. For instance, nobody in a prominent position could openly belong to the Church. If a schoolteacher publicly attended church, he or she would have been expelled.

In 1988, when we planned to celebrate the millennium of Christianity's introduction into Russia, the situation changed drastically.

The Church sought government approval to organize a nationwide commemoration of the event, but officials declared that under no circumstances could this celebration take place outside of church walls. This was the peak time of perestroika, however, when everything was changing; former dissidents were openly speaking out against the regime, and books and publications from the West were penetrating the Iron Curtain. Interest in the Church was growing, and many more people turned out at the various celebrations held that year than the government could have ever imagined. In one small town of 60,000 inhabitants, about 40,000 people took part in the festivities, whereas the local authorities had predicted a turnout of no more than 1,000. It was during that time that priests first began appearing on television, and after 1988 people started joining the Church en masse. Many of them had always been believers but had had to hide their faith. Many others, including former Party members and militant atheists, realized that their historical and national roots lay with the Orthodox Church. Many young people joined the Church in the late 1980s and early 1990s.

Then, in the mid-1990s, we saw something of a decline in people's religious interest. Although at first masses of people were publicly baptized, many of them did not remain active members of the Church. Some were baptized out of a herd mentality and never returned to the Church to take part in its everyday life. Today, if you stop people at random on the streets of Moscow and ask them if they consider themselves believers, perhaps half or even more would identify themselves as Orthodox. In most cases, however, they would not be regular churchgoers: They simply identify themselves with the Orthodox tradition and have only a limited relationship with the Church.

Thus the Church found itself in a dramatically new situation in the late 1980s and early 1990s. For over seventy years the Church had been completely separated from society, unable to influence life in the country, because any kind of "religious propaganda" in the media was prohibited. We were allowed to publish a limited number of Bibles and other books for church service, but we could not publish liturgical materials for wider circulation. After 1988 we suddenly found ourselves confronted with new possibilities and opportunities. Frankly, not everybody in the Church knew what to do with this newfound freedom. This was especially true of the older generation of priests, those who had been forced to operate all their lives in constrained conditions. Some of them had no skills in working with people outside of the Church "ghetto." Thus not everybody could make the transition and pass through the now broken wall between the Church and society. Many priests and bishops had to learn things they had never dreamed of before then. In the early 1990s many Church leaders were asked to speak to TV audiences, but television is a special medium that requires a certain charisma and an ability to "break through" the two-dimensional screen. Very few priests managed to do that.

We also had the opportunity to begin teaching religion, as many parish schools began to open again. I remember when I was serving in Kaunas in the early 1990s, I volunteered to teach religion in one of the three Russian schools in the city. Although at first the school administration reacted with suspicion, eventually I was teaching first, second, and third graders. Then it became clear that at all levels students wanted to study religion. I had to spend ten hours a week in school teaching religion to all grades. Then, the other two schools in Kaunas asked me to teach religion. Eventually I had time only for church service in the morning and teaching the rest of the day. Finally I recruited some of my parishioners, gave them some basic training, and sent them off as teachers of religion. Many priests at that time faced similar challenges, when there is so much freedom but one has neither the manpower, the resources, the time, nor the skills to take full advantage of it.

The Church is not even close to capitalizing on all the opportunities it now has. In coming decades the Church's main task, barring a sharp political turnabout in the country, is to meet the challenges of this newfound freedom.

On Church-State Relations

In Soviet times, the Church was formally separated from the state, but this separation worked only in one direction. The Church had no support from the state, but for its part the state actively intruded in Church life and collected huge taxes. Priests and bishops had to be approved by the authorities. The number of monks in monasteries was limited and regulated as well.

But even before the 1917 Revolution, the Church was not free. For a long time it was part of the state apparatus. In the beginning of eighteenth century, Peter the Great initiated reforms and eliminated the institution of the Patriarchate, installing in its place the Holy Synod, a collegium of Church leaders presided over by an official appointed by the state. During the 200 years before the Patriarchate was restored in 1918, the Russian Church was stripped of its canonical authority. One can therefore say that the Church has not been free for some 300 years.

This is the first time in many centuries that we exist completely independently of the state. Today the Church is finally separated from the state, which for once does not meddle in internal church matters. I think it is important for the Church to preserve this kind of relationship. After the collapse of communism, it became very tempting for people to fill the new ideological vacuum with the Orthodox faith. For Western people, it might be normal to live one's life without some kind of unifying state ideology. But for our people it was out of character, and many in politics and in the Church alike were seriously looking for some kind of unifying ideology. They turned to Orthodoxy as a candidate for such a role.

So far the Church has not become a part of the state, and our official position is that we do not want to become part of the state again and lose our newfound freedom. We must work out some sort of modus vivendi and modus operandi that would enable the state and the church to live side by side independently of each other, but at the same time enable the church to influence public policy in the areas of morality and spiritual revival. Ideally, the church would like to be a source of a moral authority for the people, while preserving its independence from the state.

Russia's Future and Its Place in the Larger World

I should like to share my vision about what kind of society Russia should be. The spread of American "standards of civilization" is becoming the world's number one problem. As Samuel Huntington argues, the modern world is divided among several "civilizational poles." One such pole is Western civilization, and it lives according to a liberal standard that holds the human being as "the measure of all things." This civilization is focused on the human being, on the improvement of his condition and the protection of his rights. This humanistic civilization is successful in those parts of the world where it has developed for centuries, since the Renaissance. The countries that have accepted these humanistic standards provide high standards of living and welfare support for their populations. Religion is a matter of free choice; nobody is forced into any faith, and no religion is prohibited. The humanistic civilization of the West keeps religion in the private sphere.

However, there are other civilizations. Muslim civilization is not humanistic; it places religion rather than the individual at the center of community life. Many Western and Muslim moral values overlap, of course, but many do not. Today the West takes a very tolerant approach to homosexuality, so long as no existing laws are broken. Such tolerance is unthinkable in the Muslim world. And there are many such points of divergence.

There are also several countries belonging to what one might call the Orthodox civilization. They are not necessarily Orthodox countries; indeed, I would not describe today's Russia as an Orthodox country. But these are countries where Orthodoxy has played a key role in cultural development; has laid the foundation for moral and spiritual values, for worldview. Among these countries you will find such states as Russia, Serbia, Bulgaria, Georgia, and Greece, to mention only a few. Greece, of course, stands at a crossroads between its Orthodox heritage and its current Western political orientation.

What do we see happening today? After the fall of the Iron Curtain, many people thought that it would be easy to unify the countries of the West with the countries of the Orthodox heritage that had remained until then in the Communist camp. But this was not as easy as people had supposed. In a way, we are watching a new Iron Curtain emerge across Europe, one that does not match the former frontier between NATO and the Warsaw Pact. Instead, it separates the countries of Western civilization from those of the Orthodox heritage. Note that all the eastern European countries that have successfully integrated with the West (like Poland, Hungary, and the Baltic states) are either Catholic or Protestant in their persuasion, whereas those that have been left out (like Serbia) are traditionally Orthodox.

Russia today is one of those countries that cannot live according to Western standards of civilization. This is partially the reason why the liberal democratic reformers in Russia, who came to power in the wake of Mikhail Gorbachev's reforms, very quickly fell out of public favor. They were pro-Western but they did not take into account Russian specifics, including Russia's spirituality, psychology, and national traditions. As a result, they suffered a fiasco. At this point, it is not clear who will lead Russia in the next century, but I do not think that it will be the Western-oriented democrats.

The challenge for the West is to understand that it is impossible to run the whole world by the same standard of civilization. This is one lesson of the Yugoslav conflicts. Since the times of the tower of Babel, when God made humans speak a multitude of languages, any kind of unity of humankind has been impossible by any means but the divine. Humanity is a diverse mixture of peoples, countries, cultures, languages, traditions, and laws. It is not humanly possible to have these diverse peoples accept a common standard.

The real danger is when particular standards of civilization are imposed on (or imported into) countries that are not ready to adopt them. Russia differs from the Western world in that it never experienced the Reformation, the Renaissance, or the revolutions of the nineteenth century that shook Europe and laid the foundations of today's liberal societies. Russia's standards of civilization can be different from those of the West. The greatest challenge for the West is to understand that and to let Russia develop along its own unique path, not taking advantage of its current economic weakness and dependence on the West.

Russia's Own Challenge and the "National Idea"

The great challenge before us now is to chart our country's path in the next century. During the seventy years of the Soviet era, we were told what to believe and which road our country should take. Although this doctrine was false and was imposed, at least it gave some guidance to our people. Today, nobody knows what the country's national idea is. I am confident that the Church can play a crucial rule in helping to form this idea.

I do not believe that Russia needs a unifying ideology, nor do I think that Orthodoxy should try to assume such a role. But I do believe that Russia needs a clear vision of its path and its role in the world. It would be unfair to think of Russia as a country completely unlike any other, although there are many people in our church who believe that Russia is a messianic country with a specially ordained role. But one has to admit that Russia has its own history, civilization, and culture. And after seventy years of communism, it must find its own face. Here Russian Orthodoxy could play a pivotal role. Orthodoxy is not an ideology; you can call it the "Russian national idea" if you wish, but whatever it is called, it should guide Russia's overall development, as well as the country's foreign and domestic policy. This vision, this national idea, must emerge from the people, although I am not sure what individual or organization could articulate it now. The national idea must be rooted in Russia's development before the revolution, during the Soviet period, and during the past ten years. I do not think we need to wait centuries for the national idea to emerge, but it will take at least some years.

Many people today use the biblical metaphor of Moses taking his people to wander in the desert for forty years to allow the older "generation of slaves" to die out and the new free generation to emerge. The implication is that we need to wait until the current generation disappears before a workable new national idea emerges. I do not think this metaphor is applicable to us. Every generation must take part in building the new Russia. Moreover, we cannot simply discard our Soviet past, however horrible it may have been. No foreign interventionist army forced communism down our throats; it emerged from Russia's own history and development. What we need to do is learn valuable lessons from the horrible and excruciating period of communism. This applies to the Church as well.

Many voices in the Church today are calling for its return to the nineteenth century, viewed as the golden age of Church-state relations, when the two institutions worked closely in tandem. In fact, at that time Orthodoxy was a state religion, closely supervised by the czarist regime. And we saw how it all ended in the early twentieth century, when the people turned away from the Church. The same persons who attended obligatory religious instruction in schools in the 1910s persecuted the Church in the 1930s and 1940s, burning icons and killing priests. The Church must learn a valuable lesson from what happened in 1917 and afterward, in order to find its appropriate place with respect to the state and make sure that it does not repeat its past mistakes.

Russia and the West

In the political sphere, the West should not use Russia's current economic dependence to impose its values on us. We felt this kind of blackmail when some in the West said that Russia would be denied loans and credits if the Duma approved legislation in 1998 regulating the practice of religion (the Law on Freedom of Conscience). This tactic might have worked in the colonial regimes of the nineteenth and twentieth centuries, but it will be counterproductive in today's Russia.

As for religion, Western Christians should not view Russia as a wide-open field for proselytizing. Russia is a country with a millennium-old Christian tradition, and the Church is trying hard to help the Russian people reconnect with this tradition. In the past few years, foreign missionaries have virtually invaded Russia. They come, often not even speaking the language, and start proselytizing as if this were a land of pagans, as if the country had never known Christianity. Any kind of Western mission in Russia should strive to work with the local Orthodox Church; otherwise, the mission will become a proselytizing one. When missionaries take advantage of the lack of religious education among our people by recruiting them into their sects en masse, it is unfair and antithetical to freedom of conscience. Freedom of conscience presupposes the possibility of choosing between different religions or ideologies. But one cannot be free to choose if one does not know much about his own tradition.

The Potential for Church Reform

The term "reform" does not apply well to the Orthodox Church, which is very traditional by nature. At its core, the Church is based on tradition, the unbroken chain that starts with Jesus Christ and the Apostles and continues down to our day. However, in every century the Church has had to adapt its tradition to that specific era. On the one hand, the Church must use the modern ways of approaching people, but on the other hand it must remain traditional in terms of doctrine, spirituality, and morality. We cannot sacrifice biblical values in favor of liberal ideals. Western colleagues tell us that men and women are equal and therefore women must be ordained as priests. We do not disagree about gender equality, but we cannot contravene centuries of church tradition that prohibits women from performing church services. Similarly, with the advance of gay rights, many in the West now talk about church-approved marriages between homosexuals and lesbians. In Russia, this will never work.

Nonetheless, along with what must remain constant in Orthodox ritual, some aspects of the Church's work are subject to revision, for example how we present our teaching, organize our system of theological education, and operate the system of church governance.

We should reexamine the use of Old Church Slavonic in the services. Some suggest that we should conduct services in modern Russian in order to make them more accessible. If we were to switch our services to Russian, however, we would have to drop many of our liturgical texts, which were written by ninth- and tenth-century Byzantine poets and which cannot be adequately translated outside of their original context. We cannot drop Old Church Slavonic without reforming the whole process of the church service; this is not an option for the Russian Orthodox Church. One can see how little the Catholic Church accomplished when it dropped Latin as the mandatory language of Mass; although services are now easily understood, this has not brought many more believers into the Church. Parts of the holy texts, like the Gospel and the Epistles, could indeed be read in Russian, but most of the liturgical texts should remain in Old Church Slavonic.

Today we urgently need a radical reform of the system of Orthodox theological education. The system that is now in place is a relic of the nineteenth century. It is characterized by a narrow approach, the rejection of foreign influences and ideas, compulsory rituals, and occasionally a distrust of learning, all of which stifle creativity and independent thinking. This system is a legacy of the Soviet period, when priests were constrained by the state and could not develop new elements outside the approved curriculum.

First of all, we must encourage creativity and originality of thought, instead of forcing students to mimic mindlessly the manners and thoughts of their teachers. A priest who can improvise a lively, engaging sermon will be more effective with the parish than somebody who simply recites memorized texts in the nineteenth-century style of homily. Instead of being passive listeners, students should become active learners and be given the opportunity to do their own research outside the curriculum. Some students today are systematically persecuted because they overstep the bounds of the curricula in their studies; because they stand out from the rest of the students by refusing to be content to memorize the material given to them and by trying to go further and work on their own; because they learn foreign languages more intensively then their teacher requires. Such students are sometimes accused of unorthodoxy and pride. As a result, the graduates of theological seminaries more often than not are narrow minded, inhibited, dispirited people.

It is true that the Russian Church is repelled by all things Western, non-Orthodox, and foreign. But today's students in theological schools should be educated in a spirit of tolerance and openness toward other confessions, in part by studying comparative theology and world religions. Let us not fear that such "foreign influences" will steer students away from Orthodoxy. On the contrary, they will make our priests only stronger in theological disputes with representatives of other confessions. To this end, we should also encourage educational exchanges with universities abroad. Learning ancient and modern foreign languages is exceedingly important for the priests of the twenty-first century; nobody should be allowed to graduate from the academy without speaking one of the three major European languages (English, French, or German).

Some new disciplines should be introduced to the curriculum. We must study the accomplishments of Western theologians and Orthodox theologians who developed Orthodox thinking abroad during the Soviet era. We must shift the focus from empty-minded memorization of dates and names to the thoughtful study of topics and personalities in church history. We must give our students an extensive course in classical philosophy; today they either do not study this subject at all or take only a superficial introductory course. Another important subject is pastoral psychology; many of our clergymen know absolutely nothing about mental-health issues and in their work with parishioners cannot distinguish between spiritual phenomena and diseases of the mind. Sometimes what is assumed to be the sin of despondency requires medical treatment rather than chastening and penance. Priests must be trained to recognize this.

Furthermore, the relationship between teachers and students today is unequal and often leads to spreading cynicism and loss of faith among some disciples. It is no surprise that the percentage of graduates of theological seminaries and academies who actually go on to take holy orders keeps falling year after year. We must find a fresh approach to students, one that is more sober minded, more respectful, more humane, and more Christian. The exercise of absolute power by seminary inspectors and their aides over students and their daily routines must be abolished. It is also important to diminish the influence of monks over our educational institutions. Distrust of learning is widespread in the monastic milieu. Some monks believe it to be their duty to inculcate in the students at theological schools a negative view of learning as something that is almost antithetical to faith. Very often they also cajole some students into taking monastic vows instead of starting a family, thus recruiting to their ranks people whose hearts do not desire a monastic life, but who are forced to suffer for the rest of their days.

The Church in the Social Sphere

The Church has always taken an active social position. We are involved in philanthropy, sponsoring numerous orphanages, homes for the elderly, hospices, and hospitals. However, the Church cannot possibly perform the social duties of the state—it simply does not have adequate resources. Thus, the main role of the Church is to help people survive and find their way in the current crisis. We should also try to make the state take better care of its citizens. Whatever philanthropic work we can do is but a drop in the ocean compared to the needs of the country and the capacity of the state to meet those needs.

We are developing new organizational structures so that we can work with others in positions of responsibility such as nongovernmental organizations, the armed forces, the president's administration, and the educational system. Although we are only at the very beginning of this process, we have faith that our efforts, in this sphere as in others I have mentioned, will contribute to Russia's spiritual and material rebirth.

And, of course, the rebirth of the Church itself is inextricably bound up with that of the nation. As I sought to summarize this profound challenge in a recent article published in *Nezavisimaya gazeta,* looking ahead to the future, rebirth will be possible:

- When we have theologians of a higher level, educated in ways that our present schools cannot provide. They will include experts in the areas of Bible studies, apostolic studies, church history, and ancient and modern languages. However, these experts will not emerge unless we systematically train them and unless we reform the Church's entire personnel policy to accommodate this goal;

- When we reflect on and internalize the Church's entire twenti-eth-century experience of survival under persecution;
- When we begin the process of renewal of church life on all levels;
- When the Holy Scripture assumes an appropriate role in the life of the Orthodox Church;
- When we begin systematic work to translate and publish the works of the church Fathers;
- When church service becomes accessible to common people;
- When the heritage of the Russian theological school and the experience of the "Paris period" of Orthodox theologians in exile are incorporated and implemented by modern-day Russ-ian theologians;
- When Russian theology frees itself from the "Western prison" and returns to its Byzantine and ancient Christian roots. To ensure this return, we will need fresh theological momentum and new creative approaches toward fundamental theological disciplines;
- When the new school of Orthodox theologians emerges, ready to take over the heritage from the Paris school and thus create a new theological vision for the twenty-first century. Although this school could emerge either in Russia or outside, I hope that it does emerge here, where we have all the right condi-tions for its development;
- When we reform schools and seminaries of the Russian Or-thodox Church, and when their curricula undergo reforms to foster the students' creative potential; and
- When we can create in the Church an atmosphere supportive of healthy academic theological discourse on the most vital themes of modern church life.

The Russian Orthodox Church has enormous human resources, unmatched by any other Christian church in the world. Western seminaries are closing one by one, whereas here we are experiencing a rapid growth in the number of new schools. In the West, Church supporters complain about the deficit of "calling" and lack of inter-est among people to dedicate their lives to their Church, whereas here in many of our religious schools five candidates apply for each available slot. However, we need to learn how to use this potential most efficiently, by carefully selecting personnel, attracting creative young students, channeling them in the right direction, and by encouraging them to study abroad.

Russia on the outset of the twenty-first century is ripe for a theological rebirth. The Church still commands considerable trust from the people and the secular authorities alike. To lose this historic chance would be a crime. That is why we need to engage in renewal—not only quantitatively, but also qualitatively, not only in terms of new cathedrals, but also in terms of theology, education, and mission. We have no other way.

17

CARING FOR THE
HOMELESS IN
ST. PETERSBURG

Valerii Sokolov

I have been working with the homeless since 1990; I came to this work through a chain of fortunate coincidences. At the time I myself was homeless, living without an internal passport. I have lived in such cities as Pskov, Volgograd, and St. Petersburg. At the time, I refused to cooperate with the Soviet authorities. I especially resented performing any kind of work that the state imposed on citizens. In 1989 I returned to St. Petersburg because it was strange for me to live through all the changes going on throughout the country and only hear from others about what was happening in the major cities. I remember telephoning a friend in St. Petersburg who told me that at the May Day demonstration that year some marchers were carrying Imperial Russian tricolor flags—and the police did not stop them. That's when I knew it was time to go back. I got a legal residence permit for St. Petersburg in 1994 and my internal passport in 1995.

The years immediately following 1989 were the greatest time for our country. Anybody could do whatever he or she wanted. Some used the situation to steal state property and secure their own posi-

Valerii Sokolov is the leader of Nochlezhka, a charity group for the homeless, and the publisher of the newspaper *Na Dne*, which is distributed by the homeless in St. Petersburg. Interview recorded and translated by Natan M. Shklyar.
    Interview: May 28, 1999, St. Petersburg

tion in the new Russia as the "political elite." Others, who wanted to do something useful, had the opportunity to do so, because the oppressive Soviet machine of coercion was collapsing. Whoever wanted to steal, stole. Whoever wanted to work, worked. And we were among the latter.

Our initiative was quite simple. At the time the lack of a legal residency certificate *(propiska)* was a criminal offense clearly defined as such in the Criminal Code. I disagreed with this policy. We used the more open atmosphere of that period to work with the Leningrad City Council *(Lensovet)* to address this issue. But we did not lobby council members; instead, we worked with the homeless. We proposed that the City Council grant the homeless food coupons. In the wake of the general reform and the impulse toward democratization all over the country, the council agreed. Easier said than done, however. Who would be distributing these food coupons? There was no mechanism in place. So the city authorities told me that since we had come up with this idea, we should become this mechanism. Thereupon Nochlezhka ("overnight hostel") was formed as the agency designated to register the homeless.

The homeless in St. Petersburg are quite fortunate. In contrast to Moscow, St. Petersburg today functions without the *propiska* system. Moscow is an example of the "crisis of authority." The authorities there have not been able to figure out the appropriate control mechanism, since they cannot use Soviet-era oppressive methods but neither have they learned modern, more subtle, nonauthoritarian methods of control.

Take one example. Today we publish the newspaper *Na Dne* (At the Bottom), which the homeless distribute to earn money. Our colleagues from Odessa, Ukraine, and Minsk, Belarus, have borrowed our experience and started similar projects, with some success. However, in Russia itself this initiative is having a very tough time. We tried to launch a similar publication in Novosibirsk, but we encountered great opposition from the regional authorities. Ironically, the St. Petersburg city administration has done very little for the homeless, whereas in Novosibirsk the oblast has sponsored a homeless shelter. Naively, we assumed that the authorities in Novosibirsk would welcome our initiative, but they dislike giving their homeless the kind of independence that our project gives them in St. Petersburg. They want to give their homeless access to the shelter only in exchange for performing some form of public service. The shelter administrators suggested that we let the homeless spend the night in the shelter in exchange for selling the newspapers. But we did not want to sacrifice our principles in this way. I believe that a state agency charged with sheltering the homeless should provide free access to everybody who needs it, without imposing any kind of economic conditions, as long as this practice is consistent with broad social policy goals.

We are still trying to expand our initiative to Russia's regions, hoping that people will start publishing similar newspapers locally. Usually we advertise the project in the local press, but those who respond want to know first of all how much we will pay. They assume they would be working for a local branch of our agency, not starting their own indigenous group. This is a serious problem, typical of the kind we started having after 1991. From 1988 to 1991, enthusiastic activists, who believed in their cause and wanted to make a difference, started many civic initiatives, but today people expect to be paid for their services. Some even tell us: "We no longer believe in anything. We are prepared to work with you, but at least you should pay us something."

Another of our major accomplishments was registering the homeless to vote in two national elections (1993 and 1996). St. Petersburg is perhaps the only city in the world where this has ever happened. It was extremely hard work, but it was worth it. We made certain that there were no violations of rules at the polling stations, so nobody could doubt the validity of our work, and the Central Electoral Commission accepted it. In 1996 we helped more than 2,000 homeless people register to vote in the presidential election, and television gave heavy coverage to the long lines in front of our polling stations. During this time we increased our registration database by over 1,000 people, for the most part those who were living in St. Petersburg without residence permits. These people had good jobs and incomes, but they had simply never bothered to obtain permits; our polling station was the only place where they were eligible to vote.

Since 1992 we have been providing the homeless with legal counsel, most recently with the help of the Soros Foundation. We have two lawyers and two social workers on our staff. Usually we help our clients draft proper legal documents, citing the relevant provisions of the law. The most common problem our clients encounter is real estate fraud. Every week we air a local television program, an informal talk with the "hero of the day." One program exposed a swindle involving the privatization of a large communal apartment. At first the police investigators assigned to the case refused to cooperate with us, but our program changed their attitude and made a difference.

Our greatest success is our newspaper, *Na Dne*, which began publication five years ago, in 1994. Originally, we had no foundation support and started with our own money, using our own Russian methods. As a matter of fact, the first Russian newspaper called *Na Dne* came out in Moscow in 1912. Named after the famous play by Maxim Gorky, it made a huge splash in Russian society by exposing the horrors of life at the very bottom of the community. So in 1994 we revived this newspaper, but we can do little to emulate the kind of shock that Gorky's play produced in Russian society at the turn of the century. Right now we are running a project, Tell Your Story, designed to give the homeless an opportunity to describe what it feels like to be on the streets. We hope that this project will give the public a new perspective on the homeless problem. At first our circulation was 30,000 copies, but now it is only 10,000, although the paper has grown from four pages to sixteen. *Na Dne* comes out every two weeks. In May 1999, we started a new newspaper, *Senatskaia Ploshchad* (The Senate Square)—my own crazy idea to raise money and help finance *Na Dne*. If we could make *Senatskaia Ploshchad* profitable, we could perhaps make enough money to foot the bill for the rest of our operations. We distribute this paper free of charge in hopes of attracting advertisers in large numbers.

Another accomplishment: In 1998 we successfully lobbied the city administration to launch a program of preventive action against homelessness. As a result, the city established a center to keep track of the homeless who once had the St. Petersburg *propiska*. The center issues these homeless people special residence permits that legalize their status; thus the police cannot abuse them, as officers would if the homeless carried no documents at all. Our own workload has been lightened by the work of this agency, which now registers all those who used to be legal St. Petersburg residents, while we still keep track of all the other homeless. And because this registration agency is now part of the bureaucratic machine, it will be impossible to curtail its activities, so it will work in perpetuity. Since we first helped create this agency, we have had a falling out with the administration of St. Petersburg governor Vladimir Yakovlev; city officials tried to deport the homeless in large numbers beyond the city limits during the election campaign in 1998, when I was running for the city Legislative Assembly. Two years earlier, the state had pledged to open several shelters a year, but had failed to do so. They decided to solve the problem by physically removing the homeless.

We lobby both the administration and the Legislative Assembly. Usually we pick a group of assembly members whom we deem to be closest to us politically and start talking with them, planting seeds of ideas in their heads. Eventually they begin thinking that the ideas are theirs, and then they are more likely to work hard to push them through.

We do not advertise our activities. Word of mouth is the best means of promotion. For instance, we regularly receive letters from more than forty prison facilities requesting us to send newspapers, cigarettes, or clothing. We did try to help, but right now we have no resources.

We have about thirty people working in our various projects and agencies. Some income comes from the export of handcrafted birch-bark boxes to Great Britain. We are also discussing a joint venture to export cedar oil to Great Britain. We get some help from the Russian émigré community, mostly private benefactors. I do not like to engage in fundraising: My philosophy is that people who want to help the homeless will find us. If I have to go to somebody and explain to them the need to help the homeless, that's a different story. I also like joint ventures where there is mutual benefit and profit. We can form a business partnership, make money together, and then each side can use the funds for whatever it wants.

Our total budget is $200,000 a year. We do not depend on Western foundations for our existence, although we do rely on their support. We have financing from the British Know-How Fund, which sponsors a "social advertising" project aiming to influence the public creatively through the use of images. Many social problems are so localized that society as a whole is unaware of their scope and impact, for example the spread of AIDS, diabetes, cancer, and homelessness. Creative advertising technologies can help people develop a subconscious awareness of social problems and find within themselves a desire to help. Our partner is one of the largest British advertising agencies. We have also had talks with the Mott Foundation about financing our regional chapters, but they were not enthusiastic about our work—it was not global enough, they said. Homelessness is a truly global problem, however: It touches on all aspects of life and affects a remarkably broad cross section of society.

Aside from my work with the homeless, I take an active part in local politics. However, I keep my personal political ambitions separate from Nochlezhka. I first ran for the State Duma in 1995, using my own money. For the duration of the campaign, I resigned from my regular duties at Nochlezhka to ensure that nobody could accuse us of being politically partial. I do not belong to any existing parties and believe that average people who are disappointed in the current regime should organize and create their own party.

Western donors have much to learn about Russia. One of the problems here is excessive reliance on governmental structures. Take one example: In 1995 I submitted to TACIS a proposal for a grant of 200,000 ECUs to implement a project that would have dramatically improved the situation for the homeless in St. Petersburg. Although the initial response was favorable, we were ultimately turned down. When I telephoned to find out why, I was told that TACIS had consulted with Russian government officials, who replied that if TACIS funded a nongovernmental initiative that might become more effective than initiatives by the government, this would undermine Russian statehood.

Often we face a lack of understanding about our work. Some people are offended: Why should we help the homeless when there are other social groups that need urgent care, including the sick, the elderly, the handicapped? Why should we spend our energy helping people who are already "wasted" and empty. My response: They are still human beings and citizens, they simply lack *propiska*. The main problem with Western aid agencies is that they try too hard to nurture a cooperative relationship with the authorities. In fact, if they are working with the authorities currently in power, that means they do not believe that a truly democratic alternative can emerge in the future. But people who vote at the polls can indeed overthrow the powers that be, as happened in St. Petersburg in 1996 when, in part as a result of our efforts, Yakovlev defeated incumbent mayor Anatolii Sobchak.

Our greatest disappointments of the past nine years have been when certain Western partners whom we trusted in good faith used us for their own needs and never gave anything back. For example, we worked with one German organization that used our name in their fundraising efforts in Germany, which brought them substantial capital. They would encourage German "good Samaritans" to make tax-deductible contributions to help the Russian homeless, whose photographs they obtained from us. They even gave people receipts for their donations. What the individual donors did not know was that we never saw that money. In this way, the group stole about DM1.5 million from us. I find it quite pathetic when people use the tragedy of the homeless to make money for themselves.

In contrast, our partners in Scotland are very professional and honest. All of our dealings with them are out in the open. If we agree to enter into a joint venture together to make money, we clearly set out the division of labor and profits. If they want to give us financial support, we also clearly outline the terms of agreement. When there is an equal partnership, work thrives. But when one partner tries to deceive the other, an unacceptable situation arises. There are 6 billion people in the world, and ultimately, through trial and error, we will find the partners we want.

Of course, I have my own vision of how the problem of homelessness should be addressed. We live in the real world, however, where the state as well as the nongovernmental organizations lack resources, so we have to make do with what we have. I have a vision for a system of social infrastructure that would enable any person to lift himself up from homelessness and assume a dignified place as a member of society. This system would address the many problems faced by the homeless, including dependency on drugs and alcohol and lack of faith in one's own self. We need a structured network of psychological counseling and emotional support to help these people believe in themselves. Under such a system, the homeless can climb higher and higher until they attain complete reintegration into society.

The situation is different in the West. These nations have long-established economic and social systems. In the course of my work I often travel to Scotland. I notice that the homeless there occupy a certain niche that leaves very little room for upward mobility. Potentially, a homeless person can move up in the world: get a decent job, even have a house with a garden, and deal with all the problems of "normal" life like car payments, parking fees, and mortgages. But at the end of the day, he is still viewed as a former homeless person, which affects how society treats him. Maybe this system works in Scotland. On the other hand, what is happening in Russia today might be instructive to the West. Our homeless live on the edge and have learned to survive in a hostile environment. This might be a crazy idea, but I believe that if they were given a business to run (of course, under certain conditions), they would be incredibly success- ful because they are used to fighting against the odds and have be- come naturally entrepreneurial. As human beings and as survivors they are incredibly flexible and thus have great potential. Of course, one cannot just give them money and tell them to run a business; it is crucial first to provide them with a framework of psychological sup- port that will give them the confidence they need.

18

WHAT FUTURE AWAITS THE RUSSIAN PRESS?

A Prognosis

Iosif Dzialoshinskii

Today it would be impossible to find a single person in Russia who is satisfied with the condition and performance of the press in general, and the regional press in particular. Everyone vehemently criticizes the newspapers, radio, and television. I won't repeat or rebut the charges; and I will say that most of them are just. But listening once again to the invectives against the press, I recall the years of my youth, spent at the regional newspaper *Leninskoe znamia* (Lenin Banner) and at the republic-wide Communist Party newspaper *Sovetskaia Moldaviia* (Soviet Moldavia), and I realize what a gigantic leap forward the former Soviet press has made. At least, a significant portion of the press has moved forward.

Understandably, such a swift transformation could not avoid various pitfalls, sometimes quite severe. But I react much more positively to an unkempt, sweaty running man than to a well-touched-up, flawlessly dressed, and respectable corpse. Nevertheless, the Russian

Born in 1945 in Azerbaijan, **Iosif Mikhailovich Dzialoshinskii** grew up in the Far East but later moved to Moldavia to begin his journalistic career. He worked for several newspapers there, then earned his Ph.D. in philology at the journalism school of Moscow State University; afterward, he held research and teaching positions in Moscow. In 1993, together with his partners, he founded the Institute for Humanitarian Communications, which he still heads. A civil rights activist, Dzialoshinskii has published numerous books and articles and often appears on TV to discuss media issues. Translated by Antonina W. Bouis.

press has developed in such a way that we need to consider where it is going and what kind of future awaits it.

The Past

In the years 1991–1995, Russia made the third attempt in its history to escape from the trap of totalitarianism. The first two attempts (1825 and 1917) ended with even greater clampdowns on the individual. The necessary, but extremely painful, transition from Soviet totalitarianism touched the foundations of state and society. So abrupt and simultaneous were these transformations that the ensuing crises were disjointed and leapfrogging, violating the usual cause-and-effect paradigm.

The real (and some would say only) result of the reforms was glasnost. The press, the mass media, turned into an important, and perhaps the most authoritative, social institution of those years. And yet, while promoting the values of democracy and market relations in society, Russian journalists did not apply those principles to themselves. It was a golden age for freedom of speech; the press could criticize communism as well as the current regime, while being paid quite well by that same regime. You could say whatever you wanted, without thinking about any economic consequences. With the lifting of censorship, the press nevertheless retained state subsidies; prices of publications were laughably low, and circulation rose sharply. While fighting for Russia's transformation to a market economy, only a few editors tried to imagine what that market economy would mean for them personally and for the publications they headed. Few tried to change their own economic base or the management of their publications.

New publications continued to crop up with no reason for existence except to satisfy the desire of their ambitious founders. For instance, in the period 1993–1997, the number of registered periodicals in Russia rose by 45 percent. At the same time, the countrywide subscription circulation fell by about 32 percent. Even if we add retail sales and take alternative subscriptions into account, the trend was still negative.

In Moscow alone there are still fifteen daily newspapers of quality. In the city of Yekaterinburg, with a population of 1.5 million, an average annual income in 1998 of just over $1,600 per capita, and a monthly advertising market of $2 million (before the August crisis of

1998), there were 170 periodical publications, a dozen radio stations, and twelve television stations. Television's share of the advertising market in Yekaterinburg was approximately one-third, between $500,000 and $700,000 a month. Those twelve stations operated on $700,000 a month, but 80 percent of the advertising revenue went to only three of them. The question arises: What were the other nine stations living on?

This press system was needed only by those who worked in it and those who gave money to it. Even the so-called Russian media empires were behaving like socialist enterprises rather than capitalist ones. They were not counting their money.

However, the euphoria of the early perestroika years quickly ended. Glasnost itself needed certain guarantees, the most important of which were a developed civil society, coordinated market transformations, and the development of democratic institutions based on establishing a truly effective judicial and law enforcement system.

Absent such guarantees, freedom of the press quickly dried up, and journalists felt deceived. It turned out that renaming publications and changing founders was not enough to solve all the problems. After the economic and political cataclysms came a wholly predictable drop in people's interest in mass media. The circulation of newspapers and magazines fell several times and is unlikely ever to return to those earlier levels. Some newspapers have ceased to exist.

Having felt the cruel hand of the market, many journalists started asking for a return to socialism. In fact, in January 1994, the editors of several large newspapers threatened a strike, demanding financial subsidies from the government. The Union of Journalists of Russia, the Committee on Information Policy and Communications of the State Duma of the Russian Federation, and the Russian Federation Committee on the Press all played the same game, even if not in total harmony, trying to shelter the mass media from the vicissitudes of the market—and they almost succeeded.

However, Russian society, having moved from one condition to a completely different one, made entirely new demands upon information subsystems in general and on journalism in particular. Russian journalism responded to these demands by broadening the repertoire of the mass media, changing the priorities of its activities, revising criteria for personnel evaluation, introducing new technologies, and reorienting the professional mindset.

Another problem for journalists that arose in those years grew out of the need to find a new professional, spiritual, social, and political identity. Tens of thousands of workers in newspapers and magazines, radio and television, now had to determine for themselves how they would behave. Many had to overcome decades-long professional principles and goals and develop altogether new criteria for self-appraisal. The rapid changes in those early transition years led many Russian journalists to suffer mental breakdowns. Perceptions that had once been rigid began to fluctuate, to crumble, and were then replaced. Much of what journalists had taken as incontestable truth turned out to be errors, lies, or illusions; and what used to be considered erroneous, suddenly turned out to be the truth.

It was particularly difficult to define one's political stand. The thinking of most Russian journalists in that period made up a rather bizarre mix: ideas of openness to the West, recognition of the market, and adherence to democratic values jostled with populism, concepts of social justice under a powerful state, elements of paternalism, and faith in Russia's great historic mission. This uneasy amalgam of limited economic liberalism with moderate cultural nationalism and notions of sovereignty formed the basic sociopolitical position of many Russian journalists. (In fact, many still hold these views today.)

The search for a new professional identity was complicated by the need to choose from among several concurrent ideologies that Russian journalists used to explain and justify their activity.

One of these ideologies orients the journalist toward messianic, enlightening, and propagandistic action. Under this philosophy, journalists contend that they express the highest interests of the state and society; therefore they have the right to manage (and sometimes even to manipulate) the minds and actions of the broad public. For such a journalist, the audience is an object of action, an object to be mastered.

Another ideology, one imported from the West, allows journalists to regard themselves as unprejudiced purveyors of the news, getting information and passing it on to society without bearing any responsibility for how it would be used, or by whom.

A third professional ideology, derived from the best examples of Russian editorial writing, requires the journalist to work toward solving specific social and human problems.

Naturally, there is a fourth ideology—to earn as much money as possible by offering the audience those news items, impressions, and images for which it is willing to pay the most money. In this case, a journalist regards himself as an instrument for satisfying the clients' desires. The audience is not a partner in communication, but a consumer of services: "The client is always right."

These approaches to the meaning and organization of journalism differ from one another in every essential criterion of professional self-appraisal: the basic goals of the journalist as set by himself (or by someone else); the intended audience; the means by which the writer plans to reach his goals; and the methods and technology he uses.

It is a difficult professional choice, and most Russian journalists have yet to make it.

New kinds of knowledge were now required. Thousands of seminars and training sessions have been held in editorial offices and schools to help journalists understand how to manage and market newspapers, determine editorial policy, and design advertising policy. American journalists were of great help; they visited even the most remote newspapers and patiently explained to their Russian colleagues how to publish newspapers and magazines, or run television and radio stations, under market conditions.

However, the American experience did not translate very easily into Russian reality.

The Present

The functioning of journalism in Russia today is determined by the four institutions that consume its product.

First, the government. Not only does the government determine the rules of the game but it generates, commissions, and consumes media products. The government can buy journalists or force them to comply with its demands. Coercion can take many forms, exploiting, for example, the need to request office space from local bureaucrats, or the fear that the authorities might turn off the electricity or raise the rent. But the problem is not only that the state is actively interested in journalism; many journalists themselves see the government as the most important, if not the only, source of public vitality. Over 70 percent of journalists rely on government agencies as topics for stories and as sources of information.

Second, big business. Russia's criminalized business is very interested in having the media operate in a certain way. Because very few authentic businesspeople seriously believe that media investments can be profitable, organized crime controls journalism and its entire support system, both directly and indirectly. Bribery, pressure of various kinds, and invitations to join various prestigious associations are among the weapons used.

Third, the intelligentsia. At the dawn of perestroika and glasnost, the only groups controlling the media were government representatives and the intelligentsia. The intelligentsia was the principal supplier of media content. And then, as circumstances changed, the intelligentsia was shunted aside. Nevertheless, it still continues to influence the media, particularly through the use of information associations and inducements to attract journalists to them.

Finally, civil society. Journalists take an active part in public organizations, and many become leaders of civil society groups.

The government wants journalists to give it a pleasant face, to polish its image; it hands out subsidies for that. So journalists fulfill official commissions. The business community wants journalists to push their interests. Journalists (for appropriate compensation) prepare and publish commissioned articles in great quantities, with enthusiasm. The intelligentsia wants journalists to bring to the public certain theories, myths, and values they have created. And since the intelligentsia can pay nothing, it writes its own articles and pressures the media to publish them—whether or not those ideas and theories meet the profound needs of the population. The components of civil society also want the press to help them solve their problems.

Surrounding these four structures, on the periphery of the system, are the average readers, viewers, and listeners, who, truth to tell, are of no great interest to many practitioners in the media because they bring little profit and cause much trouble.

And what do the journalists want? In Russia today, according to the Union of Journalists of Russia, there are more than 100,000 professional journalists, that is, people who consider themselves to be professional journalists. These are people who are accustomed to a certain lifestyle, a certain social position, and a certain professional behavior.

Analyzing the relationships among these four elements of the Russian media (and leaving aside the daily kaleidoscope of flickering news items on the TV screen), we find that we are all in the dramatic

situation of losing our illusions. In many respects, Russia has re-
treated from the ideas that gripped people's minds during the first
period of political and economic transformation.

In journalism, one consequence of that retreat is the desire of the
Russian nomenklatura to remind journalists who is boss. Regional
leaders are especially active in trying to housebreak journalists, although the federal authorities, beginning with Evgenii Primakov's
government, also began severely limiting access to information. In
the second half of 1999, with the approach of elections to the Duma
and the presidency, pressure on the independent press intensified.

The Future

Even in these complex conditions, however, Russian journalists are
energetically defending their right to professional independence.
They are fighting for the enactment of federal laws that would put
an end to any possibility of governmental interference with the
press. They are actively lobbying for the passage of draft legislation
"On the Right to Access to Information." They are demanding legal
regulation of radio and television; in the absence of a law regulating
television, broadcasters end up so slavishly dependent on the executive authorities that one cannot speak of them as independent media.

Information legislation in the regions is beset with particularly
acute problems. During our research on the legal framework for
mass media in the regions, we found that most often regional lawmakers see the media as an instrument of government influence on
political and economic development.

Moreover, freedom of speech and other human rights in the different regions are so sharply differentiated that Russia in effect has
eighty-nine different political systems. Compare, for instance, freedom of speech guarantees in Sverdlovsk oblast with those in auto-
cratically governed Kalmykiya.

The next focus of the journalists' fight for their future is the creation of a functioning market for mass media.

In the Soviet years, a system was created, perfect in its own way,
for organizing press activity, complete with predetermined circulation figures, planned subscriptions, fixed prices, and so on. That system guaranteed journalists comfortable circumstances. After journalists obtained their freedom, however, they discovered that
freedom had its down side. The market in which they found them-

selves was not at all the way it was described in textbooks. Trying to adjust to this strange new environment, only a few publications followed a standard market path by improving the quality of their product, modifying it to meet consumer demand, or attracting advertisers. Most editors resorted to very different methods: Publishing commissioned materials under the guise of journalistic exposés, renting out their premises, not paying taxes, using undeclared cash, and so on. During this period, some regional newspapers fawned on government agencies. Editors asked regional authorities for financial and other kinds of support; in exchange, they had to provide informational and political services. All this led to a corrupt press.

Those interested in a healthier development of the Russian press want to increase the transparency of the advertising and information markets, audit circulation figures of print media, and issue reliable ratings of television programs. To the extent that such efforts bear fruit, advertisers who today doubt their ability to evaluate the effectiveness of their media advertising will gain confidence.

Russian journalists are also grappling with the issue of ethical self-regulation. In England, for example, no one would think of rushing to the courts if a newspaper should print inaccurate (as distinct from libelous) information. There, if a journalist violates one of the unwritten but well-understood rules of journalism, he can lose his job and even be drummed out of the profession. In Russia, unfortunately, a professional community has not yet formed. Many journalists feel no responsibility before their colleagues (much less before their readers or viewers), and this had led to many violations of professional ethics. Taking advantage of such breaches, several conservative legislators are calling for harsh laws that would protect society and the state from irresponsible journalists. In order to avoid such measures, many Russian journalists feel that the time has come to create their own institutions for regulating media operations and managing relations with the public and the state.

Russian journalists are once again keenly interested in professional development and have evinced great interest in *The Charlotte Project,* a book that recounts an experiment by an American journalist who was dissatisfied with her professional development and sought remedies. The book was not translated into Russian until 1998, even though it was published in the United States in 1994.

The ideas the book propounds were discussed intensively in training sessions for Russian journalists run by the Institute for Humanitarian Communications in 1999. The participants severely criticized the Russian media community for its widespread assumption that the function of journalism is purely to gather and disseminate information. This shift to a philosophy of "pure information" accompanied the shift in the public attitude toward journalists as hired hands who could be used to transmit all sorts of information, as long as it had some semblance of veracity. This attitude, in turn, has led to an increasing alienation between journalists and their audience, on the one hand, and frustration among journalists, on the other.

Russian journalists at the training sessions were very interested in how the idea of "civil journalism" could be integrated into a conceptual and technological system enabling their occupation to attain a new level of professionalism. They particularly liked the idea that the means of mass communication had first of all to help the public influence politicians to understand the true interests of citizens. Many journalists from the regional media have gone much further. They want to give journalism a human face, make it belong to the people, linking journalism with the profound need of Russians to express themselves and understand their place in life. An interesting example of this kind of journalism is the magazine *Severiane* (The Northerners); the story of its founding which was contributed by one of its founders, Ol'ga Lobyzova, can be read in Chapter 19 of this volume. Such projects are happening in other regions of Russia, too.

An important result of these seminars was the formation of an "invisible college" composed of participants who advocate the idea of civil and socially responsible journalism. The Institute for Humanitarian Communications has the basic goal of stimulating the activities of the mass media so that they bring citizens into a dialogue that could ultimately solve social problems and create a civil society.

These training seminars, together with the publications of the Institute for Humanitarian Communications, have served as catalysts for a powerful transformation process in Russian journalism, which is coming to realize the vulnerability of a purely informational approach and which is trying to find an effective and comprehensible philosophy for its professional activity.

Obviously, future development will depend on the path that the Russian state and society take. The most pessimistic scenario assumes that the resistance of certain elements of society will ruin plans for the country's transition to a market economy and democracy. The chances of this happening are very low, but they exist. If such a backlash should indeed occur, Russia would face the danger not only of internal catastrophe but of external catastrophe as well. As for the press, it is clear that such a scenario would lead to the restoration of a totalitarian grip over the mass media.

Another scenario, which many analysts consider more likely, assumes that in the near future, Russia will become a moderately authoritarian state with an economy that mixes state control with capitalism. Should this scenario come to pass, the government would in the first instance try to control the mass media through economic and legal means.

In the final analysis, Russia's transition from an industrial society to an informational one will lead to the establishment and development of information and communications consortia, which will publish newspapers and magazines as well as produce audiovisual products. Such integrated information enterprises will make full use of new technological capabilities. Since these consortia will be steadily moving away from government influence, the authorities will try to hinder their development. In particular, they will use the pretext of combating media monopolies.

As the country moves along the path of market reforms, many publications will fall by the wayside. The periodicals that do survive will become more businesslike, contemporary, and responsive to the changing demands of the public. A determining factor in the increasing competition of newspapers with other media will be the quality of their product. Naturally, all this will require that journalists adjust to the accelerating pace of change.

Gradually, journalists will come to realize that the reader, the viewer, and the listener must be treated not as a mere recipient of information or as an object to be manipulated or educated, but as a living, doubting person seeking an effective way of organizing his life. Such an approach will bring us closer to a true dialogue directed toward answering the perennial question: How should we live?

In summing up, I can say that journalism in Russia today is undergoing a period of unique transformation. Like our society in general, it has emerged from the totalitarian shell and is trying to evolve into a normal structure of civil society. Some things work, and some do not. But unless the Russian press can become an authoritative, independent institution, no other transformations in Russia will be possible.

19

MY LIFE, MY FATE

Severiane and Russia's North

Ol'ga Lobyzova

Fate Foreshadowed

After starting to work at the city newspaper at age fifteen, I shifted to the theater. No, I don't want to describe the colorful opening nights, the life of an ordinary actor, or even the innovations of directors. The wardrobe master and light technician, the cloakroom attendant and stagehand, the ticket collector and hairdresser—they, too, deserve at least a share of the applause when the play ends and the curtain falls. The distinctive smell of the theater, its indescribable magnetism; perhaps you will sense them better when you meet, not the celebrated prima ballerinas and stars who are brilliant even when they come from the provinces, but people of the modest theatrical professions, those who are more likely to be devoted for life to their chosen work, their theater.

In those distant "stagnant" 1970s, a diverse group of people chose that path: Those of a philosophical bent or just the opposite; outright failures ("I don't give a damn") or people leading difficult lives

Born in 1955 in a provincial industrial town near Gorky (present-day Nizhny Novgorod), **Ol'ga Grigor'evna Lobyzova** wrote articles for a local newspaper when she was only fifteen; she continued her journalistic career at Gorky State University, where she studied history and philology. After graduation, she pursued a career in radio journalism while publishing articles in various newspapers. After moving to the Far North in 1986, Lobyzova continued her award-winning work in radio and journalism. She is an active member of several journalistic professional associations. Translated by Anna Kucharev.

and perhaps suffering some kind of breakdown; or those for whom the theater was a transitional stage before their final descent to the social nadir.

But I was taking my first timid steps in journalism and, naturally, couldn't express my thoughts about all this in a clear and striking manner. It was more like a premonition of a life theme, my first encounter with the breathtaking iceberg of life's diversity, whose hidden underwater mass a "bookish" schoolgirl could only dream about.

Then there was a passion for Pushkin and Dostoevsky, and the question of psychologism in contemporary Soviet literature, the subject of my senior thesis. Along with my studies and a turbulent student life, library vigils and merry little feasts, scholarly conferences and tours along small Russian rivers, talks "about life" and cracking the "granite of science," I continued to work with the mass media in Nizhny Novgorod. I remember to this day how I wound up in a boarding school for mentally retarded children, where I was confronted with tragedy, pain, devotion. . . .

Before I defended my thesis, I began working in radio broadcasting at the Kaprolaktam manufacturing association, one of the oldest and largest enterprises in Dzerzhinsk, the nation's leading city for the chemical industry, which employed more than 30,000 workers.

At that time, in addition to printing newspapers with large circulations, municipal enterprises and research institutes established radio editorial boards. We worked with municipal and provincial radio broadcasters, meeting at seminars and elsewhere simply to discuss problems of life and work. Nearly all of us were young; there was a spirit of competition and camaraderie between us. We valued the intonation and emotion in radio that gave us an advantage over the print media; after all, the papers, especially the official press, were blinkered and dried out as could be.

These lines may seem an odd assembly of reminiscences and unrelated thoughts. Actually, they aren't. Somehow they deftly and logically fall into place, row after row, following my own conception of my professional career. The embodiment of this concept of life was the appearance, survival, and development of the people's magazine *Severiane* (The Northerners).

For five years thereafter I worked as an editor at the radio station of the Plastik manufacturing association. For the first time, I was responsible for virtually everything, including technical, ideological, and, of course, diplomatic issues. Soon, however, this favorite brain-child, the contacts I made, my thorough knowledge of the problems of management and workers, suddenly began to burden me as being petty, demanding, and predictable. The limits of my activities seemed narrow and the paths well-worn. "Somehow I need more air here. . . ."

But I didn't feel like wasting away in some fatal rapture: If I didn't try to stretch the limits of this compulsion to change now, as soon as I could, while I still felt excited about my work and had the desire to have an effect, to make a foray into the unknown, I believed that such enthusiasm would be impossible later. Life would move along under its own momentum, and I would be left to regret unclaimed and, therefore, missed opportunities.

I sent job inquiries to the radio and television committees of Russia's five northern regions. Why there? It seemed to me that the epi-center of major events was there, life was in full swing there, far away from everyday routines, out there in the harsh conditions of the Far North. At the peak of their accomplishments, a different kind of character was formed: The northerner.

The first to answer me was the committee at Salekhard, in the Ya-mal-Nenets region (itself a part of Tyumen oblast). They suggested that I send several transcripts of my radio broadcasts as a sort of business card. It was still that euphoric time when everyone was talking about the Tyumen' North. It didn't didn't take much work to find an enterprise in my own city that made special equipment for the natural gas industries of Yamal and to interview people directly involved.

The broadcasts turned out to be of high quality. The enterprise was refining a powerful technological process to a high degree of precision, and the workers talked about it simply, graphically, and professionally. I sent a small package of text with my "creations" to my northern colleagues and awaited their reply. They responded dryly, even crudely, writing that they had received my package, and that the broadcast had been aired, but that it could have been even better. They didn't bother to introduce themselves and scrawled some kind of unintelligible hook instead of a signature. How was I supposed to address the "hook?" I answered the arrogant northern-ers in about the same spirit but sent them a few more transcripts.

Soon after dispatching my harsh epistle, I received a phone call. It was from Anatolii Konstantinovich Onel'chuk, the chairman of the

Yamal-Nenets Autonomous District TV and Radio Committee. At that point, my sense of impasse intensified, grew strong enough to be palpable. His energetic voice sounded clear and enticing, like the voice of hope:

"Ol'ga Grigor'evna, were you offended by me?"

"And were you by me?"

And we both laughed at the same time. He suggested that I work with them a while to prove myself, and to see how *they* worked. My vacation time was approaching and I agreed without hesitating. I agreed without asking who was taking on what obligations, including the material ones; after all, even then the North was a distant and expensive "pleasure" for those of us who earned very average wages. But I was accustomed to being responsible for myself, always and in everything, especially since initiative, as we say, is punishable.

The last days of July 1985 in Moscow, as I was departing, were scorching; on arrival in Salekhard I noticed that the vegetation was tender and somewhat sickly, as if it hadn't gathered up enough strength. There were little islands of poplar fluff, like snow that hadn't melted, and big-eyed daisies with green, still immature centers, not bright yellow ones. Instead of the usual concrete beneath the airplane's wheels we saw bumpy, camouflage-colored metal plates—this was a military airfield, and it apparently had served as such for a very limited time. It's true what they say, nothing is more permanent than the temporary. From my first steps in Salekhard I discovered that everything here was on a temporary basis, as if the inhabitants were just about to beat a retreat and all who could, would abandon these deserted, cold, God-forsaken, sparsely settled parts. And then everything would revert to how it had been hundreds of years ago.

Salekhard stretches along the bright-blue Ob River, immense in its lower reaches. The TV and Radio Committee was—and still is—located in one of the city's squat, listing little houses, the former house of a merchant, without plumbing or basic amenities. But, thank God, such quarters are slowly becoming exotic: Perhaps even before these lines appear in print, my colleagues will celebrate a house-warming in a modern building, specially equipped and designated for TV and radio journalists.

When they do, I hope they carry with them from their old "Radio House" what I felt most strongly during my first hours and days with them—a kind, creative atmosphere and a passionate involvement with their work. They knew how to work and how to relax;

for Salekhardians in those years winding up the day at a *kapustnik* (an evening of amateur stand-up comedy) in the radio committee was lucky and very desirable.

A journey in an old all-terrain vehicle with constantly slipping track belts took me through the mountains of the polar Ural region into Europe—along the routes of the summer nomads—and back into Asia. Here were the quarters of reindeer breeders, people who had never been seen before, whose remarkable way of life flowed in close harmony with nature; The vast distances and the peaks covered with snow that hadn't even melted by August, all worthy of Nicholas Roerich's brush. It was precisely after I came into contact with this multidimensional world of the tundra, so open and yet so secret—was it from the past? the future?—that my heart was taken once and for all by Yamal, a spacious land that belied the blunt heaviness of its name.

Once the North enters a person, it never releases him; it will compel him to return even after years of separation, in spite of the circumstances. *Severiane* features a column entitled "The Attraction of the North," in which people describe how they wound up in the North, how it received them, how it displayed both unexpected tenderness and stunning capriciousness. The North—is it salvation? Oblivion? Escape? Despair? Hope? Impasse? The topic is endless and unique. The leitmotif of each person's life are three numbers: The day, month, and year when he arrived in the North.

April 9, 1986, is marked as my first working day in the North. After working a little more than a year at the radio station, I transferred to the regional newspaper, *Krasnyi Sever* (The Red North). Thus, without suspecting it, I took several more steps toward founding *Severiane*: Innumerable assignments, primarily into the Yamal interior, and then the launching of *Polyarnaya Zvezda* (The Northern Star) as a weekly, the first among the regional northern newspapers. Everyone created, searched for, and tested their own conceptions, styles, approaches. The search for form and content went on concurrently; this semiofficial organ did not put pressure on other newspapers, and journalists had splendid opportunities for self-expression. Evolution, ethnography, culture, economics, society. . . .

I wrote about old women from the tiny half-deserted village of Nori; about the Kuton'uransk bakers, who baked the most delicious bread under ghastly circumstances; about the search for wives for the reindeer breeders; about the boy with heart trouble abandoned at the Radio House, who suddenly acquired both a family and his health. . . . At any rate, in the end, there was always room for hope in the conclusions I drafted. I didn't come across any absolutely hopeless situations or insurmountable circumstances. After all even death, no matter what anyone says, is the apotheosis of life, its conclusion and quintessence. Besides, the weekly was no longer that boring little four-column rag, whose style and size were predetermined and unchangeable. It had already become a symbiosis of a newspaper and a magazine, from which both formats gained. We worked with inspiration; we thought more about the newspaper, new heroes and publication topics, and less about ourselves. During perestroika the circulation of the regional newspaper reached its peak—20,000 copies for the nearly 500,000 inhabitants of the Yamal-Nenets Autonomous Region. Ordinary people with their opinions, dreams, and problems, occupied the pages of the newspaper, at first timidly and then more and more confidently.

Severiane: The New Color in the Palette of the Yamal Mass Media

Right up to 1991–1992, with the dissolution of the USSR and the start of the "parade of sovereignties," the concept of a Yamal-Nenets Autonomous Region was formal, not geographical. The address was written clearly and definitely—Tyumen oblast, city of Salekhard. Most newcomers sought a quick ruble without even suspecting that they were in Yamal. The Tyumen regional administration dictated everything, even the smallest rules of the game. Our editorial staff had to request permission from the Regional Printers and Publishers Agency for even the pettiest editorial expenses.

But in the early 1990s, the Moscow center let go of the reins, lacking the power to hold them so tightly any longer. Yamal was one of the first regions in the country to begin the battle for its sovereignty, and it was finally recognized as a full-fledged subject of the Federation. In retaliation, Tyumen oblast immediately expelled our newspaper. Yes, yes, imagine that the *Krasnyi Sever*, after becoming a weekly and switching from outdated type to modern offset methods, had to be printed in the city of Tyumen, 2,000 kilometers from Salekhard, Yamal's capital city. We had to send the film to Tyumen with airplane crews, and we picked up the printed copies the same way.

It is only now that one of the best printing complexes in the Urals has come to be located in Salekhard; all that remains is to master the technology and train the specialists.

I was dispatched to Moscow to bring home the truth to Mikhail Poltoranin, then minister of the press. My editor, however, didn't assign me any unachievable goals. "You probably won't get to see the minister. So at least get through to one of his deputies. Explain that our situation is critical: The population and regional authorities cannot remain indefinitely without a publication of their own."

I nodded my head in agreement, but in my heart I swore to be loyal to my own newspaper: I would meet with Poltoranin himself no matter what and would try to convince him that we urgently needed help. Backed by the support of Vladimir Arteev, the region's representative in the Supreme Soviet of the USSR, an energetic man of authority and a good friend of our newspaper, I bolted forward after waiting in the minister's reception room for more than three hours. My turn had come, but with no luck . . . Tyumen oblast officials had beaten me to it through a direct telephone connection (their intelligence system had worked efficiently); Ivan Kiapik, the director of the oblast's graphic publishers, had already telephoned Poltoranin. When I walked into the minister's extensive office, he was standing beside his desk, gesticulating menacingly and inquiring loudly:

"Ah, you're the one who wants to appropriate the Salekhard printers and our equipment? You're the one separating yourself from everyone and hoping to survive independently?"

Nothing doing. After being stuck in the reception room, I wasn't about to be overcome by these overbearing cries, but charged into battle straightaway:

"What equipment, Mikhail Nikiforovich? Dating from the times of Ochakov and the conquest of the Crimea? Leave it for yourself, maybe it will be good for a museum exhibit. But first, you should also hear from the other side that's been dragged into the conflict. And you ought to have a look at our newspaper. How do you like it?"

And I shoved a few copies of *Krasnyi Sever* under his nose. Somehow he became kinder instantly. He even said that, if we were to continue to produce such quality work, we would be fully capable of claiming a decent place in the nationwide championship of regional newspapers.

This was how we won the internecine war. Right up until the establishment of our own graphic base, we successfully published the paper, doing all our own prepublication work at the editorial-publishing complex of the *Krasnyi Sever.*

The Yamal region was visibly divided into rural, agrarian, industrial, and urbanized areas. For a long time, the contrasts between life in these different areas were scandalous. The asphalted model town of Nadym was planted with parks and gardens, had straight rows of upright five-story buildings, was well supplied with food products and manufactured goods, and offered its citizens sufficient salaries. Virtually next door, right there, the villages and settlements of the Nadymskii district drowned in mud and decrepitude, offering neither normal living and working conditions nor prospects of any kind.

Settlers from other parts of Russia, many of whom were security guards or janitors, valued only money in their new lives up north. They were frank to the point of shamelessness: "We'll be honest: we came here to take. To take everything if possible." These people regarded with condescension the stable, permanent population of the rural areas and of Salekhard itself, which suffered the same poverty as the hinterlands that were not favored by the oil and gas generals. The immigrants felt they were the true masters. He who pays the piper calls the tune. And that is why the question arose of transferring the regional capital from unprestigious, pitiful Salekhard, forever needing financing from the leftover rubles in the budget, to the multistoried, brick-and-concrete city of Novyi Urengoi.

If you looked at Yamal only as a rich storehouse of natural resources, then you would feel compelled to grab everything valuable quickly and with a minimum of effort; you wouldn't care whether the grass even grew. However, not everything is as simple as it may seem to worshippers of the Golden Calf. Yamal is an ancient land. It contains not only oil and gas but archeological monuments and prehistoric settlements as well. It is the homeland of a unique Arctic civilization—the few remaining indigenous peoples of the Far North.

Our newspaper began publishing these themes emphatically, taking a lofty civic perspective. The editorial staff initiated two expeditions: Along the "501st construction" route (everything connected with this project until then had been classified secret); and along the Ob River, from its source to its estuary, to attract attention to the environmental problems suffered by this greatest of Siberian rivers.

But, judging from our circulation figures and subscription rates within the region, the people of the industrial parts of Yamal were not very excited by these topics. We have not yet succeeded in attracting their interest.

Much has changed, nonetheless. Common sense and decency have prevailed. A Salekhardian, Yurii Vasil'yevich Neelov, a true native son and a man who thinks with a long-term perspective and judges matters sensitively, has become the governor of Yamal. Plans that previously seemed strange and unrealistic have now become achievable. The naked rationalism of the newcomers, who often spent most of their northern sojourns living out of suitcases and who never became intimates of this land, was replaced by filial concern for it and for those populating it. Land of my father, my birthplace—for Russians, these values are eternal.

Nor did what was happening elsewhere in Russia pass by Yamal. Builders, transport and road workers, oil and gas workers, all experienced the effects of the Russian economic crisis in full measure; employees of financial institutions and pensioners also began feel the pinch.

The social programs that Governor Neelov began implementing at that time were unprecedented. A bare listing of his innovations would take up too much space. I will merely emphasize that, as a result of these programs, the Yamal-Nenets Autonomous Region in recent years has become a relatively successful Siberian area, even compared to Russia as a whole. Both the young and old are coming here, some to begin their northern lives, some to end their working years, counting on some measure of security in their old age. Who knows? Perhaps given chronic Russian instability, this dashing from one extreme to another, and the intensification of destructive tendencies, it may turn out that the regional authorities have taken on more than they can handle.

As is now absolutely clear, Yamal is an extremely rich source of raw mineral wealth, a tasty morsel for those who maneuver in big business. Time will tell whether the region's indigenous power structures will serve only as a buffer softening the confrontations between the oligarchs and the general population, or whether they remain an urbanizing force striving to achieve an equilibrium of interests. For the time being, Yamal is an outpost of stability, encompassing migratory streams of various forces and directions. These forces may exceed even the assimilating, expansionist boom of the 1960s and

1970s. And all the more do they recall the tragic times of the 1940s and 1950s, when Yamal was part of Stalin's enormous Gulag Archipelago; the notorious, tragic railroad, the so-called Stalinka or 501st construction, passed right through Yamal.

*   *   *

Comparable to those migratory waves, not in size but in terms of influence and missionary zeal, was the migratory stream that had arisen earlier, in the 1930s, comprising educators, scholars, and zealots whose educational center was Leningrad. All these migratory streams left their mark on Yamal's history as well as on the lives of the local inhabitants. Because of the heat of their passions, and the accompanying conflicts, Yamal could never be considered as some abandoned, God-forsaken corner of Russia, far removed from the storms and anxieties of the center. I don't know whether such forgotten places do exist in our country, but it is obvious that Yamal, always colorful in its nationality mix, its social makeup, and the scale of events it witnessed, is not one of them.

Yamal is an area of priority interest to Gazprom, which extracts more than 90 percent of Russia's natural gas here. Yamal also has more reindeer than anywhere else in Russia (reportedly more than 500,000 head); the indigenous peoples keep faith with the traditional way of life inherited from their parents and grandparents—raising reindeer, fishing, hunting. The industrial development of Yamal is proceeding, one way or another, with unavoidable consequences: The withdrawal of more land from traditional uses and, along with that, the increased slaughter of reindeer for food as the tundra population gets younger and more children appear. Able-bodied young native men and women of the tundra now often have a secondary and secondary-technical education. Radios, tape recorders, television sets, and snowmobiles are no longer exotic objects in their everyday lives.

At the same time, there are a host of other problems. Supplies of bread and a variety of essential goods are adequate in some places, not so in others, but this problem is being addressed. As for another kind of "bread"—information—the situation is not going as well. What about the native people of the tundra? They are virtually deprived of any printed publications. Those northerners who at one time subscribed to many newspapers and magazines, who read books and thought about them, are now living on starvation rations:

Their living standards are steadily declining, in spite of the measures taken by the regional authorities, while the cost of periodicals and their delivery is sharply increasing. Moreover, most journalists of what was once our "central" mass media are completely uninterested in life in the Russian boondocks. As a matter of fact, observing life in the Russian regions doesn't even cross their minds; business trips are now expensive, and most journalists have no desire to leave the confines of the Moscow Ring Road. Radio and television correspondents, to be sure, are more mobile and ubiquitous, but their cavalry raids into the provinces are, more often than not, superficial; capital city snobbishness prevents them from seeing much, from penetrating into the essential nature of the Far North.

And see how many once authoritative publications have become yellow tabloids or have changed their editorial policy! The market dictates its own rules. Without a moment's hesitation, those who determine mass media content now offer readers and viewers a menu of dishes with different sauces (titles, covers), all made up of the same components—politics, crime, sex, entertainment. The people, fed to the point of satiety, are now forced to choke on this diet, which is served up along with the hot spice of reporting on the "elections." Whether this diet is to people's taste or adversely affects their health is of no concern.

The time when everyone heedlessly believed everything that the mass media reported, however, has passed into oblivion. Russians, exhausted from constant stress, who grew up in authentically humanistic traditions notwithstanding Marxist utopianism, now "vote with their feet." The mass media are not simply losing their authority, they are being rejected. The collapse in newspaper circulation on a hitherto unknown scale is related to this mood; it does not stem only from social and economic conditions.

Ordinary, simple folk are more interested in the life that is being lived nearby. They want to know more about their own land, about the customs and traditions of the peoples that have inhabited it from ancient times, than about famous individuals. They want to learn from people, whether their teachers are household names or ordinary men and women just like them.

I reached these conclusions after attending many journalists' seminars and meetings in Moscow, after listening to the advice, recommendations, and desires of venerable analysts of the central and regional mass media, and after reflecting upon these things myself. It may be banal to say it, but those who are drowning must learn to save themselves. Rejuvenating newspaper readership will be possible only after the newspapers return to those readers and place them at the center of their work.

People of the older generation are experiencing difficulty with the destruction of Russia's basic moral values, the receding into the past of that which only recently was proudly called the Soviet way of life. The baby is being thrown out with the bath water: For many older Russians, the meaning of what they had lived for, experienced, worked for, is lost. In spite of the fact that society is forever indebted to them, it does not attempt, either materially or morally, to save this life experience, these unique grains of history contained in so many ordinary lives, from devaluation and oblivion.

These destructive processes, fortunately, are not so absolute in the provinces. The very existence of *Severiane,* I hope, will become a small offering to the veteran residents of the North. From the very first issue, they have considered the magazine theirs. They write to us, suggesting topics, issues, and heroes. These letters, I hope, will in time become the core of the magazine and make it truly an authors' and readers' publication, without contrived, ingratiating, composed letters. Life devises plots that make any fabricated compositions pale. Sincerity, optimism, and naïveté, always the strong as well as the weak points of the provincial press, will always find a response in the readers' hearts, helping them withstand deepening depression, dejection, apathy, and despair.

On April 2, 1999, the first issue of *Severiane* saw the light of day. One might get the impression that *Severiane* is victoriously marching around Yamal, sweeping all obstacles from its path. Actually, this isn't the case. For almost everyone involved, the magazine is an optional field of activity. Harassing authors, working out a distribution plan with an eye to reaching the remote corners of the region despite the inadequate transportation system, meeting with functionaries, determining strategy and tactics, organizing each issue and tracking the process of its creation from A to Z, and then doing everything so that it reaches the reader as soon as possible—all this has been my work and no one else's. It is probably an absurd, old-fashioned pursuit, and from the point of view of businesspeople a naive and ridiculous one. But I do this without any pay, without any financial or technical support, even—imagine this—without an office and facilities where our creative activists might meet. So all this is not as simple as it may at first seem.

Perhaps I'm impatient; perhaps the genesis of any undertaking is exactly like this rather than being dropped down ready made from the sky. Especially since the magazine, the infant—how to say this more gently?—the "child" is still illegitimate, having no official birth certificate. But, like every living, helpless being, it is wailing, calling for attention, begging to eat and drink; it can't survive without diapers, without its own cradle and other small items essential to life. The question of how best to bring up the anxious offspring has not yet been decided. Nonetheless, people who have never had any relationship with this new being but who have sensed its value have decided to "adopt" it brazenly and highhandedly.

In our country everything occurring in other areas where the initial accumulation of capital is actively proceeding, occurs in the mass media as well. Banal envy, fierce competition, under-the-table games, excessive ambitions, elementary lying—qualities always brilliantly expressed in journalism (as in any other creative profession), are now more thickly entangled with new forms of commercialism and careerism. Basic professional principles are violated when bureaucracy prevails over creativity. And when this conflict occurs within an individual person, eating away at his soul, it is especially tragic.

But the brighter the light, the darker and more intense the shadow. One is unthinkable without the other. But we should ask: Is it worth paying more attention to the shadow? After all, the shadow exists to set off and emphasize the all-penetrating, victorious power of the light. This is especially noticeable in the North.

Prognosis and Fears

As this is being written, the third issue of *Severiane* is in progress. If everything goes as planned, we will have been able to publish a fourth issue in 1999, and will satisfy readers with continued publication in the year 2000.

To some this may seem very little. Four forty-eight-page issues of a magazine in A4 format for the year. Oh, but that's a lot! Its publication was not subsidized by the 1999 regional budget. In fact, expenditures for the already existing mass media were drastically cut.

No matter what I am involved with, no matter where I am, no matter what sort of work I'm doing, one way or another my thoughts return to *Severiane*. I'd like to avoid mistakes, choose a tone of voice that rings true, not moralize tediously, not lecture; but instead create the kinds of conditions, the atmosphere of sincerity, that will lead people to seek us out and open the storerooms of their personal life experiences.

I am absolutely certain that uninteresting people do not exist, that every life has something that merits attention, conceals discoveries, illuminates the heights of human spirit and the depths of frailty. Every life is grand, whether epic or tragic or melodramatic—depending on the viewpoint of the one evaluating it, the one who becomes its chronicler. The tone of the story, and the degree of the journalist's invasion into the author's narrative—all of that is important. Remember Pushkin's words: "The darkness of lowly truths is dearer to us than the deception which ennobles us." To exaggerate, to smooth over, to pass over in silence—or to tell the honest truth, no matter the consequences. So you are left face to face with your professionalism and your conscience.

At the same time, it's frightening to rely solely on the permanent residents of the North. What if it turns out that they too will pontificate, repeat what has already been said a thousand times? Meanwhile, young people remain in the thicket of their own concerns. Vladimir Pavlovich Polushkin, *Severiane*'s artist, a like-minded person who is close to me and, I'm not afraid to say, a real friend and comrade-in-arms, understood my doubts and shared them right away: "It's the start of the school year, we'll go to the grade schools and high schools, we'll meet with the kids, talk to them, design a questionnaire. We'll get information—we'll decide how best to reflect what interests the youth."

And Valentina Nikolaevna Kiseleva, our third comrade, the managing secretary, the most sensible of all of us, although eternally doubting and self-critical, insists on an impeccable writing style, harmoniously combining contemporary and eternal themes.

We are all very different, and this helps us avoid monotony, but we are similar in other ways—in our anxiety about the state of *Seve-*

riane, for example. Our alliance forces us to recall the ironic couplet from our childhood:

> In a single tub did wise men three
> Sail in a storm across the sea,
> If the old tub had been stronger—
> Our tale would now be longer.

Life will show how wise we are, but it's a fact that there are plenty of storms and that the tub could stand to be stronger. Meanwhile— may it be smooth sailing for us. We'll wake up some day and, instead of an old tub, we'll find ourselves piloting a modern, seaworthy vessel neither too big nor too small, but just right, so as to reach the most secret corners of Yamal and tell our readers about the people who live there, about their joys and troubles, their problems and victories.

At a time when we see the erosion of the previous political power structure, the weakening of central governmental authority, and the shift of decision-making authority to local officials, old relationships between regions vanish and new ones appear. The division of the Russian land once again, as in the past, into appanage principalities, and the continuing predominance of centrifugal over centripetal forces, mean that for the moment there is still no reason to travel beyond the borders of one's own region. Besides, the model of a regional magazine has not been worked out yet, and there is enough to do within these confines.

The emergence of the Arctic Agreement several years ago, which unites the countries of the Arctic Circle, consolidates the northern regions of Russia (nearly 70 percent of the country's area), and revives global international projects like the Northern Sea Route, gives us hope that the time is not too distant when *Severiane* will be in greater demand. Do you believe, as we do, in the importance of the "human factor" in executing such projects, in the fruitfulness of personal contacts, and in the need for information about the people of the world's northern territories?

These thoughts may seem naive, but if greater demands are made, greater efforts will be put forth. No wonder they say that every good soldier carries a marshal's baton in his pack.

Making predictions can be a dangerous matter, especially when it concerns your own work. What if we call a prediction simply the vector of an arrow shot from a hunter's bow? Where will this arrow, which promises much, trembling with impatience and pulsating with life, land?

If everything turns out the way it should, and if we are not mistaken in what is most important in our work, our magazine will be not just another medium of public information but a social, unifying, and constructive phenomenon. An embodiment of patriotism, humanism, kindness, and understanding, in whose sphere of influence people will want to be not only readers but writers, suggesting topics, feeling that it is their own, a part of their lives.

We must fight for this. It is worth fighting for.

20

THE RISE AND FALL OF ENVIRONMENTAL PROTECTION AS A NATIONAL SECURITY ISSUE

Aleksandr Knorre

The problems of environmental protection in Russia (and throughout the territory of the former Soviet Union) in the past few decades have become a topic of public attention both within the country and abroad. Chernobyl and the Aral Sea have become global symbols of environmental catastrophe. Campaigns to protect Lake Baikal, the Siberian taiga, and the Ussurian (Siberian) tiger have major international public resonance. The world has shown unfeigned interest in Russia's natural habitats and concern for their fate. This is not surprising—Russia, with her enormous territories, is one of the world's principal treasure troves of natural resources, and their condition to a great degree will determine the environmental state of the entire planet.

Reports by the news media about the environmental situation in Russia and statements by politicians have created the impression

Born in 1956, **Aleksandr Georgievich Knorre** studied geography at the Moscow State University and for many years worked as a soil survey engineer at a research institute. A Greenpeace member since 1989, Knorre became one of Russia's leading environmental campaigners, and in 1993 the executive director of Greenpeace Russia. In 1999 he became the head of the Moscow office of the International Research and Exchange Board (IREX). Translated by Antonina W. Bouis.

that the entire country has turned into an enormous zone of environmental calamity. But what is happening in reality?

According to the chairman of Russia's State Committee on Ecology, Victor Danilov-Danil'ian, 55 percent of the country's territory is not touched at all by human activity and another 20 percent is affected only slightly. One may argue about the criteria for that evaluation, but it is clear that the greater part of Russia is not in a zone of environmental crisis. That is not the situation, however, for those parts of the country where most of the population lives.

Thus, it is estimated that at least 25 percent of the population drinks polluted water that is not up to sanitary codes. Almost three out of four large cities have air pollution beyond the parameters judged acceptable by international sanitary and environmental standards.

The situation may appear catastrophic in specific areas; as a rule, this definition is automatically extended to the environment in general. But that is not at all the case. All the pollution indexes quoted by critics have been measured at relatively limited sites. A mere five to ten kilometers outside most cities, pollution becomes relatively slight or even unnoticeable.

A number of Russia's rivers have been polluted by various industrial processes, but, for instance, in the delta of the Volga—a river that receives the greatest outflow of toxic waste in the country—local residents have no fear of drinking water straight from the river; it is practically harmless.

Yes, there are quite a few industrial plants that pollute territory thirty to fifty kilometers, and even a hundred kilometers, distant— for instance, the nickel complexes in Norilsk and the Kola Peninsula. However, in relation to the area of the entire country, even those large sites are minuscule, covering only fractions of a percentage of Russian territory.

And although there are several megalopolises in Russia, it would be strange to talk about the *natural* environment in these cities. And it would be even stranger to talk about environmental destruction or catastrophe there.

The horrifyingly vast eradication of forests that took place in recent decades has decreased by several factors, and the country's forests as a whole are not in danger of falling to the axe. It is true that in six or seven regions located near countries that import timber, forests are being felled in great numbers. But even in these regions, with the exception of a few territories, the volume of annual cutting has dropped from Soviet times.

And even radioactive pollution is no greater now than it was at the time of the Chernobyl catastrophe. It is true that the nuclear sites have become much more *dangerous,* but for now, thank God, they haven't started exploding.

When we speak of the greatest *existing* nationwide dangers, rather than potential dangers, we should focus on one thing—the destruction of biodiversity as a result of the leveling of natural forests in the border regions oriented toward timber exports.

Russia's "contributions" to global problems belong in a separate category: The destruction of the ozone layer accompanied by climatic changes and polluting emissions in the form of stable organic chlorine compounds.

I will return to the existing danger sites that could be the source of genuine catastrophe when I examine issues of environmental policy. At the same time, a genuine catastrophe for the country is the state of the population's overall health and (here the word is truly appropriate) the catastrophic effect of the environment on public health.

According to numerous public health officials, only 10 percent of the infants born in Russia are healthy. Official data from Russia's most industrially developed regions show that 40 percent of all illnesses there are directly related to pollution, while citizens living in regions with a cleaner environment have a significantly longer life span. In my opinion, the scope of this problem is not fully appreciated. Most people living in extremely difficult economic circumstances believe that an improvement in the standard of living will lead to an overall improvement in well-being. This assumption characterizes government policy on all levels: "First feed the people, and then. . . ." But the problem is that for a great many people, that "then . . ." may never come.

Even Danilov-Danil'ian admits that there is "a marked weakness in environmental policy." However, even here this official is not being forthright. There simply is no environmental policy in Russia— the existing policy could actually be construed as intending to *destroy* environmental policy.

I probably should begin not with the year 1989, when cutbacks were made in all Soviet environmental protection agencies, but with the 1991–1992 period. I find the fact that the Russian government under all its prime ministers (except the administrations of Evgenii Primakov and Vladimir Putin, on which there is no data) intentionally violated applicable Russian environmental protection laws and did not back down from their decisions even when these violations became widely and publicly known. Was this not one of the reasons for the diminished interest in environmental problems among the population? Naturally, many (if not all) regional politicians reflected this disinterest.

Here are some examples:

Yegor Gaidar: The construction of sites for atomic energy, which had been halted after the Chernobyl catastrophe, was "unfrozen," and a government program for the development of twenty-six new nuclear reactors was approved.

Viktor Chernomyrdin: More than twenty government edicts that authorized the "transfer of territories covered with forests of the first group into nonforested ones, for aims not tied to forestry management" (put more simply, granting permission to build roads, dachas, and industrial enterprises in the forests) did not undergo the required environmental review. A curious, and highly dangerous, decision of the Supreme Court of Russia is related to these edicts. The court ruled that the government's actions were illegal. Appeals by the government, however, got the court to reverse its decision, and the plaintiffs—the citizens of Russia—lost because they missed the three-month deadline for bringing their suits. The government's illegal decisions are still in force.

Sergei Kirienko: The government gave permission to build a highly dangerous plant for destroying chemical weapons without the state environmental review required by law.

Sergei Stepashin: Under pressure from Exxon, the government gave permission to discharge drilling solutions from oil platforms directly into the ocean in the Far East, despite the fact that this practice is explicitly banned by the applicable law—the Water Code of Russia.

However, these examples merely illustrate the federal government's indifference to environmental issues and its often consumption-oriented approach. In examining the consistency of environmental policy, I must note that, surprisingly, the "strongest" decision in environmental protection was the 1988 joint decision of the Central Committee of the CPSU and the Council of Ministers of the

USSR establishing a State Committee on Environmental Protection as an organ set above other institutions and ministries. Since then, however, the committee (now called the State Committee on Ecology) has been losing ground. Over the years it has not only ceased being administratively senior to other ministries, but actually has lost its ministerial status. There have been nine reorganizations of the committee. Its policy control over water, forests, and radioactive materials has been withdrawn. It has suffered innumerable staff cutbacks, while the total number of state officials in other federal agencies has grown. The Ecology Committee has approximately 6,000 state inspectors, while the number of people working for the Forestry Service approaches 200,000.

The attack on environmental issues is evident in other areas. The Center for Sanitary and Epidemiological Control, which was relatively objective in its assessment of the environment in areas where it could affect the population, was stripped of its independence and made a branch of the Ministry of Health.

The State Atomic Agency has lost its control over military nuclear sites, which are now subordinate only to the Ministry of Defense. Incidentally, military nuclear sites are the most potentially dangerous sources of pollution.

Except for two prosecutor's offices mandated to protect the environment (and one of them, the Moscow office, exists only for political reasons—to give the city another level of control over the oblast), the entire system of these special-jurisdiction prosecutor's offices has been subordinated to the territorial prosecutors. In practice, this means that there are practical legislative barriers that prevent the nature-protecting prosecutors from appealing the decisions of regional authorities. And since the regional prosecutor's offices of general jurisdiction almost always depend on the local authorities, the special prosecutors have their hands tied.

At the same time, the authorities have reduced the remaining rights of the environmental organs. Thus, the State Committee on Ecology is not able to stop or suspend the work of harmful or dangerous enterprises. The only way it can act is by turning to the courts. But more about the courts later.

It is interesting that despite the profound economic crisis and the acute need for money, the Russian government has not permitted the introduction of environmental taxes or fines. Without going into the details of legal finances, I can note that the system today contains a legal loophole that can reduce by a factor of a hundred or even a thousand the fines that enterprises must pay for polluting the environment. Therefore, industries are simply not interested in reducing pollution. To make the scale of this abuse clear, the Baikal Cellulose and Paper Plant made actual payments of fines that were 3,000 times lower than the amount shown on the "invoice" issued by the government regulatory agency. Similar examples can be found among many other industrial enterprises.

It is also interesting to note, for instance, that the Space Agency and the Ministry of Defense do not pay at all for polluting the environment. The Space Agency doesn't even pay for the pollution created by commercial launches of space vehicles.

The judicial system is a special area. In the early 1990s, environmental litigation was relatively widespread. Several dozen lawsuits filed throughout the country contested various antienvironmental decisions made by the authorities. For the most part, the state organs lost. Our greatest achievement was the repeal of the presidential decree that allowed radioactive waste to be brought into the country. However, the situation has changed substantially since then. Without casting aspersions on the objectivity of the Constitutional Court, I must mention its decision in the summer of 1998. The court ruled that almost all cases dealing with complaints about decisions made by government authorities at the federal and regional levels were henceforth to be solely within its competence. Nongovernmental organizations (NGOs) can no longer bring suit on the level of the municipal courts. Private citizens will have even more trouble trying to litigate. Bringing a case before the Constitutional Court is difficult in any event, and even if the case were placed on the docket (quite a rare event!), the trial itself might not take place for two or three years or longer. In the meantime, the disputed decision will remain in force.

The federal authorities' noncompliance with the law unties the hands of the regional authorities, too. I do not know of a *single* region where the local authorities have not violated environmental legislation. In some regions, the authorities try to hide such violations, whereas in others they practically flaunt them. Thus, in Bashkiria, a dam was under construction in a national park that would never, under any circumstances, be considered legal. Yet the president of the Republic of Bashkortastan authorized that construction on the grounds that the project complied with Bashkir laws, which in his interpretation at least supersede federal laws.

In summing up the sad situation, I must reaffirm that there is no environmental policy in Russia. Instead, we have a collection of handsome, formal decisions with almost no meaningful content, and the practice of ignoring environmental laws on the part of executive authorities on all levels. But why limit the problem to the executive branch? Lawmakers themselves have decided that any draft law affecting the environment must go through an environmental review in order to be considered by the Duma. However, these reviews are simply not conducted.

Many environmental problems related to pollution could be resolved simply by using the pollution control equipment already on hand. Several scientists have shown, for example, that the normal use of that equipment would cut the volume of waste dumped into the water supply by one-half. And this measure would not require additional expenditures.

On the whole, with a small measure of goodwill, with adherence to a few basic rules, and at minimal cost, the situation could be radically changed. The following measures are needed:

• Environmental legislation must be obeyed, first and foremost by organs of the executive branch. Regardless of what these government officials may feel about the laws. Regardless of what "benefits" may accrue to the country if the laws are violated. This applies primarily to the mandatory environmental reviews.

• Payments of fines for pollution must be made in full. They must not depend on profit. They must depend only on the amount of pollution, and they must be uniformly assessed regardless of the form of ownership of the enterprise.

• Punishment of government officials who violate environmental (and any other) laws must be inexorable. This demand is already contained in the presidential decree, but it is not applied universally.

• The actual function of protecting the environment must be concentrated in one institution or ministry, which must not itself be involved in exploiting resources and which must have the legal and administrative levers to stop the violating enterprises.

• Judicial and law enforcement systems must work. Citizens must have the right to defend their environmental rights in court.

The public environmental movement became the first alternative philosophy to contest official Party and government policy in the Soviet Union. Starting in the second half of the 1960s and continuing for two decades, environmental issues were almost the only area in which views and opinions that digressed from the official line were allowed, albeit in a limited way. Debates over the fate of Lake Baikal and the project to reverse the flow of northern rivers involved scientists, writers, and politicians; and for all the limits on these debates, they went far beyond the framework of narrow technical and scientific discussions, ultimately influencing the formation of public opinion. For many people, these debates were an opportunity to "blow off steam"; for others, they were a life's work. It is no accident that many well-known politicians came up through the environmental movement, including Boris Nemtsov, Yegor Gaidar, and Aleksei Yablokov. For instance, Nemtsov was one of the leaders of the movement to stop the construction of the Gorky (Nizhny Novgorod) atomic station. Now, the buildings that were to be part of the power station house a liquor factory instead.

Along with learning the truth about their past and what had happened in the nation for seventy years, Russians discovered the truth about the environment in which they live. And the interest in that issue kept growing. Public opinion polls in 1990–1991 showed that environment ranked second or third among the problems that most concerned Russians. In the late 1980s and early 1990s, there was not a single politician who did not include protection of the environment in his platform. It was so easy then, criticizing the Soviet regime, blaming the Soviet system for all the environmental problems, and promising, promising . . . Naturally, it was that attention to environmental problems that helped many of today's politicians get ahead. However, few of them remember that now.

Ecology is no longer a fashionable topic. According to sociologists, in 1998 the environment ranked only from ninth to twelfth in a list of major public concerns. Of course, one of the most important and obvious reasons for this drop in interest was the dramatic decline in the country's economic and social condition. As an ecologist put it in the mid-1990s, people were much more worried about getting bread than about the heavy-metal particles that could be falling onto them from the sky.

But it would be a mistake to think that people completely stopped caring about the conditions in which they lived. There are numerous examples of that. It is enough to travel beyond the big cities, full of politics and big business, to see that people in their own place, in their own "small homeland," are still worried about forests and rivers, about the earth that feeds them and the air they breathe. The problem is that, as a rule, they simply don't know how to oppose the indifference—and often the destructive actions—of the authorities, local and federal, the brazen and unpunished embezzlement of resources for short-term gain, and the flagrant flouting of the law.

My work in the past few years has brought me into contact with hundreds of people from every walk of life to talk about the environment. I can testify that ordinary people have not grown any less concerned or interested over the years. For instance, a young police officer, as he arrested activists demonstrating against atomic energy, said, "You're absolutely right. If it were not for my uniform, I'd be with you." There are many instances like that. I believe that the lower ratings in opinion polls is not a function of lower public interest in environmental protection so much as it is a loss of trust in the regime, a loss of hope that the government can solve any acute problems, including environmental ones.

Along with many other factors, this mood reflects the growing gap between society and government, between daily life and politics. Note that the greatest interest in environmental problems occurred in the early 1990s—the period of the most widespread social activism in Russian society and the greatest trust in the new Russian government. The credit of trust was very high then; however, in subsequent years it has been completely used up.

And what happened to the public movement itself? The boisterous wave of enthusiasm of the late 1980s–early 1990s gave rise to many environmental organizations. A decade later most of them, with very few exceptions, have either trampolined their activist members into politics, have moved under the government's wing, or have become mere shells of their former selves. Today there are more than a thousand public environmental organizations in Russia, but less than 5 percent of them are capable of doing real work. The rest are very weak and have few members. The reasons for this vary, but I have mentioned the two most significant ones—the lack of a financial base and the low level of social activism among ordinary people, who have little faith in the possibility of positive changes in the current situation. The state is in no shape to support public movements, and moreover it has little interest in encouraging them. Unlike political parties, environmental organizations are of no interest to Russian business. To be sure, there are rare exceptions, for example when support of environmental programs or organizations helps create an attractive image for business.

We must bear in mind, moreover, that the whole concept of independent public movements (not only environmental movements) has appeared quite recently in Russia, and the mechanisms for ensuring their stable existence have simply not developed fully. Therefore, it is not surprising that almost all environmental organizations working in Russia today rely on support from abroad. This applies both to branches of international organizations in Russia and to organizations that were founded locally thanks to grants from overseas. Most environmental NGOs active in Russia are also financed by Western foundations.

I must point out that the flow of money from overseas being sent as environmental aid or loans on the state level is being used irrationally. Research done by the Federal Environmental Foundation shows that most of this money is expended on management projects, while allocations for practical solutions to environmental problems are much smaller (for instance, in the Urals region they are 4.5 times less). Yet, given a nonexistent environmental policy, chronic noncompliance with environmental (and other) laws, and the miserable salaries of government officials, it is useless to attempt management projects.

Foreign support of public policy organizations in Russia is not limited to finances. In the past ten years, Russia has learned the methodology and strategy of NGOs, without which the development of a civil society is unthinkable. Much of what has come to Russia from abroad has been modified and adapted to Russian conditions, although with great and continuing difficulties. Russian society developed for many decades in isolation and suspicion, and at first it did not trust, and sometimes simply did not understand, innovations from the West. I remember the incomprehension with which

Greenpeace's first steps were greeted in Russia and what fantastic motivations were attributed to its actions; it is only now, several years later, that its goals and aims are being assessed more or less objectively. Perhaps the greatest achievement in the 1990s has been the creation of a special niche in the motley spectrum of Russian public life for these environmental organizations, which have brought new views and approaches to long-standing problems, adding their contribution to the development of pluralism and democracy in Russia.

It goes without saying that the help and support coming from abroad creates its own problems. No sooner does a public organization touch on the interests of the regime or big business than the old accusations about foreign interference come up. And there may be a total lack of consistency in these charges. For instance, Greenpeace, which speaks out against the use of atomic energy, is regularly accused of defending the interests of international oil companies. At the same time, when it acts against oil pollution, it is denounced as an ally of the international nuclear lobby.

The same inconsistent and unreasoned approach and the same accusations of hurting Russia are used not only against organizations but against individual activists. The names B. Mirzoyanov, L. Fedorov, A. Nikitin, and Grigorii Pasko have become well known in Russia and abroad. Their main crime was trying to tell the truth about the environmental threats posed by Russian military chemical and nuclear sites. All four were charged with divulging state secrets, despite the fact that they were merely exercising their constitutional right, since Article 42 of the Constitution of the Russian Federation states: "Everyone has the right to a healthy environment, accurate information about its condition, and compensation for damage to health or property as a result of violation of environmental law." The Law on State Secrets explicitly prohibits classifying as secret any information on the condition of the environment. We know that the official investigators in each of these cases were unable to build a case on divulging state secrets; in the end all the cases, which had great public resonance, were dropped in one way or another (although the "case" of Captain Nikitin formally continues, and Pasko was given a suspended sentence on the absurd charge of "exceeding his official capacity").

I am not suggesting that a government policy designed to suppress the environmental movement was behind these incidents, which took place in different years. Rather, each of these cases involved the interests of specific groups that wanted to cover up their own mistakes and abuses or to "defend the honor of the uniform." But one can't help noticing how easily state organs (investigators and courts) are prepared to accept the charge of malice when actions of environmental activists are concerned.

Russian society is not easily abandoning the habitual suspicion and mistrust that were bred into it over decades. In the minds of many, accusations of damaging the defense capabilities of the state still do not require thorough proof. But it is clear that with every year the situation is improving. The atmosphere in society is changing; there is a growing desire to learn the truth about the conditions in which people live and to protect the environment without turning to the authorities for help. Therefore, the role of public environmental organizations is not decreasing; in the future, it will continue to grow. In light of this, it is hard to overestimate the value of the international support being given to Russian public organizations. Today, that support is an integral and indispensable condition for the development of civil society in Russia. And without that civil society, without dynamic international cooperation, it is impossible to imagine what Russia will be like in the twenty-first century.

Part Five

Preserving the Culture, Modernizing Education

21

A SAD TALE ABOUT
A HAPPY FATE

Irina Prokhorova

It has long been a commonplace that Russia is a literature-oriented country, where social and political processes are traditionally viewed through the prism of literary manifestos and the everyday strategies of invented characters. And ever since the young Russian culture stepped onto the European stage during the Romantic period, Romantic thinking to this day has been the linchpin of our society's development and self-evaluation. It should come as no surprise that the role models for the young generation are still Chekhov's dreamy young ladies, mad, disheveled geniuses, perpetually suffering Hamlets, noble knights of the revolution, bold and dashing thieves, and so on. And if a young person endowed with a life-affirming personality, a thirst for activity, and a desire for success (both creative and material) should try to bring that Romantic dream to life, he will inevitably encounter hostile incomprehension and snobbish prejudice, lectures on the incompatibility of serving God and Mammon, and demonstrative scorn and indifference about his choice.

What does come as a surprise is this: It turns out that Russian literature has also predetermined the attitude of Western society to-

---

Born in 1956, **Irina Dmitrievna Prokhorova** earned her doctorate in English literature from Moscow State University. After a career writing for TV and literary journals, she became the editor of the *Literary Review* magazine in 1986. In 1992 she founded the independent literary journal *Novoe literaturnoe obozrenie* (New Literary Review) and in 1995 an eponymous publishing house, which she owns and operates. Under its auspices, Prokhorova publishes two literary journals and several book series on literary criticism, philosophy, history, cultural studies, and fiction. Translated by Antonina W. Bouis.

ward Russia, despite the multivolume efforts of Sovietologists and historians, the revelations of spies, and plain common sense.

Moved by compassion for the mysterious and "eternally feminine" Russian soul that has been languishing under the yoke of totalitarianism, and captivated by the "universal sympathy" of Russian literary heroes, members of the economically developed international community leaped at the chance in the early days of perestroika to save the Sleeping Beauty. But when the Beauty awoke and bared her vampire teeth, when the money thrown at building a new life in Russia sank into the sand like golden rain, then disillusionment naturally followed; the Beauty was quickly reconstituted into a monster that was to be avoided at all costs. As an angry representative of a Moscow branch of a Western foundation once told me, "There's no one to work with in Russia. There are no structures here, only personalities!"

You can imagine what it felt like to hear that after seven years of hard work creating a leading philological journal and a model publication in the humanities. I doubt that this bleak conclusion would encourage my numerous colleagues in the business of publishing books and intellectual periodicals. So then, who are these "personality structures" who not only think but also act, create, and achieve success—and yet, as far as their own compatriots and foreign well-wishers are concerned, appear not to exist?

Once Upon a Time . . .

. . . there lived in the Soviet Union at the end of the Brezhnev era of stagnation a young woman, who, like most of her professional colleagues, sat in the library, wrote her dissertation exposing and condemning a bourgeois approach toward art, read banned books, and along with everyone else gathered around tables in the famous Moscow kitchens roundly denouncing the "damned Communists." And then, like a thunderbolt from the sky, came perestroika, and the astonished woman, like Dorothy from Kansas, found herself in a new, mysterious, and unknown land.

That amazing time in the early 1990s in Russia has not yet found its faithful chronicler. It was an astonishing era, both in its joyous perception of the world and in its wealth of opportunities. Intoxicated and emboldened by sudden freedom, the young woman decided to start her own "highbrow" literary journal bearing the long title *Novoe literaturnoe obozrenie* (New Literary Review). Here she planned to publish the best criticism by the best specialists in Russian literature from all over the world and (without the censor's heavy hand) to open up a heated debate over the path that the new Russian studies in the humanities should take.

Her friends, upon learning of her project, tapped their fingers on their temples and brought forth a hundred incontrovertible arguments against the timeliness and potential of the idea. At first glance, the circumstances were not very conducive to a cultural initiative. In the early 1990s, publishing was an enormous lure for organized crime.

The printing presses, with all their technological backwardness, had not yet developed market instincts and were laughably cheap, as was paper, which was still allocated to printing houses at "state," that is subsidized, prices. Added to this was the huge demand for entertaining literature . . . more precisely, the real hunger created by many years of a forced diet that prescribed militantly didactic and ideologically pure products. And finally, the Soviet centralized system of distribution had not yet been destroyed. As a result, one hastily translated and poorly published mystery novel could guarantee its publisher a mansion in Miami.

So there was nothing strange about the way the young woman, with her project, her endless refrain of "please" and "merci," and her request to print 5,000 copies of a fat scholarly journal, caused the fat printing house ladies, who looked more like brothel madams or gang leaders, to laugh at her. And why shouldn't they laugh, when at the same time the young woman was there with her journal, a no-neck dressed in a track suit with tattoos all over his body arrived, pull from his pants pocket a crumpled wad of bills with many zeroes, and generously pay the ladies, who out of gratitude for his gentlemanly ways would three days later give him 500,000 copies on gray paper of another hard-boiled novel like *Tough Tommy* or *The Ear Eater*.

But that was only one side of the coin. On the other, this was a precious and brief moment, when the old vertical axis of power was destroyed and the bewildered political elite dropped the levers of influence. It was only during that period that you could create an independent periodical that questioned the entire system of scholarly priorities and authorities and that proclaimed its own cultural policy, without being squashed by an irate and infuriated establishment.

By the way, I was not alone in my search for new ways of self-realization. Cultural magazines of every stripe were springing up like mushrooms after a rain, and some were astoundingly bold and original. Alas, not many managed to survive the unequal battle with hyperinflation, tax robbery, lack of even minimal financial support, and economic chaos. However, some did survive and were even tempered in the struggle (for example, *Kinovedcheskie zapiski* [Film Critic's Notes], *Seans* [Séance], and *Khudozhestvennyi zhurnal* [The Art Journal]). And by 1995, the situation in the publishing market had changed radically. First of all, the initial wholesale demand for popular literature had been met, and the market began quickly differentiating, responding to the acute demand for new cultural publications, mainly in general education, economics, and the humanities. Crime publishing became a bit more civilized and centered in the monstrously large publishing houses, which before had exercised monopolies in official textbooks and political propaganda materials. The abandoned territory was filled by the cultural publishers, and the flow of serious literature grew stronger. In just a few years, several hundred publishing houses (private as well as privatized government presses, primarily university presses) appeared, each publishing from just a few titles to twenty to thirty books a year in every branch of scholarship. As a group, these publishers now produce a lion's share of Russia's high-quality cultural output.

Nevertheless, they can't be considered fortune's favorites, since they started up and in large part continue to exist in an information vacuum; the new bosses of the expanding mass media with admirable stubbornness destroyed the culture sections of newspapers as well as the cultural review programs on television and radio, insisting that their audiences didn't want such content. The utterly destroyed (and still not repaired) distribution system for publications didn't bring any joy, either.

Publishing activity for obvious reasons was concentrated in Russia's two major industrial and cultural centers: Moscow and St. Petersburg. Both cities were swamped by an abundance of intellectual publications, while the rest of the enormous country was still without books or periodicals. The impossibility of absorbing the monstrous, monopolistic prices for postage has forced society to turn to the methods of our great-great-grandfathers—the country is now filled with wandering book peddlers. Not a day passes by that some bearded young man who looks like a theoretical physicist (and most often is one) does not appear on the doorstep of *Novoe literaturnoe obozrenie* to buy up magazines and books, pack them in his backpack, and head off into the vast expanses of Russia, only to return in a few months like a wild comet.

Since the former government bookstores until quite recently adhered to sacred Soviet traditions and refrained from burdening themselves by carrying a large number of books they did not understand when small "intellectual literature stores" run by the owners of scholarly journals or by passionate book lovers began to open first in Moscow and then in other cities. Today, the capital has at least a dozen such bookstores (Ad Marginem, Geliia, Grafoman, and Eilos, for instance), where you can buy or order almost any serious book published in post-perestroika Russia. In the past two years, foreign literature bookstores (such as Shakespeare and Company and Pangloss) have opened, as well as many bookstores on the Internet.

All this apparently chaotic and antediluvian infrastructure, with its book peddlers, quasi-legal bookshops, fragile publishing houses, literary clubs, and small art galleries, has turned out to be astonishingly stable and vital; it even survived the monstrous financial crisis of 1998. Wouldn't it be nice if the government were pleased and rewarded its modest heroes, who have worked so zealously for the renaissance of culture? Oh no, the government continues to shed tears over the loss of sacred sites and the destruction of cultural values; it tirelessly showers awards on well-worn and moth-eaten Soviet cultural figures, declaring them to be national treasures.

What is the root cause of this amazing myopia (if not night blindness) that prevents both domestic and foreign statesmen from seeing what is in front of their very noses—not just "personalities," but fully operating structures that deserve their attention and support?

Parallel Worlds, or the Battle Between Light and Darkness

As the perceptive reader may have guessed, it's all the fault of obsolete Romanticism. According to Romantic theory, a person must exist in an eternal duality: The earthly material world and the lofty sacred world. Usually human life exists on the earthly plane and only rarely, in an inspired moment, can an artist penetrate into the other world, becoming an intermediary between the parallel forms of existence. Essentially the same thesis was formulated more prosaically by the founder of the Soviet state, Vladimir I. Lenin, when he announced with characteristic decisiveness that the modern world had two cultures (he labeled them "bourgeois" and "proletarian," but let's not be sticklers here). Lenin and his followers turned this idea quite successfully into real life: In Soviet Russia, under the pressure of totalitarian censorship, two parallel cultural worlds were formed—the barren, official, Soviet one and the creative, unprotected, underground one.

The most amazing aspect of this is that in post-Soviet Russia—despite the development of glasnost, freedom of speech, and the independent mass media—this structure of cultural thinking has survived intact. During perestroika, all new nongovernmental cultural initiatives (unless they happened to have been created by major mafiosi like the sculptor Zurab Tseretelli and supported by the powerful lobbying of local and even federal authorities) were automatically considered by bureaucrats (and even by the public) as underground art, as illegitimate amateurism. Meanwhile, the former state institutions, however pathetic and weak they might be, were still considered full-fledged representatives of Russian culture. Moreover, this dualistic cultural worldview was influenced by the new economic concepts. The strong entrepreneurial activity elicited stormy debates within the stunned cultural community—talk of the shadow economy, criminal business dealings, and other matters about which the intelligentsia had little comprehension.

Within public opinion there gradually emerged a bizarre amalgam of concepts of high and low culture, "transparent" and "shadow" activities, positive and negative poles. As a result, the old Soviet cultural institutions (which for the most part had not reformed but had simply powdered their noses—all those ministries of culture and higher education, most of the schools and institutions of higher learning, the Book Chamber and the Lenin Library) not only preserved their official status but acquired high marks as legal, honest, and "transparent" structures. Meanwhile, the specialized lycées and gymnasiums, museums of contemporary art, art galleries, literary clubs and salons, cultural publishing houses, and "highbrow" periodicals founded by enthusiasts, were psychologically exiled to the underground. In addition, they were "awarded" shadow status, and as we all know, where there is shadow, crime cannot be far behind.

That was the simpleminded logic. (When I began publishing, some of my colleagues, upset by the quick boost in my journal's popularity, which they had not expected, shamelessly said almost to my face that I was publishing the journal with "dirty criminal money.")

Let us linger a bit on the concepts of light and shadow, for this dialectic in Russia is particularly odd. First of all, the usual identification of shadowy activity with crime in Russia requires correction. For instance, under the Soviet regime, the source of criminal, antilegal thought was the state itself, whereas the foundations of civil society and democratic consciousness were formed in the subversive, illegal, and "criminal" (from the point of view of the authorities) milieu of opposition-minded intellectuals. As for corruption and unwillingness to pay taxes, the dominance of these phenomena in Russia suggests that they are not regrettable deviations from the norm; they *are* the norm. They reflect the instinct for self-preservation, a natural reaction of the social organism to archaic and inflexible Russian laws, which bear no relationship to the realities of contemporary life and thought. In the classic words of nineteenth-century Russian literature, bad laws can be corrected only through bad execution.

And now, the second point. In the late 1940s, the brilliant Russian playwright Yevgeny Shvarts wrote a prophetic play called *The Shadow*. A shadow separates itself from its owner, proclaims itself a human being, and nearly acquires the throne as well as the hand of the princess. As is customary in a fairy tale, all ends well; the owner of the shadow, a young scholar, commands: "Shadow, know your place!" and it obediently lies down at his feet. But that is a fairy tale. In real life, the "shadow" side of Russian culture is constantly usurping the right to sovereign rule. All the "official" institutions mentioned above, all the innumerable academic research institutes in humanities and the university humanities departments run by former teachers of Marxism who quickly entrenched themselves with the aid of new tricks, are nothing more than shadows, phantoms, and soap bubbles. Nevertheless, they eagerly simulate activity; this boils down to emitting cries about saving culture (that is, themselves). They successfully continue their vampire existence thanks to the injections of new money.

In essence, contemporary Russia finds itself in a unique situation: The infamous "shadow" intellectual infrastructure has assumed the creative, educational, and enlightening functions of the traditional, official cultural institutions, now fallen into a state of profound stag-

nation. One can say without exaggeration that genuinely free scholarly and artistic thought today circulates only in that community. All
those literary clubs, bookshops, salons, and literary prizes, when
taken together, constitute a forum of intellectual ideas and a base for
a new cultural strategy.

In *Novoe literaturnoe obozrenie*'s first year of publication, we initiated a scholarly conference under the journal's aegis, and it soon
became the most prestigious and popular event for Slavicists. In
1998 I founded a second journal, *Neprikosnovenny zapas* [Private
Stock], where Russian and Western intellectuals began exchanging
ideas and thoughts about the world and their own existence.

This "through-the-looking-glass" aspect of cultural life in Russia
appears to be hardest to understand for people who have grown up
under a system of Western democratic institutions, where the administrative and social agencies, however imperfect, nonetheless reflect
the structure of society. You cannot help sympathizing with a Western colleague who tries to set up a joint cultural program with Russian institutions that have names that seem to speak for themselves,
and suddenly discovers that in fact these institutions have no structures at all.

However, please forgive me if in the heat of my polemic I have ex-
aggerated a bit and portrayed things too darkly. Western and Russian foundations are not completely blind and helpless, of course; it is
thanks to many of them that we function as well as we do. I imagine
that the grateful Russian community has long since raised a monu-
ment to George Soros, because his numerous and diverse programs
of support have stimulated many intellectual initiatives. I simply
want to stress that no foundation in Russia that I know has clearly
defined and deliberately implemented priority support for *new* cultural initiatives.

But wait, someone will object, what about all the programs to develop new communications technologies? In fact there are quite a
few of them, but it seems to me that at some point the passion for
developing mass media has overshadowed the essence of mass media: They are not a goal in themselves, but only and above all a
means for circulating developed ideas and interpretations. If there is
no support for the elements in society that give rise to such new
thinking, then the new information technologies will be left with the
sad fate of circulating old flawed myths and false fairy tales.

Instead of an Epilogue

If the reader should get the impression that I am complaining, then he would be mistaken. I am simply trying to describe as objectively as possible certain characteristics of cultural life in contemporary Russia. Personally, I am happy with my fate, which has allowed me to change my life abruptly and enrich it with new experiences.

Let me add that we have no intention of accepting a shadow existence. We are seriously discussing setting up an association of independent publishers, founding a specialized book fair for intellectual literature, and making a stubborn assault on the mass media. And so on.

Of course, as I look at my friends and colleagues, who wrench funds from their meager family budgets in order to print an arcane book, or who spend their evenings moonlighting and their days teaching Greek and Latin literature and medieval French poetry in the lycée they themselves founded, I sometimes catch myself thinking, "Perhaps all those ideas about the mysterious Russian soul and its universal sympathy aren't so wrong after all."

22

IT'S NOT EASY
BEING A SCHOLAR IN
MODERN RUSSIA

Vadim Radaev

The 1990s were not the easiest time for academic work in Russia. What difficulties and temptations did scholars and researchers encounter during those years? Who left and who remained? How were problems of financing resolved? Finally, what does the accumulated experience then suggest about the future of scholarly research in Russia?

After completing my graduate degree, I worked for more than twelve years in one of the major institutes of the Russian Academy of Sciences, doing research, teaching, and trying to organize collective projects in economics and sociology. I should like to describe my personal experience. Naturally, this kind of experience is always limited. Nonetheless, I will refrain from supporting my arguments with

Born in 1961, **Vadim Valer'evich Radaev** earned his doctorates in economics from Moscow State University and in sociology from the Russian Academy of Sciences. He has had a prolific research career in various institutes, producing four books and over a hundred other publications on topics ranging from Russia's shadow economy to its new entrepreneurs. Radaev has taught at the Higher School of Economics in Moscow, the European University in St. Petersburg, and the Moscow Higher School of Social and Economic Sciences. He is currently chair of the economic sociology department at the Higher School of Economics and is director of InterCenter, an independent research institute. Translated by Marian Schwartz.

the all-too-familiar statistics on the brain drain and reduced financing for scientific research. I realize, too, that the view I am setting forth is largely subjective. I believe, however, that many of my Russian colleagues would agree that the situation I describe is fairly typical.

The End of the Romantic Period

I arrived at the Academy of Sciences as a young doctoral candidate in economics in early 1987, at the very height of perestroika. From a formal standpoint, very little had changed yet. Party and Komsomol organizations were still in full operation, department directors handed out assignments, ad hoc research collectives wrote memoranda to the Central Committee and Gosplan. But I could already feel a powerful ferment. A sense of impending freedom and new opportunities was gaining strength.

It all began when the older generation suffered a sharp rift in its ranks. Some scholars ("men of the sixties") began actively criticizing the existing order and fighting for increasingly radical reforms. Their popularity among young people was unquestioned. We listened to all their speeches and read everything they wrote. The other "old men" did not much care for this. They attempted to voice restrained criticisms of the reformers' outbursts, but more often they kept silent and stepped back, yielding the field of battle.

At that time, capable young people were eager to join the academy. The prestige of scholarly work was still relatively high. They began to take up new perestroika topics that seemed very bold at that time: Civil society and social stratification, bureaucratism and alienation, chronic shortages and denationalization of property. Many of the "orthodox" snorted skeptically but were patient, afraid to be written off as "retrogrades." On the whole, attention to young people intensified, and thirty-year-olds quietly began moving up the ladder. Soon after, international borders opened, opportunities arose to make periodic trips abroad, and learning English became a matter of some urgency.

This was a time of glorious plans. Unfortunately, it did not last very long. Around 1990 there was an obvious break, and soon after that the academic sciences ran into a whole gamut of problems related to staffing, finances, and organization.

New Temptations

For all that has been said about the shortage of funds for academic research, the main problem has always been the lack of qualified personnel. It's always harder to find capable people than it is money. And the swift erosion of professional staffs in the early 1990s was the first grave blow. It turned out that young people had more attractive prospects than the Academy of Sciences. Those on whom hopes for the future had been pinned began to leave the academy—and the country. At the same time, it was getting harder and harder to lure graduates of the best institutions of higher education into the academy. Finally, within a few years, the flow of young scholars began to dry up altogether.

It was in 1990 and 1991 that young people began to go abroad to study en masse. Since the prospects for actually leaving were often terribly vague, they kept their plans to themselves until the last moment. A person could look at you with clear eyes and talk enthusiastically about his creative plans, projects, and new field research, but at that very same moment his visa application was sitting at one of the foreign consulates.

The moment of departure came amid declarations of mutual devotion and promises of support on all fronts. And then our young colleagues disappeared. Since e-mail was still something exotic, as a rule, working ties were broken. With the spread of the Internet, to be honest, not much has changed in Russia. These colleagues left for another world, tried to become part of it, and plunged into a round of new concerns and worries. And, for them, problems back home faded into the background. Of course, everyone swore they'd be back in a year, but then they stayed on another year or two, and then longer. By way of insurance, places nobody needed were held for them in an academic institute, but everyone knew they would not be back.

These new quasi-emigrants showed up in their native country on infrequent trips during vacations to do a little quick field research, because most of them had to specialize in Russian studies regardless of their personal professional preferences. They stopped by to talk about old friendships and at the same time "to take down information." They vanished quickly: "You know, I'm really short on time right now, but next time . . . "

In the process of this "creeping emigration," people got divorced and started new families. Having become "citizens of the world," they indulged in feelings of nostalgia for Russia, that primordial Russian sentiment that grows with distance from one's birthplace.

Some began to return, but not to their old jobs, of course. Upon arrival they quickly resigned from the institute because they were paid so little there and weren't being offered high-level positions right away (the old fellows being in no hurry to part with their own jobs). Their brand-new Western diplomas had still not been officially recognized, and it is extremely difficult to create your own research organization if you spend six or more months a year abroad. Therefore, they looked for jobs mainly in the offices of Western firms or foundations; more often than not, they had to forget about their old scholarly passions. They would say: "What can you do? Such is life."

People often ask me, "Why did you stay?" Indeed, I did have opportunities to go to the West in 1991. And I had my share of doubts, too, I confess. But it turned out I had many reasons for not just getting up and going. I had a family. I had a certain professional status, and I didn't want to sit down at a student's bench all over again or waste time interviewing junior assistants. My professional plans to create my own group of young researchers were starting to bear fruit. Finally, and most important, after many trips abroad I realized that although I could live anywhere I pleased, I wanted to live in Russia. This was no manifestation of unadorned patriotism but the result of a fundamental choice.

Many of those who remained in Russia did not stay put in one place either. Some went into business and did quite well for themselves. Others tried to make it in economic consulting. Still others went into politics. Nowadays, while continuing to exploit their "scholarly" status whenever they can, and not disdaining to cite their academic degrees, they are engaged in completely different matters. The most energetic have formed commercial firms that have taken up quarters in their old institutes and solicit orders for research work. Strictly academic research has moved off into the shadows. Only those who did not want (or were unable) to do anything else engaged in academic research—those who were either the most talented or the most helpless.

Why didn't I leave academia back in the early 1990s? After all, I had offers to jump into consulting or politics. In part it was stubbornness, an ambition to beat the odds, to be "different from everyone else." In part it was a reluctance to abandon my beloved work. In order to resist that siren's song, I had to observe a strict personal principle: Research must be kept completely separate from politics and commerce. That left only professional work that had no relation to business.

At the time, the rhetoric of survival reigned supreme. It was constantly asserted that you could not conduct non-business-related research under those circumstances. The constant refrain of the era was: "You have to live on something, survive somehow." All too often this kind of rhetoric served as justification for leaving the country, leaving the profession, or simply doing nothing.

Soon thereafter, I became the director of a small research subdivision consisting of young colleagues. In the next five years its staff turned over completely. Some left, and I found and invited others to join us. At first, people's departures irritated me, threw me for a loop. But I soon worked out two defensive rules. The first: Don't judge anyone (if they leave, then so be it). And the second: Don't hold out any hope for those who leave, because almost no one ever comes back.

Organizational Crisis

In parallel with the exodus of capable researchers, the institute's financial problems became more acute. I soon stopped asking the office for money for foreign travel so as to avoid a predictable refusal. Asking for money for research in a deteriorating situation also turned out to be completely hopeless. More important, though, was the fact that with the beginning of liberalization in 1992, it became utterly impossible to live at all decently on the frozen salary of a research associate. Realizing this, the institute's directors sharply reduced the requirements for labor discipline among employees. The directors switched over almost entirely to flex time, and they stopped checking up on moonlighters, a practice about which they had been quite strict back in the 1980s. And flex time, as we know, is good for individual employees and small groups but disastrous for a major hierarchical organization. The result was an organizational crisis that led to the institute's de facto fragmentation. Groups and individual researchers stayed on and continued to work, regardless of the difficulties. You could count them on your fingers. Others did practically nothing. But both groups began to engage more and more in their own scientific and nonscientific affairs on the side. The institute was turning into a "roof" to shelter the most diverse types of activity.

Periodic attempts were made to reorganize the institute. Once, I remember, I was drawn into developing fairly radical plans to cut staff. The goal was seen as throwing the "ballast" overboard and qualitatively improving working conditions for those who were left, the most capable associates. But all this remained on the level of bold plans. In most instances the administration did not have the heart to dismiss anyone. Actually, the staff was cut anyway—as a result of attrition. The problem was that it was the most energetic who were leaving, while the "ballast" stayed right where it was. And although new personnel have been turning up at the institute since the mid-1990s, unfortunately, they are not very impressive professionally. The staff has continued to deteriorate. A sure sign for me was that I no longer had any desire to bring anyone in to join us, as I had earlier. With time it became clear that as a matter of principle these large hierarchical structures cannot be reorganized. They possess tremendous inertia and are capable of surviving through extended periods of decay.

One of the important reasons for the current decline of the Academy of Sciences is rooted in the institutional separation of research and teaching that was characteristic of the Soviet period. Systematically, and over many years, only individual associates of our institute gave lectures. Even the creation of departments of academic institutes in universities—an important and necessary change—did not turn the situation around. For most "academics," lecturing is alien and little understood. Many are locked into a relatively narrow specialization and cut off from vital interaction with future young colleagues. Apart from this, the influx of young people into the institute has dropped off. And then these "academics" complain that none of the capable people are coming to them.

All these years I have always taught in various universities as an adjunct, and I have seen that the isolation of academic research has reflected poorly on the universities as well. Even in the leading institutions of higher education, only a very few teachers, who are chronically swamped with classroom hours, retain the motivation to do systematic research. And since competition from practicing re-searchers is negligible, education is largely turning into training by alien standards: Academics are teaching something they have never done themselves in a serious way.

Survival Strategies

The early 1990s were a difficult time for research from the psycho-logical as well as the material point of view. More than once I got the impression that no one needed all this work. Hardly any major conferences were held, and many regular seminars stopped alto-gether. Conference activity mostly shifted abroad. Domestic dia-logue among Russian researchers was destroyed because conceptual conventions had eroded and a common language was lost. Every re-searcher was cultivating his own garden and speaking in the lan-guage of the few foreign books he had managed to read by then.

At first we operated largely on sheer enthusiasm. Then we learned to write applications for Western grants and started modifying our style of work accordingly. A sad comment went around: "Today no one talks about ideas; everyone talks about grants." This was half a joke and half the truth. Trips to the West (always at the expense of the receiving side) were a good source of material support (apart from the opportunities for additional teaching). To this day, these trips are viewed largely as a way of making a little money on the side. A line of demarcation runs through the scientific community—between those who travel and do have grants and those who sit at home and do not.

Many scholars have begun purposefully seeking out contacts with their Western colleagues. They might latch onto some research topic and supplement their work for a miserable sum (by today's stan-dards). And who would dare reproach colleagues for this when their salary amounts to $15–20 a month, when one dollar will only take you halfway across Moscow in a taxi?

Participating in a research project with Western colleagues also raised one's professional prestige. Simultaneously, though, a serious trap lay hidden there. The cooperation, as a rule, was unequal. Whoever paid the money called the shots. In addition, it was felt that Russian specialists had a lot of learning to do in order to reach international standards. As a result, the overall concept of the pro-ject was proposed (and often strictly dictated) by its Western directors. They also took on the work of interpreting the results. And the local specialists collected information or gave life to other people's questionnaires. There have been examples of genuine partnership, but at first they were relatively rare. There's no doubt that, apart from money, any cooperation brings certain professional benefits as well. But I had to turn down such proposals many times. I do not dispute that at the time both my colleagues and I lost out in the material sense. Now, though, I have no regrets about time misspent.

Today, when we evaluate the results of the 1990s, we have a right to say that a certain, albeit small, number of professionals were able to demonstrate a principle: Even with the most drastic shortage of funds, one can conduct research without bending to serve someone else's interest. Later it became clear that in addition, one can earn a living by pursuing that kind of professional work.

The Role of Western Foundations

Western sponsorship played an enormous role in the survival and development of the Russian research community in the 1990s. Today there is hardly one even slightly prominent Russian researcher who is not indebted to some Western foundation—and often to several. This has meant money for field research, equipment, publications, and travel. Without exaggeration one can say that nearly all the leading academic research programs and many of the more advanced educational programs in Russia in the 1990s were made possible by Western funds. I would not like to think what would have happened to basic research in that period if half a dozen major Western philanthropic foundations had abandoned Russia. As for my own research, most of the projects simply would never have happened.

True, two noteworthy Russian funds did appear that used funds from the Russian budget to finance and support basic research: The Russian Basic Research Fund and the Russian Humanities Research Fund. This is obviously better than nothing, but the work of these funds, unfortunately, has not solved the basic problem. It has become clear that there are extreme difficulties with organizing serious projects under such grants. The reasons are several. First, the sums allocated are insufficient for conducting any kind of large-scale fieldwork; there is only enough to supplement salaries for associates and to acquire basic equipment. Second, even these relatively modest sums are subject to all taxes (the government has resumed its old practice of shifting funds from one pocket to another), and the institutes deduct overhead from their own associates at the maximum allowable rate. Third, sums are transferred very irregularly, making it difficult to plan any kind of fieldwork. Finally, grants are not transferred in their full amounts. As director of the projects, I was supposed to receive, from each of the two funds, 75 and 53 percent respectively of the amounts approved under the competition, but then I was asked to deliver my final report and shut down the project. After August 1998, one of these funds declared total default on the major international two-year grant we had won. Thanks only to Western donors, who more than graciously assumed not only their own obligations but the obligations of the Russian side, could the project proceed successfully, with only six months' delay.

It would be nice, of course, to work with Russian money, but for the time being we have to admit that for practical purposes all relatively major and significant empirical projects have been carried out with the support of Western (primarily American) foundations. Their grant policies are fairly liberal; I would not say that they dictate conditions in any unreasonable manner. However, they do shape the strategy of academic research in Russia to a significant degree. And unfortunately, hardly anyone here is concerned about that.

Unexpected Relief

At a certain point in the mid-1990s, when everyone was still talking about the general crisis and decline, I suddenly felt that things had become easier. Many attractive professional offers had materialized. Moreover, the same work that previously had been conducted almost exclusively on pure enthusiasm, began to generate various requests and hints at offers of monetary reward. We began to secure research grants regularly. Although the number of sponsoring foundations was extremely limited, it turned out to be not that difficult to get grants; despite the high stakes, the actual competition was not great. Of course, our past persistence was bearing fruit. We had gained authority and made a name for ourselves within a relatively closed circle of experts.

The financial status of our own academic institute began to stabilize. More and more space in our building was being leased. The federal budget settled some of the debt it owed the academy. Along with this, the institute concluded some fairly major economic agreements that brought in extrabudgetary funds. However, after covering expenses for supporting the cumbersome infrastructure, the resources allocated specifically for the needs of research were hardly thrilling.

By the mid-1990s, participation in the creation and development of the new educational institutions attempting to introduce Western higher educational practices had become very important to me. I had the good fortune to work in three such institutions: The Moscow Higher School of Social and Economic Sciences, the Higher School of Economics, and the European University in St. Petersburg. Today, except for the Higher School of Economics, these are small "chamber" institutions of higher education, as it were, that have been called upon to demonstrate that we can work differently in Russia, and can produce a Russian "product" that meets Western standards. Thus far not enough students are graduating from such institutions to alter the situation in the country drastically, but very soon these graduates will be playing an important role in the new research community.

At first these new institutions began each new academic year as if it were to be their last. Gradually, though, they achieved relative stability. In addition to my own increasingly steady teaching income, I began to gain confidence that I could always find as much professional work as I desired. And although my colleagues, whenever they met, complained of their hard life just as they had before, there was the sense that by the latter half of the 1990s many of them had already found and furnished for themselves professional niches. I began to receive questions like "How are you poor people doing?"—usually asked out of inertia with a thinly disguised smile.

Professional credentials—both my own and those of my colleagues—began to improve noticeably. We began to know our way around the Western literature, we each had completed several decent projects, we had written new books. Without ceasing to learn from our Western colleagues, we stopped gaping at them. And a feeling of professional dignity is a matter of no small importance in any business.

The old problems with publishing research articles vanished. There were more journals, and their backlogs of unpublished submissions dropped. You didn't have to hustle anymore; the editors themselves were asking for materials on virtually any professional topic. At times, journal articles were published with a speed that any

Western colleague would think fantastic—in a couple of months. True, not as many of these published articles are being read. Formerly, every article in any leading publication was an event noticed by one's colleagues. Today, you have to publish three articles in different publications for a Moscow colleague to read even one. In the provinces, as before, scholars must be content with the limited number of post-Soviet journals that are available there.

Actually, there are still problems with the publication of monographs. Nowadays this is not a question of political connections and ideological purity but of money. Publishers are interested in publishing different kinds of textbooks and primers, for which there is a huge demand. You have to camouflage your monograph as a supplementary textbook; then everything becomes much simpler.

On the whole, the level of competition in the academic sphere throughout the 1990s has been extremely low. The same people keep running into each other in various settings—and that, of course, is both good and bad.

What Lies Ahead

What if the Western foundations were suddenly to close up shop? What can the Russian researcher fall back on? Theoretically, there are three possible sources: The government, business, and Russian noncommercial organizations.

Unfortunately, Russian business has shown no particular interest in research, especially if it falls outside the framework of the current state of the economy. The exceptions usually have to do with the researcher's personal acquaintances, who might throw in some resources out of friendship. Institutionalized support of "bright ideas," however, is extremely undeveloped. Actually, even before 1917 Russian entrepreneurs contributed to hospitals and children's institutions and willingly patronized the arts, but much more rarely did they help the universities. This tradition of sorts appears to have been continued today.

Nor do I hold out much hope for financial nourishment from the newly created noncommercial organizations. Russian philanthropic institutions are weak and themselves are looking for foreign grants. True, a special type of noncommercial organization has arisen—political parties, which are accumulating tremendous assets. As election campaigns approach, they will give intellectuals a chance to

make some money. However, the "research" they request is very specific. And I have no desire to compromise my principle of separating
research from politics.

Our overall prognosis about the future is that if there is going to
be additional support for research and educational programs from
Russian resources, it is going to come from government agencies.
Whether we like it or not, the most realistic alternative to Western financing is the resources of the government and the agencies directly
dependent on it.

Although strengthening the role of government structures will not
(as many fear) lead to the nationalization of research, state control
over research would increase, dooming some independent research
and educational organizations to extinction or merger. Those that
are the largest and strongest and that are most firmly undergirded by
state orders will remain, as will the smallest, which can combine
maximum flexibility with minimum expenses and few high expectations.

From the point of view of staffing, the participation of women in
the social sciences will continue to increase (as is clearly visible in the
field of sociology). Another important factor is the gradually increasing flow of young researchers returning to Russia after getting
their education in Western universities. We need to bring back at
least some of these young people. In the final analysis, such changes
encourage professional standards oriented more toward international experience.

What Is to Be Done

Everyone says, "Give us more money." In and of itself, though,
money will solve nothing. We need to restructure institutions. Above
all, we need to overcome the serious split between research and educational activity. Should the government issue yet another edict?
That's laughable. Or, as some feel, shut down the academy and
transfer all the financing to the universities? In and of itself, this will
yield nothing, either. You can't make a teacher prepare and deliver
more than twenty hours of lectures a week and then write strong articles as well, even if you shower him with golden rain.

How is this problem to be solved? We must find institutional
forms that closely link universities and effective research teams. In
recent years quite a lot has been accomplished: Departments of aca-

demic institutes have been introduced in universities, while the institutes have launched their own state and nonstate universities. All these steps, however, are still not enough. Institute departments have proven to be detached from university life. Educational programs in universities under the Academy of Sciences mainly provide supplementary higher education. The usual baccalaureate degree, with its abundance of general, nonspecialized disciplines, is not within the reach of academic institutes. Nor is that their task.

I envision the following ideal model for a combined institutional form. A department is created in an existing university. It is made up half of staff teachers and half of staff researchers, all working in a single efficient research center. The researchers teach as adjuncts in the given department, and the teachers engage in research by holding joint appointments in the center. This arrangement would ensure close ties between the institutions and make possible the gradual reduction in the costs of specialization.

Because such institutional arrangements are not always possible, we must improve the status of research work in universities and learn how to evaluate it correctly. At the moment, university teachers consider research to be optional, because whether or not you conduct research, your salary and your total teaching and administrative load will not change. No one is likely to give you time off to write your dissertation. And honoraria for scientific publications (if they are paid at all) do not compensate for the effort expended. We need a system that weighs the staff teachers' research load equally with their teaching and administrative load. At our disposal is a universal criterion—the publication of books and articles in leading scientific journals.

The next problem concerns the relationship between government-supported and independent universities and research centers. Which should get the emphasis? It used to be said that state institutions were useless under the new conditions, but now criticism of the new, primarily nongovernmental entities has intensified. We do need stricter controls, including licensing, over academic programs, and we must more actively develop standardized measurements for academic programs. Standards, however, should not be like directives. In setting standards and improving academic programs, we need to study more closely the experience of the new, so-called model universities: The Moscow Higher School of Social and Economic Sciences, the European University in St. Petersburg, and the Higher

School of Economics (Moscow). One useful step would be to initiate partnership programs between universities in the capital and those in the provinces, such as that initiated on a large scale by the Open Society Institute. Meanwhile, new small educational institutions, for their part, have already created a diversity of curricula that has made the educational monsters sit up and take notice.

In the future, education will tend to become more and more open. The number of people receiving higher and continuing education will grow, in part through the development of open universities and new forms of distance learning. The future also lies with the development of "through" education, which begins with a high school or college preparatory department at a specific university, moves into the usual five-year program, and concludes with graduate study and a master's degree for students who have distinguished themselves.

Academic institutions will have to go on earning money—through tuition fees, additional educational services, contracts, and research grants. They will have to work more actively with government structures, which will be functioning not only as monitors but also as clients. Especially important is federal interaction with regional and municipal authorities. Most important, we must not lose a sense of proportion. A clear-cut distinction has to be made between the commercial and the noncommercial, between programs initiated by clients and those by researchers. Commercial contracts that bring in the most money cannot be allowed to dictate their own terms. It is important for the nation to maintain its own strategic course.

*   *   *

The same month I wrote these lines, in July 1999, I quit the Russian Academy of Sciences, where I had worked for more than a decade, and moved to a new university that in a mere five years has grown from nothing into one of the country's leading educational centers. This move promised a complicated but professionally more interesting life. My colleagues at the academy commented, in words that were simultaneously flattering and bitter, that one of the institute's last hopes had departed. Whether I remained or departed, however, would have changed nothing. Academic institutes may persist for a long time, but Russia's future will spring up elsewhere.

23

EXPERIMENTING WITH
LIBERAL EDUCATION
IN RUSSIA

The Break with
Soviet-Era Conventions

Nikolai Koposov and Dina Khapaeva

Canterbury, England. August 18, 1991. "You don't read the newspapers and you don't watch television. How are you going to keep up with the news while I'm away?" Our British professor friend put this question as he was leaving for his vacation in Italy. "Not reading the newspapers is part of our Russian cultural tradition," we replied. "And you'll tell us the news when you return." Meanwhile,

Born in 1955, **Nikolai Evgen'evich Koposov** studied European history at Leningrad State University, where he also earned his advanced degree. He worked and taught in France, Great Britain, Germany, and Hungary under various exchange and visitor programs. His research interests include the epistemology of history and intellectual history of the social sciences. In addition to his current teaching responsibilities at St. Petersburg State University, he is one of the founders of Smolny College for Liberal Arts and Sciences, St. Petersburg, a joint undertaking with Bard College.

Born in 1963, **Dina Rafailovna Khapaeva** studied ancient history at Leningrad State University, where she earned her doctoral degree. She pursued a career in sociological research and worked in numerous European institutions, publishing articles in several languages. Khapaeva is currently director of external relations at Smolny College for Liberal Arts and Sciences. Translated by Anna Kucharev.

in Foros, on the Black Sea, Mikhail Gorbachev's communications with the outside world had already been severed.

We learned about the coup late that same evening. The next few days we spent in front of the television. The BBC struck us as being the eighth wonder of the world. We felt as if we were present in Moscow finding out about events the instant they occurred. We couldn't believe what was happening. A political coup backed by the military had broken out in Russia! And the hundreds of thousands of people, in a nation of slaves, who rose up against the coup, had decided to risk their lives and fight for freedom. Russia seemed to be a different country, and the Russians a different people, quite unlike those we knew when we departed for Paris that day in 1982.

. . . The airport customs agent, a red-haired woman, had already spent an hour rummaging around in our suitcases. The mountain of confiscated books and papers kept growing. Behind the glass partition, we saw the frightened faces of our friends who were seeing us off. No politics at all from that agent. Just the ordinary Soviet-style mockery of human beings . . .

"Look your homeland in the face for the last time," we had said to each other. We felt certain we would never return. Admittedly, it took several years of the reforms for us to believe that the authoritarian past would not return. But after the failure of the August 1991 coup, we could no longer relate to our country with fear and contempt, as we had before.

We were not alone, though, in having misjudged the durability of the Soviet regime. The collapse of communism came as a complete surprise to many Sovietologists (to say nothing of the Soviet people themselves). For this there were many reasons. One of them had to do with the very concept of totalitarianism.

The West had long regarded the Soviet Union as the totalitarian regime par excellence, although in the 1980s some historians and political scientists began to doubt whether even Stalin (not to mention his heirs) had actually controlled people's behavior and consciousness so thoroughly. As often happens (remember the debates comparing Russia to Byzantine autocracy or French absolutism?), it turned out that the "ideal model" for totalitarianism had vastly simplified reality. Not that totalitarianism did not exist: Rather, Soviet society was far more complex and contradictory than the conventional concept of totalitarianism allowed. But this hitherto forbidden concept had extraordinary success in Russia in the 1980s. Calling communism "totalitarian" meant identifying it with fascism, thereby depriving it of legitimacy. The simplicity and persuasiveness of the totalitarian concept made it an effective ideological weapon. More subtle analytical constructs seemed unnecessary: It was enough to say "totalitarianism," and the entire course of Soviet history could be explained.

Except, of course, for the final act in the drama. If the Soviet system of repression were as absolute as it sometimes seemed to us, struggling against it would only have been tilting at windmills. Besides, there would not have been anyone to fight. In the end, though, the same concept that had influenced the Russian public's mindset and helped communism to collapse made it more difficult for us to foresee the impending event. In a sense, the rigid concept of totalitarianism proved to be an obstacle to understanding both Soviet and post-Soviet reality.

The most important lesson of the abortive 1991 coup was: Don't underestimate the complexity of the world. If the Party-state machine eventually failed as an instrument of repression, that was because the dichotomies of good and evil, freedom and slavery, were not its only operational logic. Every element of the Soviet system contained various whimsically intertwined—and at times mutually exclusive—principles. The communist grand design proved to be inseparable from the history of European humanism—in terms of continuing as well as replicating that humanist tradition.

Today, thinking about communism "dialectically" seems a relatively safe pastime. And it may therefore not be very interesting. But let's try to apply the lesson of the world's complexity not to the Other, but to ourselves. Not to the abandoned "evil empire" of the past, but to the very intelligentsia in Russia that considered itself the diametrical opposite of the Soviet system, while constituting at the same time an integral part of that system. The intelligentsia in Russia today is going through a profound crisis; after communism's collapse, it found itself deprived of a key element of its identity.

Indeed, the idea of the intelligentsia in Russia cannot be separated from the idea of the Russian government. From the time of its emergence in the second half of the nineteenth century, the intelligentsia staunchly opposed the czarist regime; later, it simply extended this opposition to the Soviet regime. As in the past, you can still hear talk of how the intelligentsia epitomized at its very core rejection of the Soviet system, and as such served as the very force in society that destroyed that system. (You can also hear a paradoxical, but typical, elaboration on this theme: Today the intelligentsia is suffering from the market reforms in Russia—and from the irresponsible policies of the same postcommunist Russian government it had helped install).

Any description of the travails of the intelligentsia, the repository of the highest humanist values and yet the victim (in the heroic version, also the unmasker) of those in power, takes the form of a subject followed immediately by a predicate. If you say "totalitarianism," you would tell a tale about the control of minds. If you say "intelligentsia," your tale will be about faith and suffering. Nor does it matter much that neither tale is consistent with the other. After all, if total control had been in effect, there would have been no place left for spiritual opposition; and if opposition existed, then control was not total. Words have meaning not because they describe reality, but because they are used in a certain way by people who aspire to something, loathe something, dream about something—and who express their hopes and fears in words. Let's remember this—it may help us tell a different tale.

Of course, it's impossible to deny that the Soviet regime suppressed free thinking and viewed the intelligentsia with suspicion. Or that a significant part of the intelligentsia supported the October Revolution, and only later became disenchanted with it. Or that communism became a gulag, but never entirely renounced its humanistic ideals or the hope of turning those ideals into reality—a reality that the intelligentsia, in Russia as well as beyond Russia's borders, had long associated with that doctrine. Or that the communist leaders were pragmatic men who understood the benefits they could reap from exploiting these ideals in such a way that they could integrate the intelligentsia (which they could not do without in any case) into the Soviet system—a goal that would hardly have been possible without all kinds of compromises. Or that the intelligentsia, for its part, was doomed to search for acceptable forms of coexistence with the regime—not at the cost of hypocrisy so much as of self-deception.

Enormous psychological energy was invested in this self-deception. It gave rise to extremely perverse reactions, including bitterness and intellectual barrenness. There was still enough energy to lie to oneself, but not enough to create. The general public believed that only an insignificant minority of the intelligentsia found the courage to struggle against the system; the majority of intellectuals, in this view, timidly sympathized with the minority and merely persisted in deceiving themselves. But it was the intelligentsia that gradually became the bearer of humanistic values; it was from this milieu that most leaders of the democratic movement came. Meanwhile, the hypocritical repetition of the words "liberty, equality, fraternity" cost the Soviet regime too much; and on that rainy day in August 1991, the generals didn't dare issue the command: "Fire!"

From these observations, a far more contradictory picture emerges than that depicting a confrontation between totalitarianism and the intelligentsia. Most of the Soviet intelligentsia, which had coexisted with Soviet rule for decades, did not consist of Sakharovs and Solzhenitsyns. The many adaptation strategies essential for this coexistence could not disappear in a single hour on August 21, 1991; they continue, although in ways that are not always positive, to influence the intelligentsia's sense of identity. Recall the bewilderment that ensued at the end of the 1980s, when the shackles of censorship fell away and when, instead of a gallery of masterpieces or a burst of creative energy, the eyes of Russian society saw a void. Consider also how many of our colleagues continue voting for the Communists. Any hope for a renaissance of the Russian intelligentsia will be vain until we acknowledge the link between today's intelligentsia and the Soviet system—our common bond.

Of course, not all members of the intelligentsia sought compromise with the Soviet regime, but neither did they all wind up in camps and psychiatric hospitals. After all, "someone" continued to attend Party meetings, bestow and receive advanced degrees, take examinations on the history of the CPSU. These numerous "someones"—we ourselves—needed the operational means to secure our psychological comfort. Now it's more important for us to understand how this arsenal of means is at work in our present-day lives than to proclaim ourselves the uncompromising fighters against the Soviet rule of the past.

One of the most important methods of our psychological self-defense was the ideology of professionalism. This was a spontaneous reaction against attempts to make life, and especially scholarship, an ideological instrument called upon to serve the building of communism. Clearly not many persons decided to question Marxist ideology openly. On the contrary, we would say that "Marxism is good for everyone, but philosophers, rather than scientists and scholars, should study it; scientists will be of greater service if they do their own work, and not just reiterate Marxist truths." Saying this was relatively safe. Of course, even this stance required a certain degree of courage and constituted a form of protest. Nonetheless, it amounted to a certain self-deception among those dissatisfied with the limited extent of their own opposition. While requiring total ideological conformity in theory, the Communist leaders rather soberly understood that this was neither possible nor necessary; it would suffice if academics simply kept their distance from politics.

Keeping one's distance from politics meant not allowing oneself to reflect on any profound issues—assuming, of course, that you didn't want to think about them in orthodox Marxist terms. The Soviet regime permitted, if not encouraged, various forms of pseudo-opposition in order to avoid the growth of real opposition, creating a vast kingdom of crooked mirrors in which only a few persons could distinguish between the false and the true. Because the autonomy of science was acceptable to the regime, it served as a comparatively safe form of protest.

Of course, this form of compromise, just like any other, had its price: The intelligentsia could retain a certain degree of autonomous professional activity, but on condition that its members undertook the enormous labor of "self-education." One could think only within certain limits, beyond which it was dangerous to stray. Going beyond those limits, one had to persuade oneself, was not so much dangerous as absurd, and even unworthy. How could this be done? Naturally, by sanctifying one's chains, by creating a belief system in which the rejection of freedom actually became a manifestation of virtue.

The ideology of professionalism was just such a belief system. Aspiring to narrow specialization is the professional affliction of most scientists. It represented the utmost in respectability—after all, its adepts were no "scientific bureaucrats," but "real scientists," acknowledged leaders in their fields. The autonomy of science was an ever-elusive ideal that one had to continually reestablish, and with a certain degree of risk. Becoming a professional seemed an achievement, almost a heroic feat. But we remembered the price we paid. In order to justify the tactic, we had to convince ourselves that there was no alternative; to do so, we had to condemn, and in the most severe fashion, those who refused to pay this price, those who feared the regime a little less than we did, those who allowed themselves, if not acts of dissidence, then at least periods of simple reflection, "daytime excursions" into the forbidden realm of theory. It's no surprise that for such narrow professionals, the word "intellectual"—with which they readily labeled such people—became almost a swear word.

Proclaiming that professional rather than moral, civil, or cultural values were the epitome of perfection; rejecting philosophical reflection in favor of pursuing narrow professional interests; and retreating into purely academic discourse with utter disregard for political or social issues, did make it possible to achieve impressive results. These results, of course, served as a definite line of defense against Marxist discourse, limiting its penetration into the domain of scientific debate. The quest for scientific truth (the more private the truth, the safer it was) helped overcome many moral problems that arose in Soviet daily life. At the same time, this ideology of professionalism turned its adherents into very convenient citizens of the Soviet regime.

The extreme hostility these adepts had toward "speculation" of any kind led them to equate any philosophical or epistemological thought that was not directly related to a narrowly professional topic with Marxist normative discourse. As such, it was to be discarded as irrelevant. Even the most intellectually open-minded scholars made establishing impenetrable disciplinary barriers against Marxist ideology a point of honor.

One would think that the need for complex mechanisms of adaptation to communism would disappear after the system collapsed, and that the perverse reactions—such as the ideology of professionalism—underlying these mechanisms would no longer be necessary. Nonetheless, perestroika was the very time when such devices flourished. This phenomenon was related to the intelligentsia's general transformation, which in turn led to the emergence of new groups in Russian society on the cusp of the 1980s and 1990s.

. . . When we returned to Russia soon after the August 1991 coup, we were astounded by the evidence of a revolution in the most minute details of everyday life. During those August days, our friends had been in Palace Square in St. Petersburg and in front of the White House in Moscow. Thanks to their stories, we relived, this time from the inside, the events that we had earlier watched from afar. By then, most of our friends had embraced politics, business, or journalism as their life's work. Of course, all of them vowed to return to the field of history, but in the meantime, they "simply didn't have time for anything." And we were about to leave the country again. . . .

But it wasn't those colleagues who had once been the hope of their teachers—those who now so easily abandoned their academic institutes and departments (which they were just about to inherit), and whose departure, in the eyes of the academic world, was a betrayal of their calling, a moral failure, almost like our own departure abroad—who astounded us. It was our colleagues who continued to annotate Herodotus and date fibulas from the routine excavations in Pontius Heraklea, as if nothing at all had happened, who most surprised us. And apart from their "absorption in their work," demonstratively triumphing over the destroyed world order, you could guess that on the other side of this posture was the painful desire to create the impression that everything was just as it had been before.

At that time it seemed that only those who were incapable of doing anything else—including being able to secure a minimally acceptable standard of living—remained in the Russian academic world. The university survived in those years largely thanks to those who had nowhere else to go, or who hadn't managed to leave. Their situation seemed nearly hopeless. For a number of years there was a feeling of total stagnation. The only thing that was not destroyed or subjected to doubt was academia's system of professional values, since it occupied a very marginal place in the public consciousness during the years of turbulent changes. This system remained untouched and survived intact. Is it any wonder that the ideology of professionalism became the only method of bringing back a lost era?

Of course, it is not professionalism itself that's bad; it is the ideology of professionalism. Not so much because it is an ideology, but because it assumes an extremely simplified concept of the individual: His value is seen not in his uniqueness and in the richness of his inner world, but in the degree to which he can master a number of standardized skills. Under this notion, talent has no place. Professionalism expresses the values and aims of the petit bourgeois: Accessible to all industrious, hard-working people, it transforms mediocre abilities into something perfect, levels out diversity, and does not push for another, higher measure of the individual. Professionalism, like the social sciences, is a middle-class ideology that attained an almost perfect form in the USSR.

Today, the ideology of professionalism obstructs the path to innovation in three closely related areas: The modernization of the educational system, the resolution of the crisis in the humanities, and the development of Russia's intellectual life. More generally, it hinders the formation of a new Russian intelligentsia.

"Does French intellectual life interest you?" a French colleague asked us when we first arrived in Paris in 1982.

"Yes," we replied. "We have already attended two concerts."

This true story, which we often laughed about later with our French friends, was never popular in Russia. The reason is simple: Most of our compatriots were simply not familiar with the phrase "intellectual life," just as we had not been when we arrived in France. At that time we decided that it meant cultural life, since it followed from the context that what was meant was something different from scientific life. If it wasn't scientific and it wasn't cultural, what was it? In our picture of the world, there simply was no place for a third something.

Today, we understand the term "intellectual life" to mean a particular realm of culture—and a particular type of discourse—where an initial philosophical understanding of the results of basic research in the disparate sciences can emerge and be juxtaposed with other findings. New problems and new approaches can thus arise and help determine the further development of thought in these disciplines. In other words, this is the point where scholarship intersects with the life of society. It is because of intellectual life that the renewal of scientific thought takes place (at least as far as the social sciences are concerned), for it is in the real world that scientific intuition usually finds its roots. And thanks to intellectual life, scholars are able to make their contribution to the formation of public opinion and to the development of society.

Does it follow that nothing analogous to intellectual life ever existed or now exists in Russia? Not necessarily, but, in any case, from our comments about the ideology of professionalism, it is clear why this aspect of culture remained undeveloped. Responding to the problems of contemporary life was the very thing that professionals were forbidden to do. They could have responded in unforeseen ways; to be more precise, the distillation of new data on societal trends into scientific theories could threaten Marxist dogma. Of course, such general distillation of ideas did occur, but in private, secretly, during the nightly talks around the kitchen table that were an inseparable part of the Soviet intelligentsia's daily life. These secret colloquia were little known to the general public and remained unnamed and unacknowledged. And consequently, they became distorted. The transition from the private space of the kitchen to the public space of the scientific institution led to an automatic switching from "reflection in general" to stereotyped professional discourse.

Even in today's democratic Russia, intellectual life has not undergone any particular development, nor has a dialogue arisen among intellectuals and society about contemporary problems, such as the role of intellectuals in public life, or the state of affairs in science and education. In today's Russia, culture and economics, politics and science, remain extremely isolated from each other, despite the fact that many new politicians and businesspeople came from the ranks of the intelligentsia. But in leaving their academic disciplines, our friends aspired to become professionals in fields that were new to them—politics, business, journalism—precisely because of their conviction, generally shared, that the main evil of the Soviet regime was the lack of professionalism among those in power. When our friends returned to their desks as historians, anthropologists, sociologists (if the opportunity arose), they once again withdrew into a world of professional discourse and professional interests. If the word "intellectual" in Russian has begun to have a more favorable connotation, this is because it now means professionals "like those in the West" who accomplish something—unlike members of the Russian intelligentsia who talk on and on about nothing. Small wonder that intellectuals in the true sense, who advocate certain philosophical principles, discern connections between many disciplines, and make their observations known to society at large, virtually do not exist in contemporary Russia.

A free and robust intellectual life is essential for Russia today. As an ingredient of that "social glue" whose secrets sociologists probe, its integrating force is exactly what Russian society needs. A vigorous intellectual life, beyond being the essential condition for Russia's becoming a democracy, is important for other reasons as well. Without it, the intelligentsia will hardly be able to create a new self-awareness more appropriate for our times. Without it, the crisis in the social sciences will not be overcome, nor will intellectuals be brought down from the ivory tower in which practitioners of the ideology of professionalism tried to immure them, so that they might turn and face society's problems head on.

Several years ago, during a discussion among scholars on teaching history at a recently founded university, the dean of St. Petersburg historians declared: "We are traditionalists. We are certain that the scholarly methods we use will still be good for another 200 years. And then we'll see if we need other methods."

The methods he was talking about were, of course, not Marxist at all. Although his generation of historians graduated from the "iron school of Marxism" and absorbed its analytical categories, the best of that generation do not in the least regard Marxism as their own.

What our colleague alluded to are techniques of historical research. It is customary to think that Soviet historiography, like the other social sciences, suffered heavily from ideological domination, as well as from the low professional level of our researchers and instructors in higher educational institutions. For a long time we held this view ourselves. In the late 1980s we helped found the Soviet Association of Young Historians, which advocated the de-ideologization and technological modernization of historical studies. Only later did we realize that the very domination of Marxist phraseology had triggered a drive for technical competence. We found quite a few high-class Soviet historians who were completely fluent in modern historical research methods.

The most attractive of these methods were those as far removed from the theory of history as possible. We favored the study of origins, paleography, and archival research, but we regarded with guarded alarm the methodological revolution in twentieth-century historiography led by the French Annales school. Underlying our reservations was the conviction that every theory is by definition evil; the determination of facts is the essence of historical research. This analytical system was the canonical authority to which our esteemed colleague in St. Petersburg appealed. Today this is not a matter of generations. In 1999 a young historian created a storm in Moscow by publishing an article entitled "Forward to Herodotus," in which he pronounced all general historical constructions obsolete and argued that future historiography will center on the telling of tales, albeit on the basis of serious historical criticism. Although most historians did not approve of the article's extreme tone, many judged it as the "confession of a generation."

If this was so, what does it mean? Of course, it would be easy to say that after the dissolution of the Marxist paradigm, the ensuing methodological chaos can be overcome only with the help of internationally accepted theories. These chaotic tendencies, however, exist well beyond the borders of Russia. It is a widely held view that the social sciences, and history above all, are in a crisis, that post-modernism has cast doubt upon their capacity to ascertain true knowledge and be useful to society. In contemporary French, English, and German literature, one encounters the idea that all the troubles of the social sciences come from excessive absorption in theories: Philosophers must be banished from the ranks; scholars must work as the positivists of the nineteenth century did. Both the West and Russia have their postmodernists as well as their intellectual conservatives (actually, they are two sides of the same coin). Pure reason lacks confidence in its own powers. Other theories, which claimed to possess a more or less unified explanation of social life, including functionalism, structuralism, and psychoanalysis, also arouse skepticism. This is no localized phenomenon, nor can it be explained using localized reasons.

The crisis in the social sciences elsewhere can also be related to the collapse of communism. If the social sciences are seen as a response to the Communist utopian experiment and as the justification of a middle way between capitalism and communism, it is not surprising that many of their programs were considered as confronting Marxism. When Marxism began rapidly losing its attractiveness, the urgency of legitimizing "the third way" also diminished.

In our view, the most important thing the social sciences have to say about the human being is that they articulate and substantiate a particular cultural, anthropological ideal. For example, a historian who discovers one or another dimension of human individuality in the past expresses his view about what a person is or should be. Thus, for Marx, man's principal purpose and the main measure of his worth is the class struggle. During Russia's "brilliant three decades" (from 1950 to 1980), the concept of the individual as the subject (not the object) of culture triumphed. With the establishment of social stability and the extensive growth of universities, that time of "the paradise of intellectuals," this concept, introduced by professional transmitters of culture, was broadly attractive. It accorded with the strategy of the "third way" and with the values and aims of an intelligentsia that had moved away from orthodox Marxism, with its theory of class struggle; at the same time, the concept maintained a general humanistic-socialist orientation. In the USSR, this evolution was no less obvious than it was in France, for example, although, of course, its public manifestation was more difficult. Thus, Russian scholars invested much intellectual energy in the history and theory of culture because one could to some degree express in symbolic language what one could not say openly. Accordingly, the finest achievements of Soviet social sciences in this period relate specifically to the history and theory of culture.

But does it not follow from this that in Russia today the main problem is that the intelligentsia has no equally obvious cultural-anthropological ideal it finds essential to affirm? An ideal that could inspire a new generation of scholars to create for Russia "its Athens, its Rome, its Renaissance"? Man as a subject of culture has triumphed over man as a subject of class struggle—but now the professionals have nobody to hide from in that ivory tower. The psychological springs of creative energy that inspired generations of scholars have run dry. Paradoxically, this has happened precisely during a period of colossal changes, when the Russian intelligentsia's creative energy is needed as never before. After all, if the social sciences serve as the ideology of contemporary democracy, their crisis means a crisis of democratic values. In Russia, whose future is much less predictable that that of America, for example, the danger of such a state of affairs is especially obvious. What can be done in these circumstances?

These reflections brought us to the idea that we need a critique of the social sciences, both as a particular symbolic system and as a particular ideology. Reducing the individual to a subject of culture was a notion derived from the evolution of the social sciences after their inception at the end of the nineteenth century. This historical context might explain why it was simply impossible to formulate a new ideal of the individual within the framework of the social sciences. It follows that without a review of the basic certainties of the social sciences, a substantive intellectual renewal is impossible, much less a new flowering of intellectual life. Initially we gave little thought to what a new ideal of the individual might be. Most of our attention was focused on the symbolic forms that have hindered its formulation.

*   *   *

In Paris in the early 1990s, we worked on a project critiquing the social sciences. The social sciences, we thought, were insufficiently reflective; practitioners had adopted a limited number of analytical calculations, whose origins they thought little about. It was this uncritical attitude toward themselves, together with a certain intellectual laziness, that explained the contemporary crisis. The focus of our work therefore became analyzing the thinking of researchers in the social sciences, particularly historians. We were interested in exploring logical errors and contradictions in thinking that would shed light on the logical conflicts that imperceptibly direct our thought patterns.

In critiquing the social sciences, our favorite instrument became the study of the history of ideas. History, especially comparative intellectual history, allows us to see the chain of random circumstances that give rise to the contradictory, logically inconsistent ideas used by the social sciences to construct a vision of the world. We could imagine no better method of "making strange" our habitual forms of thinking or of adopting a critical distance in relation to oneself. This approach to the history of ideas received a positive response in France, where we had worked for a long time, as well as in Russia, to which we finally returned. At the same St. Petersburg University that we had been forced to leave in the late 1980s, we organized a seminar, "Critique of the Social Sciences," which soon developed into a project entitled "A Comparative Dictionary of Major Historical Ideas in Russian, English, German, and French." The project has inspired a series of analogous initiatives in other countries, directed by the major German reference work, *Geschichtliche Grundbegriffe*.

More than seventy researchers from Russia, the United States, France, Germany, Italy, and other countries have agreed to take part in this initiative, projected to last for several years. It is too early to sum up even the preliminary conclusions. We hope that the three-volume edition under preparation will become an important instrument for critiquing the intellectual foundations of the social sciences, as well as for advancing mutual understanding among international scholars. This initiative, of course, will also help the Russian social sciences become a more integral part of the world scientific community.

Enthusiastic as we were about being engaged in a critique of the social sciences, we always thought that the project had a predominantly negative cast, as if it were mainly groundwork, clearing the terrain, preparing instruments for something else. A more positive program was needed, but we didn't know where to find one. In the meantime, we had lived in Russia for an entire year, conducting our seminar, and we didn't just know, we almost physically *felt*, how much had changed in the country. After the failure of the

1991 coup, we gradually began to evaluate the future of Russia with great optimism. Russia, yes—but not the Russian academic world. That seemed an utterly immovable monolith. As far back as 1994 and 1995, we had been telling everyone, and putting it in writing as well, that fresh shoots would not grow for an unpredictably long time in soil where professionalism had been so carefully cultivated by ideologues. Indeed, very little of intellectual interest was taking place in the Russian academic world. But our judgment also reflected the ineradicable habit of thinking in terms of the totalitarian model, a habit that prevented us from accurately evaluating the changes that had been appearing as far back as the early 1990s.

In the constantly changing world of today's Russia, even a bastion of conservatism like the academic world can not remain unchanged. The internal controls exercised by the learned patriarchs over their flocks, which were so effective as little as seven or eight years earlier, had weakened considerably. Having just returned from France, where rigid hierarchy and unquestioning subordination to the master are the rules of the functioning academic world, we discovered in Russia, to our surprise, an unprecedented degree of intellectual freedom. Life had become decentralized, and a scientific career was no longer the only choice for a scion of "a decent family." Salaries of university instructors sharply lagged behind (and continue to lag behind) the subsistence minimum, and most of our colleagues worked on the side wherever they could, often in nongovernmental institutions. Their welfare now depended much more on their personal initiatives that on the decisions of academic bigwigs. Students, graduate students, and young instructors who differed with university officials could leave for careers in journalism, business, or politics, thus weakening academic authority. The intellectual disorientation following the liquidation of communist dogma also played an important role: A flood of everything, of the familiar and the partially familiar that had been hidden behind the remnants of the Iron Curtain, surged into the void. Most of our colleagues were unfamiliar with contemporary Western theories, and they could not attune themselves to them well enough to endorse some ideas and criticize others. Enclaves of intellectual freedom, pockets of "no man's lands," appeared within the territory of the social sciences. These factors encouraged brilliant and creative people, especially among the young. At the same time, the struggle for survival under completely new circumstances helped many elderly colleagues discover unsuspected talents in themselves.

During our absence, a new generation of students had come of age, very unlike those we had taught in the 1980s. They were better educated and more self-reliant, independent, and critical. This is only one of the reasons for the proliferation of new educational programs in Russia, some of which attempt to take into account the interests of young people and depart from the usual standards of Soviet higher education. These unsystematic but persistent educational experiments strike us as a hopeful factor in the evolution of the Russian academy. We also took part in one of these experiments, using our seminar. First, however, a few words about the traditional Russian educational system.

Soviet institutes of higher learning operated on a comprehensive eight-year program: Five years of basic university education and three years of graduate school, ending with defense of one's doctoral dissertation. Narrow specialization was the hallmark. A student entering the university at age seventeen would choose his profession (for example, history), but also a narrower specialty (for example, the history of medieval France). Although Party ideologues required institutes of higher learning to prepare not so much "real specialists" as "real Communists," the institutes of higher learning themselves did not aspire to that goal. The natural self-defenses of professional communities against the incursions of Communist ideology required support for high teaching standards; and, incidentally, the education provided in quite a number of institutes of higher learning was not bad. But the ideology of professionalism also led to an extremely elitist attitude toward students: The very few who wound up in a position to reproduce precisely the guild system of values of their professors received the faculty's attention. It was simply not accepted practice to be concerned about the rest. The university aspired only to recreate itself. The ideology of professionalism approved the hierarchical abyss that separated students from professors and endorsed the didactic teaching methods that, for all intents and purposes, excluded classroom discussions. Students were supposed to master, and reproduce, ready-made knowledge.

Of course, views on the goals and methods of education, like the ideology of professionalism itself, have by no means lost their popularity within the Russian academic world. A sociological survey we conducted at St. Petersburg University in the summer of 1999 showed that more than two-thirds of the instructors continue to consider the narrow professional preparation of a "pure scholar" to be the main goal of a university education. Echoing throughout those responses is nostalgia for a world that had passed into oblivion ten years earlier. Students, though, think otherwise: More than half of them do not share the view of their professors on this matter. They see an academic career as only one of many possibilities, and by far not the most attractive one. Business, the arts and letters, and politics also occupy their thoughts.

Note, however, that more than a quarter of the instructors are more or less free of the ideology of professionalism; they do not share the university's ideal of self-perpetuation. These are usually instructors who participate actively in the new educational programs that rely on fee-based teaching; they cannot avoid weighing the extent to which consumer demand affects education.

The first of these new educational programs appeared in the late 1980s and expanded rapidly during the first half of the 1990s. Even now, institutes of higher learning are being created every year. The number of institutes of higher learning in St. Petersburg has more than doubled in a decade. Although the new nongovernmental institutes are usually much smaller than the old state ones, we are nonetheless observing a large-scale phenomenon.

Will the Russian intelligentsia survive under these circumstances? We have no doubt that it will. The intelligentsia may go on to renew itself and at least partially overcome its lack of social responsibility, recovering from the effects of the once dominant ideology of professionalism. Subordinating science and education completely to the laws of the market naturally would be just as deplorable as making these disciplines depend completely on the state. In bemoaning the destructive influence of the market economy on the Russian intelligentsia, critics often forget about the market's healing properties. The shock therapy of fee-based private teaching has forced the intelligentsia to evaluate its place in the world more realistically. Indeed, a greater sense of reality, along with the extraordinarily substantial help of Western foundations, is what has allowed the academic world to survive and to live fairly well, at least by Russian standards. Of course, quite a number of colleagues are inclined to complain about life, and not without reason. Nonetheless, the hopeless anticipation of the imminent end of the world, widespread in the early 1990s, already coexists with a more optimistic worldview.

We are now taking part in one effort to broaden general university education: Smolny College, founded in 1997 as the first college of free arts and sciences in Russia, a joint project of St. Petersburg University and Bard College in Annandale-on-Hudson, New York.

The Smolny College project complements our earlier project of critiquing the social sciences, described above, and we believe it can help provide practical solutions for the crisis in the social sciences. Had we been told ten years ago that we would be organizing an alternative traditional education program at St. Petersburg University, with the support of the chancellor and many instructors, we would have thought we were being mocked. However, Smolny College is emerging, although not without a battle (some colleagues publicly assert that we are backed by the CIA and World Zionism). But even early critics now concede that Smolny College can make the university more competitive on the education market, create a healthy intellectual tension within the university, and force a review of outdated practices.

No one expects liberal education to triumph immediately in Russia. The point is not to eliminate professional education as a whole but to attain a reasonably balanced and well-thought-out relationship between the two. Our experiment can provide new ideas and approaches that will be useful for the design of other educational models and can help uproot academia's entrenched and rigid attitudes toward broad education in general. Of course, in order for this to happen, talented students must attend. This is precisely what we are counting on.

Actually, Smolny College has been in existence for two years, initially as a program of open courses attended primarily by students from other university departments. Each semester, many more students applied for these courses than we could accept. Among them were those who, like ourselves, were deeply dissatisfied with the narrow specialization and didactic methods of the existing education system. They embraced the chance to actively design their own education and have the right to speak and be heard in class, rather than just listen to a professor pontificate from the rostrum. They were drawn by the nonstandard choice of lecture subjects and the diversity of approaches. Each course centered not on an academic discipline but on an issue that could be understood from different disciplinary perspectives and traditions of thought. Something intellectually fresh and new was taking place at Smolny College: A critical attitude toward the university from within, and a critical distance in the style of discourse.

In 1999 Smolny accepted its first full-time students. Those who entered needed to come to a college of liberal arts and had interests too broad to fit into the usual academic canon. Where else in Russia can you study sociology and learn to write poetry, master playing the piano, acquaint yourself with the theory of complex physical systems, and get an idea of modern management? Incidentally, the study of music, management, and modern theoretical physics could turn out to be mutually enriching. In a word, we have good students. And we believe that the instructors are just as good.

Returning to our project critiquing the social sciences, Smolny College provides a liberal education that cultivates independent critical thinking, is not bound by the conventions of one or another discipline, and mobilizes the most diverse approaches to solving the problems that life presents. Is this not a model for rejuvenating the social sciences? To be sure, a liberal education does not aim primarily at the preparation of researchers and scholars. A good researcher, though, is not someone who knows more, but someone who thinks better. What we lack now is not so much knowledge as creative thinking.

But for us at Smolny, the cultural project is perhaps the most important thing. A liberal education presupposes a goal other than a professional one. Mastery is achieved not by one who can reproduce the conventions of a professional environment, but by one who can create his own profession and change it if necessary. Not by one who resembles his colleagues, but by one who has become a unique, creative individual. A democracy of sociologists, undoubtedly, is possible. Is a democracy of poets possible? Is this not a challenge?

A liberal education also helps students become citizens of a society committed to dialogue. We want to turn Smolny into a cultural forum where many logics intersect and diverse cultures meet, a place where individual self-expression is joined with a polycentric, infinitely diverse world. As an international educational project, Smolny will invite Russian and foreign students and professors to study and teach together.

For us, belonging to an international intellectual environment is the most important element of our identity. In this, we are typical of many people born in Russia during or after perestroika. Hundreds of liberal-arts scholars of our generation have lived, studied, and worked abroad, continue to travel abroad often, have broad professional contacts, and in Russia work in close contact with foreign institutions. They have developed their own worldview, belonging to the Russian as well as to the international environment. We call this phenomenon "Russian cosmopolitanism." Smolny College has become one of the first facilities in Russia dedicated to translating this cosmopolitan outlook into an institutional framework attractive to the emerging leaders of our country.

24

THE ARCHITECTURE OF HUMANISM IN RUSSIAN HIGHER EDUCATION

Evgenii Kniazev

Today there can be no cut-and-dried assessments of the path Russia has taken in the realm of academic activity. We have shed our ideological blinders, but we have lost our competitive edge and our intellectual potential in many fields, and we have allowed the research and educational base of our institutions of higher education to decline.

The new openness of higher education is largely due to expanded and deeper international cooperation. My work in this area of university activity began in 1988. At that time, I was dean of foreign students at Kazan State University. In 1991, my responsibilities were broadened to include the international department, which registered passports and visas for university associates. I faced my first problem: How was I to manage two absolutely unconnected subdivisions, organize my own work, and achieve success? Much later I learned that at the time, all alone, for many weeks at a stretch, I was

Born in 1955, **Evgenii Anatolievich Kniazev** earned an advanced degree in applied mathematics at Kazan State University, Tatarstan, where he stayed to teach cybernetics and computer science. In 1988 he was appointed dean of international students and in 1991 was named head of the university's department for international programs. Kniazev has worked closely with various American and European universities and exchange programs. Since 1996 he has been one of Russia's leading advocates of university governance reform. Translated by Marian Schwartz.

engaged in what amounted to SWOT analysis. (This system of analysis, popular among strategic management specialists, entails identifying the "Strong" and "Weak" internal aspects of an organization, as well as its "Opportunities" and external "Threats.") This brainstorming resulted in two projects.

To begin with, I was able to talk the university rector into launching Kazan's first small enterprise, the Univex Academic Research Center. We began to design nontraditional international projects: Seminars and Russian-language courses. In learning how to make money from educational activities, we mastered the basics of entrepreneurship step by step and learned to keep track of our cash flow, rejoicing in every ruble or dollar earned. This was good training, and we made good students and a good team. There were six of us in all, young doctoral candidates, and this occurred just eight years ago. Today one of us is a banker who has survived the country's multiple (and now chronic) crises. Another is a trade representative for Tatarstan in the United States. The third owns a small finance company. The fourth is one of the leading experts in the Ministry for State Property Administration. The fifth is a leading marketing specialist. And I am still at the university and consider it my calling.

The second project was to reorganize the system for administering international cooperation programs at the university. What a wave of opposition and misunderstanding among university officialdom this project provoked! I had to respond to so many accusations— that I was indulging my personal ambitions, encroaching on traditions, criticizing the university as inflexible! I looked at myself in the mirror, and had to agree with the indictment. But as I came to work each day, performed routine, monotonous work in my cramped little office, and supervised the boring ladies who worked for me and were constantly bickering among themselves, I suddenly realized that Mikhail Gorbachev's already skidding perestroika had begun, and would end, with us. Simply carrying out orders from above was not for me.

My project aimed to create a completely new structure to administer international contacts, expand the university's international activity, and raise its significance and status. The focus was on providing information and organizational services to undergraduates, graduate students, and teachers. Today ours has become the university's most advanced department. We have the most modern technology; a team of educated, experienced, and young specialists; a modern, businesslike approach to our work; and a congenial atmosphere.

Responsible, independent, and professionally qualified workers are the key to success in any undertaking. The director can supply everything else. I have seen my principal task as seeking out initiatives for our team and creating incentives for their effective implementation. What don't my colleagues end up doing! We publish an information bulletin on international cooperation in higher education, *Globus,* which we send out to all regional institutions of higher education, and we cannot keep up with demand. We prepare and execute the most unexpected international projects for entrepreneurs, farmers, teachers, and journalists. We assist those who want to get an education abroad and offer services in the transfer and registration of passports and visas. We have an e-mail station where novices first learn to use the medium and then set up their own mailboxes. We maintain the European Documentation Center, the Spanish Cultural Center, language and culture courses for participants in international programs, and printing services. The income this brings in allows us to support the infrastructure at a high level: Modern computers, Internet access, copying and printing equipment, and our own specialized library of reference works, periodicals, and electronic databases. All this gives our colleagues interesting work, a broad perspective, authority, and pride in their involvement in this necessary and important business.

Our experience in organizing international activities at Kazan State University is known far beyond the Kazan city limits. The journals *Evropa* and *The Chronicle of Higher Education,* as well as national and local newspapers, have described our work. Television reporters like to spend time with us; they know they will always find interesting and useful information here, a commodity that our society has in all too short supply. Even the Voice of America and the BBC have honored us with their attention.

Over the past five or six years, we have secured about $4 million from foreign sources for technical equipment, joint scientific research, educational projects, and international travel. Against the backdrop of a protracted economic crisis and an acute shortage of budgetary funds, this figure is quite encouraging.

However, it is not the material and financial component alone that has been important. University colleagues have been able to acquaint themselves with the achievements and experience of European, American, and Southeast Asian universities. Eight or nine years ago, we could not have dreamed that the university's international contacts would encompass every continent; that our partners would number more than fifty well-respected universities and organizations in the leading countries of the world; that our scholars and teachers would be successfully participating in major international projects; that eminent foreign professors would be teaching in our lecture halls; or that American, German, Swiss, Belgian, Japanese, and many other foreign undergraduates, graduate students, and postdoctoral students would be regularly attending the lectures of our professors. The university and its academic staff have passed the test of openness, with honors.

Beyond the strictly academic vantage point, international travel has enriched us with invaluable experience of university life in the most diverse corners of the planet. This experience has forced us to take a critical look at how we manage our own work. The social and economic cataclysms in our country, and the impoverished status of science and education, demand that the university respond effectively. International programs of academic cooperation are one way to do so.

The first major grant we received, from the European Union, was for implementing a joint European project called "The University in a Changing World." Representatives from Belgium and Spain were our partners. This project allowed nearly sixty colleagues and students of the university to spend time in Europe. As coordinator of this project, I worked hard to direct work into constructive channels. Each participant (many of whom found themselves abroad, in a completely new environment, for the first time) studied a very specific area of the work of our university partners and made suggestions for improving the analogous activities at our alma mater.

Thanks to the active participation of the university leaders, including the rector, pro-rectors, and directors of the principal offices (the people who make the decisions), and after stormy debates at the start, we were able to submit a work plan to our colleagues from the Catholic University of Leuven and the University of Granada covering five topics:

- studying the socioeconomic and political characteristics of educational administration in a federative state;
- strengthening the interdisciplinary approach in research and education;

- organizing continuing education programs and expanding the range of educational services offered;
- emphasizing the broad international dimensions of university life; and
- examining issues common to university administration elsewhere.

Thereupon, university activities moved into completely new areas.

We established the Information Center on Issues of International Cooperation and the Library of Reference Literature. A year later, in 1995, the rectors of ten major institutions of higher education in Kazan signed an agreement giving the center the status of a regional center for international cooperation. Today the center serves all the institutions of higher education in our city, including some 300 regular clients—scholars, teachers, graduate students, undergraduates, and administrators.

We created the Department of Continuing Education and an interinstitutional noncommercial organization, the Forra Fund for Business and Community Development. The department markets new educational programs and examines fee levels, multimedia applications, and certification. The university's income from providing these additional educational services has already equaled the regional and federal funds allocated. We are closely studying foreign experience in continuing education, and we know what our colleagues from the Urals, from the Nizhny Novgorod and Tomsk State Universities, as well as from the Moscow University of Statistics and Information, have achieved, which is even more than we have.

The Forra Fund owes its existence to the exceptionally active moral and material support of the International Research and Exchanges Board (IREX), the Chamber of Trade and Industry of the Republic of Tatarstan, and Organic Synthesis, a Kazan-based corporation. The Forra Fund assists the market-oriented and political transformations in our republic by involving the intellectual elite in the resolution of the problems facing our society. During the three years of the fund's activities, including seminars, conferences, publishing projects, study courses, and exchange programs, two elements stand out: Joint work among scholars and practitioners, and the integration of national and foreign experience.

Three examples of the fund's activities will suffice. Together with the Monitor Company, affiliated with Harvard University, the fund organized a competition among young entrepreneurs, economists, and students to evaluate the international competitiveness of Tatarstan's industries. The five winners, who demonstrated an exceptional understanding of the ideas of Michael Porter and an ability to apply them in practical work, received an opportunity to spend two weeks at Harvard Business School. The fund published a multi-criteria business rating handbook, *Business Leaders of Tatarstan,* which uses the same methodology as *Forbes* and *Fortune* and was the first publication of its type to appear in Russia. Finally, the fund held a major conference on attracting foreign investment to Tatarstan's economy, attended by representatives from the Troika-Dialog Bank, the KPMG consulting firm, and the World Bank's Institute of Economic Development, as well as by leaders of the republic's government, enterprises, and banks—about eighty people altogether.

The fifth topic of our work plan (to me the most important one), examining issues we had in common with university administrations elsewhere, was taken up when half the time allotted for the whole project had already elapsed. By then we had accumulated enough information and ideas about management in foreign universities, and I had recruited the chief administrator of the Catholic University of Leuven, Karel Tavernier, a man with enormous practical and theoretical experience. After four years of close collaboration, and now that we are friends (I'm certain he thinks so, too!), he often jokes about our first meeting. What first flashed across the mind of this estimable administrator, who is experienced in all the subtleties of running a university, when I showed up at his office, was: "Does this young Russian really think that I'm going to go to work for him?"

But now Professor Tavernier does so, and with great pleasure. He has many friends in Kazan. He knows my university well, generously shares his experience, and actively influences our new approaches to administrative problems. I see him as a mentor and reliable partner. I would add only that today he and I are involved in three international projects.

In the course of this activity, which has consumed all our attention, we have been able to bring together a working group, including directors and associates from various subdivisions of the university as well as teachers and outside experts, whose members have been laboring for three years on a completely voluntary basis. This group is made up of pro-rectors, faculty deans, directors of administrative services, and people of various ages, experience, and social status. They have become initiators and participants, analyzing the effectiveness of the system of administration at Kazan State University and seeking ways to improve it.

We have studied modern university organization and administration in the United States and western Europe. We have absorbed the ideas of the strategic approach to university administration and have achieved good results by utilizing these methods. A university mission statement, approved by a conference of professors and university teachers, has become an important component of our charter.

We have drawn up a development strategy and convinced the university community to endorse it. Drawing on the university's mission statement, we have formulated seven policy statements relating to education policy, scholarly research, culture and education, regional policy, relations with international partners, social policy, and university development.

These policy statements constitute the program for the university's rector during his second term and serve as the basis for the joint activities of the university's Academic Council and its various commissions and administrative units. Funding to implement reforms in our system of administration has come from foreign sources, including the European Union's TEMPUS/TACIS programs, the Flemish Scientific Society, and the World Bank.

We have aroused community interest in finding our own solutions to the prolonged economic crisis, and perhaps we have even ignited a spark of confidence in the public by the very fact of our existence. We have worked out a concept for reforming our system of administration, which will allow us, while remaining a classic research university, to become more entrepreneurial and more integrated with forums of international cooperation.

The first conference of directors of academic and administrative subdivisions of the university, which was held in mid-June 1999, supported our proposals, notably the idea of separating administrative and academic management. The Administrative Council will remove nonacademic issues from the agenda of the university's Academic Council, which for many years has spent more than 80 percent of its time adjudicating these very questions! The Administrative Council will coordinate interaction among departments and smooth out conflicts over the allocation of resources. The Academic Council will concentrate on academic quality and on implementing and fine-tuning the mission statement. An office of the general manager will ensure executive discipline and adherence to standards, regulations, and the budget. A system of efficient resource administration and an integrated system of assessment and self-evaluation are other important elements. In all this, we have benefited enormously from the experience of such marvelous colleagues as John L. Davies from England; Anthony W. Morgan, James L. Ratcliff, Paul T. Brinkman, and Bruce Johnstone from the United States; Peter A. M. Maassen from the Netherlands; Robin H. Farquhar from Canada; Herbert R. Kells from Denmark; and Paul Verdin and Karel Tavernier from Belgium.

Along the way, we encountered skepticism and lack of trust, envy and suspicion, huge cultural differences, and the language barrier. However, this has been interesting work, and it remains so for me. Moreover, by studying other universities, we have come to a better understanding of our place and mission in Russian society. We have become more sensitive to the requirements of the region, our students, and our partners. Finally, we have come to envisage more clearly what we expect of the future and what kind of university we want to be. I think that we have learned to stay our chosen course in Russia's current environment of swift and turbulent change.

Russian institutions of higher education are doing much interesting work in administration reform. At Rostov University, procedures of technology transfer, patenting, and other innovative activities are being perfected. In Tver, administrators are introducing new information technologies into university operations. Many institutions of higher education are launching new services and departments to encourage international cooperation, attempting to build their relations with local business circles along new lines, creating administrative systems for continuing education, and developing distance learning.

From my talks with colleagues from other universities, I have noticed that there is much duplication of effort; we are deplorably lacking in information about one another's experience, ideas, accomplishments, and failures. For this reason, one cannot overestimate the importance of the "Universities" project. For over two years, under the aegis of the Salzburg Seminar, project director Raymond Benson and his colleagues from Middlebury College (Vermont) and Salzburg (Austria) have created a constructive and open atmosphere for the serious and creative exchange of experience in administration, organization, and technological changes. Directors and specialists from the leading Russian universities work with renowned specialists from Europe and North America.

Today the Salzburg Seminar serves as perhaps our sole opportunity to have serious, instructive discussions with these partners. It was there that I learned of the innovative approaches adopted at Nizhny Novgorod State University, where administrators are successfully applying matrix structures and effective material stimuli in the organization of their work, and where they pay great attention to normative and regulatory activity. At the seminar I became acquainted with the impressive results of the integration of institutions of higher education in Novgorod Veliky and Novosibirsk, heard about the successes of Tomsk State University in developing continuing education programs, and rejoiced at a successful initiative at Yekaterinburg State University, which has begun publishing a journal *Universitetskoe upravlenie* (University Administration).

* * *

The past ten years have changed me personally. Until the early 1990s, my research career as a mathematician was working out quite successfully: My dissertation defense, interesting work as a dean, lecturing, and interacting with young people. Then came the offer from the rector, and (naturally!) the Party committee, to take up administrative work in developing the university's international ties. And so, beginning in 1988, the academic and the bureaucrat within me have been making their peace. At first it was hard to reconcile the two different types of activity, but later I became more and more convinced that university administration in the new conditions is intriguing work. At a certain moment I made a paradoxical discovery: Even though we may engage in both research and teaching in a university, we know so little about the essence of the institution. We approach university administration so uncreatively, and at times so unprofessionally, that we feel at sea in the new conditions.

The primordial question for Russia has always been: "What is to be done?" What I must do is something I decided for myself. Strategic university administration, its theory and practice—that is what interests me today as a scholar and as an administrator. I have not abandoned my work in mathematics; I still give lectures and direct student research. Moreover, I have found many applications for my mathematical knowledge in the modeling and research processes in education and the university. The past ten years have brought me experience, knowledge, information, and contacts with leading specialists in university management all over the world. Apparently, thanks to my creative streak (though this does not sound altogether modest), I have realized that this sphere interests me as an area of scholarly research as well. As the young people say, I have "switched my orientation."

I should like to record the enormous impression that many books and publications on university management published in Europe and America have made on me. I am altogether envious when I see that university education abroad is under the meticulous gaze of researchers; that scholarly analysis and opinion invariably accompanies decisions made on issues of higher education administration; and that university administration abroad, especially in the United States, is a professional sphere of activity.

*　　*　　*

Our principal accomplishment along these lines is probably the team of like-minded thinkers we have assembled. Our university is dear to us. We care about it and want to make it better. It is with these people that we are pursuing yet another line of reform, one that is most important for me personally.

We are creating the Center for Strategic Analysis and Planning at Kazan. This center will be an analytical laboratory for conducting research in university administration and will function as a continuing education institute for administrators of institutions of higher education. Our prototypes are the Center for Higher Education Policy Study at the University of Twente (Netherlands), which is widely known in western Europe, and the Center for Educational Policy and Leadership at the Anglia Polytechnic University (Chelmsford, England). Preparations are already under way for opening an analysis laboratory with the financial assistance of the World Bank's Innovation Project. The first modules for a training program for university administrators, which is intended for administrators in higher education in the wider Volga-Urals region, are ready. With funds from the European Union, an information guidebook on university strategic management for Russian institutions of higher education is being readied for publication, and an Internet web site is being created for posting useful information on university administration.

Why am I so enthusiastic about this? Because to develop our universities, we must first strengthen their autonomy. Because I am convinced that the social base for reforms in universities should be broadened. Because university administration should become a professional activity. All this requires training university administrators, and professional training is impossible without a scientific understanding of Russian and foreign practical and theoretical experience, without systematized knowledge, without publications. Nor am I free of my own personal ambitions and selfish plans. The idea that my colleagues and I are part of something that is completely new for us, and for the entire system of higher education in Russia, gives me strength and inspiration. Without false modesty, I can say that I want to be at the head of this work, the principal "culprit" in its success.

In an institution as conservative as a university, resistance to innovation will probably continue to persist. The roots of this resistance, I believe, lie in the resilience of the administrative-command tradition in our society, the all-encompassing and all-pervasive authority and tyranny of the bureaucracy, and our people's lack of confidence and ignorance of their own power. The problems of our society are reflected in the universities as in a single drop of water. This is why the formulas for overcoming our troubles are also of a general nature—decentralization, open international cooperation, transparent decisionmaking, and an emphasis on nurturing the best creative forces and professionalism.

*   *   *

A few words about the assistance that Western countries provide to our country in the field of higher education are in order. Without any question, this help will preserve our institutional relevance for the near term. Nonetheless, this aid must become more effective, better targeted, and more pragmatic.

Funding for centers of academic excellence should not be dispersed and spread thinly among too many recipients, but should be allocated to provide vigorous levels of support for the most deserving. It is unwise to allow ourselves to be guided by mere political or transitory interests and divorce the potential of Russian higher education from the solution to these problems. One can, and probably should, admit that Russian society acutely needs humanization on a broad scale. Foreign investors are perfectly justified in not wanting to risk supporting enterprises or institutions capable of "dual use" military and civilian production or research. Specifically for this reason, our army of many thousands of university specialists in the exact sciences, by all accounts, has not seized sufficient attention and support from international organizations and foundations. Many celebrated scholars and young talents are departing, or have already left the country. Seductive offers from abroad are easier to come by than support for their work here, in Russia.

This trend is leading to the devastation of our scientific schools, the loss of top-notch specialists, and—it's not hard to predict—Russia's increasing technical and technological lag behind the industrially developed countries. The country's economic revival and the resolution of its most acute social problems will require more than just political will and financial backing. These goals require a scientific-technical potential, an educated public, a public consensus, and society's unified efforts. Today, foreign support is largely humanitarian, as I see in the example of my university, but we must not forget that a university, like a nation, is a unitary organism, a unitary family, a community.

In my opinion, specific adjustments should be made in the planning and execution of Western assistance programs for Russian education. First, we should not drive a wedge between humanities scholars and natural scientists by helping one to the detriment of the other. And second, we must help stop the brain drain from Russia by creating conditions that allow scholars to profitably pursue their creative work at home. It is my deep conviction that Western assistance would be more effective if it were focused on the more advanced Russian universities. Bringing these universities up to modern levels of organization and supporting the academic process is far from simple; it cannot be achieved by providing only a limited number of hard-to-get grants in a few specialized fields. Everything in a university is interconnected and interdependent: scientific research and teaching; administration and infrastructure; the humanities, the natural sciences, and the exact sciences. It is impossible to combine coherently modern curricula, methods, and style of work in some spheres with archaic ones in others.

At the turn of the new millennium, harmony should be the indispensable characteristic of a university. Cultivating and supporting harmonious universities that meet the demands of the era in Russia should become not only the key to effective Western humanitarian assistance to our country but also the guiding principle in Russian educational reform. Centers of academic excellence could serve as models to stimulate all other institutions of higher education. The mentality of my fellow citizens is such that it is easier for them to trust examples of successful work and to follow the example of "our own" than that of foreigners. It has been pounded into our heads so insistently that we are different, that we are following our own path. Recall what Fedor Tyutchev said: "Russia cannot be understood with the mind or measured by a common yardstick; it has a special imperative, one can only believe in Russia." I do not subscribe to this opinion! I am convinced that we are talented and enterprising, and that we can and will work and live like other civilized countries! If only we could be a little more demanding of our leaders of all ranks and a little more patient and trusting, work a little more and talk a little less.

Western assistance programs should direct special efforts to supporting university libraries and telecommunications. Information is food and fresh air for science, it is a window on the world. It is instructive that our Kazan State University library, the oldest in Russia, which counts more than 5 million volumes, including more than 10,000 ancient manuscripts, has been forced to cancel its subscriptions to many scholarly journals, something that did not happen even during World War II. Adequate library service and communications systems ensure the minimum conditions for scientific research activity, the basis of a university education; they also prevent Russian higher education from becoming isolated from the world academic community because of our economic problems. We cannot allow this huge country, which has survived such hard times, to be thrown back into the chaos of ignorance and embitterment. If that were to happen, then all of humanity would be the loser.

The West should not trust bureaucrats in the federal center or in the regions but instead should work directly, and more intensively, with institutions of higher education and scientific collectives. There are quite a few intelligent and decent people in the federal and regional organs of educational administration. However, they are functionaries, cogs in the system; they articulate and defend the system's interests and are detached from the real academic process, from the academic product, which is created "below," in the universities. But the system will be strong if it is made up of many effective institutions of higher education and if it meets the demands of the times. The system will be strong if it provides institutions of higher education with the important services and resources they need. Today, institutions of higher education in Russia do not get either. Federal and regional authorities have to give us more autonomy and administer us from a distance, using the tactics of mediation.

However, universities and institutions of higher education as a whole are too important as public institutions to be condemned to live in isolation from one another. That is why the weakness of the old vertical system of management must be offset by expanding horizontal connections: Professional associations and contacts, integration among institutions, and networks of cooperation extending to other disciplines. As the greater Volga-Urals region's oldest and leading institution of higher education, Kazan State University is continually proposing joint projects to develop academic infrastructure and telecommunications and to work out coordinated programs for advancing the interests of science, education, and culture in our region. Our international connections are open to the entire higher educational community and student body of the republic.

When we Russians think carefully about what awaits us, we conjure up our own visions of the country we would like to live in. Some probably dream of Florida and other demi-paradises. But those who want to live and work here, those who can work and know what to do, those who have faith, picture the future Russia as a civilized country of enlightened, law-abiding citizens that is swiftly developing and helping others.

We must replace false patriotism, based on a belief in military force and the myth of inexhaustible natural resources, with pride in ensuring for our citizens a high quality of life reinforced by the reliable protection of their rights. In our own profession, we must reject hollow incantations about the high level of Russian education, which conceal the reluctance or inability of the authorities to make the development of our intellectual potential a paramount concern. Here I include all official levels, from ordinary departmental director and university rector to minister, head of government, and national president. Miserly salaries for history teachers in high school and mathematics professors in the university need to be raised, of course; but just as important is the opportunity to work, the opportunity to be in demand. A good system of education, to my mind, is inextricably linked with the flourishing of our graduates, with mutually enriching connections to the business world, and with the active participation of the academic community in solving regional, national, and even global problems.

I see my role in performing a great deal of creative and effective work and in becoming a recognized leader surrounded by talented, proud, well-meaning, and cheerful people. I want my university to be known and respected not only in the Ministry of Education but also in the corridors of local power and abroad; I want the research and development work of our scholars to bring glory and prosperity to the university; I want the diploma and education received at Kazan State University to be valued far beyond the borders of Tatarstan and Russia. If we, the thirty- to forty-year-old scholars, teachers, and administrators who have been working at Kazan State University can achieve this by the end of our careers, we will be able to say that the glorious traditions of our university live on.

25

A Theater for
Oneself

Vladimir Mirzoev

In the word "Rossiia," the Russian ear can hear a chain of random meanings: *rosa* (dew), *siianie* (radiance), *rost* (growth), *rasseian'e* (dispersion), *messia* (messiah). Actually, the last word in the series requires philological cleverness and a rich imagination, which nature has given us hyperboreans in great abundance. A rich imagination is, perhaps, our main national trait, our gift from above, and at the same time our curse. In any case, we are convinced that we have a mission in History as a nation, a special role in the Divine Comedy. But Westernizers and Slavophiles, politicians of the right and the left, intellectuals and the staff of the Federal Security Services, all have their own understanding of that role. Some are frightened by this discord, and there are occasional hysterical cries in the mass media that we urgently need a "national idea" (read: To replace communism sleeping in the deep), otherwise we will perish.

I don't think there is any cause for fear: Russia for the first time in many years has the chance to bring its citizens out of an infantile sleep. Let everyone defend his own opinion, let everyone learn to carry on a dialogue and recognize the possibility of an alternative turn of thought. Therein lies our salvation. The works of Albert Ein-

---

Born in 1957, **Vladimir Vladimirovich Mirzoev** studied theater directing at the Russian State Academy for Theatrical Arts and produced several plays before emigrating to Canada in 1989. During his years in Toronto, Mirzoev directed plays in many theaters, in Canada as well as the United States. After returning to Russia in 1995, he has been a resident director at the Stanislavskii Drama Theatre, a guest director in various Moscow and provincial theaters, and a director of several TV documentaries. Translated by Antonina W. Bouis.

stein should be published in the Rabelaisian print-runs that were used for the classics of Marxism.

That is why I thought that the best format for my remarks is a dialogue. The form is also good because within me I have, as does every thinking person in Russia, various voices arguing among themselves. Sometimes there are two, sometimes three or four. And believe me, it's not schizophrenia. It's just that it is impossible to give a simple answer to a single vitally important issue today. Everything is confused and mixed up in our house. We are going to have to track reality anew.

1

First Voice: The most inspiring acquisition in Russia in the last eight years is, of course, the ability to choose. And not only the political choice that has resulted from the introduction of a multiparty parliamentary system. Along with the refusal to build a Tower of Babel (that is, a utopian society), the existentialist paradigm of Russian society has changed. Emigrating or putting one's energy into the country's renaissance, wearing ashes while mourning the imperial "fraternity" of peoples or mastering the spiritual wasteland left behind by the Soviet regime—all these are typical and fatal questions facing our intelligentsia today. Russians have had to master the theory of relativity rapidly: Previously we were forced to live in a world without any alternatives to the one "true faith," a world where a few million of the most cynical, narrow-minded, and easily bought citizens usurped the role of high priests. They called themselves "Communists" but essentially they were feudal, self-proclaimed pseudo-aristocrats.

Second Voice: Let's assume that for the theater, the cannibalistic regime was an inexhaustible source of inspiration. After all, the art of the theater in any society is to play the role of the trickster, the violator of tribal taboos. The Soviet regime had a taboo on almost everything: Unorthodox ideology, erotica, freedom of movement, aesthetics—the list can go on and on. Before 1991 the theater provided the breathing space where the nation, enslaved and exhausted by prison camps and wars, could rest, could breathe the air of Aesop's fables, could enjoy their hidden meanings, hints, and metaphors.

First Voice: But why the theater, rather than film or music?

Second Voice: There are several reasons. The language of the theater in the twentieth century became more and more the language of poetry rather than the everyday telling of an interesting story. This allowed us to speak obliquely about things that were considered dangerous and shameful for society. But for all that, unlike symphonic music, the theater remained a democratic institution. Here the laborer, the intellectual, and the Party boss could meet, laugh together, and have ice cream during the intermission. The movies were too literal and lifelike. There wasn't enough of the theater's elusive and ephemeral qualities, its subtexts. And also, since filmmaking in Soviet times was a sinecure, only the "right" people, ideologically correct comrades, were allowed to work there. White crows like Sergei Eisenstein were ruthlessly chased from that fat field.

First Voice: But weren't theater people also fired, didn't they too perish in the camps? Think of Aleksandr Tairov, Vsevolod Meyerhold. When Tairov lost his child—the Kamernyi Theater—he lost his mind. Meyerhold was executed in the Gulag.

Second Voice: That is true, of course, but it does not refute my thought that the theater was the unique provocateur in the Soviet Union, the many-faced trickster who cast doubt on the reinforced concrete of socialist idols and who always managed to evade punishment. Individual unacceptable artists could be destroyed, but the very atmosphere of a dangerous and half-hinting conversation was indestructible. An actor's free, albeit totally illusory, expression of will on the stage reflected everyone's secret dream—to be free of fear, to be Someone. Actors had the status of national heroes.

And so: In my opinion, the "spiritual wasteland" you mentioned above is what today's theater has actually encountered. The good old taboos are gone, but new ones have not yet appeared. One might think, what could be better for an artist? It's a paradox: The absence of censorship has deprived us of energy, we seem to have fallen into emptiness. In the eyes of society, actors have ceased to be idols and have turned into ordinary performers; the profession has lost its status. Any rag of a newspaper can publish invectives against the government. But soon enough the "elite" that is shamelessly enriching itself at the expense of the silent majority will be forced to shut the mouths that are too open.

First Voice: But you must agree that someone has to take on "original sin" and become a property owner, to take over what used to be held in common, that which the Soviet mentality considered "no one's" property—factories, oil fields, theaters. Isn't it natural that the lucky owners turned out to be former bureaucrats?

Second Voice: In other words, you're trying to say former Communists? Yes, it is natural, especially since they were the ones who created a bloodless revolution from above. The people never did dare do anything, even though the Soviet Union had a fifth column the size of four-fifths of the population. The Communists realized that they quickly had to change the overhead sign, otherwise they might lose everything. The Party nomenklatura established the first commercial banks back in 1987. However, there is something unnatural in that story of speculation.

First Voice: And what is that, if it's not a secret?

Second Voice: For instance, theater directors were given the freedom to handle real estate as they wished. They rented up to 30 percent of their theater space to various small companies: Restaurants, travel agencies, stores—and now they are hauling in money. The same thing is happening in factories and educational institutions. A question: Why shouldn't a theater director work at making the theater flourish instead of, say, putting on a strip tease?

First Voice: But actors and other workers in the theater get a bonus added to their pathetic salaries from that money. (The major Moscow theaters pay their actors $15–20 a month.)

Second Voice: If only that were so! Only part of those profits show up on paper. Tens of thousands of dollars (called "black cash") ends up in the administrator's pocket. And that scheme works throughout the land, not only in theaters. The vicious circle of payoffs among the nomenklatura turns the law into a pathetic parody.

First Voice: But what can you do? . . . The inability to differentiate between what is "mine" and what is "the state's" is a common trait in *Homo sovieticus.* According to Marx, the destruction of private property was supposed to lead practically to a rebirth of the spirit of the early Christians. Instead it led to alienation from elementary morality. Are you seriously maintaining that some other category of former Soviet citizens would not have done the same thing?

Second Voice: Steal?

First Voice: Yes, get rich at the expense of the less clever and less swift. Party and Komsomol leaders are not the most dangerous types. Their egoism was at least regulated a little by their past experience. I can just imagine what would have happened to the "underground man" (that is, the dissident intellectual) if power had come into his impatiently trembling hands. He would have turned the remains of the hated Evil Empire to ashes. Unconsciously, perhaps, but he definitely would have done that. It's just like asking a hippie family to run an atomic submarine.

Second Voice: Well, let's say you're right. . . . However, what great future are the "Red Directors" and former Komsomol lads preparing for us, now that they have turned into capitalists overnight? What can be expected, say, from a theater director who has saved a decent fortune and doesn't know how to use it? Being an independent producer is too much trouble. Opening a sausage factory will lead to questions like, "Where did you get that much money, comrade?" And if questions don't come up now, they might later, after the next change of scenery on the political stage. And so the theater director keeps his money in America somewhere, perhaps in the bank account of his great-niece, drives around in a cheap Zhiguli, and trembles in fear, anticipating the thunderbolts that will drive him across the border. In any case, the money as well as the people will be lost to Russia forever.

First Voice: Why forever? The government is seriously discussing an amnesty for those who exported capital illegally. Tomorrow that director will buy himself a theater as his private property or he will become its largest stockholder.

Second Voice: That's just what I mean, and we'll have what we see now in entrepreneurial theaters: Trite French comedies and home-grown melodramas played by three actors on three chairs so that they can travel more easily from town to town, playing to provincial audiences. Total dependence on the box office will kill the evocative language that distinguishes the art of the theater from TV soaps— and that makes the Russian theater a unique phenomenon in European culture.

First Voice: OK, OK, don't get upset. Let's talk about mutations in stage language. After all, we're not such Marxists that we need to reduce everything to economics.

Since 1991, or more accurately since the start of perestroika, when Russian civilization became a fully open system, the theater started greedily adopting "foreign" languages: Modernist dramaturgy and music, modern dance, unusual materials for the stage, unusual people—"eccentrics," as Chekhov used to say.

In 1987–1989 I staged Samuel Beckett, Howard Barker, Paul Claudel, and August Strindberg. This list of authors would have been impossible under Sof'ia Vasil'evna (the code words the intelligentsia used for *sovetskaia vlast'*, the Soviet regime). The audiences enthusiastically filled in the blanks in their experiences with *difficult* plays. Experimental studios and laboratories grew like mushrooms after rain back then. Unused cellars and dusty conference halls filled with the ghosts of Partycrats were quickly converted to newborn theaters and art galleries. The state subsidized all this marginal activity without a murmur, apparently hoping to distract intellectual young people from politics, and later, from privatization. I may be wrong and there may have been nothing more to it than the true romanticism of renewal.

Second Voice: The postmodern theater of the mid-1980s used the poetics of deconstruction, and that refreshing gesture was an expression of destructive energy vented into the air. Although there weren't many people who picked up on it then: The critics were stunned into silence, as if they had water in their mouths. They're all left-brain folk; analysis always precedes experience for them.

First Voice: The audience didn't always understand that language, but they loved the emotional charge.

Second Voice: Be that as it may, the idyll soon ended, it just wasted away. The nouveaux riches took over the cellars for warehouses. And the repertory theaters were taken over by dreary petit bourgeois elements. There was a new audience: Poorly educated and weary of the drama of daily life. This audience wanted to be entertained, not made to think. "Fill myself up with information or, God forbid, philosophy? Go find yourself another fool! My brain is composted enough at work, I want to relax." That was the typical argument of the new audience, and theater administrators quickly echoed it.

First Voice: But even in Shakespeare's day people like that attended the theater. That didn't keep playwrights from writing at the peak of their own ideals and creating great works.

Second Voice: And so now we've moved to Shakespeare and other classics. No one has dared to bring up Beckett or Harold Pinter in our repertory theater—they would be misunderstood and fired.

First Voice: It's possible that Russians need the classics, the canon, now more than ever—as a symbol of stability and dependability. Sitting on a powder keg for ten years is hard on the nervous system. Canonic art, oriented on tradition, gives people what the state cannot give—psychological foundation, support. If there is no law, then you need at least consistency. Just as a child who can't read likes to have the same story read to him over and over. That gives him the illusion that he can get around in a frightening and hostile world.

Second Voice: Exactly—illusion is the operative word.

First Voice: So what? Isn't the art of the theater by definition illusory? The question is what that illusion serves. Did you know that in Greek and Roman days madhouses were built next to theaters? The ancients thought that the theater had a healing effect on the human psyche. In my observation, theater always plays the role of a complementary system in relation to the primary reality—life. It is a kind of compensatory mechanism that helps regulate the collective unconscious of a nation.

Second Voice: I must note parenthetically that Russians have a particularly unconscious unconscious.

First Voice: No argument from me. But the time for reconstruction has come. The theater must not be the catalyst for destruction, when the soul of the audience is in ruins as it is. It should offer a model of new spiritual programs, scan versions of the future and positive versions at that. In our present situation the best medicines are sacred laughter and high tragedy. But note the resistance that tragedy encounters.

Second Voice: Which illnesses are you planning to treat, if I may ask?

First Voice: The classic ones: Cynicism, greed, spiritual apathy, and various social neuroses.

Second Voice: I see. Then we must simply determine how your "sacred laughter" differs from ordinary guffawing. If one tries, one can find profound meaning in anything, even the swift degradation of artistic taste. The primitiveness that is TV will soon come to the theater. The alliance of bureaucrat and shopkeeper will do its work.

First Voice: Don't exaggerate—our culture has a pretty good immune system if it survived "developed socialism." The art of post-Soviet Russia, for all it might try, cannot manage without the primitive. After all, it is a different country now with new rules of the game. Of course, this isn't the country's infancy, but a new reincarnation of its culture. And the problem is that an enormous part of the Russian intelligentsia (and not only the intelligentsia) does not wish to take the new rules of the game into account. Writers unconsciously extend the lost reality in their imagination. They use obsolete codes and are angry at the "unenlightened crowd" because it has suddenly become unreceptive to their art. They are substituting the art of self-hypnosis, spiritual masturbation, for living creativity and intuitive knowledge of reality. This lack of correlation leads to decadence that likes to dress up as "tradition." A kind of travesty in reverse.

Second Voice: In that sense the situation in repertory theaters is very sad, since they are given for life to old people whose fate is inextricably entwined with the fate of the USSR. The average age of chief directors of Moscow theaters is sixty-five. Among them there are people like Tat'iana Doronina, who has turned the Gorky Moscow Art Theater into a totalitarian preserve. For some mysterious reason she stages trite and totally unnecessary productions season after season. The actors are terrified when that Party lady arrives. Doronina perceives herself, at the very least, as a queen. A gigantic space in the center of Moscow is being wasted, free tickets are handed out among schoolchildren and pensioners. The theater collective is paralyzed by the evil will of a single mediocre person. And everyone is silent.

First Voice: You must agree that these "old people" (among whom there are forty-year-olds who have prematurely aged morally) simply have no other way out. The state isn't prepared to give them a dignified old age free of anxiety.

Second Voice: Of course not. Not every high-placed bureaucrat has built himself a million-dollar house. By the way, do you know that between 1991 and 1999 the number of civil servants has grown five-fold?

First Voice: What are you proposing? Do away with repertory theater? Break up the permanent troupes? That's equivalent to destroying Russian dramatic art. That school and its traditions can survive only in conditions of stationary theater and direct inheritance of mastery: From one generation to the next. After all, our craft is not just technique, it has its own irrational component, its subjective magic. This will vanish in an instant if the actor's "family" is replaced by random connections.

Second Voice: Perhaps . . . However, the dysfunction of the old model is obvious. It was obvious back in the Soviet period, when "family members" were chained to one another and to their building like galley slaves. We did not have (and still do not have) a rational mechanism of self-liquidation for a dead collective. For changing the leadership. The monarchist principle in the theater, the monarchist principle in the regime—believe me, it's not accidental. It was the cause of many tragic breakups: Just think of Anatolii Efros or the forced emigration of Yurii Liubimov.

First Voice: Then we must create new models.

Second Voice: Without destroying the old ones? Do you think that's feasible?

First Voice: Of course, the most painful thing is that the new generation of professionals, who are much more suitable and are not deformed by censorship and double morality (they are now twenty-six to thirty-six years old), does not have its own spaces. They have no place in which to carry on a dialogue with society.

Second Voice: But you seem to have found yourself a good place. Academic theaters invite you to do productions. Entrepreneurial theaters, as far as I know, are at your service, too. Then what's your problem? Altruism is suspect nowadays, it stinks of demagogy at a hundred paces.

First Voice: First of all, we're not talking about me but about a tendency. And second, two or three exceptions merely prove a sad rule. Just a year ago I had a plan. I thought: We need to create a theater within a theater. To bring together young actors on some project, ignore sabotage and grumbling from the "living dead" (that is, the so-called main repertory troupe). When the administration discovered that we could attract another audience, that the media would write about us differently, that we were always sold out—it would start to help us. But nothing of the sort. The theater administration is quite happy with a "swamp" and the lack of initiative from the workers. And third-rate performances suit them, too. Because it's easier to fish in muddy waters. They don't want to attract unnecessary attention. And the administrators keep their money in a different bank—a bureaucrat doesn't make money on plays. He'd happily get rid of the theater, but then he wouldn't have that cozy spot. That's the entire mathematics involved.

So then I gave up on my idea of a theater within the theater, just another utopia, and decided to stay a free agent. I work on various stages, without expecting special support or encountering fierce opposition, either. They're not too crazy about me, nor I about them. But I have an audience, a fact they admit reluctantly. However, to try to change something seriously, to try to build a fundamentally new Theater—sorry, no go. Young directors don't have their own performance spaces, and therefore all their work is a constant and disillusioning compromise with the half-dead establishment.

Second Voice: And what do you propose?

First Voice: I propose creating (with the help of American cultural foundations, for instance) several independent spaces: In Moscow, St. Petersburg, perhaps in other major cities. These companies would sign a contract for one or two seasons with producers, directors, actors. Everything would be done on a competitive basis.

Second Voice: And why not bring in the city authorities? Especially since the Evgenii Primakov government passed a resolution supporting the creation of alternative models for theater.

First Voice: And where is Primakov now? You're looking for last year's snow, dear fellow. City authorities, just like the federal ones, are busy with politics and have no time for the theater. They have their own great play, "The Mother of All Plays." And they won't have time for the theater for a long, long while. So if we don't want to lose a generation of talented people, we have to look for real alternatives now. Especially since the theater, at least in part, is capable of keeping itself afloat: Expenses are recouped much more quickly than in film. But even more important, if performance spaces are created where unique plays appear, over time the Russian government will want to subsidize them. It prefers to bring up children who are already born.

Second Voice: You bet: Unborn children have to be fed with your own blood. And what, pray tell, will be so unique about these plays?

First Voice: Well, perhaps nothing more than the fact that they will represent contemporary Russian playwriting. You're not going to deny that the plays of the best young playwrights—Mikhail Ugarov, Maksim Kurochkin, and Ol'ga Mukhina—are almost never produced. This is a sad but not accidental fact. The artistic language of their plays is alien and incomprehensible to the establishment.

Second Voice: Perhaps it's incomprehensible to the audience, too.

First Voice: That can be tested only in work. A playwright whose works are produced develops differently—much more intensely and harmoniously. By the way, one could organize all these independent spaces into workshops for contemporary drama, modern dance, and so on. Young people have nowhere to continue their studies, nowhere to exchange experiences. The gerontocracy, exiled from politics, has found itself a safe haven in culture, where the "era of the last General Secretaries" still reigns. It's turning into a real disaster.

Second Voice: Why can't such workshops be organized at repertory theaters?

First Voice: Attempts have been made more than once—at the Lenkom, at the Chekhov Moscow Art Theater, but they didn't work. Every time the effort died at the root, before it even began. Apparently the atmosphere of cynicism and despair is not very conducive to experimental strivings.

So: It is in establishing independent performance spaces for everything that is fresh and aesthetically radical in our theater that the West could help Russia.

Second Voice: Where Western money goes now is a deep, dark secret. Either straight into the pockets of bureaucrats or to mend holes in the budget that formed because of the thievery of those very same bureaucrats. It's a vicious circle. Don't you see?

First Voice: That means the West should change its system of financing cultural projects in Russia. Bureaucrats must be excluded from the chain, they must lose their absolute grip on financial flows. Russian society cannot exercise any financial control whatever over such income streams. On its side, the state has not only power and force but seventy-five years experience operating a totalitarian regime in Russia. Fear and apathy are still in our genes and our mentality. The immorality and brazenness of bureaucrats and bandits alike is the flip side of the coin. The cause of this phenomenon must be sought in the very servile fear of life among our people, which allegedly can be put to rest with money. It can't. Bureaucrats and bandits, you're making a tragic mistake!

Second Voice: Let's set emotions aside. If I understand you, you are talking about the system of grants. Such a system of subsidizing culture exists in Canada, for example.

First Voice: Absolutely right.

Second Voice: I must disillusion you: The system doesn't work. It turns out that the bureaucratic machine (in the guise of various councils and collegia) devours almost half of the money given by the state. Second: The principle of grant distribution is quite subjective and politically motivated. There isn't enough pie to go around, which means that a caste of "the chosen" is created. And who chooses them? Friends and colleagues.

First Voice: I'm not surprised by what you tell me about Canada. That country budgets for its own culture, about which it allegedly cares, less money than the German city of Munich. In that sense, the only thing Canadians and Germans have in common is a love of beer. Of course, Canada is a young country, and a country of immigrants.

The newly arrived have to master the elementary bases of life and learn the new rules of the game.

Second Voice: In that sense, Russians today are like immigrants who changed their citizenship virtually, without ever getting up from their chairs.

First Voice: Yes, but you can't reproach Russians for being indifferent to culture. No sooner does a new Russian attain a little social status than he, like Eugene Onegin, rushes off to the theater. Let's get back to grants: In my opinion, the system could work without a clumsy bureaucratic allocation system. The important thing is not to create a scuffle beside the feeding trough.

Second Voice: Cultural figures, according to your model, turn out to be like spongers: Useless but so nice it's hard not to feed them. And yet, we're talking about the survival of the nation. Dysfunction and degradation of the arts inevitably leads to the death of all other institutions.

First Voice: Don't forget, there's still religion.

Second Voice: All we need is theocracy after the Communist delirium!

First Voice: Let's not confuse God's gift with an omelet.

Second Voice: And don't you confuse the inquisition with theater directing. You of all people won't have a good time if a theocracy should come to Russia. Even though you admire Paul Claudel, your plays are far from being Catholic.

First Voice: It's time for all of us to clear up one simple truth: Culture is perhaps the only sphere in which man is fully free. Free from all constraints—religious, national, even ethical. Only in culture does man truly imitate the Creator. Only here can unlimited experimentation take place.

Second Voice: Yes, yes, and then young people who take the experiment too much to heart will start testing its effectiveness on their compatriots. Saint-Simon's utopian socialism was merely an amusing fairy tale, was it not? And the cult of violence in Hollywood films is merely a pleasant tickle for the viewer's nerves. Yet the former "Easter egg" hatched Russian communism, and the latter has hatched unmotivated murders in American high schools.

First Voice: What a comparison . . . Let's take a break, otherwise we might dump too many things into the same pile.

Second Voice: They say that Americans like garage sales as an informal method of socializing.

Once upon a time plays had many acts, and a play could last five or six hours. Today the optimal time for a play is two hours and fifteen minutes, two hours and forty-five minutes at most. Exceed that and the audience gets bored. It looks as if film has imposed its time restrictions, its rhythm, on the theater. Which confirms yet again that we are musical creatures and that any algorithm can be imposed from outside. Especially when it is tied to the principle of pleasure. It's not bad or good—it just requires attention. . . . Musicologists maintain that music is usually about a century ahead of its time. Beethoven, for example, anticipated the cataclysms of the first half of the twentieth century. The best contemporary composers have moved away from the principles of atonal music and are rediscovering polyphony. I don't know about you, but I find that encouraging.

Especially since, graphically speaking, the sequences resemble DNA chains.

By the way, about DNA. The average Russian, like the average American, is a mixture of bloodlines, like a good exotic cocktail. For example, I myself have seven: Armenian, Georgian, German, French, Arab, Jewish, and Russian. It is very hard to define ourselves ethnically but very easy to do so culturally. The United States as an ethnic mix is properly considered the archetype of future humanity. But Russians wouldn't mind auditioning for the part.

2

First Voice: Every nation, even the most eccentric and most prone to dangerous fantasies, if it intends to survive in history, sooner or later finds that its mysterious mechanism of self-regulation is working. In that sense—hail, old man Bacon!—a nation is like the human body with its instinct for survival, despite the obvious advantages of suicide. Probably this is the cosmic principle of self-preservation of all living things right up to final entropy, decline, and subsequent metamorphosis.

Second Voice: But people do commit suicide frequently enough. And weren't the Revolution, the Civil War, the genocide of the best part of the population in Stalin's camps, and the loss of millions through emigration a form of suicide on the part of Russia? I'm afraid that Igor Shafarevich is right: Having to choose between Eros and Thanatos, the Russians chose the skeletal embrace once and for all.

First Voice: However, it was the Communists themselves who dismantled the system.

Second Voice: In order to privatize the country, which they considered their private property anyway.

First Voice: We've talked about that already. Nevertheless, my prognosis for the next ten years is optimistic.

Second Voice: That's because you have dual citizenship, and if things should take a turn for the worse you can pack up in three days and move your family to Canada. It's easy for you to talk about variations of life and freedom of choice. And what would you have the average person do?

First Voice: Well, I think a trip abroad, for just a few years, wouldn't hurt anyone. You get the right distance in relation to your own culture. The experience of communicating and—most importantly—thinking in a tongue that is not your native language has an enlightening effect, leading you out of the labyrinth of orthodox ideology, which, as you know, is just one step away from paranoia. . . . Perhaps I have a greater degree of freedom of choice than my actors. I emphasize: Perhaps. But I made that choice back in 1993—to be with them during the crossing of the desert, to work in Moscow, to try to change at least some things.

Second Voice: My goodness, what a marvelous fellow you are! Things won't change in Russia until everyone who had the least connection to the Soviet regime dies out. Now, you, for instance, were you in the Komsomol?

First Voice: Of course I was. You were inducted automatically at age thirteen.

Second Voice: So was I. So: Until you and I die, everything will remain as it is.

First Voice: I don't agree with you. Thievery and cynicism come from above. The bureaucrats of all levels are tied together. It's their example that is corrupting.

Second Voice: Ah, yes, "our wise, good Russian people," how easily you are corrupted!

First Voice: If the government and the Duma are represented by people with a different mentality—neither angels nor saints, but simply professionals who are not indifferent to the fate of their country—and if those people can give the country normal laws and most importantly will want to obey them—

Second Voice: Cleaning up the Augean stables will take more than one generation. Once you start, it will stink to high heaven.

First Voice: Nevertheless, someone's going to have to start. I hope that it will be our generation. I wouldn't want us to go down in history as apolitical weaklings and neurotics.

Second Voice: You know, Thomas Mann has a marvelous essay on that topic. He writes that politics in Germany was always considered a dirty and undignified job. The German character is too romantic to take the crude reality of political games and find a drop of common sense in it. Therefore, Mann concludes, when a German does go into politics, he behaves like a filthy pig and sheds rivers of blood—in complete accordance with his perceptions. So: I have a troubled surmise that deep in their hearts, Russians consider not only politics but economics—in fact anything that returns a profit—a dirty and sinful business. Just look at how quickly the young intellectuals who appeared on TV in the early 1990s degenerated. They were people of our age and our circle. And it turned out that they had nothing to counterpoise to the cult of stupidity, bad taste, and crazy money that came from advertising. Isn't it clear that if they had come to power, their generation would have used it just as ineptly? Look at an Anatolii Chubais or a Sergei Kirienko. I don't think that they're in any sense better than Yurii Luzhkov or Boris Berezovskii. They're just as pushy and have the same distorted sense of historical reality.

First Voice: Come, come. Chubais, Yegor Gaidar, and Kirienko were all forced to make compromises with members of the old nomenklatura who knew little about economics—that's why their reforms were so half-baked and unproductive. Yet you work with directors who, in your opinion, don't have clean hands. You stage your production despite or, shall we say, in parallel with your knowledge of their "off-the-books accounting." So the question is: Why?

Second Voice: Because I love my craft and I have no other way. For now.

First Voice: And perhaps the young reformers were hostages of a similar situation. . . . But you are right, it's not about politicians. The average person is merely an object, the new material of history, and the Russian especially. The concepts of "personal initiative" and "personal responsibility" were eroded for centuries in Russia. We need a system aimed at the renaissance of the very concept of Personality and Individual Uniqueness. The value of human life in Russia is still barbarously low.

Second Voice: What kind of a system would this be?

First Voice: For a start, the state must at long last carry out real, and not fictitious, liberal economic reforms. Leave decent people alone, not skin them three times over with absurd taxes that don't fill the treasury so much as push the entrepreneur into crime. Under present circumstances no honest business can make a profit. And the government should strip the crooks of their semilegal "covers." Today you can buy yourself off any criminal charges at the Prosecutor General's Office, even the most clear-cut ones. In this situation, the criminal bosses have become practically the pillars of society, a special privileged caste.

Second Voice: I hope you realize that this is no accident. Why should the former Communist nomenklatura breed strong and honest competitors? Today they are working in small businesses, where they are relatively controllable and loyal, but tomorrow they'll move up and start dictating their terms. Our bureaucrats are not used to competition. They like to be the boss, but without the stress and rivalry. And they can keep wealthy crooks out of power on "legal" grounds.

Besides, if the entire society, because of the idiotic tax system, is forced to cheat a bit, then bribe-taking among bureaucrats has smooth sailing. This frees them psychologically from responsibility. That's why everything in our economy is made to make the "chosen" richer and to keep the rest of the people ("cattle" in their terminology) in their shameful poverty. Our middle class is embryonic; society consists of the poor and the millionaires.

First Voice: Our middle class prefers emigration to a political struggle for its rights.

Second Voice: That's preferable for everyone now. Bureaucrats are happy to get rid of the critically thinking part of the population, their potential rivals. The West is no less pleased to consume Russian brains. Leaving for the West, the scientific and cultural elite makes room for the mediocrities.

First Voice: And what is the way out?

Second Voice: Either a true democracy or a new form of fascism. It doesn't matter what it's called: A presidential republic or a theocracy.

First Voice: But you must admit that the most passionate of today's Russian elite are the repatriates. Those who have lived in the West and got an injection of the Protestant ethic and then returned to

Russia after 1991. They are rarely deceived by the virtues of living abroad, they had the experience of surviving in an inhospitable environment (relative to their previous experience), and they have developed a strong immunity to social stress. These are not false patriots; their feeling for their homeland is much more objective and no less emotional than ours.

Second Voice: Yes, if you don't praise yourself, no one else will. However, what is it you're suggesting? That the entire Russian intelligentsia emigrate and then all come back one fine day?

First Voice: I've already told you that this wouldn't be a bad idea, however utopian. But here's the thought I have: America and other Western democracies could create special programs for those Russian intellectuals who want to acquire the experience of living in another culture. For instance, Russia absolutely requires such experience in contemporary ballet and filmmaking. We're at least thirty years behind. We need contemporary projects. Not one or two, but many. Let's say that in three or four years we have a boom in the film industry, it's inevitable. And then those professionals could change something in both the aesthetics and the economics of filmmaking. And by the same token, in the way people think.

Second Voice: You, dear friend, are a complete romantic. You can't be allowed near politics. The American film industry is much more interested in promoting its own products in our huge market. Why the devil should they help their Russian competitors, who know local conditions much better than they do as it is?

First Voice: You're talking about narrowly focused industry people, merchants, who don't see beyond their own noses.

Second Voice: I'm talking about normal, patriotic businesspeople. Hollywood is not only a Dream Factory but a source of wealth for the nation and especially for the national elite.

First Voice: I'll never believe that America is so short sighted. Russia has too strong a sense of identity to become a cultural colony. Anyone's. We easily adapt to foreign influences and turn them into part of our own psychological makeup. In that sense, we very much resemble Americans and Jews.

Second Voice: But the United States and Russia are still, if not enemies, then rivals.

First Voice: Only a crude consciousness, which evidently characterizes politicians the world over, puts military potential at the cornerstone of the arch. War always follows. We arm ourselves because we do not understand one another. Lacking understanding, we have no trust in each other and we are afraid. Fear leads to aggression. It's classic psychopathology. In fact, Russian cultural genes are no less universal than American ones. We compete with one another because we have similar roles in world history, we are actors in the same style. In its radical nature, the American experience of individualism is comparable to the Russian experience of collectivism. And now both concepts are being shaken back and forth. The Russians have shifted toward the pole of individualism and, as usual, we know no limits in our movements. (Russians in general tend to act without a sense of limits.) In the meantime, Americans are mastering collectivism. What else can explain "political correctness" if not an Orwellian influx into democracy? The new millennium is setting in our two countries the goal of intensive "language" exchange (naturally I am speaking of "language" in structuralist terms). Therefore, America is vitally interested precisely in the renaissance of Russian film rather than in cultural expansionism. Do you know how some scholars at Oxford decipher the letters GOD? "Generator of Diversity."

Second Voice: But for some reason, intellectuals never come to power, either in America or in Russia.

First Voice: Perhaps we should thank God that they don't. They have too much imagination and fill a different function in society. Politicians and military men, however, should not think that they are God's representatives on earth. Dialogue is the only acceptable form for the relationship between people and government. This concept—a socially acceptable moral imperative—is having a difficult time taking root in our soil, where arbitrary and unchecked power has always been the norm. But now the authoritarian model is reaching its ignominious end—first of all, in the minds of the people. The nation no longer is willing to live under servile, humiliating conditions. Any government that does not take that into account is doomed.

Second Voice: That brings tears to my eyes. Emotional and pathos-filled rhetoric always affects me like teargas. But I'd like to know then why the people's wrath in theaters hasn't swept away the directors. As everybody knows or surmises, they are behaving in arbitrary fashion.

First Voice: Because they will be replaced by people exactly like them, or worse. (A theater director is not selected by the troupe but is appointed by the Ministry of Culture.) Because they have "protectors" at all levels of the pyramid. After all, they feed their bosses, who then feed theirs. It's like the wrapper on the "Try to Take It" candy bar: There's a little girl making a dog beg, holding up the candy, and on that candy wrapper is another picture of a girl making a dog beg, and so on. An infinity of evil that makes your head spin. But in the year 2000 Russia will have another government.

Second Voice: Honest and incorruptible.

First Voice: No need for sarcasm. Russia is an irrational country. Inexplicable things and sudden metamorphoses often occur.

Second Voice: Here's a random thought. Near Copenhagen there is a statue of the Little Mermaid. Some miscreants have already cut off her head with an acetylene torch twice, and then, once a hefty sum was paid to them, left the head on a deserted street. After which the head was neatly welded back on. That is vandalism, Danish-style. The other monuments that were erected in the sixteenth, seventeenth, and eighteenth centuries are still there untouched. Now think about the fate of monuments in Russia, particularly in the twentieth century. They are constantly being taken down and replaced with new ones, as if in an effort to destroy the past along with its inevitable mistakes.

First Voice: Is that some kind of a metaphor?

Second Voice: I imagine that we just won't be able to start from a clean sheet.

While I was writing these dialogues, there came a new scent of human sacrifice: The second Chechen war started. In several cities in Russia, terrorists blew up apartment buildings. This took place at night and the people asleep in the buildings were not soldiers but women and children, peaceful civilians. . . . The most incredible rumors are circulating: That these monstrous acts of terrorism were committed by Russian special services in order to ruin the elections, to declare an emergency situation in the country, and to provoke an invasion of federal forces into rebel Chechnya. As if the Chechen invasion of neighboring Dagestan, the vicious murders of hostages, and the entire bandit regime of self-proclaimed Ichkeria were not already sufficient grounds to start military action. . . .

For all the bizarre quality of these rumors, you can see a rational grain in them, a hard-to-find bit of sense: People do not trust their government 100 percent, they think that this government is prepared to sell its soul to the devil just to stay in power.

Of course, this demonization of the higher elite did not happen overnight or for no reason. But another thing is also clear: The Russian tendency to mythological thought is genetic. I can accuse myself of that to the fullest extent. Even though it is more natural for a person working in the theater to think this way than, say, the mayor of Moscow. (Recently Mr. Luzhkov said on television, "Mr. Berezovskii is the devil, Satan." Perhaps he meant that Mr. Berezovskii had tempted the mayor? I can't say for sure, but honestly, that phrase didn't sound at all like a metaphor.)

I can offer other examples of mythological thinking:

Example No. 1. I am given my salary at the accounting office of the theater. And the cashier behaves inappropriately: Very hostile, even aggressive. She behaves as if she were paying me personally, out of her own pocket, for work that I had either not done or had done badly. The reason? Laughably simple: The bills physically pass through her hands, she mentally makes them hers, and she considers the work of a director to be a priori not worth one penny.

Example No. 2. I am convinced that there will be no civil war, no bloody rebellions in Russia, and that even the separatism of Chechnya will not set ablaze the entire northern Caucasus. And what is the basis of my optimism? If you like, the law of composition. After all, history has its composition, its predetermined harmony. In the twentieth century, Russians have made a colossal sacrifice. Tens of millions of citizens—the best and brightest—died in Stalin's camps. I'm not even mentioning the wars and revolutions. I don't know to whom that sacrifice was made. I doubt that it was to the Creator of all that exists. But I do know that thereby we have earned at least 150 years of relative peace, a respite from bloodshed and violence; we have earned cultural renaissance. Is that naive? Perhaps, but I've already said that Russians have a rich imagination. And this text was merely meant as Theater for Oneself.

26

RUSSIA'S LITERARY REVIVAL

From Authoritarianism to Intellectual Freedom

Aleksandr Ageev

To understand the unique aspect of the current literary situation in Russia, one must fully comprehend the role that literature has played in Russian life throughout the nation's history, especially during the many decades before the reforms of Mikhail Gorbachev and Boris Yeltsin, when Communist ideology predominated.

Russia has never been truly free—the evolution of its social thought (philosophy and the social and political sciences) and publishing (the printing of books and the press) was always held back by the constraint of fierce censorship. In consequence, virtually the only realm in which *ideas* of any sort could develop and, most significantly, be brought to the attention of the public, even in a mediated form, inevitably became fiction and belles lettres.

This circumstance appreciably distorted the scale of aesthetic values to which both writers and the public gradually came to orient themselves. Artistic craft, aesthetic originality, and novelty of form

Born in 1956, **Aleksandr Leonidovich Ageev** earned an advanced degree in philology and taught literature at Ivanovo State University. A prominent literary critic, he has been widely published in many "thick" journals, including *Znamia, Novyi mir,* and *Oktiabr',* as well as in newspapers. In 1991 he moved to Moscow to become an editor of *Znamia,* where he directs the literature department. Translated by Anna Kucharev.

were valued far less than the writer's ability to respond to the current burning issues of the day. The writer was perceived not as an *artist, virtuoso,* or *master craftsman of the word* but primarily as a *teacher of life,* a *prophet,* and a *thinker.* Two great Russian writers (better known in the West than any of the others), Leo Tolstoy and Fyodor Dostoevsky, each in his own way expressively represents the archetype of the Russian writer proper—that is, the writer who considers the art of the word to be a means of transforming man and the world. In the end, both men resorted to direct advocacy of their religious and sociopolitical ideas, with Tolstoy casting doubt on the moral value of art itself in his tracts on aesthetics. Aleksandr Solzhenitsyn was, and remains, the last of these writer-prophets; his literary talent simply loses importance when seen against the vast scale of his social and historical role in a particular historical era.

In a Russia seized by the thirst for changes, every spiritual movement (represented by both Tolstoy and Dostoevsky, and—in his own way—Solzhenitsyn in recent times) was perceived as a version of a liberating, revolutionary movement. Most nineteenth- and early-twentieth-century Russian writers were far from supporters of revolution, but public opinion nonetheless subsumed their work into a revolutionary context.

The Communists, who came to power in 1917, understood very well literature's principal importance as a social institution, and they used the traditionally eminent authority of literature in Russian society to accomplish their own ends. During Soviet rule, this authority ceased being a matter of free social choice; it was inculcated, using the full force of the entire state propaganda machine, so that in the end, literature became its most significant aspect. The writer saw his status raised to an unprecedented height, the Party and the state lavished their attention on him, and he received privileges and perquisites that served to separate him socially and materially from the majority of the population, which was impoverished and had no rights.

In exchange, the writer was required to give up his creative freedom and write "at the bidding of his heart, and our hearts belong to the Party," as the official Soviet classic writer Mikhail Sholokhov put it. At the same time, admission to "the rank of writer" was put under rigid ideological control and was sharply restricted (only a member of the official Union of Writers could be considered a "writer," only he had access to privileges and perquisites, only his books did not encounter obstacles on the way to the reader; the rest, if they were engaged in literary work but were not listed as employed anywhere, could be sentenced to administrative exile for "parasitism," as was Joseph Brodsky in 1964). A few resisted this kind of official temptation and perished during the years of repression or were persecuted their entire lives. The rest compromised with their own personal artistic natures (I'm referring here to genuine writers, not the third-rate hacks who constituted the majority of orthodox "Soviet writers"), and their literary lives became dramas of talent betrayed by their own hands.

The Communists, having carried out a "cultural revolution," conquered illiteracy (albeit at the cost of mediocritizing culture) and developed high schools and higher education in their own way and for their own purposes (and in so doing dramatically increased the formerly very thin strata of "educated people" in Russia). In this way, they were able to cultivate Soviet literature and, with its help, the genuinely average reader. By the end of Communist rule, this reader readily devoured enormous editions of practically any sort of literature. The tastes of this average reader were formed by Soviet schools and propaganda, but in general they were standard tastes, similar to those of the general reader in any country—appreciating realistic literature that was reminiscent of classical models. From the mid-1960s to the very end of Soviet rule, the strange phenomenon of "book hunger" was evident at nearly every level of the population. A book (a good book) became a prestigious consumer item for all strata of the population. During Nikita Khrushchev's "thaw" of 1956–1964, the status of the writer was elevated even higher. Apart from the customary official aspect, a measure of spontaneous societal trust in writers and in their authority appeared, since they were often leading dissidents and human rights activists. The example of Solzhenitsyn was particularly compelling.

In short, just as in prerevolutionary Russia, writers were expected to oppose the regime intellectually. By that time, Soviet rule had become completely stagnant, decaying internally and rapidly losing society's support. The Andrei Siniavskii and Yulii Daniel trial in 1965, Solzhenitsyn's expulsion to Germany in 1974, the exile of many other writers in his wake, the development of samizdat and tamizdat (underground publishing within the USSR and abroad), and the weakening of the Iron Curtain, through which a carefully measured but substantial influx of new artistic and philosophical ideas came from the West—all this promoted the authority of literature and writers.

The years of perestroika (1986–1991) were marked by a final and unprecedented stir of public attention to literature. Besides their earlier polemical articles, novels, and stories, Anatoly Rybakov's *Deti Arbata* (Children of the Arbat), Daniil Granin's *Zubr* (Bison), Vladimir Dudintsev's *Belye odezhdy* (White Garments), and Solzhenitsyn's works (published in Russia for the first time) became the banners of perestroika. The circulation of the "thick" journals in which all these books were published surpassed the million-copy mark. (The number of subscribers to *Novyi mir* [New World], where Solzhenitsyn was published, was nearly 2.7 million in 1990, and the publisher simply could not cope with the demand, with the result that the last four issues of the journal did not get published that year.)

The "serious press," a far cry from cheap tabloids and entertainment pulp fiction, had never had such circulation figures anywhere.

It seemed as if the entire nation was reading these literary journals, that writers had unlimited power over minds. Already this seemed abnormal, almost hysterical to some. The euphoria of the early years of perestroika, when the population learned the monstrous truth about Soviet history in shocking detail, seemed to be growing into a kind of narcotic dependence. I recall that in my article, "On the Harm of Literature," I asked myself and my compatriots: "If everyone in the country is reading, who's working here?" The intensity of interest in literature was also heightened by the general instability of the situation in the USSR and the real, harsh ideological war that, because of the backwardness of the press in those years, unfolded right on the pages of the literary publications. Moreover, writers were often more candid than politicians, who maintained an attitude of restraint virtually until the last days of the regime with regard to the "socialist choice" on which Gorbachev insisted.

This wave of interest in literature, unparalleled in magnitude, began playing itself out back in 1991, when it seemed to many that perestroika had reached an impasse and that the complete breakdown of the socialist planned economy confronted the nation with a real threat of hunger and collapse. A five-year ideological discussion, which thereupon divided society into two hostile camps without bringing victory to either side, psychologically exhausted the people in the extreme, particularly the middle intelligentsia, the main body of readers. A landslide began, a serious decline of circulation, which continues to this day. My first critical articles were published in the monthly magazine *Znamia* (Banner) (where I work and am published), which had a circulation of 1 million copies in 1990; my most recent pieces in 1999 appeared in an edition numbering only 9,500 copies.

* * *

The last "heroic" period in the history of Russian literature ended in January 1992, when the former "Soviet people" woke up one day in a different country. Western observers, it sometimes seems, are inclined to underestimate the harshness of the shock that most Russians experienced (they had just been cut adrift, without the Union of Soviet Socialist Republics) during the first few months of actual economic reforms, which Gorbachev had delayed for such an inexcusably long time. The point wasn't even so much the steep drop in the standard of living or the loss of savings eaten up by inflation—people in Russia have always known how to suffer and live in poverty, and they still do. The shock was primarily psychological: No one knew how to *act* in the proposed situation, and hence it seemed as if the will of the majority was paralyzed.

Perestroika's "liberal-progressive" rhetoric (and writers were partially responsible for this) was in large part starry-eyed, optimistic, and detached from reality. It contended that Russia, with its great human and creative potential, once freed from the fetters of the administrative-command economy, would immediately blossom under free-market conditions. Almost no one wanted to consider that the species *Homo sovieticus,* a type of dependent individual lacking in creative initiative, had actually evolved during the long years of Communist rule. No one had prepared people for the difficult, lengthy, agonizing adaptation to the new rules of the game. No one—including writers—could bring themselves to say that most people were absolutely unprepared to accept the new system of priorities and values that the reforms entailed; that in order to survive they would have to change radically the petrified socialist communal stereotypes that had formed in their minds during the era of distributive economics and rigid regulation of every individual's social behavior.

People had lived for many years in a badly organized, cruel, and unjust—but understandable—*Cosmos;* they had been united with people similar to themselves by a not-too-joyful but common fate. Now they suddenly found themselves cast down into creative Chaos by an invisible new life, with no agency providing leadership or risk insurance. The former Soviet individual had nothing against the rights he was granted, but he couldn't even imagine their real price— the personal responsibility for his own life and work that he would henceforth have to bear.

From a distance and in theory, it didn't seem that difficult. But freedom became a trial that was nearly unendurable for the general population's mentality. The nation experienced stress, which easily slid into a depression from which Russia is only now very slowly beginning to recover.

Literature was also among the victims of this mass depression, or more accurately, the role literature was accustomed to playing in Russian life. This was a unique moment of truth. Freedom had suddenly arrived (and along with it, requirements); the opportunities that accompanied freedom revealed the degree of society's actual demand for literature (which proved to be lower than that expected in Russia, but wholly within worldwide standards). Freedom also revealed the price of the propagandistic clichés about "the nation that reads the most" and about the social stability derived from the intelligentsia's proficiency in the humanities.

Reading fiction systematically proved not to be among the most stable of the intelligentsia's skills. Moreover, the change in the national psychological and economic climate led to the marginalization of the mid-level service intelligentsia, of which there was a surplus. It was these people who were the first to wind up on the street as a result of the closing down of many useless offices where it had been possible to exist, peacefully albeit meagerly, shuffling papers nobody needed. For some reason, it was in this environment (according to not just my own personal observations) that the "reevaluation of values" was the most radical: A person who only yesterday had been incapable of surviving a month without devouring four or five of the latest "thick" journals and without discussing the prospects of Russia's Christian (or national, or economic) renaissance with his comrades was now reading only cheap novels and the sports pages, watching only Hollywood blockbusters on television and video, and passionately engaging in some petty speculative business.

In short, the average reader turned his back on literature, and the prestige and status of the writer's profession declined accordingly.

The entire powerful government infrastructure comprising the economic foundations of literature collapsed then and there—the system of book publishing (limited but cheap paper and printing services, book sales, and relatively high royalties that depended little on print runs) and the system of privileges and perquisites.

At first (and later as well) the state was not at all concerned with the fate of literature: It wound up at once as the private business of private people. And then and there—deprived of the government protection and high social status—literature was forced to enter into competition with cheap novels (formerly artificially suppressed and now luxuriantly flourishing), mass literature, and pulp fiction, which at first was translated and then was domestically produced. (The new reality furnished many plots for all this crime fiction.) "Serious literature," needless to say, could not endure this competition, having in the meantime acquired an inferiority complex and having wasted a huge amount of energy to no purpose in the battle with this inescapable "evil." The very idea of the separate coexistence of two cultures, which simply had different natures and functions, could by no means penetrate the heads of writers and critics who were accustomed to the strict hierarchical structure of socialist culture.

Paradoxically, writers who had themselves just become liberated from the all-suffocating censorship publicly and loudly demanded that the government prescribe or at least set strict limits on its competitors' activities. In turn, the competitors defended, entirely reasonably, the free choice of the reader (already seen as a "consumer"), who preferred to entertain and distract himself instead of following the acknowledged "masters of the word" to peer into the darkest remote corners of the Russian soul and Russian life.

The "serious" literature of the perestroika and post-perestroika years was predominantly gloomy and hopeless; above all, it demonstrated the bewilderment of its creators, who had wandered into a kind of existential impasse in their attempt to reflect the Russian historical experience of the bloody twentieth century. The works of Liudmila Petrushevskaya, Vladimir Makanin, Andrei Bitov, Nina Sadur, and many other talented writers whom the new era freed from the underground astonished us not only by their power and deep penetration into human psychology but also by the glaring absence of even a hint of a future "light at the end of the tunnel." Essentially, they refused to collaborate with the reader, who was accustomed to getting not only questions from literature but answers as

well. But the pendulum had somehow swung too far in the other direction. Answers were not forthcoming. Petrushevskaya expressively
entitled one of her best (and most gloomy) works *It's Nighttime*.

The crisis in Soviet and post-Soviet consciousness, even though it
was analyzed by the nation's best pens, did not bring back to literature the readers who had abandoned it. In the meantime, the generation of writers mentioned above and the marked pathos of their
post-Soviet works have dominated the best literary magazines of the
past decade. These writers, having encountered many difficulties in
Soviet times, were already mature masters who had captured the
imagination of readers; they became something akin to the present
literary establishment, by turns serving as laureates of all the literary
prizes, the main characters in all the critical discussions, and the
"plenipotentiary representatives" of Russian literature for Western
readers. Despite all my respect and love for the works of the writers
of this circle, I cannot refrain from venturing the speculation that
they are nonetheless fin de siècle writers: Their spiritual roots lie too
deeply in Soviet soil—not the healthiest environment, it should be
said, even for powerful talent. Their experience is priceless, but it is
also rapidly depreciating—its unkind gravity is vanishing before
one's eyes—in proportion to the turbulent changes taking place in
real life.

It should be noted that literature in Russia has always been
slightly ahead of society, has led it, in a certain sense, indicating the
desired path of development and furnishing it with moral reference
points. Now it looks as if the situation is directly the reverse—literary consciousness, formed back in Soviet times, lags behind the evolution of life. Perhaps the main problem in our literature is its extremely unclear, dare I say skeptical attitude to such a fundamental
value as freedom.

Variations on the standard plot roam from one literary work to
another (and we're talking about works of high literary quality): An
individual attains freedom but finds no happiness in it, simply does-
n't know what to do with it. No argument here—the structure of
Russian life throughout the nation's history has inevitably produced
a type of contemplative person, a dreamer, a visionary, since this life
did not require the activist and life-affirming elements in a person all
that much. The doer in Russian classical prose was, as a rule, either
a foreigner or a crook, while the true Russian hero sought from life
not so much *freedom* as *truth*. Here the specific nature of Russian

life—always strictly regulated, not challenging the individual to take creative initiative in practical action—gave rise to the particular nature of the national consciousness and, correspondingly, to the specific character of its literature. The instinct for freedom did exist, as it does in any creature possessing reason, but it was, to put it bluntly, weakened by the circumstances of life itself.

Vladimir Makanin, one of Russia's major contemporary prose writers, has been preoccupied with this issue in his work for quite some time. Nearly all the main characters in his works, as far back as the Soviet period, undergo the agonizing process of individual self-definition, of displacement from a close circle, the "collective," the community that spawned and shaped them. To keep from dissolving as individuals in the depersonalizing collective (which the family can also be), nearly all of them escape. In the story "Pustynnoe mesto" (Deserted Place), an entire philosophy of escape is worked out. It's a pessimistic philosophy: "There is no purification in escape—there is only a craving for, a kind of prolonged attraction to a deserted place, and nothing more. A craving that exhausts itself in the escape itself, runs its course on its own, like chickenpox or measles."

And completely in keeping with this philosophy, Makanin's characters run in place. The "craving" deceives them, the "deserted place" horrifies them, "the childhood disease" of freedom—"chickenpox or measles" as we are slyly told—passes. And those who have been given more than others, who had a powerful start, gained momentum, and wound up beyond the "ring of the Ural Mountains," like Bashilov in the story "Gde skhodilis nebo s kholmami" (Where the Sky Met the Hills) or like Ninel Nikolaevna and Goloshchekov in the story "Odin i odna" (One and One). They are doomed to lonely nostalgia for their "village," their "collective," their "brood," from which they broke out by yielding to their "craving."

Yes, there is no purification for them in the instant of freedom. On the other hand, in Makanin's words, "this instant is small and seemingly even meaningless; however, a man has valued it and will always value this instant, and, if you ask him why, he'll shrug his shoulders—saying, 'you, brother, are a fool.'" In the Soviet era, this collision had no resolution, because that "freedom" about which Makanin and his characters agonizingly reflect was still a theoretical and philosophical category, and the questions "What for?" and "Why?" arose almost from the realization that attaining real freedom was impossible. But since then, life in Russia has changed in a radical way. Literature that had been bold and advanced in Soviet conditions (since it even had the impudence to think about freedom) has begun to lag noticeably behind rapidly changing life.

"Literature lags behind life" was a favorite thesis of official, standard Soviet criticism. But, strange as it seems, it is now true. Everything has been turned upside down.

The time, of course, is "Nighttime." Russia is experiencing a time that is not the most psychologically comfortable for writers or readers. But economic chaos and the spiritual crisis of the former Soviet individual does not change the simple fact that it has fallen to our lot to live in the great era of reconstruction of the entire world order. Russia was the site of the jolt that initiated this landslide-like process, which has given the country, for the first time in its difficult history, actual (not "internal," not "spiritual," not theoretical, not hypothetical) *freedom*. And, finally, a new type of individual has appeared, a person who knows why he needs this freedom. This individual, however, lives among a multitude who remain internally unfree and who are horrified, like Makanin's characters, by the "deserted place." This in itself constitutes our most important moral and aesthetic problem. How Russian literature helps solve this problem will be its most profound challenge in the years to come.

*   *   *

Knowing the history and specific characteristics of Russian literature, I have been deeply interested in observing over the past ten years how it has evolved without anyone's control, how its secularization and emancipation—not only from ideological Communist blueprints and from the state but also from certain venerable yet timeworn aesthetic traditions—have taken place. This evolution has proceeded in the most diverse ways, at times ludicrous and intriguing, at times dramatic, accompanied by tumultuous discussions. (Sometimes the topics of the discussions themselves have been ridiculous; for example, serious critics have spent much time arguing about the role and function of so-called obscene vocabulary in a literary text, or they have attempted to draw the line between erotica and pornography, since these kinds of themes and devices, which were strictly forbidden in the past, have now appeared in Russian literature and assumed their normal places.)

Literature was becoming colorful and diverse right before my eyes, losing the unity that had been constructed by theoreticians of socialist realism, splitting apart into a multitude of autonomous and fully self-sufficient literatures. In order to describe this scene, critics were forced to invent a myriad of temporary terms such as "the other literature," a phrase introduced by Sergei Chuprinin, or "artistic prose," coined by Mark Lipovetskii. Literary trends multiplied and were also given florid names—such as "metametaphorism" and "turborealism." The underground came out of the basement noisily, in carnival fashion, but its creative potential, as later became apparent, was not very great; its most vital aspect, *sots-art* (a sardonic reference to socialist realism), is represented by the work of Dmitrii Prigov, Yevgenii Popov, Vladimir Sorokin, and several others. Western Slavicists are very familiar with these writers, but almost no one in Russia reads them: Their aesthetic novelty drew on an all-too-perishable substratum. The language and ephemera of everyday life in the Soviet era and their reinterpretation in parody form, which makes up the essence of *sots-art,* disappear and are rapidly forgotten. The aura of scandal surrounding these writers also faded quickly, while the overuse of literary devices that had at one time been effective led only to the trivialization of talent. Prigov finally became something akin to a literary showman, more interesting to society-page journalists (when he appeared at any public function or gala event) than to readers and serious critics. And Sorokin, after the publication of his novel *Goluboe salo* (Blue Bacon), is making forays into the bestseller genre.

Most of the poets and prose writers once ranked as avant-garde were by no means all avant-gardists. Those writing within one or another influential tradition (neoclassical, neo-acmeist), such as Sergei Gandlevskii and Sergei Soprovskii, simply were not published in the censored Soviet press. Now they have emerged from semilegal poetic circles to come before a wider audience and, having matured as artists, have immediately taken their rightful places in the new literary establishment.

The literary arena was rapidly expanding. Former dissidents and external and internal émigrés once more entered the general literary stream. Noisy, scandalous, marginal groups and trends that irritated traditional tastes but advertised themselves skillfully began to appear. The critics nurtured on such concepts as the "literary process" (actually, what they meant here was not so much process as "progress," in which literature was supposed to get better and better), were at first greatly annoyed by all this diversity, understanding neither where it was all headed (the fact that literature must constantly *move in the right direction* was understood implicitly) nor which concept they could possibly use to describe it all. This is why critics of the older and middle generations (such as Anatolii Bocharov, Viktor Kam'ianov, Stanislav Rassadin, Valentin Kurbatov, and many others) occasionally felt open or secret nostalgia for Soviet times—unfree and difficult for literature but comprehensible—and began speaking about the "crisis in literature." They rose up in openly conservative opposition to the literary innovations that annoyed them.

In a certain very limited sense, they were right. Much of what floated up to the literary surface during these years and enjoyed a brief notoriety was simply froth and failed to live up to general expectations. But these critics did not appreciate the revolutionary nature of the situation, when *everything* became possible in literature, nor did they approve of or support the powerful creative potential inherent in it.

In 1991, irritated by the many-voiced chorus of critics complaining about the "crisis in literature," I myself wrote an article entitled "Synopsis of the Crisis," in which I did everything I could to welcome this crisis. I characterized the situation as follows:

> The picture that we are witnessing is a really motley one that can shock the outside observer. Our literature is now experiencing that extremely rare transitional point when it contains everything: All the stages of the evolution that awaits it are not spread out over time, but are revealed all at once, the way the "cultural layers" of several centuries are laid open in the cross section of an archeological dig.

From a creative standpoint, the situation even then seemed to me extraordinarily fruitful, as it still does. We were observing and we continue to observe neither disintegration nor entropy (even if it is destruction, it is the destruction of a prison) but creative Chaos, as the ancient Greek thinkers understood it. The Cosmos can arise only from Chaos—this is what I always kept in mind as I observed the literary scene in post-Soviet Russia, which sometimes annoyed me, too.

In the meantime, pessimism about the literary situation in Russia is to this day widespread and influential. In a society that has turned its back on literature, that has stopped subscribing to the "thick" journals and does not buy serious books, the desire to somehow justify such a cooling off to culture is very strong. Explanations such as "Good literature has disappeared in our nation"; "There's nothing to read"; "Thick journals have died"; "Gallows humor and pornography reign supreme in contemporary literature"; and "The craft of writing has declined" are quite popular in the semieducated circles that are cut off from active participation in literary life and that once made up the collective "social clients" of Soviet literature.

The facts attest to the complete opposite. Unabashedly mediocre, dull, uninspired but ideologically impeccable prose and poetry produced by an army of more than 10,000 official Soviet writers in an almost planned system predominated in the enormous stream of Soviet literature issued by Soviet publishers. The reader had to search for pearls in this enormous heap of, metaphorically speaking, dung. Given this frank vulgarity, mediocrity, and falsehood, even those writers who were simply honest about everyday life (such as Boris Mozhayev, Vasilii Belov, Yurii Nagibin, Valentin Rasputin, Anatolii Pristavkin, and several other prose writers of a very average aesthetic level) seemed like very good writers in comparison. The best journals of the Soviet period (such as *Novyi mir* and *Yunost'* [Youth]) were nonetheless forced to devote the greater part of their pages to the mediocre literature of the writers' bosses, printing endless, multivolume epics about the grand revolutionary past, about socialist collectivization and industrialization, about the war and postwar peace building. For some reason, there was an especially large number of books (under the paternal leadership of the Communist Party, to be sure) about the natural resources of Siberia, the Far East, and other exotic places.

All this useless ballast was forcefully cast overboard in the very first years of perestroika, freeing up space, at first for the enormous expanse of literature forbidden under Soviet rule and then for completely new, young literature.

I can state with complete assurance, both as one who is sufficiently close to the scene by virtue of working at a "thick" literary journal and as a critic who by professional necessity knows the state of affairs in contemporary Russian literature: Never in Russia's history has there been a decade in which so many writers with mature, fully developed talent, whether in prose, poetry, dramaturgy, or criticism, have appeared. There are so many of them and they have appeared

so suddenly that no one has had the time to be surprised and astonished by this outpouring; after all, in the previous era it took years
for something even relatively new and fresh to appear.

And here the change in quantity has immediately generated a
qualitative leap. In just a few years, the level of literary standards
has risen to an unprecedented height. Every list will be incomplete,
but it is impossible not to mention here at least several names of
writers who made their debut very recently. They are principally:
Viktor Pelevin, Dimitrii Bakin, Oleg Yermakov, Andrei Dmitriev,
Aleksei Slapovskii, Yuri Buida, Mikhail Butov, Vladimir Berezin,
Aleksandr Borodynia, Vladimir Sharov, Anatolii Korolev, Aleksandr
Melikhov, Aleksandr Terekhov, Anton Utkin, Mikhail Shishkin,
Irina Polyanskaya, Olga Slavnikova, as well as many, many others.

This is by no means a snobbish urban literature centered in
Moscow—many of the prose writers I have named live in the
provinces: Oleg Yermakov in Smolensk, Aleksei Slapovskii in Saratov, Olga Slavnikova in Yekaterinburg. Many have only recently
moved to Moscow: Yurii Buida from Kaliningrad, Andrei Dmitriev
from Pskov, Anatolii Korolev from Perm. This is genuinely new and
young prose, achieving a level of craftsmanship, inner freedom, and
readiness to reflect and speak about issues that the older literature
could not reach.

A similar scene can be observed in poetry, where an entire generation of brilliant poets has appeared in the past ten years. Once begun, the list is impossible to complete. It includes Timur Kibirov, Ye-
lena Fanailova, Vitalii Kalpidi, Aleksandr Levin, Maksim Amelin,
Aleksei Purin, Leonid Shevchenko, Shampal Abdullaev, Denis
Novikov, Danila Davydov—and so on to infinity.

What unites all these very diverse, utterly dissimilar prose writers
and poets is a high level of literary and—I will not be afraid to use
the word—philosophical culture. They have come to literature enriched by diverse life experiences and carrying weighty intellectual
baggage. There has never been so cultured (in the best sense of the
word) a generation in our literary history. After all, Soviet literary
tradition viewed any intellectualism with almost open hostility and
relied on "natural talent," on the man from "the bottom" possessed
of little culture who was easy to shape ideologically and aesthetically and to render dependent on the prevailing literary norms and
customs.

In the past few years, a school of literary criticism has developed simultaneously with the new prose and poetry that is capable of understanding and evaluating its quality and significance. The names of Andrei Nemzer, Aleksandr Arkhangelskii, Vyacheslav Kupritsyn, Mark Lipovetskii, Mikhail Zolotonosov, Evgenii Shklovskii, Andrei Zorin, Aleksandr Etkind, and many others, are familiar to anyone involved with literature. As head of the bibliographic section at a "thick" journal, I can say with certainty that the intellectual and aesthetic level of even average criticism, sometimes even written by a greenhorn critic, is now very high. Unknown young men and women fresh from their student desks come to us bringing their first manuscripts. Very often these are the writings of fully mature critics who do not have to be taught anything. (In Soviet times, editors used to love to instruct a talented person for a very long time, since a young person, as it was then considered, by definition couldn't write anything worthwhile—he "didn't know life.")

In short, there are now, as never before in Russian literature, many young and talented writers who have something to say to society and who know how to say it. What is alarming, however, is the drastic reduction in the number of readers who are capable of hearing them. I have already described the natural and understandable reasons for this reduction. It isn't just that Russian society, after the stress it has undergone, is experiencing a devastating spiritual and cultural apathy, epitomized by the rupture between writer and potential reader. The point is also that the normal channels of communication in culture—the entire system of cultural communication—were destroyed in the breakthrough era and have not been reconstructed to this day. The old system was poor, no argument there; it was constructed for purposes of propaganda, but it operated after a fashion. The new system is being created with toil and in agony, but in the meantime it is fragmented and ineffective.

I am referring primarily to book publishing. The first post-perestroika years were marked by the most difficult crisis in this field, which is so very critical for cultural evolution. The monsters of state publishing collapsed and their privatization was long and hard, rife with endless scandals, while the newly emerging private publishers were initially preoccupied with making money and as a result set no cultural goals for themselves. They published (often through copyright pirating) an enormous amount of purely entertaining, lowbrow reading matter, which brought quick and easy profits because the Soviet regime had treated consumers of such products so badly that they eagerly bought these previously unavailable books.

It was now possible to publish any book—but only if you had the money, of course, to pay for the cost of printing. Unfortunately, money is precisely what talented young people of letters have always lacked. Meanwhile, books were published anyway. Money was found by various means—sponsors were discovered, friends and admirers of the gifted appealed to—but all of these efforts were chaotic and haphazard. Most significantly, the public simply could not find out about books published in this manner, since the state system of book distribution had collapsed along with the state system of book publishing. Many talented prose writers and poets published books at their own expense and then were left penniless with unopened packages of unwanted copies of a print run that nobody knew about.

In those years, libraries were dramatically reduced to beggary (they are still all government-run in Russia), and hence they stopped replenishing their collections with new books. Books published in Moscow did not reach the provinces, nor did provincial editions get to Moscow. There was practically no specialized reporting on books (even of a strictly commercial nature); no print media reported on new books or advertised them. Book circulation continued only because of the efforts of a few enthusiasts, who carried heavy packages of books from city to city. (It is worth mentioning that the postal service also became inordinately expensive, thus closing down still another channel of communication, while the cost of surface and air transportation sharply increased as well.)

At that time, the "thick" journals, which continued to appear in spite of their desperate financial straits, saved the day. But for such an enormous country there were (and remain) few of these journals, and they could not accommodate every author worthy of publication. Besides, their readership was sharply reduced, not to mention the fact that they could only pay their authors symbolic royalties. It became impossible to survive on a literary paycheck in Russia; and this was equally true for all writers, venerable ones as well as beginners.

Nonetheless, nothing could prevent the growth of new literature. The enthusiasm of its creators proved to be stronger than the nearly insurmountable economic competition. Writers such as Zufar Gareev, Aleksandr Terekhov, and Vyacheslav Kupritsyn earned a living any way they could, most often by working at the proliferating glossy entertainment magazines and tabloid newspapers, or by writing pulp fiction under pseudonyms, as did Irina Polyanskaya and Iulia Latynina.

Generally speaking, most of the new writers share a broad intellectual profile and are much more dynamic and resourceful than their older comrades in literature. Poets do not disdain to write book reviews and other semibusiness prose, and moreover they are doing so professionally. Prose writers write scripts for TV series. All this varied work allows them, in their search for their daily bread, to avoid straying far afield from literature, a profession that is not bringing them money or glory at the moment but that does give them the feeling of full creative self-realization.

An enormous number of journals, small magazines, collections of literary miscellany, and anthologies are being published for the most insignificant sums (in small editions, of course), both in the major cities and in the provinces. After existing for a short time and finding no serious financial support, they disappear quickly, but new ones appear all the time. Talented organizers of literary affairs emerge suddenly amid gifted young people, and they create out of thin air literary associations, publishing houses, and a great many publications. One of these organizers in Moscow is the writer and critic Dmitrii Kuzmin, who gathered around him creative young people and founded the Vavilon (Babylon) literary union (membership was prohibited initially to writers over the age of twenty-five) as well as the Argo-Risk publishing house. Argo-Risk published several dozen issues of a literary review in which many talented poets and prose writers made their debut, while Vavilon organized several national poetry festivals—and all this without regular financial support, relying only on money donated by occasional sponsors.

Another publisher is Nikolai Iakimchuk, who lives in Tsarskoe Selo and is the founder of the Tsarskoselskoye Literary Prize. Vladimir Abashev and Vitalii Kalpidi from Perm founded the Iuriatin Foundation (affiliated with Perm University), which publishes and distributes at no charge the books of young prose writers and poets. For a time they even published a substantial literary journal called *Nesvoevremennye zapiski* (Untimely Notes). In Ufa, Aleksandr Kasymov publishes the small literary magazine *Sutoloka* (Hubbub), in which accomplished young writers are published. The list of literary enthusiasts who have little interest in monetary profit can go on and on.

Virtually every major city, especially university centers such as Saratov, Yekaterinburg, Cheliabinsk, Samara, and Tver, has its own literary environment from which fully developed writers emerge. All these writers lead difficult and impoverished lives and must spend an enormous amount of energy not on creative work, but on earning money. Charitable giving and sponsorship grants are still very poorly organized in Russia. Local authorities in the provinces prefer to help members of the old writers' unions, whereas officials at branches of the national Union of Writers do not wish to involve themselves with talented young people who are oriented toward a new literary consciousness.

I cannot fail to mention here that the West extended its helping hand to well-known writers in this time of difficulty for literature. Benefiting from the wave of interest in Russia, these writers began to be published in the West, were invited to lecture at American and European universities, and were given stipends, grants, and literary prizes (the Alfred Toepfer Foundation's Pushkin Prize deserves special mention). Several Russian writers and critics settled in the West for a long time, including Tatiana Tolstaia, Yevgenii Yevtushenko, Mikhail Shishkin, Aleksei Parshchikov, Marina Palei, Mark Lipovetsksii, and Evgenii Dobrenko (unfortunately, nearly all of them have stopped writing). This foreign aid was spotty, and, to be sure, it did not reach those who needed it most, the youngest writers whose authority had not yet been established or whose work was simply not noticed by Western scholars. Their Russian colleagues, often individuals who were not young by any means, always gave "correct" suggestions and typically sought to confine Western scholars to traditional literary tastes.

The Soros Foundation has provided and continues to provide generous and, most importantly, regular assistance to Russian literature. It supports libraries and helps "thick" journals to survive. Without its grants, the lives of scholars in the humanities would be much more difficult and bleak. But the area that is of greatest priority for the Soros Foundation has been the support of science and education, not literature. To be sure, this support also indirectly helps literature, since it bolsters the freedom both of the contemporary cultural environment and of the potential readers of new literature.

The Soros Foundation also provides assistance in bringing the Internet to Russia, and this has a more direct bearing on the growth of new literature. The Internet is an ideal instrument for literary communication, and the Web is already filled with a great number of Russian literary sites (true enough, most of them are of poor aesthetic quality—money and opportunities often do not go hand in hand with talent). It's possible to read practically all the influential literary journals, newspapers, and literary miscellany on the Web. An on-line literary community has also emerged with its own infrastructure—electronic libraries, journals, prizes, and competitions. The potential audience on the Internet has no limits, but in reality, the poverty of most Russian writers and readers sets the limits. Internet access, for Russians, is still expensive. Nevertheless, good Russian literature will certainly continue to inhabit the Internet in the future, where it can enjoy not only unlimited distribution but also the possibility of rapid feedback from its readers.

On the whole, unfortunately, too many of the problems of the new literature in Russia can be attributed to poverty. The contemporary young writer has rights and freedom—but not the material resources to take advantage of these rights. For instance, a Russian now has the right to travel the entire world—it's difficult to overestimate the importance of such knowledge for a writer, especially a young one—but he doesn't have the money to exercise this right. And in the past few years, the West has not often been inviting young writers on exchange visits, certainly not as often as it used to.

The picture of literary growth that I have here described is, naturally, subjective and incomplete. Others may see the meaning of literary life in entirely different terms, such as the merging of literary consciousness with religious consciousness, or the renaissance of national consciousness. But I nonetheless insist that literature is part of the general process in Russia of shaping a free, active individual who is capable of radically changing our presently distressed society for the better.

Epilogue:
Will Russia's
Terrible Years
Be Repeated?

Vyacheslav Ivanov

We are the children of Russia's terrible years.
—Alexander Blok

The swift pace of events in Russia has required me to revise my epilogue to this book. It has become necessary for me to do more than simply comment on the assessments made in these essays of what has happened in Russia in recent years. Along with those authors who dare to peer into the future, I too must try to take a look at the new century. Let me try to assess the embryonic changes and gain some understanding of the possible direction of the nation's develop-

Born in 1929, **Vyacheslav Vselovodovich Ivanov** graduated from Moscow State University, where he lectured until 1958; at that time he was dismissed because of his friendship with Boris Pasternak, a Nobel Prize winner and then the target of political persecution. For thirty years thereafter, Ivanov was banned from traveling to the West. He headed the Institute for Slavic and Balkan Studies, and in 1989 he was again invited to Moscow State University to chair the new Department of the History and Theory of World Culture. He then became director of the M. Rudomina Russian Library of Foreign Literature, a position he held until 1993. A former member of the USSR parliament representing the Academy of Sciences, Ivanov is currently a professor in the Slavic Department at the University of California, Los Angeles. He is a fellow of the British Academy, the American Academy of Arts and Sciences, and the Russian Academy of Natural Sciences, as well as the recipient of numerous awards for his scholarly research. Translated by Antonina W. Bouis.

ment. Boris Yeltsin's departure from the presidency denotes the end of the historical period that most of the essays in this volume address. It is clear even now that a new era has begun; its contours are only beginning to take shape. I feel an affinity to many of the thoughts in *Vladimir Mirzoev*'s article, written in fall 1999, which juxtaposes various points of view about Russia's prospects in an imaginary dialogue. I can venture early prognoses regarding a few probable paths of future changes in Russia. That in turn requires me to review the principal features of the preceding period and think about the lessons that come to mind even now.

* * *

In the past ten years, we have heard much talk about the need for economic reforms. But it cannot be said that the reform goals were defined in a way that was clear to the broad public. It is not an end in itself to proclaim, as did the first governments assuming power after the collapse of the USSR, that the construction of a market economy was the goal, any more than the former Communist phraseology was justified in proclaiming the construction of socialism—a false goal. The goal of any of the reforms, whose success we desire, can only be the speediest improvement of the well-being of the greatest number of Russia's inhabitants, including guarantees of what everyone needs: jobs matching qualifications and providing regular pay; inexpensive housing; reasonable prices for medicines and medical services; pensions for the elderly; and education for the young (entailing adequate numbers of teachers for a modern education, school and university buildings, textbooks, and educational aids). In comparison with these priority goals, which can in principle be achieved in Russia (notwithstanding their apparently utopian nature today), all the others, on which incommensurate sums are being spent, must be deemed secondary. In a country where most people lack these primary necessities, it does not seem appropriate to maintain a huge and inefficient government apparatus that is constantly expanding in size and privileges. This includes the special intelligence services, which were inherited from the Stalinist period and are once again assuming greater significance. Nor does it seem justified to give priority to the production of the newest and most expensive weapons systems and the maintenance of a gigantic army.

But reducing such nonproductive expenditures (at present a very unlikely prospect, despite its urgency) would by itself not solve the country's economic problems. In order for real reforms to succeed, many other urgent actions are required, in particular, immediate passage of legislation on land reform, which is needed for private farming to develop quickly. Without land reform, Russia will not be able to return to the time (before the catastrophe of dekulakization and collectivization) when not only did the nation not depend on food imports and foreign aid, but it actually exported food products. The newly elected Duma is planning to resume consideration of draft land reform legislation, but the political composition of that body makes it unlikely that the law as enacted will respond to the interests of farm owners. Tired of waiting for decisions from the center, some oblasts are already beginning to introduce radical land reform on their own. We can examine the different points of view on this issue by reading *Kirill Gorelov*'s article in our anthology.

A bold start in reform came about through the private initiative displayed by many enterprising Russians in the period 1989–1992. For an appreciation of how capital arose in the early stages of development and how market relations formed, see *Arkadii Zlochevskii*'s account in our collection. The instant creation of wealth for the new Russians, and the tendency to spend it as profligately as the merchants of the past, have astonished the world. But a consumer society is not built solely on the ability to consume, to purchase everything on credit and not repay debts. It is important to start manufacturing not only weapons and planes (the current government, recalling the early years of Stalin's dictatorship, is enthralled by flying). Before anything else, Russia must begin trading with the world for its own benefit, as it did in the past. And for that there must be an assortment of items that are more edible and useful (and not for Saddam Hussein alone) than rockets, bomber planes, and submarines.

The frequent comparisons made in recent years between the economic situation in Yeltsin's Russia and that of the post-Versailles Weimar Republic can be extended in yet another way. Hitler increased military production in destitute Germany. This form of development is echoed in the program of the new Russian leadership, envisaging a substantial expansion of the military-industrial complex. The dominance of this sector in the Russian economy under Leonid Brezhnev made serious reforms impossible. We must make the same assumption in view of the new government's analogous plans.

The failures of the economic transformations that were proposed and have been partially implemented in the past eight years can mostly be attributed to the fact that development was artificially limited primarily to the field of financial capital. Capital has a tendency to flee to other countries, although with rational organization these assets could have been used for beneficial capital investments, for example in the neighboring republics, once part of the USSR, which are economically important for Russia. Capital flight without investment deprives the country of capital without substantially increasing the volume of savings of its owners, and thus in the final analysis is not good for anyone.

Among the more general reasons for the failure of the reforms begun in 1992 is the reformers' exclusive orientation on the ideas of the liberal school of economics, whose application has not proved fruitful in many other countries, either. The absence of any original economic theories in Russia since the death of Nobel Prize laureate Leonid Kantorovich has also been significant. In conversations with me, Kantorovich acknowledged that the black market was the real basis of the Soviet economy in Brezhnev's day. The legalization of that black market, with all its distortions, could have been the guiding developmental principle during the post-Soviet years.

Similar ideas are expressed by the authors of our collection. *Sergei Vasil'ev* describes how the former political elite converted its privileges into property and income. The author traces the appearance of private property among the nomenklatura to Mikhail Gorbachev's administration. But the desire for personal gain was present among Soviet leaders much earlier, back in the Brezhnev years. Mikhail Suslov, considered by many to be the primary guardian of Marxist ideology, left an inheritance of several million dollars.

Yurii Plyusnin, in this volume, demonstrates that, contrary to expectations, the reforms of the 1990s led to a sharp decline in the standard of living for the average Russian urbanite, for instance in Novosibirsk, where he did his research. I agree with Plyusnin's conclusion that the decline in life expectancy and the acute emotional stress that people feel reflect the depth of the psychological crisis brought on by the negative results of the reforms. *Nadezhda Azhgikhina* points out that the position of women has deteriorated rapidly in the reform period.

*   *   *

Capitalism has become global. It has identical or similar characteristics in every country—both developed and developing. And it is these common traits that have had a highly negative effect on events in Russia in recent years by sharply increasing material inequality. Throughout the world there are attempts to find an optimal balance between a free market (which can be either good or bad, especially if the market is not left to itself) and the mechanisms regulating it. The details may vary from country to country, but the failures of extreme attempts that dogmatically select only one path to development have been notable. In that sense, the shift in recent months toward an increasing government role in economic policy does not appear to be a sensible decision.

However, the weak side of the arguments offered by proponents of economic reform in Russia has been the unsubstantiated assertion that the free market has already had a beneficial effect on the development of many countries (*Mikhail Prusak*, among others, writes about this in our anthology). On the contrary, we can point to many complications in this theory. Nearly every free-market economy has experienced difficulties (the United States is still relatively untouched, although there are concerns about a possible crisis, and the government is considering measures to avoid it). It seems unrealistic to suppose that Russia could somehow manage to be the only exception in the world, as the extreme nationalists would hope. Russians, no longer operating on the proposition that the economy can be built "in one separate country," cannot escape the consequences of the development of modern technology. According to a view that is gaining ground, the goal should not be to wheedle yet more large sums from such institutions as the International Monetary Fund, only to have the money vanish without a trace in the bowels of an omnivorous state machine without ever reaching the ordinary citizen. Also gaining ground is the desire to define once again the place of Russia, whose countless riches should prevent the country from falling into eternal debt, in the world economic community. But Russia will have to fight for a dignified place.

There must be broad changes in the whole strategy of development for the Russian economy. It is time to stop thinking about heavy industry, the country's obsession during the Five Year Plans of the early Communist era; it is time to start producing consumer goods, to intensively develop farming, and to modernize light industry. It is time to stop focusing on the extraction of oil and gas and on the production of weaponry. Modern society has become information based. Therefore, it is most important to produce and to sell information.

And it is in this very field that Russia has an excellent chance to secure a place among the world's top-ranking countries. It is here that the country's intellectual potential can find a practical outlet. Many of the most gifted young people have mastered computer programming magnificently. The the shortage of good computers for many years did not stop them, and in fact promoted the development of efficient ways to use imperfect technology. The level of computer expertise among the public in Russia is higher than that of Germany and comparable to that of the United States. But there is talk in the United States of overproduction of computers; the country apparently has more computers than it needs to handle commercially viable tasks. But in fact it is not a question of having too many computers, but rather of not having enough new ideas for their possible applications. What has been invented in Russia (but as a rule, not implemented) would suffice for others countries, too.

Let me give two examples from areas that I have watched develop over the past decades. Primitive translation software programs are just now beginning to make money in America. Before Igor Melchuk was forced to emigrate to Canada (during Brezhnev's closed era), he and his coauthors had developed translation systems that were far superior to those commercially profitable programs. And N. A. Bernshtein and his colleagues developed the foundations of robot technology, which has wide industrial applications, in Russia prior to World War II.

The basic miscalculation of Russian governments in recent years has been the inability to understand that Russia's wealth lies not so much in oil, gas, and aluminum but in the intellectual capabilities of such large numbers of Russian people, particularly the young. According to the generally accepted findings of the economist Nikolai Kondrat'ev, who was executed during Stalin's terror, the decline that comes once an existing technology has exhausted its possibilities is accompanied by discoveries whose integration into the economy makes possible a new industrial upsurge. According to this paradigm, when economic difficulties first appear, experimental work and fundamental research in the sciences must be supported. Some of the difficulties and hardships experienced by scientists in Russia today are recounted in *Vadim Radaev*'s essay in this volume.

Ten years ago, our best biological laboratories were world class. Today, because it had not invested in new and expensive technologies, Russia was unable to participate in a series of important biotechnological and bioinformational discoveries of recent years. Here, as in other leading fields of science and technology that have suffered comparable lags, the fault lies primarily in the obtuseness and lack of civilized standards (to put it mildly) among many high-ranking officials who have recently served in office. The current government has talked about the intensive development of high technology, but for the time being it is spending enormous sums not on science but on a bloody internal war.

However, the newly elected governor of Moscow oblast, Boris Gromov, outlined in his first speeches and interviews in early February 2000 his goal to assist the "science cities," among the oblast's principal resources. Science can be used in various ways, but it is of no benefit to science to focus on military applications. As Nobel Prize–winning physicist Pyotr Kapitza once said, in such a case science would have to go back into purdah and wear the veil. The secrecy required by military research slows down the development of science. If the new government sends Russian science down that path, the loss will be both Russia's and the world's.

*   *   *

As a result of the reforms of the 1990s, monopolistic state capitalism, which under the demagogic pseudonym "socialism" prevailed throughout the Soviet period (sometimes in conjunction with the market, whether illegally as under Brezhnev or semilegally as during Lenin's New Economic Policy), was replaced in the dominant part of the economic system by a form of monopolistic capitalism in which the state sector was merged with the supermonopolies. Thus, the supermonopolies were given the right to export the country's basic energy resources, which gave rise to new opportunities for speculation. Socialism as a system for providing every citizen with all the basic necessities for living did not exist in the USSR. Therefore, the transition to a new predatory system took place without any great difficulty.

One effective means of overcoming such abuses would be to allow total freedom of access to information regarding relationships between monopolies and companies, and between government functionaries—individual (especially high-ranking) political leaders and their relatives—and state institutions (such as the Central Bank). A review of the history of antimonopoly legislation in Russia in recent years appears in *Natal'ia Fonareva*'s article.

But it is not enough to introduce Roosevelt-style antimonopoly legislation and anticorruption laws, no matter how sweeping. These laws must be executed and applied with utmost severity to those high-ranking officials who are most mired in the graft. The ancient Russian skills of embezzlement and bribery survived throughout the entire Soviet era. These skills can now be applied to the wide-ranging operations of transnational corporations, for instance in mining and marketing diamonds, and to the corresponding political spheres. Unlike in developed societies that follow the rule of law and where the state helps regulate the market, in Yeltsin's Russia (as well as during the Soviet era) the state was the main predator, working with large capitalist organizations to plunder the country's resources. In this way, the state hindered the free development of entrepreneurial initiative.

Aleksandr Auzan stresses in his essay the significance of legal and ethical factors for the future of the Russian economy. No less important is the enactment of economic legislation that would preclude the kind of theft through speculation that reigned throughout the 1992–1999 period with the connivance, if not the outright participation, of government officials. Over the years of nonownership under the Communists, everyone involved in business—from the highest officials to rank-and-file dealers and traders—lost the habit of protecting property, whether public (including the collection of taxes) or private.

It should be noted, however, that a harsh monetary and budget policy by itself is not always and uniformly a benefit: In this connection, the observations made by *Sergei Vasil'ev* regarding the recent Evgenii Primakov government, which had the support of the Communist majority in the former Duma, are pertinent.

As for the social democratic ideas that helped strengthen the state's regulatory role in many Western countries, especially in the social sector, they were profoundly alien to the former ideology, which demanded the total subjugation of the individual and his needs to the interests of the Communist Party and the Soviet regime. But in some areas (for instance, health and education), despite all the bureaucratic obstacles created by the regime, the Russian intelligentsia managed to accomplish amazing things through a system whereby the state, at least theoretically, supported the social sector. State institutions in Russia, as in the rest of the world, functioned poorly because of the low levels of personal interest among employees in the results of their work (which is why nationalizing an enterprise or branch of industry does not, as a rule, solve any problems).

But there have always been self-sacrificing individuals who worked fabulously hard—not out of fear but because of conscience—although they were paid miserable salaries and although in recent years they have not been paid at all (the new government has promised to pay salaries regularly, but it is not yet clear how these promises can be kept). The government must not permit a decrease in the level of services in areas where the USSR had achieved great success—for instance, ambulance and first-aid services and many aspects of the educational system. Tellingly, in listing the beneficial results of the first stage of the reforms, *Mikhail Prusak* mentions the preservation of free primary education and medical care for all Russians.

The main threat to to such beneficial social outcomes is the new market society, with its cult of money as the only goal and measure of success. The negative consequences of this cult for life's true values are described by Yurii Plyusnin. Russia's traditional ethical concepts are antithetical to such crass materialism. This earlier idealistic tradition prepared the way in part for the development of noncommercial organizations, described in the amusing report by *Elena Topoleva* and *Andrei Topolev* in this anthology. The role of noncommercial legal organizations is outlined by *Vladislav Grib*.

The activities begun during the two Chechen wars by such completely independent public organizations as Mothers of Soldiers show that this form of expressing public opinion is slowly developing and will not allow the mistakes of the past to be repeated without protest.

Throughout the civilized world, the importance of nongovernmental organizations (NGOs) is growing. The interview with *Valerii Sokolov* gives some understanding of how these organizations work in modern Russia. In his exceptionally interesting comments, Sokolov describes how in a short time he helped organize services for the homeless and publish periodicals devoted to them.

*   *   *

The more I study the history of Russian culture, the more I am astonished by the thousand years of striving toward a higher beauty and by the concentration on profound moral issues of universal relevance. And at the same time, reflecting upon the tragic fate of some of the best practitioners of that culture, there is much to make me despair.

Despite the mockery to which our intelligentsia has been subjected (political in the Soviet period, economic in the post-Soviet period), Russia has preserved the spiritual strength that distinguishes it from most big countries. The acutely critical remarks by *Dina Khapaeva* and *Nikolai Koposov* pertain not so much to the intelligentsia in the old sense as to modern scholars ("the proletariat of mental labor," a phrase that the physicist Umov introduced in the early twentieth century). They are the subject of *Evgenii Kniazev*'s article, which is basically a factual footnote. I will not engage in a dispute with the authors of these two articles: The very existence of numerous contradictory opinions on even such a seemingly obvious issue as the exceptional historical role of the Russian intelligentsia can be taken as a sign of these interesting new times.

The patterns of Russian culture still aspire to unite modern scientific reason with the wisdom of religious philosophy, a trend that marked the spiritual flowering at the start of the 1900s, only to be interrupted by the Communist terror. It is no accident that the thought of Mikhail Bakhtin is of such great significance in Russia and the entire world. The concept of dialogue formulated by Bakhtin and Martin Buber can serve as the basis of a contemporary understanding of democracy both within Russia (which must be freed of demagogy) and in relations among nations. The articles in this anthology (for example, the imaginary exchange of remarks in "A Theater for Oneself" by *Vladimir Mirzoev*) show how much the dialogue principle has become part of the daily life of Russian culture.

That article also allowed the reader to judge how much the theater meant and continues to mean in Russia—despite all the financial and political difficulties. A similar conclusion regarding literature can be drawn from the survey of recent literary trends offered by *Aleksandr Ageev*. *Irina Prokhorova* tells us how she managed to create and publish a new literary and critical journal that reflects the latest creative trends and therefore is popular with readers.

Among the most important achievements by the heroic members of our intelligentsia, who continued to labor over the cognizance of the highest aesthetic values despite all the years of the impoverishment of official culture, are the works of the late Yurii Lotman. His books, which reveal for us a new understanding of literature, are constantly in print in Russia and remain best-sellers.

I hope that a scholarly revision of Russian philosophy of art will return Lotman to his place as perhaps the most important and accessible author from whom we can comprehend the harmony and tragedy of the world. And if we remove from art its functional role as mirror and as entertainment and restore its higher dignity, it will ennoble us with a new flowering. I expect that this process will begin with Russian arts and letters; the prose of Varlam Shalamov and the poems of Osip Mandelstam, for example, have already dealt with the most important themes of the past century.

The resurgence of Russian spirituality is inevitable, but the suffering is still great along the via dolorosa traversed by our intelligentsia. The restoration of a police state would hinder even more the full rejuvenation of the Russian arts.

Interludes of foreign influence in Russia, like the Petrine era, are later recognized as having been necessary for the preparation of subsequent original achievements. I am certain that once again the window that has been flung open onto Europe and America will have an invigorating effect on the discovery and embodiment of new Russian talents. A convincing example can be seen in the biography of Evgenia Alekseeva, recounted in our anthology by *Elena Topoleva* and *Andrei Topolev*.

It is hard to overestimate the significance of the fact that in recent years millions of Russians have been able to touch the "sacred stones of Europe." Dostoevsky, who coined that phrase, in a speech about Pushkin called the ability to penetrate and transform oneself into the essence of various cultures the most important trait of the Russian genius. The openness of the country in recent times has been aided in large measure by the publication of numerous books written by formerly banned authors dealing with once forbidden topics. This is due to the enormous achievements of a dozen private publishing houses, demonstrating how much small and midsize businesses can do in a brief time.

* * *

I believe that certain basic characteristics have tended to recur in Russian society, from Soviet and post-Soviet times right up to the last few months of 1999: (a) a single person and his immediate, well-organized circle retaining power at any cost, protected by the might of the police system; (b) that group having unlimited freedom to continuously rob all strata of the population for their own sole benefit; and (c) that ruling group not disclosing any information on how they make decisions. Despite the appearance of effective change in certain forms, titles, and symbols, these entrenched characteristics, or at least their vestiges, make real reforms impossible.

The interview with *Aleksandr Sergeev* points out similarities of behavior among officials in Soviet times and during the Yeltsin administration. Not only did these officials behave in the same way, but in many cases they were the same people. Governor Mikhail Prusak of Novgorod remarks in his article that during the reforms his administration brought in people from the former Oblast Committee of the CPSU and other Soviet organs.

Many Russians (including the authors in this anthology) hoped that the time had come to Russia when choice was possible. The presidential elections in March 2000, which were in effect a plebiscite without alternatives and with a predetermined outcome, have cast doubt on such hopes. The difficulty of bringing the idea of democratic elections to a Russian population that is completely unprepared for it is described by *Nadia Seriakova*. *Vladimir Chetvernin* in his article[1] analyzes the fatal flaws in the Russian Constitution, which offers an adherent of an authoritarian and bureaucratic system a clear chance to become a dictator if he wins an election. Of the three scenarios outlined by *Sergei Vasil'ev*, the most likely in that case will be the third—the scenario of the "strong hand."

In order to establish the most elementary conditions for the development of democracy in Russia, the inherited forms of political investigation, surveillance, and informing on others must first be eradicated. And that requires a law enabling citizens to be free from fear, a law that formulates a categorical ban on the reinstitution of the activity of any organization like the KGB, whatever combination of letters it may use in its name. People who worked in political investigation have no place in the government apparatus and certainly not in its leadership. The tragedy of the last period of Yeltsin's administration was that on three separate occasions the head of the government was a man from the secret service. This paved the way for the present attempt to significantly increase the influence of these vestiges of the totalitarian system on the life of society. The conviction expressed by some of the authors of this anthology (and until quite recently one that was widely held) that a return to totalitarianism was impossible has been put in doubt by recent events. Even in the Brezhnev era, the former Communist ideology was replaced by total cynicism. The only stable part of the system was the police apparatus. Therefore its strengthening is an actual restoration, unlike any alleged ideological restoration, the danger of which many (especially in the United States and western Europe) mistakenly attribute to communism.

One of the most vicious signs of a return to the police methods of Yurii Andropov's day is the growth of a new secret services division dealing with the mass media. In that sense, there is a substantial difference with the almost limitless freedom of the press described by *Andrei Richter*. For authors like *Iosif Dzialoshinskii*, freedom of the press, or "glasnost" in the broad (and traditional) meaning that Gorbachev restored to the word, was perhaps the most important (and maybe the only) achievement of the entire period of reform. Since then, pressure from the authorities on the press has clearly increased. But even during the Yeltsin period, freedom of the press had criminal limitations: Those who broke the unwritten rules were killed, for instance Dmitrii Kholodov, a reporter for the newspaper *Moskovskii komsomolets,* who presumably received information on corruption in the army (a suspect in the murder is a former intelligence officer of the paratroopers).

An urgent issue, which cannot be avoided in discussing the observance of human rights in Russia, is the banning of torture during criminal interrogation. The question of torture and its variants in contemporary Russia is raised by Vladimir Chetvernin. In the Stalin era, political prisoners were tortured; the torturers, all members of the Communist Party, are living out their days in peace. Today it is almost the norm for criminal suspects to be beaten and tortured. The inhumane conditions in prisons is another grave concern. As Chetvernin rightly notes, being detained there is a form of torture in and of itself.

While serving on the presidential commission on pardons in the first half of the 1990s, I was depressed by the scope of crime in Russian society. That is perhaps the best evidence of the corruption created by the Soviet regime. The serial murderer Chikotilo, whose villainy made the whole country shudder in outrage, in his last letter to the president asked for mercy because he was a faithful Party member and KGB agent (was this not the reason that he went so long unpunished for his cannibalism?). One can only fully overcome the terrible legacy of the inhumane, despotic regime created by the Communist Party by leaving it as far behind as possible in the direction of a civilized democracy. Most members of the new, smug Duma, however, are not concerned with the interests of the population, and and they do not express their constituents' demands.

The past decade was characterized by attempts (as yet episodic) to restore the consciousness of law in society. One interesting direction, setting up conciliation meetings, is described by *Rustem Maksudov*.

No one prepared for the disintegration of the USSR, either politically or economically. The subsequent policy of the Russian government has been immoral (most glaringly in Chechnya) and also devoid of common sense and consistency: It is not clear why Russian soldiers must die to defend the government of Tajikistan, which is independent of Russia. In any case, it is clear that Russia must not feed or defend regions that can separate from it at will. Russia has no interest in holding onto them: The marvels of ancient Russian art took place at a time when the country was much smaller. For all of its morbid outbreaks of nationalism, the modern world is inexorably moving in the direction of weakening the role of national governments and borders and creating large associations like the European Union (into which Russia is being gradually drawn). In turn, these associations belong to the world community, which is growing into more of a reality with every passing year.

Against this background, extreme decentralization and the transfer of a significant number of federal functions (primarily in social services) to local authorities at various levels is a real problem for Russia. The disasters occurring in the Russian Far North show that the center can no longer handle its obligations. *Ol'ga Lobyzova*, based on her own experiences, writes about the hardships and achievements of the northerners, who are seeking their own way out, no longer relying solely on the federal authorities for help. The latter, in fact, seem to plunder more than provide support. This in turn gives rise to the tendency toward self-government observed in the regions. As *Aleksandr Auzan* demonstrates in his article, there is no real self-government yet. The weakness of the appropriate legal framework is explained by *Aleksandr Voronin*. On the one hand, there is the almost unlimited power of governors and mayors (which shows the conditional nature of all the elections held to date). On the other hand, groups of citizens organize to resist lawlessness. In describing one example of an association of local residents that successfully combated crime, Yurii Plyusnin correctly compares this episode with the traditional happy ending of a Western film.

But the Russian situation during the Yeltsin period is like a Western film without a sheriff, and therefore without a happy ending. If a strong hand does come to power in the near future, it will be a response in part to the desire of most citizens to end the lawless rampage of the mafia (which does resemble the Sicilian and Colombian variety) and gangsters. The newly elected president will also be the Head Sheriff. In that case, it is not surprising that he will depend on the power of the police. How this will affect local self-government is hard to tell.

But if we assume that cities and oblasts will continue to undertake independent planning, then we can start thinking now about new prospects. It is possible to think of a complete reorientation of the main direction of development favoring regional capabilities, which were subordinated in the Soviet era for the benefit of the centralized military-industrial complex. Thus, following the experience of Greece and a few other countries where the main source of revenue (and a very large one) became tourism, this could be the plan in the near future not only for St. Petersburg and the cities near the Golden Ring, but those in the southern Urals (where the Arkaimskii Museum and preserve is being created on the site, recently discovered by local archaeologists, of a "country of cities" dating back four millennia). Moscow does not need to remain an industrial city at all, and it would be more appropriate for the Kremlin to become, in the words of the great philosopher Nikolai Fedorov, the principal museum of the highlights of the Russian past instead of bearing the burden of a burgeoning bureaucracy. Besides the indisputable ecological advantages of this development strategy, it is important that all the measures necessary for commercially successful tourism (pleasant cities, safe and speedy travel, improved catering and accommodations, reconstruction of buildings, financing of museums and other cultural centers) will make life better and more pleasant for the local population, too. And the influx of foreign tourists will help us overcome the vestiges of tension remaining from the Cold War.

*   *   *

The primary danger for the entire country and for the intelligentsia as the center of its spiritual potential is the recent coming to power of a totalitarian government, supported by a police apparatus, and the intended union between the pro-government and Communist Parties in the new Duma. The situation is reminiscent of the Weimar Republic during Hitler's legitimate rise to power: The weak government's policy led to systematic state bankruptcy and (hyper)inflation. At the same time, extremists who wanted to use the police and militias were involved in nationalistic propaganda. With the history of the Hitler and Stalin camps, the intelligentsia must not allow itself the luxury of noninterference.

The task of the intelligentsia is to be the country's guide through the "noosphere"—the sphere of thought in the sense of Pierre Teilhard de Chardin and Vladimir Vernadsky. Russia, and all of humanity, need positive confirmation of basic spiritual values. Even those values found in the moral precepts of the great world religions should be well known to us now, but they remain unused, primarily because they have yet to be presented in the language of our own times. And this translation must be done before the absence of a universally recognized moral law leads to a new global catastrophe. In that sense, probably the most modern moral philosopher was Leo Tolstoy (who clearly demonstrated the immorality of the state, the army, and the courts). Like many later philosophers, he sought a synthesis of the religious philosophies of East and West (and through Mahatma Gandhi and Martin Luther King, Tolstoy had great influence on the course of events in the United States and the Third World).

The Russian Orthodox priest Father Aleksandr Men' was following the same path. Not long before he was assassinated, he proposed holding a debate at the Moscow State Library of Foreign Literature (where I was then serving as the elected director) on the relationship between Christianity and Islam. Men' and the Muslim clergyman who came to Moscow for the debate discussed what the two religions had in common in their concept of God. I think that the regular continuation of such discussions is very important. The conclusions of modern philosophy should be among the topics debated.

There is no doubt that one of the main problems of the twenty-first century for Russia, western Europe, and North America will be managing the relationship between the Christian and Islamic nations. Kosovo and Chechnya have shown us how not to solve the problem. Sophisticated diplomacy is not enough. Mutual enlightenment and conviction are required.

I was a friend of Father Men', and I found the breadth of his views to be similar to my own. The theological ideas of other members of the modern Orthodox Church are surveyed in the article by *Hieromonk Hilarion Alfeev*. His recounting of the events in Vilnius is of particular interest.

Mikhail Prusak notes that the appearance of forced migrants led to the creation in Novgorod oblast of various cultural associations based on ethnicity, which peacefully coexist: German groups, Jewish culture societies, the Vainakh Chechen-Ingush center, the Armenian community, and the Russian assembly. Thus quietly are born the trends of the future, so different from the nationalist-socialist madness of the past.

The new millennium will see the fruition of the dreams of Sergei Korolev, who drafted blueprints of spaceships at night in his bunk after a day of forced labor in the *sharashka* (prison for scientists). After Korolev's release, he directed the construction of his spaceships. Russia's exploration of space began with his plans (in accordance with the earlier plans of his predecessor, Konstantin Tsiolkovsky) and under his direction, for he religiously believed that humanity must move into the cosmos and that this exploration could lead in the twenty-first century to the mastery of the moon and then Mars. Russia will have an important role in such preliminary phases as building an international space station, even though there has been recent discord in the joint project.

Russia must not lose its place in these international projects, even though the short-sighted cuts in financing, particularly the reductions in training of young specialists, may interfere. If these hopes of conquering the solar system come to pass, there will be a need for clear international legal principles to prevent the danger of conflicts and piracy. Coordinated action in space will be promoted by a united global community. Over the next few centuries, humanity must become a single whole; otherwise it will perish.

Within this unity, it is probably good to preserve cultural and linguistic diversity, but not political and certainly not military differences. Let us hope that some nonbureaucratic form of world government will be able to prevent a third world war, the likelihood of which grows with the proliferation of nuclear capability in more and more countries (the latest statements of Russian politicians on this topic are not distinguished by excessive caution). In the worst-case scenario (unfortunately, not to be discounted completely), a world government will have to save the surviving part of humanity. In any case, in the near future people will have to solve several problems, which as the Club of Rome's projections thirty years ago showed, threaten the very continuation of history in the coming century. Each of these difficulties can be overcome, but only if they are constantly in our field of vision and constantly combated.

These are not theoretical quandaries, but the essence of the coming age, with the fate of every country, including Russia, at stake. One of these problems is the danger of radiation, related not only to the continuing manufacture of atomic and nuclear weapons and the probability of nuclear war but also to the possibility of another Chernobyl. No matter what complications the shutting down of unsafe atomic reactors may involve, it will have to be done. Another ecological danger demanding urgent action is the threat of global warming: We must act decisively to prevent the poisoning of the atmosphere. *Aleksandr Knorre* addresses the shocking ecological situation in his article.

Similar decisive measures are required with respect to the exhaustion of energy resources that many people (albeit with differences over the statistical data) expect in the next century. In this context, the extravagant use of energy resources by the Russian government and the monopolies appears all the more feckless. By the middle of the twenty-first century, when this issue will come to a head, controlled thermonuclear synthesis might be a new, industrially viable energy source (along with other alternatives like solar and wind power). Russia, in cooperation with other countries, has been working on such solutions, and it is important that these projects not suffer from cutbacks in fundamental research. The problem of world food shortages and hunger (which has already begun in Africa), related to the continuing demographic explosion in some parts of the world, underlines the urgency of Russian agricultural reform: It is dangerous for Russia not to have its own stable food base. The global nature of medical problems is defined by the fact that pandemics (like AIDS, which is a threat to a great part of the population in Africa) knows no borders. (In fact, AIDS came into Russia from Africa.) The fight against AIDS and other viral diseases, most importantly cancer, will require tremendous progress in molecular biology and related sciences.

And once again I must express my concern over the situation of science in Russia: After his arrest more than fifty years ago, Lev Zilber formulated the viral theory of cancer in Butyrka Prison. His imprisonment interfered with the publication and development of his theory, and then it was classified. Zilber's successors in Russia are hindered by lack of funds. Although out of political prison, Russian science has fallen into a financial trap.

Despite all this, the latest achievements in biology lead me to predict that there will be a time when, theoretically, human life will be almost limitlessly extendable, through replacement of faltering organs and through a partial physical resurrection of cloned pseudo-doubles, almost like in Andrei Tarkovsky's film *Solaris*. These achievements in science raise numerous social, religious, and psychological issues. It will be through the science of man that the difficulties related to the inexorable growth of knowledge and its practical applications will be solved, just as the successes of biology were based on breakthroughs in chemistry and physics.

Russia dreams about these future triumphs of knowledge as if they were a physical need. The sheer complexity of development in the twentieth century has been a severe obstacle in the search for workable solutions. First of all, we must try to understand an actual course of events. The next step can be prognosis. It will take much more work before we can approach a joint solution to global problems on a rational basis, without devolving into nationalist madness that has eclipsed reason in many Russian politicians and is leading the world once again to the brink of nuclear catastrophe.

Czech president Vaclav Havel has spoken more than once of the determining factor of the anthropic principle in the worldview of modern man. Andrei Sakharov examined the role of this principle thoroughly in three articles, written during his exile in Gorky and published by Pyotr Kapitza in the journal *Uspekhi fizicheskikh nauk* (Achievements in Physical Sciences). According to one formulation of the principle, the starting conditions of the evolution of the universe determine the possibility of the appearance of man. In other words, the establishment of the universe presupposes that it will become the object of observation and conscious reflection (and according to some philosophers, thereby turning it into reality, at least for us). The place given to man in these theories of physics forces us to take our responsibilities seriously. The world would be extremely absurd if after the billions of years of evolution required to create rational humans, these humans could be destroyed as a species by a few crazy politicians. To keep this from happening, we must grasp the scope of the growing threat. Today those who do not want a third world war must pay attention to Russia and the worrying tendencies that are apparent in its new government.

Of course, in the past Russia has followed profound disasters with amazing turns of fate, like those forever tied to the names of Alexander II and Mikhail Gorbachev. Even if our rational considerations make us expect the worst, we can still hope that the irrational side of Russian history will work for the better.

Even though the scenario of a totalitarian, militarized police dictatorship that strengthens the military-industrial complex, increases state control over the economy and ideology, and limits freedom of the press seems the most likely at the moment of writing this epilogue (February 6, 2000), nevertheless we cannot consider that all opportunities to resist this tendency have been exhausted. Despite the obvious passivity of a significant mass of the voters, who are disillusioned by all politicians, there are groups and associations, like the ones I mentioned earlier, independent of both politics and the state, which continue their work. Despite the weakening of activism among miners and other groups protesting economic injustice, the potential remains for their collective actions against property inequality. Parallels with postrevolutionary France in the nineteenth century bring to mind the Paris Commune and its suppression. The threat of such a social explosion can influence future Russian governments and limit their totalitarian tendencies. As the middle class and the ranks of independent farmers grow, they will also act as a deterrent to the behavior of the nomenklatura.

But these more optimistic prognoses are for a longer term than the future that is discussed in this book and its epilogue.

Note

[1] EDITOR'S NOTE: By September 2000, some nine months into the Putin presidency, Chetvernin's essay, prepared in mid-1999, with its extensive critique of tax collection procedures and the technical obstacles to impeachment, had been made less relevant by passage of major tax reform legislation and the development of a more constructive relationship between the executive and legislative branches. Since these issues constituted the bulk of the chapter, it was dropped in the final stage of publication. Chetvernin's scathing indictment of conditions in the army and the prisons remain valid, of course and are echoed elsewhere in the book, notable in the chapters by Grib and Maksudov.

Index

Abortion, 219, 226
Academic excellence centers, 352
Academic institutions, 316, 319, 320, 321
Academy of Sciences, 214, 308, 313, 320
Activism, 137, 165, 379, 415
  environmental, 292, 293, 294
Adaptation, 12–13, 15
Added value tax, 105
Advertising, 39, 109, 254, 264
  law, 37, 38, 39
  market, 37, 260
  regulating, 38, 140
Afghanistan, 224
AFL-CIO, 124
Ageev, Aleksandr, 405
Agrarian reform, 59, 60, 66, 67
Agriculture, 56, 57, 108
  cooperatives, 25, 58
  foreign programs, 110
Aid agencies, 255
Aids, 413
Air pollution, 285
Aivazova, Svetlana, 214, 216, 228
Alcohol, 39, 54, 181, 256
Aleko, 215
Alekseeva, Evgenia, 196–196, 406
Alexander II, 66, 67, 415
Alfeev, Hilarion, 412
American Bar Association, 159
Antimonopoly policy, 34, 35, 37, 38, 130
  and advertising, 39
  and entrepreneurship, 36, 40
Antitrust legislation, 40
Arctic Agreement, 282

Argo-Risk publishing house, 393
Arms race, 33
Art, 363, 378, 406
Arteev, Vladimir, 274
Arthur Andersen accounting firm, 47
Assassination, 119
Associations. *See* Nongovernmental organizations (NGOs)
Astrakhan Bread Factory, 111
Atheism, 235
Atomic energy, 54, 287, 288, 291
Authority, 25, 251, 336, 378, 380
Autonomy, 67, 71, 327, 355
Auzan, Aleksandr, 403, 409
Ayatskov, Dimitrii, 105
Azhgikhina, Nadezhda, 399

Baikal Cellulose and Paper Plant, 289
Bakeries, 51
Bakhtin, Mikhail, 405
Banks, 53, 82, 84–85, 131, 134, 360
  bankruptcy, 85, 135
  contractual disputes, 135, 136
  foreign, 12, 59
Bar association, 147–148, 153
Baranskaia, Natal'ia, 223
Bard College, New York, 339
Barker, Howard, 361
Barter system of exchange, 112
Bashkortostan, 74, 290
BBC (British Broadcasting Network), 200, 323, 344
Beckett, Samuel, 361, 362
Beijing, 213, 234
Belgium, 345
Belye odezhdy (White Garments), 380
Benson, Raymond, 349

Berdiaev, Nikolai, 9
Berezovskii, Boris, 371
Berlin Wall, 193
Berman, Harold, 173
Bernshtein, N. A., 401
Bible, 238, 247
Blackmail, 119
Black market, 399
Black waiting lists, 133
BMW, 122
Bochin, Leonid, 38
Bolsheviks, 67–68, 176
Books, 303, 307, 379, 392, 406
    peddlers, 302, 303
Brain drain, 353
Brand names, 109, 110
Bread, 51, 277
Breakdowns, mental, 15, 261, 269
Brezhnev, Leonid, 96, 237, 398
    era of, 220, 300
British Broadcasting Network. *See*
    BBC
Brodsky, Joseph, 379
Buber, Martin, 405
Budgets, 48, 53, 56, 75, 76, 85, 104
Bulgaria, 122
Bureaucracy, 49, 403, 118, 280
Bureaucrats, 354, 370
    and crime, 27, 367
    as reformers, 118, 119
Businesses, 44, 51–52, 129, 136, 138,
    166 , 196, 318
    criminalized, 93, 125, 263
    ethical constraints on, 42, 141
    shadow, 27
Business Leaders of Tatarstan, 347
Butyrka Prison, 414
Bykov, Anatolii, 164

Cadbury's chocolate factory, Chudovo,
    48–49
Canada, 101, 367, 369
Cancer, 414
Capital, 76, 77, 361
    flight, 83, 399
Capitalism, 195, 198, 400
Cars, 129, 131, 132

Catherine the Great (empress of
    Russia), 214, 215
Catholic University of Leuven, 345, 347
Caucasus, conflicts in, 68, 72
Censorship, 259, 326, 377, 383
Central Asia, 66, 222
Central Bank, 82, 135
Centralization, 33, 43, 68
Chambers of commerce, 50, 51
Charitable giving, 185, 256, 394
Charles Stewart Mott Foundation, 157,
    254
Charlotte Project, The, 265–266
Chechen war, 82, 163, 166, 375
Chekhov, Anton Pavlovich, 299, 361
Chekhov Moscow Art Theater, 367
Chemicals, 54, 287, 294
Cherkizovskii Meat Processing Plant,
    50
Chernobyl, 284, 413
Chernomyrdin, Viktor, 287
Chernyshevskii, Nikolai, 216
Chetvernin, Vladimir, 407, 408
Children, 29, 56, 57, 157, 226, 286
Chile, 164
Christianity, 214, 237, 244, 382, 411,
    412
Christie, Nils, 174
Chronicle of Higher Education, The,
    journal, 344
Chubais, Anatolii, 69, 371
Church, 235, 238. *See also* Russian
    Orthodox Church
    and state, 239, 240, 243
Circus, The, film, 221
Citizen involvement, 197, 201. *See also*
    Volunteerism
Civic associations, 138, 139, 141, 194.
    See also Nongovernmental
    organizations (NGOs)
Civil Code, 34, 149
Civil rights, 34, 183
Civil society, 136–137, 201, 206, 207,
    260, 263, 305
    development, 123, 138, 154
Claudel, Paul, 361, 368
CNN (Cable News Network), 165

Coal mining industry, 120–121, 122
Coercion, 119, 262
Cold War technologies, 122
Collective bargaining, 117, 124
Collective farms, 57, 59, 104–105, 108
Commodities and Raw Materials
    Exchange (RTSB), 107, 108
Communes, 67, 176, 216
Communications, 36, 395, 207, 306
Communism, 25, 86, 96, 323, 324, 337
Communist Party, 46, 68, 115
Compensation for damages, 128, 180,
    181, 182
Competition, 34, 121, 175, 318, 383
    and advertising, 37, 39
    among employees, 112
    law/legislation, 33, 34, 36, 37, 39
    unfair, 35, 37, 41
Computer programming, 401
Comrade courts, 146
*Conception of Judicial Reform in the
    Russian Federation*, 171, 172
Conflict resolution, 175, 176, 177
Consciousness, crisis in, 384, 385, 394
Constitution, 34, 38, 70, 145, 407
    and autonomy of Federation
        subjects, 71
    proposals to revise, 73
    rights in, 71, 207
Consumer Rights Protection Law,
    127–128, 130
Consumers, 126, 127, 128, 130, 131,
    134, 398
    associations, 61, 130, 133, 137
    KonfOP, 130, 131, 133, 134
    lawsuits, 129, 136
Continuing education, 346, 350
Contractual culture, 127, 129, 130, 136
Corruption, 151, 157, 305
Cossacks of the Kuban film, 221
Coup of August 1991, 108, 323, 328,
    324, 335–336
Crime, 174, 177, 180, 209, 408, 410.
    economic, 151, 403
    organized. *See*
Crimea conflicts, 68
Criminal behavior, 178, 184, 152

Criminal Code, 146, 251
Criminal justice, 182, 183, 185
Culture, 98, 167, 306, 334, 376, 405
    as freedom, 368
    support/subsidizing of, 56, 194, 367
    and television, 167
Currency, 45, 88, 91
Czech Republic, 101, 179

Dagestan, 375
Daimler-Benz, 122–123
Daniel, Yulii, 379
Danilov-Danil'ian, Victor, 285, 286
Dashkova, Ekaterina, 214
Day-care centers, 226
Debt, 85, 88, 89, 134–135
Decembrists, 215
Decentralization, 69, 70, 352
Default of government, 133–134, 135
Defense industries, 97
Deficits, 82, 85, 127
Democracy, 25, 202, 203, 205, 206,
    207, 213, 224, 334
Depression, national, 382
Deti Arbata (Children of the Arbat),
    380
Dirol factory, Novgorod, 49
Discourse/dialogue, 330, 374, 405
Dissidents, 118 , 379
Distribution system, 301, 302, 392
Divorce, 219
Domestic violence, 226, 230
Domostroi, 214
Doronina, Tat'iana, 364
Dostoevsky, Fyodor Mikhaylovich,
    269, 378, 406
Dovgan Corporation, 50
Drugs, 30, 181, 209, 256
Dudintsev, Vladimir, 380
Duma, 38, 55, 47, 76, 409, 411
Dzialoshinskii, Iosif, 408

Ecology, 24, 154, 285, 288. *See also*
    Environmental protection
Economic crisis, 13, 15, 18, 276, 288,
    348, 386. *See also* Financial crisis
    of August 1998

Economic liberalism, 261, 372, 399
Economic policy, 60, 88, 92, 116, 400
Economic reforms, 29, 33, 35, 69, 95,
    372, 381, 397
Economy, 28, 44, 69, 74, 83, 160, 292,
    400
  command, 45
  monopolization of, 32, 34, 35
Education, 56, 208, 313, 319, 337,
    345. *See also* Higher education
    institutions; Universities
  abroad, 344, 351
  free, 44, 55, 404
  women's access to, 215, 219, 227
Efremov, Ivan, 210
Efros, Anatolii, 364
Einstein, Albert, 357
Elderly people, 226, 279, 397
Elections, 22, 61, 166, 252, 407
Electronics, 130, 131
E-mail, 198, 200, 344
Emigration, 97, 310, 372, 358, 369, 387
Emory University, 173
Employers' unions, 120
Employment, 14, 225
Energy, 36, 88, 123, 402, 413
English, 309
Enterprises, 44, 50, 91
Entrepreneurship, 33, 40, 51, 53, 129,
    318, 343
  by government officials, 41
  and shadow economy, 42
  support of, 36, 47
Environmental protection, 284,
    284–285, 286, 290, 291
  fines, 288, 289, 290
  noncompliance by government, 287,
    289
  organizations, 293, 294
Equality, 154, 160, 213, 215, 218, 222
Escape philosophy, 385
Estonia, 29
Ethics, 24, 136, 137, 140–141, 403,
    404
  of government officials, 138, 141
  of legal profession, 153, 160, 264
  of press, 162, 264

Ethnic groups, 61, 71, 412
Eurasia Foundation, 157, 234
European Union, 124, 345, 348, 351,
    409
European University, 317, 320
Evropa journal, 344
Exchange rate, 83, 88
Exports, 45, 52–53, 88, 102
Exxon, 110, 287

Family, 16, 58
Family Code, 146, 230
Farms, 57, 58, 108. *See also* Collective
    farms
  natural, 30
  private, 44, 58, 415
  state, 27, 59
Fascism, 324
Federation of Independent Labor
    Unions (FNPR), 116, 125
Feminine Mystique, The, 232
Feminism, 213, 215, 216, 219, 223,
    228, 229, 230, 233
Fiction, 215, 382
Fifth column, 360
Figner, Vera, 217
Film, 372, 228
Financial crisis of August 1998, 81, 85,
    103, 113, 303
  consequences of, 82
  and deterioration of press, 168
  and government default on debts,
    133–134
  and NGOs, 155
Financial pyramids, 37, 38, 39, 155
Financing, 53, 85, 91, 131, 207,
    208
Finland, 66, 101
Fishing collectives, 29
Flax, 58
Fliamer, Mikhail, 179
Fonareva, Natal'ia, 139, 403
Food, 251, 413
Forbes, 347
Ford corporation, 122
Ford Foundation, 157
Foreign aid, 139, 394

Foreign investment, 48, 49, 77, 113, 352
Foreign policy, 62, 230
Foreign trade, 49, 88, 94
Forests, 53, 285, 286
Forra Fund, 346
Fortune, 347
Foundations, 306, 315
Fourth estate, 163
France, 335, 336
Freedom, 207, 336, 382, 384
Freedom House, 124
Freedom of assembly, 207
Freedom of choice, 94, 95, 358, 370
Freedom of conscience and religious choice, 244
Freedom of information, 169
Freedom of press, 168, 207, 408, 415
Freedom of speech, 193, 207, 208, 259, 264
French Annales school, 332
Friedan, Betty, 232
Friedrich Ebert Foundation, 124
Fuel, 29
Funding, 52, 196, 315, 351, 352, 367
Furniture, 53

Gaidar, Yegor, 69, 291, 371
Gay rights, 237
Gazprom, 277
Gender issues, 229, 230, 234, 244
Germany, 52, 101, 103, 105, 116, 256, 367
Geschichtliche Grundbegriffe, 335
Glasnost, 259, 260, 408
Global warming, 413
Globus information bulletin, 344
God, concept of, 411
Goethe, 11
Golubka public organization, 195
Goluboe salo (Blue Bacon), 387
Gorbachev, Mikhail, 114, 193, 241, 223, 225, 323, 343, 377, 380, 408, 415
Gorelov, Kirill, 398
Gorky, Maxim, 253
Gorky Moscow Art Theater, 364

Goscilo, Helena, 212
Government, 26, 90, 187, 208, 262, 267, 324
    agencies, 154, 172, 319
    authority, 25, 282
    and ethics/morals, 26, 141, 290, 409
Grachev, Pavel, 164
Grain market, 105, 108, 109, 110, 111, 113
Granin, Daniil, 380
Great Britain, 254
Great Soviet Myth, 221
Greenfielding, 91
Greenhouse effect, 123
Greenpeace, 294
Grib, Vladislav, 404
Gromov, Boris, 402
Group of Seven (G–7), 89
Guberniya, 66, 67, 72
Gulag, 277, 359

Harder, Sara, 232
Harvard University, 346, 347
Havel, Vaclav, 414
Hay, 29, 58
Health, 135, 286
Higher education institutions, 99, 317, 320, 321, 337, 338, 349, 355
High technology, 402
History, 332, 335
Hitler, Adolph, 398, 411
Homelessness, 226, 251, 253, 254–255, 256, 404
Hour of the Bull, 210
Housing, 36, 44, 55, 59, 103, 121, 397
    construction, 101, 102, 104
    perceived as constitutional right, 103
How I Understand Philosophy (Mamardashvili), 221
Humanism, 154, 240, 324, 326, 333
Humanities, 10, 315, 353
Human resources, 84, 109, 112, 248, 310
Human rights, 61, 71, 146, 154, 185, 379, 408
Hungary, 122
Huntington, Samuel, 240

Il'in, Ivan A., 152
Income tax, 56, 92, 93, 150
Independent labor unions, 114, 115,
  124, 125
Individuality, 333, 373
Industry, 49, 59, 277
Inflation, 35, 44
Information, 96, 97, 130–131, 200,
  264, 267, 401
  freedom to access, 169, 264,
    402
  networks, 198, 207
Inglehart, Ronald, 18
Intellectual, 305, 330, 331, 331, 333,
  336, 340, 374
  elite, 97, 98
  literature, 303, 307
Intelligentsia, 263, 330, 358, 363,
  403–404, 405, 406
  identified with government, 324,
    325, 326
  middle, 380, 382
International cooperation programs,
  343, 344, 345, 346, 352
International Monetary Fund (IMF),
  82, 123, 400
International Research and Exchanges
  Board (IREX), 346
Internet, 54, 133, 198, 200, 344, 351,
  395
Interrogation and torture, 408
Investments, 47, 48, 49, 50, 51, 52, 77,
  105
Investors defrauded, 135, 136, 137
Ireland, 52
Iron Curtain, 193, 379
Islam, 411, 412
Iuriatin Foundation, 393

Japanese self-government experiment,
  74
Joint venture enterprises, 100
Journalism, 98, 259, 260, 261, 262,
  263, 266
Journals, 317, 380, 405
Judicial system, 147, 146, 157, 171,
  173, 177, 182, 184, 289
Justice, 105, 115, 151, 152, 174
Justice of the Peace, 146

Justice system, 146, 159, 174, 175
Juvenile crime, 178, 179, 186

Kacharovsky, Karl R. 151
Kalashnikov, Sergei, 38
Kantorovich, Leonid, 399
Kapitza, Pyotr, 402, 414
Kaunas, 236, 239
Kazan State University, 342, 344, 348,
  351, 355
Kennan Institute, 63
KGB, 115, 116, 224, 407. 409
Khabarovsk, 205
Khapaeva, Dina, 405
Kholodov, Dmitrii, 408
Khrushchev, Nikita, 237, 379
Kiapik, Ivan, 274
Kirienko, Sergei, 287, 371
Kirill, Metropolitan, 237
Knockoffs, 129
Knorre, Aleksandr, 413
Kommunist journal, 220
Komsomol, 158, 370
Kondrat'ev, Nikolai, 401
Kontur industrial group, 53
Koposov, Nikolai, 405
Korolev, Sergei, 412
Kotovskaia, Mariia, 215
Krasnyi Sever (Red North), 272, 273.
  274, 275
Ktovskaya, Mariia, 214
Kultura (Culture) television program,
  168
Kuznetsk Coal Basin (Kuzbass), 114
Kvant corporation, televisions, 54

Labor, 117, 120, 124, 219, 412
Lake Baikal, 284, 291
Land, 104, 105, 217
  development, 100, 102
  reform, 59, 67, 398
Languages, 361
Law, 33, 153, 160, 173, 409
Law and the Army, The, 156
Law enforcement, 147, 150, 153, 172,
  175, 183, 185, 291
Lawsuits, 129, 163, 289
  consumer protection, 128, 136
  against government, 131, 132, 134

Lawyers, 155, 156, 159
  associations of, 148, 156, 159–160,
    404
Layoffs, 120
Lebed, Aleksandr, 164
Legal education, 153, 159
Legal nihilism, 128, 160
Legal reform, 136, 145, 146, 157,
  173
Legal services, 148
Legal system, 136, 139, 150, 159, 172,
  173
Legislation, 73, 146, 160, 222
  on accessing information, 264
  antimonopoly, 403
  bar association, 148
  competition, 33, 34
  economic, 403
  environmental, 290
  land reform, 59, 398
  media, 169
  notaries, 149
  regulating legal profession, 159
  regulating religion, 243
  of Soviet Union, 71, 218
  tax reform, 76, 93
Lenin, Vladimir I., 304
Leninskoe znamia (Lenin Banner)
  newspaper, 258
Levi's, 129, 130
Liberal arts college, 340
Libraries, 354, 392, 411
Life expectancy, 226
Life prospects and goals, 14, 21
Life support, 29, 30
Lipovskaia, Olga, 224
Literary criticism, 301, 387, 388, 391
Literature, 212, 301, 302, 333, 378,
  381, 383, 385, 386, 405
  growth of new, 390, 392
  and West, 230, 299, 411
Lithuania, 236
Liubimov, Yurii, 364
Livestock, 29, 57–58
Living standards, 83, 97, 278, 286,
  329, 381, 399
Lobyzonva, Ol'ga, 266, 409
Local self-government, 25, 27, 55, 56,
  57, 67–68, 137, 409, 410

American model, 74
operational model, 28, 73
officials, 77, 282
in rural regions, 44, 67
Lotman, Yurii, 406
LOTOS, 224
Luks joint stock company, 129, 130
Lumber industry, 53
Luzhkov, Yurii, 163, 371

MacArthur Foundation, 230, 234
Mafia, 410
Magazines, 228, 229, 260, 302
Makanin, Vladimir, 383, 385, 386
Maksudov, Rustem, 409
Mamardashvili, Merab, 221
Mandelstam, Osip, 406
Mann, Thomas, 371
Manufacturing, 33, 50, 93
Mariia journal, 223
Market, 22, 33, 35, 41, 48, 101, 105,
  108, 225, 262
  price information, 107, 108
  reforms, 63, 267
Market economy, 41, 67, 83, 86, 110,
  118, 167, 226, 338, 400
Marxism, 69, 326, 328
Maslow, Abraham, 17
Mass media, 21–22, 97, 98, 169, 281,
  306, 408. *See also* Media
  and advertising, 37, 38, 48, 130
  government control of, 264, 267
  and politics, 164, 167
Matsushita Electric (Panasonic), 130
Meaning of life, 19, 20, 21
Media, 97, 137, 148, 165, 167, 263,
  264. *See also* Mass media
  coverage of military conflicts, 163,
  166
Mediation, 139
Medical services, 44, 55, 210, 397,
  404
Melchuk, Igor, 401
Men', Aleksandr, 411, 412
Mental disorders, 15, 163
Meyerhold, Vsevolod, 359
Middle class, 46, 51, 96, 97, 104, 372,
  415
Migrants, 59, 412

Military, 294, 373, 402
Military industrial complex, 84, 122,
    410, 415
Mining industry, 115, 121
Ministry of Defense, 102, 289
Ministry of Finance, 82, 85
Ministry of Justice, 147, 213
Mirzoev, Vladimir, 397
Mirzoyanov, B., 294
Monitor Company, 346
Monopolistic capitalism, 117, 125, 402
Moonlighters, 312
Morality, 153, 160, 241, 279, 360,
    374, 378, 411
Morris, C. W., 19–20, 21
Mortgage financing, 9, 91, 103, 104
Moscow, 50, 55, 57, 100, 114, 157,
    179, 185–186, 199, 259, 410
Moscow Conservatory, 236
Moscow oblast, 101, 102, 104, 402
Moscow Prosecutor's Office, 186
Moscow State University Law School,
    152
Moscow Theological Academy, 237
Moskovskii komsomolets, 408
Municipal government, 36, 67, 132
Myth of Soviet Woman, 221, 226

Na Dne (At Bottom) newspaper, 251,
    253
National Security Council, 122
Natural farming, 30
Natural gas, 270, 275, 277, 400, 401
Natural resources, 89, 276, 284
Neelov, Yurii Vasil'yevich, 276
Nemtsov, Boris, 291
Nesvoevremennye zapiski (Untimely
    Notes) journal, 393
New Russia, 208, 209, 210, 243, 251
Newspapers, 251, 253, 260, 264, 273,
    275, 278, 279
News programs, 22, 165, 166
Nezavisimaya gazeta, 233, 247
NGOs. *See* Nongovernmental
    organizations
Nickel complexes in Norilsk, 120, 285
Nihilism, 128, 160, 217
Nikiforovich, Mikhail, 274

Nikitin, A., 294
Nishny Novgorod, 269, 346, 350
Nochlezhka, 255
Nomenklatura, 220, 371, 372, 399,
    415,
Nongovernmental organizations
    (NGOs), 135, 154, 155, 194, 199,
    200, 201, 207, 393, 404
  and citizen involvement, 196, 197,
    198, 201.
  environmental, 289, 293
Nonprofit organizations, 194, 197,
    198, 201
Notaries, 148, 149, 150
Novels, 382, 383
Novgorod, 46, 49, 51, 53, 54, 55, 58,
    60, 407, 412
Novoe literaturnoe obozrenie, (New
    Literary Review), 301, 303
Novosibirsk, 10, 13, 101, 251, 350
Novyi mir journal, 96, 223
NTV television station, 164, 167
Nuclear sites, 287, 288, 294, 413

Ob River, 271, 275
Oblasts, 47, 49, 55, 57, 61, 114, 412
Obshchina (commune) court, 175, 177
Offenders, 177, 178, 180, 184, 186
OGO corporation, 107, 108, 109, 110
Ogonyok magazine, 212, 225, 230
Oil resources, 110, 275, 400, 401
On Bases of State Service . . . , 41
On Competition and . . . Monopolistic
    Activity . . . , 33–34, 41
On Foundations of State Youth Policy
    . . . , 156
On Natural Monopolies, 35
On Protecting Consumers from Unfair
    Advertising, 38
On State Regulation of Tariffs on
    Electric and Fuel Energy, 35
On Tax Benefits for Enterprises and
    Organizations . . . , 47
On Territorial Rehabilitation for
    Repressed Ethnic Groups, 72
On the Press and Other Mass Media,
    162
Onegin, Eugene, 368

Onel'chuk, Anatolii Konstantinovich, 270
Open Society Institute, 157, 234
Organic Synthesis corporation, 346
Organized crime, 25, 26, 27, 105, 151, 263, 301, 372, 410
Orlova, Liubov', 221
Orphans, 226, 247
Orthodoxy, 241, 242–243
Our Bodies Ourselves for the New Century, 232
Outsourcing grain processing, 109
Oxford University, 237
Ozone layer, 286

Parliament, 70, 86, 206, 210, 222, 230,
Pascal, Blaise, 161
Pasko, Grigorii, 294
Pastukhov, V., 172
Paternalism, 20, 55, 220
Pavlov-Sil'vanskii, Nikolai, 175
Peasants, 105, 222, 223
Pensions, 44, 57, 111, 114–115
Perestroika, 96, 98, 115, 260, 300, 309, 343, 380, 381
    and freedom concepts, 193, 203
    and intellectual elite, 97, 328
Perovskaia, Sofia, 217
Peter the Great (czar of Russia), 66, 214, 239
Petit bourgeois, 329, 362
Petrova, Dimitrina, 182
Petrushevskaya, Liudmila, 383, 384
Philanthropy, 247, 315, 318, 353
Philanthropy and Humanitarian Aid, 199
Pinochet, Augustor, 164
Pinter, Harold, 362
Pioneer Youth, 158, 203
Pisarev, Dmitrii, 216
Planning, 13, 14, 33
Playwriting, 366
Pluralism, 22, 225, 294
Plyusnin, Yurii, 399, 404, 410
Podmoskov'e Corporation, 101, 103
Poets, 387, 390
Poland, 66, 122, 179
Police, 150, 186, 408, 411

Political correctness, 23, 374
Political parties, 61, 72, 87, 116, 205. 209, 217, 318
Politics, 25, 60,141, 327
Pollution, 285, 286, 289, 290
Poltoranin, Mikhail, 38, 274
Polyarnaya Zvezda (Northern Star), 272
Populism, 93
Pornography, 228, 386
Porter, Michael, 347
Posadskaia, Anastasia, 220
Postage, 302, 392
Postfactum information agency, 199, 200
Power, 25, 69
Pravda, 108, 223
Press, 124, 163–164, 168, 200, 225, 258, 259, 260, 264
Prices, 35, 37, 44, 88, 94
Priests, 238, 239, 246
Primakov, Evgenii, 36, 86, 264, 366, 403
Prisons, 175, 178, 224, 408, 412
Privatization, 50, 51, 69, 100, 108, 391
    of property, 43, 151, 360, 369
Pro bono legal consultation, 156, 157, 159
Professionalism, 329, 365
    ideology of, 326, 327, 328, 329, 331, 337
Profit margins, 105, 106
Prokhorova, Irina, 405
Propaganda, 411
Property, 44, 53–54, 55, 56, 71, 74, 118, 151, 154, 359, 360
Propiska (legal residency certificate), 251, 255
Prosecutor General's Office, 150, 171, 186, 372
Provinces, 12, 165, 317, 320, 390, 394
Prusak, Mikhail, 404, 407, 412
    Public organizations, 61, 156, 194, 195, 213, 263, 292–293, 295. See also Nongovernmental organizations (NGOs)
Publications, 259, 277
Publishing, 264, 301, 302, 307, 317, 377, 391
    houses, 302, 393, 406

Pulp fiction, 383, 393
Pushkin, Alexander, 215, 269, 281, 406
Pyramid schemes. *See* Financial
    pyramids

Radaev, Vadim, 401
Radiation, 286, 289, 413
Radio, 200, 233, 264, 269
Raion (district), 46, 74
Real estate, 100, 121, 138, 149, 252,
    360
Receipt revolution, 130
Reconciliation programs, 179–180,
    181, 184
Reform, 67, 82, 86, 87, 95, 123, 127,
    248
    educational, 353
    initial strategies of, 68, 45, 83, 87
    positive results of, 44–45, 404
    private farms, 398
    of tax system, 90
    university, 348, 349, 352, 353
Regions, 52, 56, 72, 111, 175
Rehabilitation services, 185, 186
Reindeer, Siberian, 27, 272, 277
Religion, 23, 151, 227, 239, 240, 405
    as free choice, 241
    legislation regulating, 244
Rent, 36
Repatriates, 372
Republic (Plato), 19
Research, 310, 311, 313–314, 317,
    320, 332, 402
    funding, 314, 315, 318
    separated from politics, 312, 319
    university, 320, 351
Responsibility, personal, 112, 119, 221,
    382
Restorative justice, 177, 178, 179, 183
Retraining, 120, 121
RHR International, 105
Richter, Andrei, 408
Rimashevskaya, Natal'ia, 220
Rivers, polluted, 285
Road taxes, 48
Robot technology, 401
Roerich, Nicholas, 272
Rogers, Carl R., 20, 21

Romanticism, 303
Rossyiskie universitety (Russian
    universities), 167
Rostov, 121, 349
Ruble, Blair, 63
Rubles, 44, 83, 91
Rule of law, 147, 153, 154, 156, 172,
    173
Rural areas, 12, 59, 67
Rus', 66
Russian Federation, 38, 39, 71, 134,
    147
Russian North, 29, 278, 409
Russian Orthodox Church, 23, 24,
    238, 246, 411, 412
    human resources, 247, 248
    reform, 244, 245
Russian-language courses, 343
Rybakov, Anatoly, 380

Sakharov, Andrei, 203, 414
Salaries, 225, 226
    for law enforcement, 150
    payment of, 56, 114–115
    public sector, 57
    for researchers, 312
    of teachers, 355
Salekhard, 270, 271, 275
Salzburg Seminar, 349, 350
Samizdat (underground publishing), 96,
    379
Samizdat magazine, 223, 224
Samsung, 130
Sanitary codes, 285
Saratov, 105, 110
Savings in foreign currency, 91
Scholarly work, 10, 309, 317
Schools, 56, 235. *See also* Education;
    Higher education institutions;
    Universities
Sciences, 309, 314, 320, 327, 328, 402
    Academy of, 214, 308, 313, 320
    financing, 84, 414
Scotland, 52, 256
Secret (intelligence) services, 221, 397,
    408
Security Council, United Nations, 158,
    164

Segodnia news program, 163
Self-government. *See* Local self-
   government
Self-perpetuation, 197, 338
Self-regulation, 140, 369
Selling air, 204
Seminaries, 236, 246, 248
Senatskaia Ploshchad (Senate Square)
   newspaper, 253
Sergeev, Aleksandr, 407
Seriakova, Nadia, 407
Severiane (The Northerners) magazine,
   266, 269, 272, 279, 281, 282
Sexual harassment, 226
Shadow, The, (Shvarts), 305
Shadow economy, 26, 42, 83, 92, 304,
   305
Shafarevich, Igor, 369
Shalamov, Varlam, 406
Sholokhov, Mikhail, 378
Shvarts, Yevgeny, 305
Siberia, 66, 114, 276, 284
Siniavskii, Andrei, 379
Sixth Russia, 11
Smolny College, 339, 340
Soap operas, 22, 167
Sobchak, Anatolii, 255
Social contract, 139, 141
Social control, 173, 177
Social Information Agency (ASI), 198,
   200, 201
Socialism, 86, 380, 386
Social partnership commissions, 117,
   119, 120
Social sciences, 331, 319, 333
   critique of, 334, 335, 340
Social services, 56, 117
Social workers, 183, 184
Society changes, 19, 30, 31, 358
Socioeconomics, 13, 43, 45, 62, 158
Sokolov, Valerii, 404
Solaris film, 414
Solzhenitsyn, Aleksandr, 378, 379,
   380
Sony, 130
Soros Foundation, 157, 230, 252, 394,
   395
Sovereignty, 261, 273

Sovetskaia Moldavia (Soviet Moldavia)
   newspaper, 258
Soviet government, 68, 116, 323, 358,
   408–409
Soviet writers, 359, 379, 389
Sovremennik magazine, 215
Space program, 33, 289, 412
Spain, 345
Specialization, 156, 174, 327, 337, 353
Speransky, Mikhail, 66
Spiritual matters, 152, 359, 386, 391,
   405, 406, 411
Splav company, 53, 54
St. Petersburg, 103, 214, 216, 217,
   218, 332, 410
St. Petersburg University, 335, 337, 339
Stalin, Joseph, 68, 71, 221, 237, 277,
   323, 401, 411
Starvation, 29, 277, 413
State, 70–71, 90, 174, 219, 240, 403,
   411
   control, 26, 174, 319, 415
   as property owner, 68, 69, 118
State Duma, 36, 38, 85, 104, 132, 146,
   159, 230
   annulment of labor laws, 117
   land purchases, 105
   and tax code, 92–93
Stepashin, Sergei, 287
Stimorol gum, 49
Stite, Richard, 214
Stock exchange, 91, 101, 107, 108,
   129, 130, 346
Stolypin, Pyotr, 67
Strikes, 116, 119, 120
Strindberg, August, 361
Strong hand, 94
Subjects of Federation, 68, 72, 73, 74
Subsidies, 44, 57, 90
Supreme Court, 132, 136
Supreme Soviet, 34, 82
Survival, 13, 20, 28, 29, 30, 137,
   312
Suslova, Nadezhda, 216
Suslov, Mikhail, 399
Sutoloka (Hubbub) magazine, 393
Sverdlovsk, 120
Sweden, 101, 102

Tabloids, 278, 393
Tairov, Aleksandr, 359
Tajikistan, 409
Tariffs, 35, 37, 58, 116, 117
Tarkovsky, Andrei, 414
Tatar-Mongol invasion, 42
Tatarstan, 74, 346, 347
Tavernier, Karel, 347, 349
Tax breaks, 50, 58
Tax Code, 92, 93, 146
Taxes, 76, 105, 88, 288, 315
    currency, 88, 89
    evasion and collection, 92, 93, 150
    personal income, 56, 92, 93, 150
    system, 90, 93, 372
    value-added, 48
Tax holidays, 47, 57
Teachers, 210, 246, 320, 338
Teilhaard de Chardin, Pierre, 411
Telecommunications, 354
Television, 22, 133, 167, 233, 239, 393
    and politics, 165, 166, 252
    regulation, 140, 264
Terem, 214
Theater, 268, 359, 360, 361, 365, 366,
    405
    repertory, 362, 364
Theft, 140, 403
Theocracy, 368
Theological education, 236, 237, 245
Theology, 248, 412
Thick journals, 380, 382, 389, 391,
    392, 394
Third Sector, The, journal, 199
Third sector. *See* Nongovernmental
    organizations (NGOs)
Thoreau, Henry David, 12
Tiger, Ussurian (Siberian), 284
Timur Teams, 194
Tobacco products, 39
Tolstoy, Leo, 378, 411
Topoleva, Elena, 198, 404, 406
Topolev, Andrei, 404, 406
Torture, 183, 408
Totalitarianism, 323, 324, 367, 374,
    415
    return to, 408, 411
Tourism, 138, 410

Trading companies, 129
Translation software programs, 401
Transport, 36, 44
Travel abroad, 44, 345, 370
Truth-in-advertising crusade, 130
Tsarskoselskoye Literary Prize, 393
Tvardovsky, Aleksandr, 223
Tver oblast, 26, 75, 349
Tyumen oblast, 74, 270, 273, 274
Tyutchev, Fedor, 354

Ukraine, 29, 251
Underground, 304, 383, 387
Unemployment, 13, 209
Union of Young Lawyers . . . (MSIu
    RF), 155, 156, 157, 158
Unions, 62, 118, 119. *See also*
    Independent labor unions
    insurers', 134
    labor, 115, 116, 122 125
    trade, 61
    women's, 219–220, 228, 230
    writers' and journalists', 260, 394
United States, 103–104, 101, 116
Universitetskoe upravlenie (University
    Administration), 350
Universities, 319, 329, 329, 337–338,
    346, 348, 354
    administration, 347, 349, 350, 351
    broader education, 339–340
    reforms, 348, 349, 352, 353
    Western influences, 348, 353
University of Granada, 345
Univex Academic Research Center, 343
Urals, 410
U.S. Agency for International
    Development (USAID), 122
U.S. Grains Council, 111
Uspekhi fizicheskikh nauk
    (Achievements in Physical
    Sciences), 414

Value-added tax, 48
Values, 18, 329, 372, 411
    hierarchy, 17, 18, 19, 167
Moral values, 172–173, 279, 378, 382
Vandenberg, Martina, 232
Vasil'ev, Sergei, 399, 403, 407